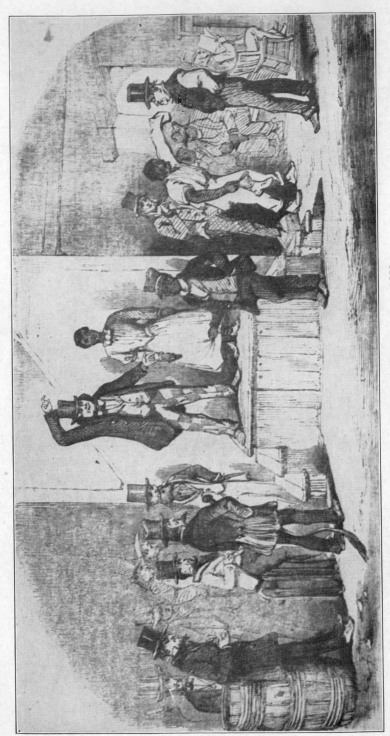

A SLAVE-AUCTION IN RICHMOND, IN 1853

From a sketch made from life by Eyre Crowe

SLAVE-TRADING
IN THE OLD SOUTH

BY

FREDERIC BANCROFT

Author of

LIFE OF WILLIAM H. SEWARD
CALHOUN AND NULLIFICATION
ETC., ETC.

❦

WITH ILLUSTRATIONS

❦

J. H. FURST COMPANY

12-20 HOPKINS PLACE,

BALTIMORE, MD.

1931

COPYRIGHT, 1931
BY
FREDERIC BANCROFT

CONTENTS

ILLUSTRATIONS

CHAPTER I

SOME PHASES OF THE BACKGROUND

Measureless superabundance of cheap land was the most conspicuous feature of agriculture in colonial days in the South. Long after the bestowal of vast royal grants, bounded by ocean, rivers, mountains or degrees of latitude, large tracts were to be had for a petty quit-rent—"the payment of a ' penny ' or a ' pepper corn ' "— and a promise to make a clearing annually or to give certain other evidences of occupation that were almost as easily complied with. At one time, 1,000 acres could be bought in South Carolina for £20, less than $100, and an annual payment of ten shillings, $2.40.[1] In 1700 the average estate in Virginia was 700 acres, while many planters had thousands of acres.[2] Peter Jefferson, the father of the third President, "patented" a thousand acres of land adjoining the estate of William Randolph of Tuckahoe, and bought four hundred more for the price of "Henry Weatherbourne's biggest bowl of arrack punch". As late as 1769-70 William Allston in four months received five royal grants in South Carolina, amounting to 4,700 acres, for inconsiderable payments and conditions. Wild land, except the most fertile, was hardly salable at any price. The crops supposed to be best suited to the climate and the soil of the South— tobacco, mainly in Maryland and Virginia, rice and (later) indigo in South Carolina and Georgia, and some of all three in North Carolina—could not be cultivated and marketed to advantage except on a large scale. With land almost gratis and a good although distant market assured, the supreme difficulty was to obtain laborers.

[1] E. L. Whitney, *Government and Colony of S. C.*, 66 (13 *Johns Hopkins University Studies*).

[2] Coman, *Industrial History of the U. S.* (1914), 32 ff. gives a good summary based on numerous authorities.

1

Substantial relief came from indentured white persons brought from England and slaves directly or indirectly imported from Africa. It was a peculiar coincidence that in 1619 Virginia should receive both the first shipload of Africans and the first 100 pauper children. White servitude was based mainly on stimulated or forced deportation, often of criminals, paupers or persons cruelly kidnaped. It became a very lucrative industry to transport indentured " servants " to the American colonies. The planter that paid the importer or creditor most secured the labor of these persons for definite periods—adults usually for four or five years and children longer.[3] At its best and according to law, the system had some beneficial features; at its worst, in practice, it was barbarous. But such laborers could not endure the climate of the Carolina and Georgia coast and were not stable enough for successful planting anywhere.

The African negro—imported very slowly, at first, and at times received with strong misgivings even by persons that most needed his toil—was suited to the miasmic lowland plantations: being cheap and easily managed, he rendered planting on a large scale both stable and profitable. According to another's conclusions from various authorities, there were only 300 negroes in Virginia in 1650 and 2,000 in 1671. By 1721, they comprised one-seventh of New York's population, one-thirteenth of Pennsylvania's, nearly one-half of Maryland's, more than one-half of Virginia's, one-third of North Carolina's and four-sevenths of South Carolina's.[4] It is supposed that in all the continental colonies there were about 75,000 slaves in 1725, a little more than 250,000 in 1750 and about 500,000 in 1776.[5]

Down to the Revolution and beyond, the enterprising and profitable slave-trading was in negroes born in

[3] Coman, 42-44.
[4] Coman, 44, 45.
[5] Du Bois, *Suppression of the African Slave-Trade*, 5, cites authorities on which these rough estimates are based.

Africa. At times, many of them were brought from the West Indies, but a great majority came directly from the Dark Continent. Because Northerners carried on a large commerce in them, there were Northern ports for transshipment to the different colonies.[6] Otherwise, the cargoes were taken straightway to Charleston or Savannah or some other port least inconvenient to the plantation regions where the Africans were expected to be worked. ✓Between the importer and the planter there was a commission merchant—unless the commission merchant was the importer— who sold the negroes publicly or privately and was responsible for the payments whenever made, whether in cash or produce. Two choice cargoes of 300 and 490 slaves from Africa were sold at Yorktown, Virginia, in 1736 and 1737, the larger by Thomas Nelson,[7] the grandfather of Thomas Nelson, Jr., a signer of the Declaration of Independence. Such trading by the large commission-merchants of excellent social standing—who were not rarely the actual importers—was almost a matter of course, especially at Charleston, South Carolina.[8] Not many years later Henry Laurens—who " sometimes held shares in the vessels that delivered slaves to him ", and " wrote of seven hundred slaves as the number his ' small business ' would receive annually by choice "[8a]—was enriching himself there as a result of his judgment of these Africans and from the high prices he was obtaining. He became a great planter and theoretically an emancipationist, without liberating any " except a few individuals ", says his candid biographer.[9] But tradition left out the " Guinea business " and embalmed Laurens as an antislavery man. The gen-

[6] Du Bois, 28, 34-35.

[7] U. B. Phillips (editor), 2 *Plantation and Frontier*, 52, quotes the advts.

[8] See *post* pp. 376-77.

[8a] Miss Elizabeth Donnan, " The Slave Trade into South Carolina before the Revolution ", 33 *Amer. Hist. Rev.*, 810, 811.

[9] Wallace, *Henry Laurens*, 47, 74-76, 444 ff., 456.

eral characteristics of the African trade were the same in 1804-07, when 40,000 were rushed to Charleston in anticipation of the prohibition to begin with 1808.[10] The cargoes were variously advertised as " very prime Congo slaves " or " prime Mandingo Africans " or " choice Gold coast negroes " or " prime Windward Coast Africans ". They might be sold either on Gadsden's wharf or alongside of it on board the slavers. The Charleston *Courier* of January 1, 1807, announced eight such cargoes, totaling more than 1,500 persons.[11]

Before the Revolution, cheap land, cheap slaves, primogeniture and entail, the great demand for tobacco, rice and indigo, and the profit of dealing in them, facilitated the building up of large slaveholding estates, especially in Virginia and South Carolina. The planters soon fancied themselves enormously rich and aristocratic, and all the more easily impressed others by living extravagantly and boasting of their ancestry. But the highest authority says: " Merchandise and trade were the foundation stones of most, if not all, the great fortunes in South Carolina." [12] During the Revolution foreign trade was cut off. The Carolina plantations, especially, suffered on account of neglect and the damage inflicted by the British soldiers.

[10] De Bow, 2 *Resources of the Southern and Western States*, 340-42, gives the figures and the names of the ships, which were largely owned by Northerners; Du Bois, *Suppression of the African Slave-Trade*, 90.

[11] Some advts. were continued after the date of the commencement of the sales. In general they were similar, but the announcement following " N. B." was somewhat exceptional.

"The sale of the ship MERCURY'S cargo, consisting of 400 prime Angola SLAVES, will commence on board, at Gadsden's Wharf, THIS DAY, the 29th inst. at eleven o'clock.—JOHN WATSON & Co. N. B. The whole of this cargo have had the smallpox, and are in an excellent condition. Produce, at market price, will be received in payment." . . .—*Courier*, Jan. 1, 1807.

[12] McCrady, *S. C., 1719-76*, 399. Gabriel Manigault, the richest merchant in S. C., and perhaps "the richest man in all the colonies", died in 1781, leaving an estate, including 43,532 acres and 490 slaves, estimated at $845,000.—*Ibid.*, 402, 404.

It is supposed that South Carolina alone lost about 25,000 slaves.[13] As India supplied the demand for indigo and held the market, the culture of that crop in the United States virtually died out. The restoration of the rice plantations was difficult and slow, for they were confined to the swamp lands near the coast and along the rivers where the flooding of the fields could be controlled. The demand for tobacco steadily increased after the return of peace, but Virginia, long spendthrift with fertile land, could not supply the same proportion as formerly of this crop.

Neither section of the colonies displayed much moral opposition to slavery. In the North, especially New England, where slavery was hopelessly unremunerative, many persons were early and resolutely hostile to the institution; but the profitable fitting out of ships for the African slave-trade was suffered to continue with impunity in different Northern ports.[14] The South, while making the most of slave property, has cherished the tradition that its colonies, as a matter of moral objection, tried in vain to get rid of the African slave-trade, but that the mother-country thwarted the efforts. If the conclusions of Du Bois, Spears and Miss Donnan may be accepted, nearly all the opposition that the planting colonies made to the African slave-trade, by putting heavy and sometimes prohibitive taxes on it, was variously due to a desire to get revenue from the trade, to shut out Africans on account of fear of negro insurrections, to prevent the depreciation of the value of slaves or to encourage the immigration of white persons.[15] There was only slight sentiment, and most of that passive, against keeping an inferior race in bondage. Accordingly the economic interests of relatively few energetic persons

[13] Du Bois, 11.
[14] Du Bois, 29, 31, 38.
[15] Spears, *The American Slave-Trade*, 97; Du Bois, 15, 42; 33 *Amer. Hist. Review*, 804 ff.

were able to dominate. " It was not until the opening of the Revolution that any honest effort was made to suppress the [African slave-] trade, except in Pennsylvania ", said Alexander Johnston, one of the highest authorities on American history.[16] Other than moral motives seem sufficient to explain nearly all that was done in either section prior to 1774 and much of what was done until after 1800.

Conflicting interests and mutual recriminations bring out the facts. The different attitudes of very high-minded men in the Constitutional Convention of 1787 illustrated how material advantages, possessed or sought, may rise above questions of general welfare or human rights. New England, having large investments in shipping and wishing to increase them, ardently desired commerce to be under the control of the national government. Maryland and Virginia, much overstocked with slaves, had, according to the census of 1790, almost four-sevenths of all in the United States. Virginia alone had 31,000 more than all the rest of the South except Maryland, and Maryland had more than North Carolina, only 4,000 less than South Carolina, and three and one-half times as many as Georgia.[17] Planters in the Carolinas and Georgia thought that tens of thousands of Africans were needed in the South Atlantic States. Luther Martin of Maryland proposed that

[16] 3 Lalor's *Encyclopaedia of Polit. Science*, 732.
[17] SLAVE POPULATION IN 1790:

Va.	292,627	*The rest of the South:*	
Md.	103,036	Del.	8,887
		N. C.	100,572
Total	395,663	S. C.	107,0⌐4
Northern States:		Ga.	29,264
R. I.	948	Ky.	12,430
Conn.	2,764	Tenn.	3,417
N. J.	11,423		
N. Y.	21,324	Total	261,664
Pa.	3,737		
Total	40,196	—*U. S. Census 1790, Population*, p. 7.	

Congress be given the power to prohibit or tax the importation of slaves because they were a source of weakness, and such a traffic was inconsistent and dishonorable. Rutledge of South Carolina sharply replied: " Religion and humanity have nothing to do with this question. Interest alone is the governing principle with nations." Sherman and Ellsworth of Connecticut and Gerry of Massachusetts were willing to postpone taking over the power to control the foreign slave-trade for a greater and permanent gain. " Let every State import what it pleases ", said Ellsworth. " The morality or wisdom of slavery are considerations belonging to the States themselves. What enriches a part enriches the whole, and the States are the best judges of their particular interest."

Everybody is familar with George Mason's denunciation of slavery as discouraging the arts, manufactures and white labor, having a pernicious effect on manners, breeding petty tyrants and bringing the judgment of Heaven on the country; but a very significant sentence that preceded it has been quoted much less frequently: " The western people are already calling out for slaves for their new lands, and will fill that country with slaves, if they can be got through South Carolina and Georgia." Cotesworth Pinckney very pointedly remarked: " As to Virginia, she will gain by stopping the importations. Her slaves will rise in value, and she has more than she wants." [18] During the campaign for the adoption of the Constitution Ellsworth said that Mason had " about three hundred slaves, and lives in Virginia, where it is found by prudent management they can breed and raise slaves faster than they want them for their own use, and could supply the deficiency in Georgia and South Carolina ", and that Mason's objections were not in behalf of freedom nor in compassion, but because importations would render the United States weaker, more vulnerable and

[18] See 5 *Elliot's Debates*, 457 ff. for the full discussion.

less capable of defense.[19] Mason himself made it clear that he was really more concerned about the safety of slave property than he was about establishing a strong national government:—" As much as I value a union of all the states, I would not admit the Southern States into the Union unless they agree to the discontinuance of this disgraceful [foreign slave-] trade, because it would bring weakness, and not strength, to the Union. And, though this infamous traffic be continued, we have no security for the property of that kind which we have already. There is no clause in this Constitution to secure it; for they may lay such a tax as will amount to manumission." [20]

Each interest obtained, temporarily or ultimately, what it most cared about when the Constitution gave Congress full control over commerce, except the foreign slave-trade until 1808. This exception allowed Carolinians and Georgians meantime to stock up with African negroes and encouraged Maryland and Virginia slaveowners to expect that thereafter their slaves would increase in value. As yet, the territory beyond the Mississippi and that to the south of Georgia had hardly been thought of.

Mason and Pinckney were both right. The cheapness and superabundance of slaves in Virginia and Maryland already made it certain that slavery would expand as an aid to pioneering in Kentucky and Tennessee and in the region that became Alabama and Mississippi. Yet that expansion would have been quite different but for a certain invention.

Prior to 1786 the cotton grown in the South was the " short-staple " or " upland " variety. Small quantities had been produced over an extensive region, but little or none of it had ever been exported and no one had yet dreamed of it as " king ". The reason was that even

[19] E. H. Scott (editor), 2 *The Federalist and other Constitutional Papers,* 577.
[20] 3 *Elliot's Debates,* 452.

after it had been gathered a skilful person could not prepare more than about a bale (approximately 400 pounds) a year for the factory by separating the seeds from the lint. This labor in addition to the cost of production made cotton fabrics far too expensive for common use.

By 1790 the '' long-staple '' or '' sea-island '' cotton—so-called on account of its peculiar quality and the place where it flourished—had been introduced and grown in considerable quantities on the South Carolina and the Georgia coast. The difficulty and, therefore, the expense of seeding it were much less. These advantages and the superiority of the fiber caused an immediate demand for it. Inventions for weaving and the development of the factory and the commercial systems in England had shown that there were boundless opportunities for manufacturing and selling cotton goods, if cheap and ample raw material could be obtained; the demand was lively although the price was high. But because successful culture of sea-island cotton was restricted to a region still less extensive than that of rice, the crop was only an insignificant fraction of what was needed. By a strange fatality the seeds provided to perpetuate the only kind of cotton that could be grown in a sufficient quantity were preventing it from being of great practical value.

With no thought of any special relation between slavery and cotton, except the sea-island kind, the South had persistently hoped that some cheap and speedy method of removing the seeds might be found. Many persons were working on the problem. Eli Whitney, a New Englander, with natural talent for invention, was in Georgia intending to go to South Carolina to teach school, when his attention was called to the great need. He quickly devised his '' saw-gin '', and patented it in 1793. It was a simple invention: by means of a revolving cylinder with saw-teeth, the cotton was drawn through a screen which was so fine that it separated the seeds from the lint. With a hand-gin one person could accomplish fifty times as much as previously, and a machine run by horsepower could gin from 300 to 1,000 pounds a day.[21] The invention had a marvelous effect, almost immediately. Although no appreciable amount of the upland cotton had previously been exported, the obstacles as to price and quantity were virtually removed. The " king " was born, but no one imagined the extent of his future domain.

Sea-island cotton for a time enjoyed special advantages; it rapidly occupied the abandoned fields where indigo had once been very profitable and even encroached on those of rice; but its best qualities were developed in only a narrow and not long strip of the coast—from the neighborhood of Charleston, South Carolina, to the mouth of the St. Johns River in Florida.[22] Upland cotton was quite different. Its wonderful expansion was nominally to turn nearly the whole South into a " cotton country ". The entire crop, which in 1792, the year before Whitney's invention, amounted to but 13,000 bales, became 461,000 bales in 1817—a thirtyfivefold increase. For many years the short-staple cotton was supposed to be especially suited to the uplands, which were usually hilly and rarely better than second-rate in quality. The fertile surface was so thin and so crudely tilled that heavy rains soon washed much of it away. The Whitney gin did not, of course, increase the amount of cotton that one person could raise; only better soil or better methods and implements could do that. The heavy hoe, and the small plow drawn by a horse, mule or steer, continued in use. In order to prosper, one must continually make extensive clearings or buy good new

---

[21] See M. B. Hammond, *The Cotton Industry*, 25-27, and *passim* for details on many points mentioned in this chapter. Coman, 150-51, gives illustrations of gins.

[22] Hammond, 19. In later years, Governor Seabrook of South Carolina indicated half a degree of latitude, 32° 10' to 32° 40', as the region "where the length, strength, and firmness of the fibre are most happily blended".— De Bow, 3 *Industrial Resources*, 137.

land and add to the number of fieldhands. Before 1820 the alluvial belt of Alabama, Mississippi and Louisiana had demonstrated where the plant would most flourish and the soil not wear out. By 1840 the crop was more than two million bales and cotton had extended its dominion over western Tennessee, much of the agricultural part of Florida, most of the best parts of Alabama, Mississippi, northern Louisiana and part of Arkansas, and was demanding Texas for purposes of expansion. Before 1850 Texas had been acquired and a flood of prospective cotton-growers was sweeping into that vast region. The maximum crop between 1840 and 1850 was 2,867,000 bales in 1849. By 1860 it rose to 4,861,000 bales. The crop had nearly doubled in eleven years; it had increased more than tenfold since 1817, and more than three-hundred-and-fiftyfold in the 68 years since 1792.[23]

This rapid expansion and increase of cotton culture would have been impossible but for two conditions: the great abundance of suitable, cheap land and the large and increasing, although insufficient, supply of slaves.

At first it was expected that short-staple cotton would continue to be grown principally in the upcountry by small farmers. But the white population was inadequate and lacked sufficient energy to improve the opportunties. More and more the South deceived itself into believing that extensive and profitable cotton culture depended on the use of slaves. The work did not require much skill or intelligence; it extended throughout most of the year and could be done by slaves of both sexes and of nearly all ages, who could be fed, clothed and kept in good health at slight expense. De Bow estimated that in 1840 there were approximately 800,000 slave to 100,000 white laborers raising cotton;[24] that by 1850 the slaves of all ages em-

[23] Hammond, 358, gives a valuable table covering production, export, consumption and prices, 1784-1897.
[24] De Bow, *Industrial Resources*, 175.

ployed in [or associated with?] the culture of cotton numbered over 1,800,000 and were more than 72 per cent of
all that were engaged in agriculture, exclusive of bread
stuffs; whereas only 14 per cent were raising tobacco, 6
per cent sugar, 5 per cent rice and not quite 2½ per cent
hemp.[25] If De Bow was right, Professor Hammond is
not far wrong in supposing that about 2,225,000 slaves
were dependent principally on the culture of cotton in
1860,[26] when the crop was about twice as large as in
1850.[27] In 1820, the regions that already or later comprised the States of Alabama, Arkansas, Florida, Louisiana, Mississippi and Texas contained probably less than
160,000 slaves—only 145,000 exclusive of the not many
thousands in Florida and Texas; but in 1860 they had
increased about tenfold.[28] It was, of course, the profitable
raising of cotton in this great region that had increased
the demand for slave labor there, which doubled or trebled
the price of slaves and enormously augmented slave-
trading.

Perhaps not one-fifth of this movement of slave population and this growth of cotton culture would have taken
place when it did, but for the tens of thousands of slaves
unprofitably employed in the Southern border States. To
these States cotton was directly a great agricultural misfortune, but it was indirectly the means of an enormous
profit to their slaveowners.

[25] Hammond, 60; De Bow, *Compendium of the Census of 1850*, 94.
[26] Hammond, 61.
[27] The tables given by Hammond, 359, and by Coman, 239, disagree.
[28] Number of slaves:

	1820	1860
Alabama	41,879	435,080
Arkansas	1,617	111,115
Florida	unknown	61,745
Louisiana . . .	69,064	331,726
Mississippi . . .	32,814	436,631
Texas	unknown	182,566
Totals . . .	145,374	1,558,863

Virginia supplied the extreme illustration of this. Even before the Revolution much of its formerly best land had been exhausted by the unvaried planting of tobacco. After the abolition of primogeniture and entail, estates were commonly sold or divided, and the showy signs of riches rapidly decreased. Before 1800 North Carolina and Kentucky had begun what was to be a damaging competition with Virginia in raising tobacco. Agriculturally, Virginia as a whole had ceased to thrive. Only planters and farmers with exceptional industry and frugality prospered merely by tilling the soil.

Many of the most revered Virginians of the Revolution and of the next generation illustrated the common workings of slave labor. Jefferson early ran in debt and his slaves increased much more rapidly than the value of their work. The net profits on his whole [agricultural] estate in 1785 were no more than he could have realized by hiring out a few negroes. To meet his obligations, he directed that his estate be leased in parts to different persons, because, as he said, experience showed that only small concerns were gainful. To pay off some bonds, he in 1793 ordered the sale of a considerable number of his slaves—probably between 10 and 20, for he obtained about £800, $2,666 in Virginia currency.[29]

[29] Jefferson's *Writings* (Ford), IV, 342, 416, 417, 418; VI, 214-15. Mr. Philip Alexander Bruce has kindly informed the author that Va. currency was then estimated at six shillings to the dollar.

Jefferson's peculiar reasoning was: " I cannot decide to sell lands. I have sold too much of them already, and they are the only sure provision for my children, *nor would I willingly sell the slaves as long as there remains any prospect of paying my debts with their labor. In this I am governed solely by views to their happiness which will render it worth their while to use extraordinary exertions for some time to enable me to put them ultimately on an easier, footing, which I will do the moment they have paid the debts due from the estate, two thirds of which have been contracted by purchasing them.* [Italics not Jefferson's.] I am therefore strengthened in the idea of renting out my whole estate; not to any one person, but in different parts to different persons, as experience proves that it is only small concerns that are gainful, & it would be my interest that the tenants should make a reasonable gain."—IV, 416-17.

It will be remembered that Thomas Mann Randolph, the first, was left as an orphan to the care of Peter Jefferson, the father of Thomas; that the two Thomases were like brothers; and that Thomas Jefferson's daughter, Martha, married Randolph's son, Thomas Mann Randolph, the second. Eleven years before Jefferson's death, his son-in-law, a few years before he was elected governor of Virginia, sold several families of negroes within sight of Monticello, where he and his family lived much of the time.[30]

Writers on planting, architecture and society in Virginia have been lavish with their superlatives in describing the William Byrds, " Westover " and life there. With the third generation came adversity, and after the death, in 1814, of the widow of the third William, " Westover " was sold for a small sum. But few if any writers have mentioned what became of the slaves. Shortly after his mother's death Richard Willing Byrd advertised as follows:

" On Thursday the 19th of January next [1815], if fair, otherwise, on the next fair day, I will expose to public sale, at Westover, in the county of Charles City, *Upwards of an Hundred Likely Virginia born Slaves.* Among them are coarse carpenters, shoe-makers and blacksmiths; also good washers and plain cooks, and house servants of both sexes. I do not know [another] such a valuable number of good negroes. * * *

At the same time, upon a credit of six months, I will sell, *Ten Fine Mules, two Waggons, and an excellent Chariot.*" [31]

In 1819, when slaves were still cheap in Virginia, Francis Corbin wrote to Madison: " Under the best management, . . . it [farming by slave-labor] does not afford us two per cent upon our capital, and often brings us into debt." [32]

[30] " The Subscriber will offer For Sale several FAMILIES OF NEGROES, at the Albemarle May Court, for cash or on a credit as may suit the purchasers. THOMAS MANN RANDOLPH the [then] elder, of Albemarle county.—Richmond *Enquirer,* Apr. 12, 1815.

[31] Richmond *Enquirer,* Jan. 5, 1815, and many other days, of course.

[32] *Mass. Hist. Soc. Papers,* Jan., 1910, p. 261.

Bushrod Washington, a Justice of the Supreme Court of the United States and a nephew of the first President, inherited Mount Vernon and 400 acres, but not General Washington's slaves, for these were liberated. When the Justice was president of the American Colonization Society he expressed a hope for abolition and called slavery the only stain on our political institutions. Not unnaturally his slaves looked forward to freedom after his death, especially as he, like the most revered of Americans, had no children. Such expectations did not, of course, increase their industry. In 1821, the Justice wrote that he had " struggled for about twenty years to pay the expenses of my farm, and to afford a considerable support to those who cultivated it, *from the produce of their labor*. In this way to have balanced the account would have satisfied me." But he had annually paid from $500 to $1,000 to make up the loss.[33] Although he frankly informed his slaves that their hopes were vain, they neither ceased their longings nor were any more considerate of his lack of profits. A valuable cook and two other slaves ran away " without the pretence of a cause ",—slavery and a natural desire for freedom not being counted. The cook safely reached the North, but the others were recovered, after an expense of about $250. And the Justice believed that nearly all of his male fieldhands were intending to try to escape when he returned to his circuit. His negroes, he said, had become insubordinate and " worse than useless ". In August, 1821, he sold, to two Louisiana planters on the Red River, 54 (of his total 90) for $10,000—an average of about $185 each for all ages. The Leesburg, Virginia, *Genius of Liberty* of August 21, 1821, contained this item:

" On Saturday last a *drove* of negroes, consisting of about 100 men, women, and children, passed through this town for a southern destina-

---

[33] 21 *Niles' Register*, 71. Presumably this included his living expenses at Mount Vernon. Nor was anything said about the value of the natural increase of the slaves, which must have amounted to a few thousand dollars.

tion.—*Fifty-four* of the above unhappy wretches were sold by *Judge Washington,* of Mount Vernon, PRESIDENT OF THE MOTHER COLONIZATION SOCIETY."

The Justice considered that he had been very generous because he took special pains to prevent the separation of husbands and wives and let these planters (who promised to keep them together) have them for " $2,500 less than the price which I [he] had at first fixed upon ". According to ideas and practices in Virginia at that time, the Justice's acts and reasoning were exceptionally considerate and honorable.[34]

Like many others, the amiable James Madison in his old age, finding that his slaves and farms did not produce enough to cover the expenses of maintenance, doubtless including his own living, sold some of his best lands and a dozen of his negroes to keep things going safely.[35]

After fifteen years of inquiry Jesse Burton Harrison—a scholarly man and the father of Burton Harrison, Jefferson Davis's private secretary in Confederate days—expressed the opinion in 1832, that " a very great proportion of the larger plantations, with from fifty to one hundred slaves, actually bring their proprietors in debt at the end of a short term of years, notwithstanding what would once in Virginia have been deemed very sheer economy; that much the larger part of the considerable landholders are content, if they barely meet their plantation expenses

[34] Niles, who in his Baltimore *Weekly Register* had credited erroneous reports about the sale and made very sharp comments, seemed to conclude that the Justice's explanation would be considered a vindication.—21 *Niles' Register,* pp. 1, 39, 70-72, give the original report and the Justice's long statement.

Somewhat similar cases were probably not rare in Md. Representative Weems's brother had a gang of slaves who had been so unprofitable that either some of them or some of his lands had to go to pay his debts. As the lands were hardly salable, the slaves expected to be taken in execution and scattered. A Louisiana planter bought twenty in families.—*Cong. Debates,* 1828-29, 183.

[35] Martineau, 1 *Retrospect of Western Travel,* 191-92.

without a loss of capital; and that, of those who make any [strictly agricultural] profit, it will in none but rare instances average more than one to one and a half per cent on the capital invested."[36] Evidently Corbin's estimate of the average profits from planting was not too low. The experiences of Jefferson, Madison, Bushrod Washington and many others of equally high standing were not exceptionally unfortunate. Purely agricultural conditions in Virginia grew worse rather than better. And intermittent fear of slave insurrections and a growing sentiment in favor of colonization and of gradual emancipation were additional circumstances that had much significance.

Before the end of the eighteenth century the rapidly increasing proportion of slaves in the seaboard regions south of the Potomac was viewed by thoughtful persons with grave misgivings. All history had demonstrated that where slavery existed plots for freedom were inevitable. And in the South rumors of them were nearly everywhere sufficient to keep fear alive if not alert. It was a slave conspiracy in Virginia in 1800 that prompted the first legislative effort toward colonization, the purpose of which was to eliminate free negroes. Apprehension of uprisings helped to bring the American Colonization Society into existence, in the winter of 1816-17. But as soon as this society manifested vigor and a somewhat antislavery purpose, opposition to it, in the planting regions, increased faster than support. Insisting that it was the free colored population in a slave State, not slavery, that was the great menace, the proslavery men expected to find a sufficient remedy in exiling or enslaving the free negroes and dispersing many of the slaves by their sale or removal to the new States and the Territories.

Late in the summer of 1831, a band of slaves under the lead of Nat Turner massacred about three score white

[36] 12 *Amer. Quarterly Review* (Dec., 1832), 390.

persons near Southampton, Virginia. Turner fancied that he was called of the Lord and heard voices from the air and read messages in the sky and on the leaves, ordering him to free his people by murdering their masters. This insurrection was accepted by many persons as conclusive evidence that both more slaves and all free negroes should be sent away. But many Northern States as well as all Southern barred free negroes, for it was generally assumed that they were either vicious or likely to become paupers. Believing that as a result of actual or feared insurrections Virginia and other States were taking pains to sell to the traders the most dangerous slaves and criminal free negroes, Alabama, Mississippi, Louisiana and other States passed laws forbidding all importations for sale.[37]

These barriers against Virginia's outpouring of slaves were cited as conclusive evidence of the inadequacy of the remedy by dispersion and that the State would ere long be inundated by its own negroes. Antislavery men in Virginia took advantage of the conditions to urge gradual abolition, which they wished to begin by freeing all slaves born after 1840. This plan, ably championed by Thomas Jefferson Randolph—a common grandson of Jefferson and of the first Thomas Mann Randolph—was much like Jefferson's of about half a century previously. These wise, but still unappreciated men, were enthusiastic colonizationists, hoping that all negroes, or enough to remove serious dangers, could ultimately be sent to Africa or the West Indies.

Why their efforts were futile will be evident when we know more of the slave-trade and of the importance of slave-rearing.

[37] See *post* p. 270 ff.

CHAPTER II

EARLY DOMESTIC SLAVE–TRADING

In colonial days, strictly domestic slave-trading in the South was secondary and mainly in American-born negroes, who, as a rule, were the only slaves fit for house-servants or even partially skilled laborers. In cities, still small, there was at times considerable trading of this kind, apart from the sale of slaveholding estates for division or debts. While primogeniture lasted it obviated the sale of many estates, but subsequently such sales became so common as to be almost the rule rather than the exception.

The domestic trade was well developed, especially in Maryland, Virginia and South Carolina, before the end of the eighteenth century.[1] The Fredericksburg *Virginia Herald* of February 5, 1799, made a remarkable showing in advertising the following lots of slaves for sale:

"a valuable negro fellow", about 28 years old, who knew something of carpentry and was an excellent sawyer;

two valuable young men, one an excellent shoemaker and the other a nailor, "in which a great bargain" might be realized;

two excellent ship-carpenters, for sale or hire;

15 likely young negroes belonging to the estate of William Bruce, then lately deceased, to be sold at auction;

"a likely young negro wench, 17 years old";

"a middle aged negro woman * * * with her two male children, the eldest four years of age";

another mother, 21 years of age, with her two female children.

Moreover, William Lovell had three carpenters and " a

---

[1] The Charleston, S. C., *City Gazette and Daily Advertiser* of Feb. 25. 1796, contained 14 advertisements about the public or private sale, hiring or purchase of a total of 288 slaves besides "a number". Not one of them seems to have come directly either from Africa or another State.

young wench " whom he would hire out on bond and security, and some unnamed person wished to buy a female house-servant of good character. It also contained advertisements of these forthcoming auctions in the adjoining county of Caroline:

" 25 negroes consisting of men, women, boys and girls, the property of James Dunlop, Jr., of Great Britain ", for whom Edmund Pendleton, Jr., was attorney;

18 negroes of the same kind, belonging to a Timberlake estate;

and two good sawyers and a girl about 12 years old (together with two work-horses), all to be disposed of to the highest bidder to discharge the debts of their deceased master, Reuben Thornton.

The issue of December 3, 1799, offered three lots of slaves for sale, privately: a man and a woman on short credit; " a wench and four female children "; two millers and four coopers (all of whom were also bakers), two men laborers, three women and five children. On the 23d, 12 or 15 men, women, boys and girls were to be sold for cash in front of a tavern. There were also advertisements of prospective sales in other counties: on January 13, 1800, " if fair, if not, the next fair day ", the executor of the estate of William Fauntleroy was to sell, at Westmoreland Court House, " to the highest bidder, for ready payment, about 40 likely Virginia-born slaves, consisting of men, boys, women and children ". Two similar sales from the estates of decedents were soon to be held in Middlesex county: one of twenty-odd negroes, and another of between 40 and 50. And the owner of the Wilderness Tavern property— which in little more than three score years was to be famous in military history—wished to rent it, two good blacksmiths with their tools, and a good hostler.

Of the 22 slave-advertisements in the issues of these two days only one mentioned the word *family*. It was in an announcement of a sale by John F. Mercer—a personal and political friend of Jefferson and at different times a holder of high offices in both Virginia and Maryland— saying that on December 10th, he would sell, in Stafford county, several families, who had been reserved from previous sales. Were they to be offered only in families? If they could be so disposed of prior to December 10th, then the terms would be " much moderated ", and the public would have timely notice in the newspapers. Otherwise they would be " offered at public sale in such manner as the bidders may require ". As all but four days of the time is known to have elapsed without any change in the advertisement,[2] it is almost certain that the family ties of these negroes, except mothers and small children, were disregarded.

Among all those vendors there was apparently not a regular trader; but it would be rash to suppose that there were not some among the purchasers. At this time traders were buying in Maryland and Virginia and selling in South Carolina and Georgia.

When estates were to be disposed of there was no hesitancy about mentioning the name of the late master—in fact, it could not well be avoided, and it greatly helped to attract attention and to increase the financial returns. When one or a few slaves were sold, it was usually because their cash value was desired, and therefore the most marketable were selected, such as superior laborers, skilled mechanics or young mothers with one or more children. In such cases, especially when mothers with young children were offered, the vendor commonly concealed his identity and requested any one interested to " enquire of the printer ", who acted orally as a connecting-link.[3]

---

[2] It was unchanged Dec. 6, 1799. Immediately subsequent numbers are lacking in the Library of Congress file.

[3] The following are fair samples:

" FOR SALE, A likely young Negro Man, *By trade a Cooper. Enquire of the Printer.*"

" FOR SALE, A LIKELY YOUNG NEGRO WENCH, With a Male Child.

Very similar and also other features were appearing in the Richmond newspapers about this time. Without explanation, Wilson Cary Nicholas, the future Governor of Virginia, was advertising that he would soon sell " 100 prime negroes, consisting of men, women, boys and girls ", at Warren, Albemarle county.[4] A few buyers, some evidently traders and other probably planters, were advertising for considerable numbers, one for boys from 7 to 15 years old.[5] And the fact that in five out of eight slave advertisements in the Richmond *Virginia Argus* of December 24, 1803, the negroes were described as " Virginia-born ", indicated that native Africans were still in the market and were less desirable.

The interstate trade came with the early economic demand for it. Although for many years prior to 1803 South Carolina forbade the importation of negroes from

Price 350 DOLLARS Cash.—Apply to Richard S. Hackley."—Both advts. in the Fredericksburg *Va. Herald*, July 2, 1799.

"FOR SALE, A WENCH and four female children, about 16, 9, 5 and 2 years old.—For terms, enquire of THE PRINTER."

" FOR SALE, A NEGRO MAN, ABOUT 38 years of age, very healthy and strong; he has been principally since a boy engaged in hewing, sawing, planing and polishing furniture, and is well acquainted with taking care of horses, and hard labor in general. His present owner having no such employment for him, is the cause of his being offered for sale. He can be recommended as faithfully honest.—For terms, apply to *The Printer hereof*."—*Va. Herald*, respectively, Aug. 16 and Sept. 3, 1799.

" FOR SALE, A LIKELY Negro Wench, 18 years of age, with a healthy Male Child, two years old—Enquire of The Printer."—*Va. Herald*, Sept. 17, 1799.

[4] Richmond Semi-Weekly *Enquirer*, Nov. 22, 1805.

[5] "NEGROES Wanted. Enquire at WILLIAM DAVIDSON'S near the Market."

"Wants to Purchase, FROM FIFTY TO ONE HUNDRED NEGROES, In Families.—Would prefer them in an entire gang, from one person.—Apply at this office, or Tappahannock, by letter, addressed to M. Between this and first Oct.—The number, ages and sex is required."—Richmond, *Va. Argus*, Sept. 14, 1803.

"CASH WILL *be given for* 12 *or* 15 *BOYS, from* 7 *to* 15 *years old.* Enquire of the Printers."—Richmond *Enquirer*, Feb. 1, 1805.

Africa, they were openly brought in from Savannah. In 1796, and doubtless at other times, Savannah importers of large African cargoes maintained regular agents in Charleston and advertised the fact.[6] The " calling out for slaves for their new lands " was inevitable on the part of many settlers advancing and spreading out in the Southwest. The increase of slaves in Tennessee from not quite 3,500 in 1790 to more than 13,500 in 1800, and in Kentucky from 12,500 to more than 40,000, must have involved much trading. From 1800 to 1810 Tennessee's slave population augmented 31,000 and Kentucky's 40,000. Many thousands, hundreds of whom were imported Africans, were also taken to regions now known as Alabama, Mississippi and Louisiana. Fieldhands, house-servants, carpenters and blacksmiths, who were cheapest in Maryland and Virginia, were demanded. South Carolinians and Georgians had long been drawing on these States for the better class of slaves.[7] The operations of interstate traders had become so common by January, 1802, that the grand jury of Alexandria county, in the District of Columbia, described " as a grievance, the practice of persons coming from distant parts of the United States into this District for the purpose of purchasing slaves, where they exhibit to our view a scene of wretchedness and human degradation, disgraceful to our characters as citizens of a free government ". Numerous victims of slavery were said to have been collected and lodged in places of confinement until the desired numbers were obtained and " then turned out in our streets and exposed to view, loaded with chains as though they had committed some heinous offence against our laws. We consider it a grievance * * * that the interposition of civil author-

---

[6] Their advts. about negroes from the " Gold Coast ", the " Isles de Loss " etc. can be seen in the Charleston *City Gazette and Daily Advertiser* of July 4, Aug. 26, 1796, and other dates. See also *post* p. 377 n.

[7] *Life and Adventures of Charles Ball* (Pittsburgh, 1853), 12, 29 ff.; Phillips, *Amer. Negro Slavery*, 165-66, 188-89, 2 *Plantation* etc., 55, 56, 70-71.

ity cannot be had to prevent parents being wrested from their offspring, and children from their parents, without respect to the ties of nature." [8]

By 1810 several regular traders had appeared in Fredericksburg and were advertising in laconic, businesslike language. John Stannard said: "I WILL GIVE CASH for a few LIKELY YOUNG NEGROES." John Crump was less concise but equally effective: "I *wish to purchase* Thirty or Forty Negroes, in families, for which I will give the cash." [9] A few months later Anthony Buck advised the public that about January 20, 1811, sixty negroes would be wanted, for which cash would be given. "It would be desirable to have a few families." [10]

The war of 1812 checked the trade for a few years, then it became more enterprising and profitable. [11] Little Winchester, situated in farming country in the Shenandoah Valley and unsuited to slave labor, was sufficiently known by 1818 as a source of supplies to tempt several traders wearing labels on their hats offering "Cash for Negroes". Yet the historian that cites the fact, strangely represents that not the presence of the traders but the expression of indignation against them was typical. [12] It was hardly more typical than was the protest in Alexandria in 1802. Both were rare exceptions. In this part of Virginia there were numerous earnest advocates of colonization, which in 1818 was in the first flush of popularity. Of course they and many other persons hated traders. On this account, slave-sellers—either wishing to avoid antislavery criticism or being sympathetic with the slaves to be sold—sometimes expressly barred the traders. But it was much more significant expressly to invite

[8] Alexandria *Phenix Gazette*, June 22, 1827, quotes the document.
[9] *Va. Herald*, Sept. 12, 1810.
[10] *Va. Herald*, Dec. 1, 1810.
[11] Torrey, *Domestic Slavery in the U. S.*, 32-34, 41, 42, shows that it was common before 1816.
[12] Prof. U. B. Phillips, *American Negro Slavery*, 192.

traders, which John Randolph had already denounced in
the House of Representatives. Turning to a file of a
newspaper of this time, published in Warrenton, only
about 30 miles from Alexandria and about 40 miles from
Winchester, these advertisements were found:

* * * "for sale several Likely Negro Girls, From twelve to eighteen
years of age, for Cash." * * * [13]

* * * "For Cash, a likely negro woman, with her four children, the
eldest a boy, about eleven years of age." [14]

"A Likely Young Woman, about sixteen years of age." [15]

"Will be sold for Cash or good Bonds, 3 LIKELY NEGRO WOMEN,
One with a male child. No objection will be made to traders purchasing.
Enquire at this office." [16]

The names of all the other sellers were mentioned with
their respective advertisements; but to have given one's
name when inviting traders would have needlessly incurred
criticism. Traders came with increasing frequency to all
three towns, because they were not disappointed. In each
there was later at least one resident trader, or resident
agent for some large trader, and in Alexandria there were
usually several.[17]

[13] Warrenton, Va., *Palladium of Liberty*, Jan. 15, 1819. For brevity, only
the main part of each advt. will be quoted.

[14] *Ibid.*, Jan. 22, 1819.

[15] *Ibid.*, May 7, 1819.

[16] *Ibid.*, Feb. 4, 1820. See also *post* p. 27 for a more urgent invitation to
traders.

[17] Here are samples of later advertisements in Winchester:—

"NEGROES WANTED. CASH will be given for fifteen or twenty likely
negroes. Apply at Capt. Bryarly's tavern. JOHN B. WILLIAMSON."

"NEGROES WANTED. THE subscriber wishes to buy 20 or 30 likely
negroes, from 12 to 25 years of age. Any person having such for sale, may
for further information apply at E. M'Guire's hotel, in Winchester, where
the subscriber will generally be found.—THOMAS DYSON."—Winchester,
Va., *Republican*, June 23 and Aug. 18, respectively, 1826.

And in the same year, trader Samuel Garey was in Cumberland, Maryland,
far up in the mountains and close to Pennsylvania, flaunting cash to tempt
owners of "likely" negroes.—Cumberland, *Maryland Advocate*, Oct. 28, 1826.

In 1851-52, the Campbells, large interstate traders (see *post* pp. 121, 316 ff),

The lower counties of Virginia and Maryland naturally supplied the largest numbers for the market. A visitor in Fredericksburg in the summer of 1835 found a trader with a slave-pen containing about 150 whom he was planning to take overland to the New Orleans market.[18] This was undoubtedly N. C. Finnall of the New Orleans firm of Finnall & Freeman, who since early in that year had been advertising for 200 slaves between the ages of 15 and 25.[19] Instead of 200, they are known to have bought nearly 300 in about six or eight months.[20]

About the same time, James Vass, who seems to have been a miller, was advertising: " I want to purchase 10 or 12 negroes, chiefly young females, to go to the most healthy section of the Southern country. Should it be an object with any person or persons wishing to dispose of such, they can be satisfactorily assured that the negroes are wanted for the exclusive use of a private gentleman well known here, and not for sale ". [21] Evidently " breeders " were desired. A vendor, apparently not a regular trader, but eager to sell to anyone with cash, had " 5 or

had a regular agent in Winchester.—Stowe, Key to Uncle Tom's Cabin, 145, quotes his advt.

For evidence of the traders in Warrenton see post pp. 59 n., 370, and for those in Alexandria see chapter three.

[18] Ethan Allen Andrews, Slavery and the Domestic Slave Trade (1836), 164-65. Andrews, a Yale graduate of 1810, taught ancient languages in N. C. University, 1822-28, and for several years had been the head of a school in New Haven, Conn., when in 1835 he was sent to investigate slavery and the domestic slave-trade in Md., Va. and the D. C. His trip resulted in a little volume that has lasting historical value and charming simplicity. Subsequently he acquired much distinction by his Latin textbooks etc.

[19] Va. Herald, Aug. 19, 1835.

[20] Besides the 150 in the yard in July, 1835, 30 were sent on the "Virginia" from Richmond, Dec. 11, 1834; 50 from Norfolk on the "Ariel", Jan. 17, 1835, and a total of 67 from Alexandria on the "Uncas", Feb. 5 and March 26, 1835, and on the "Tribune", Feb. 26, 1835. Three of these shipments were consigned to "Theophilus Freeman" and one to "Freeman or N. C. Finnall".—The manifests are in the Library of Congress.

[21] Va. Herald, Aug. 19, 1835. An advt. in the number of Jan. 17, 1835, indicates that he was a miller.

6 slaves, consisting of men, boys and one woman ". He preferred to dispose of them by private sale, but if that could not be done, they would be auctioned off, for cash, in front of the hotel. Whoever wished to know more should inquire of the printer.[22] Another vendor, hiding behind the editor instead of the printer, was equally secretive but more obliging: he offered a " negro woman, with one or more children, to suit the purchaser—all uncommonly likely ". [23]

In marked contrast with these anonymous advertisements were three announcements of forthcoming sales in adjoining counties. Mann A. Page had " 15 or 16 likely young negroes consisting of boys, girls, women and children " to be sold at auction for cash (" no postponements on account of the weather ") at the front door of the Orange Hotel, at Orange Court House. He was evidently of the slaveholding aristocracy, as his name suggests, for he gave notice that " gentlemen wanting good house servants of tried faithfulness, will find this a good opportunity to supply themselves ". [24] In Caroline county, John Washington, the administrator of Elizabeth Washington, would likewise dispose of one man and two girls, on courtday; and Lucy Hundley, administratrix of Wm. K. Hundley, a few days earlier would sell at a tavern called Needwood, " two likely young negroes ". " Traders will do well to attend the sale." [25] Indeed, it was hardly possible to prevent their buying at public sales; it was rarely attempted, for they were usually welcome. Here they were expressly invited. Persons of high standing needing money sold their best negroes because they would bring most. It was the money, not the purchasers or the slaves, that mattered.

[22] *Va. Herald*, March 21, 1835.
[23] " FOR SALE, A NEGRO WOMAN, with one or more Children, to suit the purchaser—all uncommonly likely. The woman is a first-rate Cook, and can weave plain Cloth. Enquire of the Editor.—*Va. Herald*, Feb. 7, 1835.
[24] *Va. Herald*, Jan. 7, 1835.
[25] Both in Richmond *Enquirer*, Jan. 1, 1835.

The conditions in Richmond, Petersburg and other cities were not unlike those in Fredericksburg.[26]

Thanks to the rising value of slave property, Virginia was rapidly recovering from the antislavery influences of the eighteenth and the early nineteenth century, but in Maryland those influences increased. Both are shown by these facts: between 1790 and 1860 Maryland's free negro population increased more than tenfold (although a few thousand were colonized in Africa), Virginia's considerably less than fivefold; Maryland's slaves decreased one-sixth, Virginia's increased about 200,000.[27] Because slave property in Maryland was less secure, more troublesome and, in relation to other opportunities, less profitable than in Virginia, it gave less prestige and slaveowners were more easily reconciled to emancipation, colonization or sale. Yet, in case of sale, a much larger proportion of masters than elsewhere wished to show or to affect humanitarian considerations; and every vendor liked to be told, and still more to tell others, that his slaves were " bought by (or for) a planter ". And where escape to the North was tempting and easy, property interests demanded that slaves should be sold on the first

[26] Here are samples of the enterprise of traders in Richmond and Petersburg in 1835:—

" CASH FOR 200 NEGROES.—We will give the highest market price, in cash, for two hundred likely Negroes, from 12 to 25 years of age. Every person who intends to sell, will do well to give us a call, near Seabrook's Warehouse, where we are prepared to keep them safe and comfortable, whether for sale or otherwise.—THOS. M'CARGO & CO."—Richmond *Enquirer*, Dec. 31, 1835.

" NEGROES! NEGROES!!—I have stationed myself at the Bollingbrook Hotel, in Petersburg, to buy Negroes. Persons wishing to sell, either in Town or adjoining counties, will do well to give me a call, as I expect to pay liberal prices for such as are likely, of both sexes, from 12 to 30 years of age—Mechanics and house servants in particular.—Any information directed to the subscriber, will be attended to promptly.—RICHARD R. BEASLEY."— Richmond *Enquirer*, May 8, 1835.

[27] See Census table of slave population 1790-1860, *post*, opposite p. 382.

suspicion of an intention to run away. Under such conditions slave-trading was sure to thrive.

The counties comprising what is called the Eastern Shore of Maryland demonstrated what slave-trading became under the most favorable influences. Of the nine counties let us consider the six where the most data can be found. The trading centered in the countyseats—Cambridge (Dorchester), Princess Anne (Somerset), Centreville (Queen Anne), Snow Hill (Worcester), Easton (Talbot) and Salisbury (Wicomico). During 1830-40 there was a considerable decrease in the slave population in each of the five counties where the population is known, and the total decrease was nearly 4,000.[28] That some decrease, instead of a still greater normal increase, was mainly due to slave-selling cannot be doubted when we know the number and the activities of the traders.

A search through an incomplete file of the Cambridge *Chronicle* discloses not less than 15 traders endeavoring to make purchases in Dorchester county during 1831-35. And there were three other large buyers, one or all of whom may not have been purchasing strictly for their own use. Besides these 15 or more there were probably several times as many petty traders, agents or helpers that did not advertise but made purchases or obtained fees by bringing vendors and dealers together. It was common to appeal for such assistants. A regular trader thus advertised for many of them:

[28] Countyseats	Counties	Slave Populations 1830	1840
Centreville	Queen Anne	4,872	3,960
Easton	Talbot	4,173	3,687
Cambridge	Dorchester	5,001	4,227
Princess Anne	Somerset	6,556	5,377
Salisbury	Wicomico	Figures lacking	
Snow Hill	Worcester	4,032	3,539
		24,634	20,790

—" Census 1870 " Population, pp. 36-37.

" N. B.—Persons desirous of engaging in this business as agents, either in town or country, can procure employment, and obtain liberal commissions, on application to the subscriber." [29]

A like search of the Princess Anne *Village Herald* indicates that the traders were fully one-half or two-thirds as numerous in Somerset county. From broken files of Centreville and Snow Hill newspapers it is apparent that they were not at all scarce in Queen Anne and Worcester counties. The advertisements in one county often named agents in other counties and requested reprinting there. Easton was but little behind Centreville and Princess Anne. It is believed that at least 40 or 50, perhaps 60 or 80, regular traders of various degrees operated in these six counties for short or long periods between 1831-35. Few except the rather small traders and agents were actual residents of the region. The others came only to make their purchases; their sales were elsewhere.

The traders were so numerous because slaves in large numbers were nowhere else so cheap, and trafficking in them had strong attractions for persons of certain types. From 1829 to 1832 John Bull, buying on the Maryland and the Virginia peninsula of the Eastern Shore, offered to pay what he called the highest prices for slaves to go to the Louisiana market: for first-rate young men from 18 to 24 years of age, from $400 to $450; for women of the same age, $250 to $275, or $280, for first-rate.[30] Although only exceptionally good slaves brought such prices there, they could be resold in Alabama, Mississippi and Louisiana for nearly or quite twice as much. Such conditions excited the imagination and appealed both to very energetic men and also to many that were too proud or too indolent to farm or lacked the talent, capital or inclination to earn a living at any ordinary business or labor. If they could

[29] N. Hight, Cambridge *Chronicle*, Feb. 8, 1834.
[30] Snow Hill *Messenger*, Dec. 6, 1830.

assist in a few successful speculations, they were sure to
flatter themselves that they had a genius for judging
negroes. And they at once considered that they rightly
belonged to the slaveholding class and were superior to
all other non-slaveholders, however thrifty or prosperous.
The agents needed no capital; the petty traders but little,
for the large dealers were always ready to give a premium
for prime slaves.

But advantageously to buy many of the best slaves
required much cash and great activity in all directions.
Some of the traders seemed to be ubiquitous. Where
opportunities did not appear they must be found or
created; and a good opportunity was worth a long
journey. One H. Robertson was so anxious to obtain fifty
negroes between the ages of 8 and 25 that he promised
the highest cash prices, with or without competition,
and without requiring certificates of character.[31] It was
not unprecedented but very rare thus virtually to advertise for the vicious, although it was much less rare to
speculate in them. In the spring of 1833, the firm of C.
S. and J. M. Knight regularly made the round of seven
counties of the Eastern Shore: Cambridge was their
headquarters; one partner, stationed at Easton, each week
visited Centreville and Chestertown, the countyseats of
Queen Anne and of Kent, and the other partner went
from Salisbury to Princess Anne and Snow Hill.[32]

In 1830, the firm of Woolfolks [two or more], Sanders
& Overley, wished to purchase "200 negroes for the
New Orleans market". One Woolfolk was living at Salisbury; Sanders & Overley were at Princess Anne; and
there was an agent at Snow Hill. Thus the firm was
active in at least three counties.[33] The two or more
Woolfolks soon dropped out but were happily not lost

[31] Centreville *Times*, June 16, 1832.

[32] Cambridge *Chronicle*, May 25, 1833; Snow Hill *Messenger*, May 6, 1833;
see also the photostat of the Centreville *Times*, Apr. 19, 1834, *post*, opposite
p. 32.

[33] Snow Hill *Messenger*, Dec. 6, 1830.

from historical view. In 1835 Overley & Sanders, while keeping headquarters at Princess Anne, Somerset county, also scoured Dorchester and Talbot counties.[34] In 1840 they were still " in the market prepared to buy FIVE HUNDRED NEGROES of all ages and descriptions " and they had regular agents in Easton, Cambridge, and in Belle Haven, Accomac county, Virginia.[35]

To make the largest possible profits, traders in Maryland and Virginia not infrequently pretended to be planters from the lower South buying for their own use, or to have orders to purchase families for some unnamed and distant " planter ". When the large firm of Woolfolks, Sanders & Overley, was seeking the " 200 for the New Orleans market ", they also assured the credulous public of this: " One of the firm wishes to buy families for his own use, and will give for them the highest prices ";[36] and of this: " One of the firm intends declining the trade after the present year and wishes to purchase family negroes for his own use." [37] " After the present year " was evidently used in the pickwickian sense of *long after,* for this feature was so satisfactory that it was still running as late as May, 1831.

Early in 1830 Richard C. Woolfolk was advertising in Princess Anne and Salisbury that he would " give more than any other purchaser for likely young negroes, viz.:—fellows, women, lads, small girls, and families ". " Mr. Sanders " was his agent.[38] (Everywhere traders of all degrees were very careful to put " Mr." before references to one another, until riches or some distinction brought a military title.) And to the readers of the Snow Hill *Messenger* Woolfolk was proclaiming: " I

[34] Princess Anne *Village Herald,* Jan. 13, 1835; Cambridge *Chronicle,* Oct. 3, 1835; Princess Anne *Somerset Herald,* Oct. 23, 1838.
[35] Princess Anne *Somerset Herald,* Nov. 24, 1840.
[36] Princess Anne *Village Herald,* Sept. 14, 1830.
[37] Snow Hill *Messenger,* Dec. 6, 1830.
[38] Princess Anne *Village Herald,* May 11, 1830.

☞ Notice.

I wish to purchase fifty NEGROES of both sexes from 6 to 30 years of age for which I will give the highest cash prices; those having such to dispose of, would do well to give me a call before they sell to any one else as I am determined to give higher prices than any purchaser now in market, or may hereafter come; all communications addressed to me in Centreville on the subject will be immediately attended to by
ALEXANDER S JONES
February 8 1833

UNDERTAKING,
& Carpentering !
—o-o-o—

The subscriber, who has been engaged for the last ten years in the above business, takes this method of informing the public generally, that he is now prepared to do any work he may be favoured with. He assures all those who may be under the painful necessity of calling some one to attend funerals, that he will do every thing necessary for such an occasion—he has a good two horse carriage and will send as usual, coffins to any part of the county, free of charge, and will when practicable give his personal attention.

As I intend to keep for my assistance an experienced hand, I flatter myself from past favours, that I shall still be encouraged by a generous public.
EBIN COVINGTON
C. Ville, Oct. 26. tf.

☞ Cash for Negroes,
—oo—

The subscribers wish to purchase a number of likely young

NEGROES.

of both sexes, from the ages of twelve to 30 years; for such they will give the highest cash prices. Persons wishing to dispose of their slaves, will do well to call on Jas. M. Knight, at Mr. Reese's hotel in Centreville who will attend immediately their calls; or a line addressed to him will meet with prompt attention.
C, S, & JAS. M. KNIGHT
march 1st 1834,

150 SERVANTS

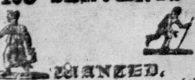

WANTED,

Of all descriptions——mechanics of all kinds from 12 to twenty-five years of age also 50 in families it is desirable to purchase them in large lots as they will be settled in Alabama and will not be separated—Persons having slaves to dispose of will do well to give me a call as I am permanently settled in this market, and at all times will give the highest cash prices. Any communication directed to me in Easton will be promptly attended to can at all times be found at Mr. Lowe'
May 5th. THOS. M. JONES.

NEGROES

wanted !

We wish to purchase 40 or 50 hands; we wish to purchase some families, & would like to purchase as many as practicable from the same plantation or neighborhood. —

Persons wishing to sell families can receive the most satisfactory evidence that we purchase for our own use &r will not separate them, by applying at the bar of Mr. Wilmer's tavern in this place,

FELIX HUSTON &
WALTER BYRNES,
Centreville Aug. 17th 1833

$150 Reward!

RANAWAY from the subscriber on the 27th instant three negro men and one negro woman,

JACOB, twenty three years old, 5 feet 6 inches high of dark complexion, very stout pleasing countenance walks stiff and smiles when spoken to.

PETER is 18 years old, about five feet six or seven inches high, slender made and nearly the color of Jacob,

SAM, is 26 years old, about five feet 4 or 5 inches high, complexion, black eyes very red and rolls them when spoken to.

CHARLOTTE is a bright mulatto about five feet eight or nine inches high

SLAVE-ADVERTISEMENTS IN THE CENTERVILLE, MARYLAND, *Times and Eastern-Shore Public Advertiser*, APRIL 19, 1834

wish to buy from 5[00] to 600 NEGRO SLAVES, and will at
all times give more than any other purchaser that is now,
or may hereafter come into this market—for such as may
suit me." One Elisha E. Whitelock was serving as his
agent in Snow Hill.[39] A few months later, Richard C.
Woolfolk was advertising in Somerset county calling for
" six or seven hundred negroes for the New Orleans
Market ".[40] The following year he was likewise saying:
" I wish to buy about 150 negroes for Mr. John Woolfolk
and myself. Large families are very desirable, as they
are not wanted for speculation, but for our own use." [41]

There were at least three Joneses trading separately in
that region during the 'thirties. Alexander S. probably
did not strip cradles, but he was at Centreville prepared
to buy all likely negroes from six to thirty years of age.
A single number of its *Times* contained a group of typical
advertisements by four traders and two " planters ".[42]
William B. Jones was ready to " pay the HIGHEST CASH
PRICES " on " any part of the Eastern Shore of Maryland
or Virginia ", and would also buy all the " likely " from
six to thirty years of age.[43] Still another Jones, Thomas
M., was appealing to the public thus:

" 150 SERVANTS WANTED—of all descriptions—mechanics of all
kinds from 12 to twenty-five years of age; also 50 in families; it is
desirable to purchase them in large lots as they will be settled in Ala
bama and will not be separated." [44]

At this time he was also widely advertised in the Washington *National Intelligencer* as an agent of great interstate traders having their Southwestern headquarters in

[39] Snow Hill *Messenger*, May 17, 1831.

[40] Princess Anne, *Village Herald*, Dec. 27, 1831.

[41] Snow Hill *Messenger*, Aug. 20, 1832.

[42] See photostat of the Centreville *Times*, Apr. 19, 1834, *ante* opp. p. 32.
In 1835 he was also acting as agent for Overley & Sanders.—Cambridge
Chronicle, Oct. 3, 1835.

[43] Princess Anne *Somerset Herald*, Oct. 23, 1838.

[44] Centreville *Times*, May 4, 1833; photostat of Apr. 19, 1834, *ante*
opp. p. 32.

Natchez, Mississippi.[45] But high prices in cash were likely
to convince most persons with " families " for sale that
even a trader regularly buying separate small children
from six years of age would not make the most of his
opportunities.

Elisha E. Whitelock duly rose to preëminence among
the traders at the countyseat with the picturesque, wintry
name. In 1828 his ambition was modest; " a few likely
negroes " satisfied it — temporarily.[46] Alas, Amos, purchased near Berlin, Maryland, was so unappreciative as
to prefer freedom to being sent to the South; he even
took " sundry clothing " and wickedly rode off on his
trader-master's bay horse.[47] But adversity did not discourage Whitelock. He continued to buy for Richard C.
Woolfolk as well as for himself. By 1833 he was happily able to offer the highest cash prices for from " one
HUNDRED to one THOUSAND NEGROES of any description ". [48]
That was meant to betoken tremendous prosperity, although all the traders together could hardly have found a
thousand for sale in that county; yet it was a real distinction in a slave-selling community. And Whitelock had
risen to political importance. In those days, before pri-
maries and conventions, it usually sufficed when the local
newspaper said: " We are authorized to announce ———
as a candidate for ———." One Littleton D. Teackle
in that manner appeared as candidate for the National
House of Representatives. If solemnly pronounced, his
name might be impressive. But some envious person
charged that its bearer had been self-nominated and did
not represent public sentiment. Littleton D. Teackle and
public sentiment needed a champion. Who was better
known or more influential than Snow Hill's citizen that

[45] *Post* p. 59 n.
[46] Snow Hill *Messenger*, Aug. 12, 1828.
[47] Snow Hill *Messenger*, Sept. 2, 1828.
[48] Snow Hill *Messenger*, May 6, 1833.

would, or fancied he could make others think he would, buy a thousand slaves? Elisha E. Whitelock bravely wrote: " I * * * do affirm that I, in accordance with the unbiased and republican will of Worcester county, did suggest Mr. Teackle's name to the printer of the Snow Hill *Messenger.*" [49] Tartarin was never more important in Tarascon.

Many other traders have been found, each advertising his business in one or more counties of the Eastern Shore, during these years. [50]

More than a few cases have been met with of persons advertising as planters desiring slaves for their own use. Appearances are not conclusive, but because planters took pride in making purchases openly they rarely concealed their names. [51]

[49] *Messenger*, May 6, 1833.

[50] Where a page of footnotes would be required for even brief details, it must suffice to mention the names of traders that seemed most active:— William Ramsey, William Harker, H. S. Atwood, James Houston, Benjamin F. Cochran, James G. Gordon, Levin D. Collier, William Roach, Jr., and Leonard P. Breedlove.

[51] " WANTED.—THE subscriber wishes to purchase for his own, and brother-in-law's use, thirty likely young negroes, to take to the State of Georgia. They must be clear of fault, and unquestionable titles will be required, in *every instance*, for which he will pay the highest cash prices. During his absence from Cambridge, he refers to Mr. Wm. H. Yates, for further particulars. U. J. BULLOCK."—Cambridge *Chronicle*, Aug. 25, 1838.

"WANTED TO PURCHASE FIFTEEN OR TWENTY YOUNG NEGROES, of both sexes, for my own use, to take to Arkansas, for which the highest cash prices will be paid. Any communications addressed to me, at Warrenton, Va., will receive prompt attention.—D. B. FISHER."—Alexandria *Gazette and Virginia Advertiser*, Sept. 3, 1860.

Here are samples of suspicious advts:—

"NEGROES WANTED.—A GENTLEMAN from the South wishes to purchase 40 or 50 effective Slaves, of good character, for his own service, and among them it is desirable to have a blacksmith, carpenter, coachman, and a man cook. His address is with the Editor of the Alexandria Gazette."—Wash., D. C., *National Intelligencer*, Aug. 19, 1833.

" NEGROES WANTED.—A gentleman who is about to remove to the South, wishes to purchase, *for his own use*, thirty or forty Negroes in families.—

B. B. Lamar, perhaps a Georgia planter, wanted plantation hands, for his " own use, and not for speculation ".
He preferred families, and was ready to go anywhere on
the peninsula to make his purchases.[52] He considered his
general assurance and offering " the highest prices "
sufficient, without either telling where his plantation was
or (unlike many anonymous " planter " advertisers) referring to some bartender as evidence of good faith.
More dubious was the case of Felix Huston and Walter
Byrnes. For a long period they jointly advertised in at
least three counties (Kent, Queen Anne and Dorchester)
for 40 or 50 negroes " for the use of their plantation in
Louisiana ". They preferred families and as many as
possible from the same plantation or neighborhood. To
preclude suspicion, assurance was given that the most
satisfactory evidence could be obtained by applying at the
bar of a certain tavern in Centreville.[53] This was undoubtedly General Felix Huston — " a typical military
adventurer, ambitious and aggressive " — who in 1835
enlisted for the independence of Texas,[54] for which he
spent much money and probably neglected his planting.
In 1838 he was advertising in the Natchez *Courier* " thirty
very fine acclimated negroes " for sale.[55]

Most of the counties of the peninsula between the
Chesapeake and the Potomac had larger slave populations than those on the Eastern Shore, were more accessible, and their slave-trade could hardly have been less.
Much of it went directly or indirectly to Baltimore and

Letters addressed to the care of the Publisher of the United States *Telegraph*
will be immediately attended to."—Wash., D. C., *United States Telegraph*,
Jan. 30, 1837. See *post* p. 38, notes 57 and 58.

[52] Snow Hill *Messenger*, Aug. 30, 1831.

[53] Their advt. ran in the Centreville *Times* (See photostat, opp. p. 32) from
Aug. 17, 1833, to Oct. 4, 1834, when the only available file breaks off; and a
similar advt., without suggesting application at the bar, continued in the
Cambridge *Chronicle* for a long period.

[54] Prof. J. E. Winston, *Miss. and the Independence of Texas*, 3, 9.

[55] Wm. Jay, *Misc. Writings on Slavery*, 272.

still more to the District of Columbia. Elsewhere in rural
Maryland the difference was mainly one of degree.

A large part of the slave-trading in Maryland centered in Baltimore, the State's only large city and the
focus of its commerce. The leading slave-merchants there
daily advertised in one or more metropolitan newspapers
which went to every part of the triangular little State.
But that did not suffice; these advertisements were often
reprinted at the countyseats. In the summer of 1835 Baltimore's leading slave-trader told a visitor that there were
then a dozen or more persons " in the business " in the
city.[56] He must have meant only the well-known resident
traders, and he did not exaggerate the number. There
were probably still more resident petty traders, and the
visiting traders that came to sell or to buy undoubtedly
several times outnumbered all that were resident.[57] Ad-

[56] E. A. Andrews, *Slavery* etc., 78.

[57] The Baltimore *Republican and Commercial Advertiser* of Feb. 2, 1835,
contained the following six advertisements in a row:—

"*Again in Market.*—CASH and very liberal prices will at all times be
given for SLAVES. All communications will be promptly attended to, if
loft at SINNER'S HOTEL, Water street, at which place the subscribers can
be found, or at their residence, Harford avenue, near the Missionary church;
the house is white.—JAS. F. PURVIS & CO."

* * * Advertisement of a firm of wine-merchants.

"NOTICE.—The subscriber, at Barnum's City Hotel, wishes to purchase
immediately thirty five or forty Slaves; a few mechanics and house servants
are wanted in that number—they will be bought in families or separate—
they are to be settled in Alabama. Liberal prices will be given.—J.
BATES, JR."

"CASH AND LIBERAL PRICES will be given for NEGROES. Apply to
AUSTIN WOOLFOLK, West Pratt st. at the intersection of the Washington
Road."

"CASH, CASH, CASH.—THE SUBSCRIBER wishes to purchase a number of SLAVES, of both sexes, for plantation, for which he will give the
highest CASH prices. Apply to No. 24 South street, opposite Second street.—
NAT. AUSTIN."

"CASH FOR NEGROES.—I WISH to purchase from 75 to 100 Negroes,
of both sexes, from the age of 8 to 25 years, for which I will pay liberal

vertisements on other and not remote days help to make up a list of considerably more than a dozen active traders.[58] Where eleven traders and a firm comprising at least two or three more were found advertising in 1835, only the firm was designated by the city directory as engaged in slave-trading.[59]

Hope H. Slatter wanted from 75 to 100 negroes from 8 to 25 years of age and " particularly to purchase several seamstresses and likely small fancy girls for nurses ". As a reference, he also preferred a bartender to the " Editor " or the " Printer ".[60] He was buying for the

prices. I can always be found at Owing's Globe Inn, corner of Howard and Market streets, Baltimore; and in my absence at any time, a line left at the bar will be attended to, immediately on my return.—HOPE H. SLATTER. N. B. I wish particularly to purchase several seamstresses and likely small fancy girls for nurses. I will also purchase several families. H. H. S."

" CASH!—I WISH to purchase a number of likely SERVANTS, (SLAVES) of both sexes, from about 12 to 25 years of age, of good habits. They are not for *speculation*. I can give the most unquestionable satisfaction, as to that. Persons wishing to part with their slaves, will do well to call or communicate with me, as I will give *at all times* the HIGHEST PRICES IN CASH.—JOHN BUSK. Office opposite the Exchange, South Gay st."

[58] Besides those mentioned in the previous note were: "*James Blair*, Esq., at his office in Eutaw street", an agent of Hope H. Slatter (*Republican* etc. June 18, 1835); *David H. White*, living on Loudenslager's Hill, Philadelphia Road, seeking "thirty or forty likely young Servants, slaves for life" (*Republican* etc., Oct. 14, 1835); *E. G. Abbott*, South Eutaw st., one door south of Pratt st., desiring "a few likely negroes" and "one or two likely families" (*Republican* etc. May 8, 1835); *Moody & Downes*, 37 South st., needing "about 10 or 12 to fill an order" "for a planter's own use and not for speculation" (*Republican* etc., Aug. 21, 1835), and then *an anonymous buyer* making this appeal: "WANTED, a large number of SLAVES—single ones or in families, but will not buy to separate families without their consent. [!] The gentleman wishing to purchase is a native of Maryland, and now and for the last 20 years a resident of Baltimore. Liberal prices will be given. Enquire of the Editor."—*Republican* etc., Jan. 10, 1835.

[59] Matchett's Baltimore *Director* [sic] *for 1835-36* called Purvis a "dealer in negroes", Blair a "justice of peace", White a "tavern keeper", Moody & Downes "commission agents and exchange brokers". John Busk's occupation was not indicated, but according to the *Director for 1837-38* he was "an auctioneer". A few years later a trader was usually, but not always, designated accordingly.

[60] See *ante* p. 37 n.-38 n. for his advt.

" Southern market " and would go, or send his agent, to
any part of the State to inspect negroes for sale.[61] A few
weeks later he gave Professor Andrews his selling-prices:
" likely fellows " from 18 to 25 years old were from $500
to $650; women of the same age and quality, from $300
to $500 — the best fieldhands, from $300 to $400. And he
was enthusiastic about a sprightly, bright mulatto girl
only seven years old, as fine a servant as he ever saw,
who could intelligently run errands and market for small
articles; she was for sale for $250.[62] He had not adver-
tised in vain for little girls. Then or a few years later,
he had a large new jail, " fitted up with bolts and bars ",
on one of the principal streets. It sometimes contained
300 or 400 slaves. Antislavery callers frankly admitted
that cleanliness and order were conspicuous in it and
that the physical wants of the slaves were not neglected by
Slatter.[63]

Purvis & Company did a large business notwithstanding
their strange address: their headquarters was at Sinner's
Hotel and they lived " on Gallows hill, near the Missionary church—the house is white ".[64] They continually advertised — at times, twice on the same page [65]— in a Baltimore daily newspaper and also in rural weekly journals;
for they bought slaves of all kinds in their city and
throughout the State,[66] turning over those most suitable
for the Louisiana and the Mississippi markets to a great
firm in the District of Columbia.

The Woolfolks were born slave-traders. There were at
least six or seven of them in Maryland,[67] and Austin was

[61] *Republican* etc., June 18, 1835.
[62] Andrews, 77, 78.
[63] Joseph Sturge, *A Visit to the U. S. in 1841* (Boston, 1842), 45, 46.
He erroneously called him Hope H. Slaughter. For more see *post* p. 372 ff.
[64] *Republican* etc., July 3, 1833. See *ante* p. 37, note 57.
[65] *Republican* etc., Feb. 20, 1833, and many other dates.
[66] Cambridge *Chronicle*, Sept. 15, 1832.
[67] Richard C. and John have already been noticed. William W. and J. B.
were buying in Easton in 1828.—Easton *General Advertiser*, June 3 and 24,

the most notorious. In addition to the usual qualities of the family and of the trade, he displayed strange craft and vanity. On the first page of the leading Baltimore journal there daily appeared this brief notice:—

"PERSONS

WISHING to see the SUBSCRIBER will please call at his residence, head of Pratt street, above the Three Tuns Tavern.

AUSTIN WOOLFOLK." [68]

The purpose was to excite curiosity and to prompt the question: Who is Austin Woolfolk and why do so many persons wish to see him? In a neighboring column an index-finger pointed to the answer, beginning: ☞ "300 NEGROES WANTED", and saying that Austin Woolfolk would pay the highest cash prices for slaves of from 13 to 25 years of age and would give liberal commissions for assistance. At the same time he requested the *National Intelligencer* and the *Globe* of Washington and the *Gazette* of Alexandria to copy this advertisement "till forbid". But all that did not satisfy him. He longed for greater notoriety. What was much rarer, he knew how to command it, thus:

"A CARD.

A. WOOLFOLK wishes to inform the owners of Negroes in Maryland, Virginia, and N. Carolina, that he *is not dead*, as has been artfully represented by his opponents, but that he still lives, to give them CASH and the HIGHEST PRICES for their NEGROES." [69]

Had his humor equaled his craving, he might have anti-

1828. In the Baltimore *Republican etc.*, July 10, 1834, and many other days, Richard T. Woolfolk advertised for "20 young negroes of both sexes". There was still another. The matchless poet John Keats had a brother George, who came to the U. S. and settled in Ky. An advt. of runaways belonging to an estate of which he was one of the executors contained this: "Charles was purchased of R. Woolfolk, up the [Ohio] river, by Prentice & Bakewell, in 1818".—Louisville *Public Advertiser*, July 11, 1827.

[68] *Republican Commercial Advertiser*, July 10, 1832.

[69] Cambridge *Chronicle*, from Oct., 1832, to Oct., 1836, and Baltimore *Republican* etc. for many weeks, at least, after Oct. 1, 1832.

cipated Mark Twain's remark about himself — that the
report of his death was exaggerated. But he long continued " to inform the slaveholders of Maryland and Virginia that their friend still lives to give them *cash* and
the *highest prices* for their Negroes ", and assured them
that if they would call at his residence, Pratt street extended, they should " see the justly celebrated Austin
Woolfolk, free of charge ", and added: " N. B.—His
checks are such as usually *pass*, and will convince the
holders thereof that ' *there's nothing broke!* ' " [70]

To contemporary Abolitionists, Austin Woolfolk was
the most famous, even the most infamous, of slave-traders.
In 1826, when he was sending 29 slaves from Baltimore
to Georgia on the " Decatur ", they overcame the captain
and the mate, threw them overboard, put one of the white
men of the crew in command and ordered him to steer for
Haiti. Soon suspected and overhauled by another ship,
the " Decatur " was taken to New York, where the slaves
escaped; but one of them was captured, tried, convicted
and executed. The New York *Christian Examiner* reported that just before execution this slave made a for-
giving farewell speech and addressed it to Austin Woolfolk, supposed to be present; that Woolfolk replied with
angry profanity and said that he was glad the slave was
about to receive his deserts. Benjamin Lundy — the most
important and tireless of the early nineteenth century
Abolitionists and less violent in language than his then
youthful co-worker Garrison, yet much too violent for a
Quaker — was not content merely to quote this article.
In his Baltimore *Genius of Universal Emancipation* he
denounced Austin as a " monster in human shape, the Ish-
mealite, Woolfolk * * *, knowing *himself* to be the cause
of the death of the captain and mate * * * and also of the
poor unfortunate ", whom, " with a fiend-like assurance ",
he had insulted " with his outrageous profanity * * *.

---

[70] Cambridge, Md., *Chronicle*, Jan. 2, 1836, and many other dates.

Hereafter, let no man speak of the humanity of Woolfolk.''[71] Perhaps it was not Austin, but another Woolfolk of the same family and trade, that was present and
did the cursing.[72] Unless Lundy coveted martyrdom, it
was foolhardy thus to stigmatize a prosperous and reputable trader, whose business was then as lawful as a drover's
or a poultry dealer's is today. Publicly to proclaim in
such a trader's buying market that he had no humanity
was almost as injurious to him as it would have been in
his selling market likewise to accuse him of dishonesty.

When James L. Petigru—the famous South Carolina
lawyer, wit, Federalist and Unionist—was young a vulgar
fellow called him '' a damned rascal ''. Petigru ignored
it. Soon the fellow called him '' a damned Federalist ''.
Petigru immediately knocked him down. When Petigru's
friends expressed surprise that he should thus resent a
minor insult, after ignoring a grave one, he explained:
'' I did not care about his calling me a damned rascal, for
I knew no one would believe him; but when he called me
a Federalist, I felt that there was some truth in it, and
that if I did not resent the imputation, the bystanders
would believe it.'' Perhaps Woolfolk would have overlooked the gross appellations, '' monster in human shape ''
and '' Ishmaelite '', which were not true; but if he had
not resented the injunction, '' Let no man speak of the
humanity of Woolfolk '', it would have damaged one of the
most valuable factors of his business good-name. Woolfolk soon met Lundy near the postoffice and inquired
if he had written the article in the *Genius*. Lundy
finally admitted authorship of what must have been most
exasperating. Woolfolk then fiercely assaulted him, chok-
ing him until he was nearly breathless and then kicked
him in the head and face in a manner that might have
proved fatal. Fortunately Lundy was rescued before his

[71] Thomas Earle, *Life, Travels and Opinions of Benjamin Lundy* etc., 208.
[72] *Ibid.*, 209.

condition was as dangerous as it was bloody. He secured
the arrest of Woolfolk, who was duly tried and convicted
by a jury, — but the judge sentenced him to pay a fine of
only one dollar. These major and some minor incidents were excitedly commented on by the Abolition
press. Of course many besides the countless patrons of
the Woolfolks considered Austin justified and vindicated.
Thus Austin Woolfolk became " the justly celebrated ".
He long stood high in his low business and, like many
another in it, richly propered,[73] because so many Maryland and Virginia slaveowners were glad to receive his
" CASH and the HIGHEST PRICES for their NEGROES ".

Did masters wish to deal with some one still more kind-
hearted than that strange, anonymous buyer in Baltimore,
who desired " a large number of slaves — single ones or
in families ", but who would " not buy to separate families without their consent " ?[74] There was John Busk,
who was so tender-hearted that he could not bear to mention the cruel word slave except to explain the meaning
of the gentle word servant:

"CASH! I WISH to purchase a number of likely SERVANTS,
(SLAVES) of both sexes, from about 12 to 25 years of age, of good
habits. They are not for speculation. I can give the most unquestion
able satisfaction as to that."

Yet the rest of his advertisement supplied conclusive evidence that he was an eager speculator![75] Moreover, for
years he had been notoriously so. And John Woolfolk,
with headquarters at the office of his nephew, " the justly
celebrated ", supplied further evidence as to Busk's services. Those 150 slaves, whom Richard C. Woolfolk had

[73] A Quaker friend told Prof. Andrews about a rich trader, a " Mr. W."
[undoubtedly Austin Woolfolk], who had an establishment with a slave-pen
near the end of Pratt street where he kept his negroes until he sold them or
sent them to his brother in Louisiana to dispose of.—Andrews, 80.

[74] Ante p. 38, note 58.

[75] Ante p. 38 n.

bought, or tried to buy, for himself and John Woolfolk, did not suffice. John wanted a few score more " for his own cotton plantation on the Chattahoochee River ". His agent, John Busk, would act promptly.[76] There could have been no doubt as to who John Busk was, for his advertisement immediately followed, fairly shouting: " CASH! CASH!! " and that he " still continues the business of *buying* and selling Servants ", paying " the most LIBERAL PRICES for Young and Likely SLAVES, of both sexes "!

Some of these advertisements about buying for personal use or to fill special orders for planters may have been truthful. Most of them look like the common " tricks of the trade ". Of course planters — scores, perhaps hundreds of them, especially in the 'thirties, when several of the Southern States forbade the bringing in of slaves for sale [77] — came from the lower South to buy Maryland and Virginia negroes. Making purchases was such a pleasure and a distinction that there was no reason for secrecy, and the fullest publicity was helpful. Yet relatively few had sufficient enterprise and thrift to advertise. Most of them bought of the dealers having the best reputations or of original owners or at the auctions of large estates. The traders' tricky advertisements seem to indicate three aims: to establish a reputation for having large planters as clients; to obtain most cheaply and keep a supply of the best class of slaves; and to make large profits, whether the negroes were sold collectively or separately. If no planters came, there were always large interstate traders willing to pay a premium for good slaves. We shall see why they so often had " plantations " in the Southwest and were insatiable as to the number desired " for their own use ".

[76] Baltimore, *Republican etc.*, May 8, 1835.
[77] See *post* p. 271 ff.

CHAPTER III

THE DISTRICT OF COLUMBIA "THE VERY SEAT AND CENTER

For nearly half a century the slave-trade in the District of Columbia, although far from being the largest, was the most notorious. This federal territory, ceded by Maryland and Virginia respectively in 1788 and 1789, was ten miles square until 1846. It originally contained two so-called cities and a third soon came into existence: Georgetown, small, quaint and shabby, sprawling up picturesque heights on the Maryland side of the Potomac; Alexandria, village-like, flat and sleepy, on the opposite bank, six miles below; and Washington, spacious, little populated, having a few really beautiful public buildings on commanding sites, but otherwise slovenly, with unattractive houses and small stores scattered haphazard along broad, dusty or muddy diagonal avenues and rectangular streets. The District was the head of navigation on the Potomac, and Alexandria and Georgetown were the natural outlets for a long and wide region. Because the slave population in the District was small, the trading there was dependent on supplies brought in from Maryland or Virginia, and fully nine-tenths of it was for distant markets.[1]

The complaints in Alexandria in January, 1802, conclusively showed that this trade had considerable proportions long before John Randolph, in the House of Representatives in 1816, poured out on it his bitter reproaches. Although he had voted against the bill to prohibit the foreign slave-trade, he denounced and pointed his famous long " finger of scorn " at the conditions in the District and related how he had recently been " mortified at being told by a foreigner of high rank: ' You call this the land of liberty, and every day that passes things are done in it

---

[1] *Ante* p. 39 and *post* p. 48.

45

at which the despotisms of Europe would be horror-struck
and disgusted.' ''   Randolph and many others must have
remembered the scathing lines that Thomas Moore had
written from Washington,

" where bastard freedom waves
Her fustain flag in mockery over slaves."

Randolph appealed to his fellow-members to put a stop
to proceedings that were a crying sin before God and man;
a practice not surpassed for abomination in any part of
the earth. It was not necessary, he insisted, that this city
should be made a depot for slaves, who were bought either
from cruel masters or kidnaped; the kidnaped being of
two kinds—slaves stolen from their masters, and free persons stolen, as one might say, from themselves. In comparison with this nefarious traffic, that from Africa to
Charleston or Jamaica was mercy, was virtue. There was
a great difference between merely passing through the
District and actually making it a depot for a systematic
slave-market—an assemblage of prisons where the unfortunate beings, torn from their connections and the affections of their lives, were incarcerated and chained down,
and thence driven in fetters like beasts, to be paid for
like cattle. Cotton, tobacco and sugar demanded slaves,
and traders came to get them, as was shown by these
words of an advertisement of a sale—'' *No objection to*
TRADERS *bidding.*'' The increase in the price was the
temptation for which base, hardhearted masters sold out
of their families the negroes reared among them. That
very day he had been reliably informed of a case where
a negro by hard work and saving had paid his master for
the freedom of his wife and child and then died, and the
master on the following day resold them.[2] Thus early
the facts, in the glow of Randolph's rhetoric.

In January, 1829, Charles Miner, a Representative from

---

[2] The language, much condensed, is Randolph's in *Congressional Debates*,
1815-16, pp. 1115-17; Benton's 5 *Abridgment*, etc., 609-10.

Pennsylvania, made a more subdued exposure. The trade had rapidly increased. He quoted the advertisements of an Alexandria firm, who wished to buy " one hundred likely young negroes ", and those of two speculators, Samuel J. Dawson and Jesse Bernhard, operating independently in Georgetown and crying in their headlines " Cash! Cash! Cash! And Negroes Wanted " and " Cash in Market ". He also cited three different sales of negroes in Washington— a man, a girl aged 17, and one Margaret, 14, who was seized because her owner was hopelessly in arrears for rent. Margaret was sold in front of Lloyd's Tavern,[3] at or near the southeast corner of Seventh street and Pennsylvania avenue, northwest. Several Southern Representatives blandly pleaded total ignorance of such conditions.

What Miner referred to was only a small part of what traders had recently been advertising for in the newspapers. Besides the Alexandria firm mentioned, John W. Smith was anxious to buy " 40 or 50 " and E. P. Legg wished " 50 or 60 likely young negroes of both sexes from the ages of 10 to 25 years ". Smith especially wanted a carpenter, a cooper, a bricklayer, a calker, a seamstress, a washer, an ironer and a pleater, while Legg summarily said: " I will also buy mechanics of every description."[4] In addition to the two Georgetown traders mentioned, another, Samuel Meek, wished to make up a coffle of fifty young negroes of the usual ages, and John M. Hendricks advertised exactly like a trader, for "45 or 50 likely negroes from 12 to 25 years of age ", except that he inserted the phrase, " to work on my plantation in Mississippi." All

[3] Cong. Debates, 1828-29, 167, 175 ff.
[4] Alexandria Phenix Gazette, Dec. 30, 1828. Samuel Hunter had advertised in the same newspaper from Sept., 1826, to Feb., 1827, offering "the highest cash price for 25 or 30 YOUNG NEGROES. As the prices of Negroes are on the decline, those wishing to sell would do well to give me a call as early as convenient.—I shall be constantly at Elias P. Legg's in Alexandria, until I complete my purchases. Application personally, or by letter, will be immediately attended to."

four of these Georgetown buyers stopped at McCandless' Tavern. At the same time, George Millburn was at the Lafayette Tavern in Washington " to purchase 20 or 30 likely young negroes as agent for the Southern market ".[5] Probably there were other traders advertising in the District in 1828; there certainly was considerable petty trading apart from all that has been noticed. Yet those Southern Representatives knew nothing of it!

It was not the trade in slaves belonging to masters resident in the District of Columbia and for use there that was especially objectionable; for these slaves numbered only a few thousand and were chiefly domestic servants, with whom a greater number of free negroes competed in the labor market.[6] Thus large sales were hardly possible unless gangs were brought in from Maryland or Virginia.[7] When residents wished to buy, sell, hire or hire out slaves and preferred to attend to the business themselves, they advertised. Otherwise the business was usually turned over to one of several auctioneers that specialized in slave-trading. Richard Wright and Edward Dyer seem to have been much patronized in the 'thirties. Besides selling slaves by auction, they privately bought and sold as agents. Wright offered the public " a good bargain for cash " in a six year old girl.[8] Jilson Dove, probably a real estate

---

[5] Meek's and Millburn's advt. were in the Washington *National Intelligencer* of June 24, 1828, Hendricks's in that of June 21st, and all appeared on many other days, as was the rule in such cases.

[6]

	1830	1840
Free negroes	6,152	8,361
Slaves	6,119	4,694

Yet even here we find trader-auctioneer Dyer concluding his advertisement, as agent, to hire a slave cook and a boy or a man, with the sentence: " No free negro need apply ".—*Nat. Intel.*, Oct. 9, 1840.

[7] Apparently such a case was the sale of a gang of seventy by the administrator of the estate of T. Snowden, at the main slave-pen in Alexandria.—*Nat. Intel.*, Jan. 5, 1836.

[8] " FOR SALE.—A COLORED girl, who has 19 years to serve; she is in her seventh year, well grown, healthy and strong. A good bargain may be had

agent, wished " to purchase from forty to fifty Negroes of both sexes, from the age of twelve to twenty-five ", and to give in exchange two two-story brick houses in the business part of Washington.[9] Obviously he was agent for some interstate trader when he later " wanted immediately from 25 to 30 negroes of both sexes ".[10] As this was more than the District was likely to supply, it was an appeal to Maryland and Virginia. The trading in District slaves—which was relatively slight, spasmodic and carried on chiefly by agents—also comprised, of course, sales to settle estates, collect debts and pay for fines and jail fees.

What was shocking to antislavery residents and Members of Congress, to visitors from the North and abroad, was the use that interstate traders made of the District as their headquarters and as a depot for their purchases. Because Alexandria was the best point from which to start both coastwise shipments and overland coffles, it was long the place most favored. By 1830 Washington had drawn most of the trade from Georgetown and much of that from Alexandria. For the primary and all-important task of buying, directly or indirectly, in northeastern Virginia and most of Maryland, Washington became the center before 1835. The largest firm of traders in the District continued in Alexandria, but they did much business in Washington through regular agents. It was then—when " flush times " in Alabama and Mississippi were at the climax, and the demand for slaves by the Southwest was unprecedented—that the District of Columbia was called " the very seat and center " of the slave-trade in the United States.[11]

for cash (if early application is made to Richard Wright, Auctioneer."—
Nat. Intel., July 2, 1833.

[9] *Nat. Intel.*, Feb. 16, 1833. Earlier, auctioneer N. P. Poor offered to exchange improved property in Washington bringing 12 per cent interest for " a lot of slaves ", especially " a woman with 3 or 4 children, from 8 to 15 years of age ".—*Nat. Intel.*, Aug. 11, 1828.

[10] *Nat. Intel.*, July 25, 1840.

[11] Andrews, *Slavery and the Domestic Slave Trade*, 122.

The newspapers of Washington were the best means for the traders to reach the slaveowners in neighboring counties. The advertisements offering to buy large numbers of negroes might accurately express desires or they might be exaggerated so as to tempt masters in need of money; but calls for a few slaves of specified kinds and ages represented what was wanted. In the Washington *National Intelligencer* of April 23, 1836, the leading interstate traders and a slave-trading auctioneer respectively made these announcements:—

Franklin & Armfield, of Alexandria, had " CASH FOR 500 NEGROES " and would " give higher prices, in Cash, than any other purchaser who is now, or may hereafter come into the market ".

James H. Birch and William H. Williams, both settled in Washington, called for 400 and 300, respectively. All desired slaves of either sex from 12 to 25 or 28 years of age.

Joseph W. Neal & Company, also of Washington, put no limit to the number of negroes from 10 to 30 years of age for whom they would pay " the highest prices in cash ".

Auctioneer Edward Dyer likewise advised the slave-selling public that a " gentleman now in this city " wished to purchase, " for his own use (not for speculation) * * * a cook, male or female, a carriage driver, not older than twenty-five years, a seamstress and two or three boys and girls, accustomed to house service ", and would pay " the highest prices now going " for them.

Besides these would-be purchasers, one " N. Maddox, near Washington ", desired immediately to receive, through the postoffice, bids naming the highest price for " a handsome, intelligent mulatto; a good plain cook, waitress, seamstress and laundress, about 17 or 18 years old ", whom he had put in the custody of trader Neal. An acceptable offer would be promptly answered by mail.

This looks like a shrewd effort to obtain a fancy price for an available " fancy girl ".

The advertisements were almost as numerous on many other days and some of them (Williams's and Birch's) appeared daily for months. For shorter periods, Robert W. Fenwick " wanted immediately " 100 negroes of from 12 to 30 years of age;[12] William H. Richards had cash and liberal prices for " any number of young and likely negroes, from 8 to 40 years of age ", and George Kephart was eager for the " likely " from 10 to 25 years of age.[13] And John Lamar, stopping at Gadsby's Hotel, was " anxious to purchase, for my own use, to be sent to Georgia, * * * a first-rate cook, a smart and likely waiting girl, from the age of 10 to 20, two likely and intelligent boys, and a body-servant, for which the highest prices will be paid ". He named Dyer as one of his references.[14]

As a rule, interstate traders were directly or indirectly itinerant buyers, and a large percentage of them would " promptly attend to all communications ". William H. Williams and James H. Birch said so in their advertisements already referred to; but Franklin & Armfield and Neal & Co., without any suggestion of that kind in theirs, advised persons having slaves to sell to call and get the benefit of the high prices offered. In other advertisements, Birch and Jones, as partners [15] and separately,[16] and also Fenwick [17] clearly indicated that they expected vendors to come to them.

[12] *Nat. Intel.*, Aug. 8, 1836.

[13] William Jay, *Miscellaneous Writings on Slavery*, 270-71.

[14] *Nat. Intel.*, Aug. 8, 1836.

[15] " CASH FOR NEGROES. WE WILL pay the highest Cash price for Fifty likely Negroes from 12 to 25 years of age. We can at all times be found at Lloyd's Steamboat Hotel, near the Centre Market. Birch & Jones."— *Nat. Intel.*, May 28, 1834. A few weeks later they advertised likewise, except that they were located both at Isaac Beers' Tavern, a few doors south of Lloyd's, and at McCandless' Tavern in Georgetown.—*Nat. Intel.*, July 11, 1834.

[16] (Thomas M. Joanes [Jones]), *Nat. Intel.*, Nov. 18, 1833; (Birch), *Nat. Intel.*, June 30, 1837 and July 2, 1839.

[17] *Nat. Intel.*, Aug. 8, 1836.

Thus it was proclaimed how ready large traders were to give high prices in cash either at the homes of the masters or in the District. Ever-prevalent common talk spread all news to a score or perhaps a hundred persons for every one that read the advertisements in the *National Intelligencer*. And the inquisitive, ubiquitous, itinerant trader was abroad, chatting at the country stores and taverns, loitering, treating and asking questions at the barrooms, looking in at the county jails to see the latest arrivals, cordially greeting the slaveholding farmer, whether in town, on highway or afield, as if specially concerned about his welfare; but at all times and in all places the trader never forgot his main purpose—to buy negroes for considerably less than the interstate traders in the District would readily pay for them. Until an extensive region had been canvassed, the purchased slaves were lodged in the county jail to prevent them from attempting to escape or the master from changing his mind.

Soon these itinerant traders, with their respective collections of from one or two to a score, were on the various roads leading to Alexandria, Georgetown or Washington. The main highways from Maryland centered at or a few squares below the Capitol, like the ribs of a semi-circular fan. The largest gangs were likely to be from Baltimore, where the agents of District traders grouped selections from the best slaves received from the Eastern Shore. The women with little children were carried in some vehicle. When more than a few, the men, handcuffed in pairs, fastened to a chain and followed by boys and girls, walked in double column, and the trader's mounted assistant brought up the rear. Thus, like a butcher's drove of hobbled cattle, they shambled into the streets and avenues of Washington and often passed close to the Capitol. There was no mistaking a trader and his numerous purchases for a farmer or small planter moving to a new region with his slaves, for the mover was accompanied by his family, household effects and some stock as well as his negroes, who were rarely, if ever, handcuffed or chained. But it was impossible to know the intentions of a thrifty small farmer who, distrusting the itinerant buyers and counting very precious one or a few marketable and unsuspecting human treasures, brought them, together with some usual country produce, to the Washington market.

What might be called the daily life of local trading was in or near the taverns or small hotels,[18] at the public or the private jails, and about the country markets. When the slaveowners did not seek out the traders and request that " highest price in cash ", the impatient traders went to the markets to look for masters that might be tempted. A Southwestern trader would give more cash for a prime fieldhand or a young woman with one or two children than the average Maryland or Virginia farmer could save from years of agricultural labor. And selling at such a time enabled the vendor to explain matters at home to suit himself.

Private slave-jails for public use were never numerous in the District of Columbia. There were two reasons for this: the slaves brought into the District or bought there by the interstate traders were kept there only until a cargo or a coffle could be made up; and the public jails in different parts of the District were available for these temporary needs. This was complained of as early as 1816.[19] About twelve years later, Representative Miner showed that 452 such slaves were boarded and guarded in the Washington jail alone in the course of the five years 1824-28. He thought that the same favor was ac-

---

[18] Those most frequented by the traders in 1827-36 were Lafayette Tavern on F st. between Thirteenth and Fourteenth, northwest; Lloyd's Tavern (*ante* p. 47) ; one or more, a few doors south of Lloyd's, variously called Beer's Tavern, Mechanics' Hall and Shekell's Tavern; Robey's Tavern (*post* p. 54) ; McCandless' Tavern, Georgetown, at or near the southwest corner of what are now called Wisconsin ave. (32d st.) and M st. (Pennsylvania ave.) ; and Smith's Southern Hotel, Alexandria.

[19] Torrey, *Domestic Slavery in the U. S.*, 41-42.

corded by the jail in Alexandria.[20] And probably the jail in Georgetown was doing likewise. This exposure may have lessened but did not stop the misuse of the public jails.

Early in the 'thirties Washington Robey was conducting a tavern on the east side of Seventh street between B street, southwest, and Maryland avenue and in connection with it had a slave-pen.[21] Tavern and pen were well patronized. On a hot day in 1833 E. S. Abdy, an English traveler, went to inspect the pen, but nearly all of it except the exterior was left to his imagination. He called the place a wretched hovel, surrounded by a wooden paling fourteen or fifteen feet high, with the posts outside to prevent escape, and separated from the building by a space too narrow for ventilation. At a small window above he saw two or three sable faces wistfully looking out to while away the time and to catch a breath of fresh air.[22]

Neal & Company (for a short time Simpson & Neal) could " at all times be found at Robey's Tavern, near the corner of Seventh street and Maryland avenue ",[23] and undoubtedly they kept their numerous purchases in his pen. The firm was active in that immediate neighborhood for several years.[24]

---

[20] *Cong. Debates*, 1828-29, 176-77. In 1841 the charge was 34 cents per day. —Sturge, *A Visit to the U. S. in 1841*, 116.

[21] The Washington *Directory* of 1834 indicates the ownership and location of the tavern as follows: " Robey [,] Washington, Tavern, e side 7 w, btw B and C s " [southwest]. As Md. ave. cuts off part of the block north of C st., the *Directory* to that extent is inexplicit.

[22] Abdy, 2 *Journal of a Residence and a Tour in the United States*, 96-97.

[23] *Nat. Intel.*, Nov. 8, 1833.

[24] Advts. in 1834 and 1836 mentioned headquarters as being at Neal's " residence " [at or near Robey's Tavern] which was " immediately south of the Centre Market-house ".—Wm. Jay, *Misc. Writings*, 156; *Nat. Intel.*, Sept. 18, 1834; Apr. 23, 1836. In 1833 they called for " 100 likely negroes of both sexes, from the ages of 8 to 30 years " and, again later, for likely young negroes, of both sexes, either in families or otherwise "; in 1834, for " 150 likely young negroes, of both sexes, families included ".—*Nat. Intel.*, Feb. 16, Nov. 8, 1833; July 11, 1834.

On a Potomac boat Professor Andrews fell in with a junior member of this firm taking 50 slaves to South Carolina.[25] Supposing Andrews sympathetic, because he had lived in the South, this young trader prattled the details of his business. Every other month his firm had for years sent to the South Carolina market a collection of at least 40 negroes—probably 300 annually. Although a cargo of 75, valued at $40,000, had been lost early in 1835, Neal consoled himself with the thought that the firm had made a profit of $40,000 before suffering this misfortune.

"Flush times" were not confined to the Southwest. Slave-traders anywhere might enjoy them. Were there many slaves in the market? They were never more plentiful, answered the trader, but the prices were "monstrous high"; the original owners could have almost any price they asked, which was the reason so many were willing to sell. (That was about what John Randolph had said 19 years earlier.) "Children from one year to 18 months old are now worth about $100. That little fellow there", pointing to a boy about 7 or 8 years old, "I gave $400 for. That fellow", pointing to one about 18, "I gave $750 for last night, after dark". Seven other young fieldhands had recently been sold to Armfield. "He just made me an advance of $50 a head." "I offered the other day $1200 for two girls, and their owner got $1300, a day or two after. A first-rate fieldhand is well worth $900, and would bring it, if the owner did but know it. A good mechanic is worth $1200. Mine are nearly all fieldhands; but I shall not take a cent under $1000 [each] for the men, when I get to Carolina."[26] He was evidently expecting to make 25 or 30 per cent on money invested but a few months, at most. If 25 per cent net profit was real-

---

[25] E. A. Andrews, 145-50. He refers to the trader's name by only "N". But the fact that Neal lost a cargo of slaves at the same time and place as "N.", completes the identification. See *post* p. 277.

[26] Andrews, 147-48.

ized on 300 slaves selling at the low average of $400 each, the firm cleared $30,000 annually.

Prior to the early part of 1836 William H. Williams was modestly advertising for " a number of servants of both sexes, for which " he would " pay the highest market price ". He was then living near the National Hotel and evidently had no jail of his own.[27] While most traders preferred the tavern barrooms, Williams, at first, made a lottery office his headquarters, where losers were often glad to sell their slaves so as to buy further chances. That spring he wished to buy 300. In December he had " CASH FOR FOUR HUNDRED NEGROES ".[28] This made him appear to be abreast of fellow-trader Birch and ahead of all other strictly Washington dealers. Meantime he had taken possession of the " yellow house ", a three-story brick dwelling, covered with plaster, painted yellow and standing in a garden surrounded by trees. The whole property must have taken up most of the north side of the square between Seventh and Eighth streets and south of B street, southwest, across B street from where the Surgeon-General's Library building now stands.[29]

The jail proper was a detached building, but slaves were sometimes kept in a room adjoining the kitchen of the trader's dwelling. He advertised: " Negroes are taken on board, at the low price of 25 cents per day, from the country or town."[30] Staples, to which they had been

[27] *Nat. Intel.*, Jan. 5, 1836.

[28] *Nat. Intel.*, Apr. 23, Dec. 26, 1836.

[29] Clearly to distinguish his place from Robey's, Williams called it the " yellow rough-cast house, the first on the right hand going from the market house to the steamboat wharf "; and he advised all desiring to get the highest market price " to give him a call at his jail, on 7th street, between the Centre Market and Long Bridge, at the rough-cast house that stands in a large garden surrounded by trees, on the west [Robey's was opposite on the east] side of 7th street ".—*Nat. Intel.*, Dec. 26, 1836, and Aug. 12, 1839.

Clephane's " The Local Aspects of Slavery in the District ", 3 *Columbia Hist. Soc. Records*, 239-40, supplies some details.

[30] *Nat. Intel.*, Aug. 12, 1839.

shackled, were found in the walls of both places by the
purchaser of the property many years later. This " yellow house " property was so well known that trader Richards, after giving his " residence " as at the corner of
Seventh street and Maryland avenue, added, " and opposite Mr. Williams's private jail ".[31]   There might be doubt
as to where such important thoroughfares crossed, but
who did not know the location of " Mr. Williams's private jail "! It soon had a virtual monopoly of the pri-
vate-jail business.[32]   There, in 1841, trader James H. Birch
imprisoned the drugged and kidnaped free negro Solomon Northrup before taking him to Richmond, where he
was shipped to Theophilus Freeman in New Orleans.[33]
At Williams's jail Fredrika Bremer, in 1850, found a number of children, " kept here for a short time to fatten ",
and " some very splendid articles for sale, which were to
be sent down South ", as the keeper said./ Among these
was a girl that " had been brought up in all respects ' like
a lady '; she could embroider and play on the piano, and
dress like a lady, and read, and write, and dance, and all
this she had learned in the family which had brought her
up, and who had treated her in her childhood as if she
had been their own. But, however, her mind had grown
too high for her; she had become proud, and now, to humble her, they had brought her here to be sold." (All that,
if known, would have greatly lessened her salability as
a servant but not as a " fancy girl ".) And how did
slaves confined in such a place behave?—" Oh! They
would be unruly enough if they were not afraid of a flogging." [34]   And it may have been to this jail, rather than
to Robey's, which was much less famous, that old Joshua
R. Giddings still later referred, with vigorous tautology,

[31] Jay, 271.

[32] Sturge, *A Visit to the U. S.*, 107.

[33] *Narrative of Solomon Northrup*, 40 ff.; *Key to Uncle Tom's Cabin*, 173.

[34] Bremer, 1 *Homes of the New World*, 492-93.

as " that infernal hell which once existed at the corner
of Seventh street and Maryland avenue ". [35]

There, in his " yellow rough-cast house " " in a large
garden surrounded by trees ", for many years Williams,
like Milton's Satan,

> " exalted sat, by merit rais'd
> To that bad eminence."

His success was so rapid that before the end of 1836 he
had purchased from the fleet of the largest slave-traders
in the United States " two splendid New Orleans steam
packets "—the brigs " Tribune " and " Uncas ", coastwise slavers—and was regularly using them, one leaving
Alexandria and the other New Orleans on the first of each
month, to transport the slaves he was buying for Louisiana and Mississippi markets. He was also prepared to
carry those of others; but in his advertisement he was
as elegant and mealy-mouthed as the tender-hearted John
Busk: " Those wishing to ship had better have their servants at this place a day or two previous to the vessels
sailing." [36] Much later, he was reported to have boasted
of making $30,000 in a few months.[37] That will seem not
at all incredible when we know his methods in the Southwest.

Isaac Franklin and John Armfield, at the height of their
success, from about 1830 to 1836, were not only far in the
lead of all other traders in Maryland, Virginia and the
District, but were perhaps unequaled in all the South.
They had a positive genius for speculating in slaves.
From May, 1828, Franklin & Armfield advertised in the
Alexandria *Phenix Gazette* for " 150 likely young negroes
of both sexes between the ages of 8 and 25 years " and

[35] *Cong. Globe*, 1856-57, p. 80. It was near enough to make the reference
permissible, according to the custom of that time, for houses were unnumbered
and there were many vacant lots.

[36] *Nat. Intel.*, Nov. 7, Dec. 26, 1836; Jay, 271.

[37] Collins, *The Domestic Slave-Trade*, 29, cites the *Liberator*, Sept. 6, 1850;
but the *Liberator* gives only a news-item without details.

that they had a long lease of a three-story house on Duke street, which had formerly been occupied by a General Young. Armfield lived there and attended to buying and forwarding the slaves to the New Orleans and Natchez markets, where Franklin disposed of them.

Because they were purchasing in the cheapest markets and selling in the dearest, they could afford to pay higher prices in cash than any other purchasers for 500 or for " any number " of " likely " young negroes. Such offers attracted petty traders and needy masters, and most masters were needy some time. For a considerable bonus, even large traders—like Neal, when he resold seven at " an advance of $50 a head "—were occasionally glad to give Franklin & Armfield a choice of the most " prime ". For months, in 1833, they published the names of their leading agents—all, except in one place, well-known slave-trading *companies* comprised of two or more persons— in Richmond, Warrenton, Baltimore, Fredericktown and Easton.[38]

By 1834, Franklin & Armfield were said to be sending from 1,000 to 1,200 slaves a year to the Southwest;[39] and,

[38] " CASH IN MARKET. WE will pay Cash for any number of likely Negroes, of both sexes, from 12 to 25 years of age, Field Hands. Also, Mechanics of every description. Apply to

R. C. Ballard & Co.	Richmond, Va.
J. M. Saunders & Co.	Warrenton, Va.
George Kephart & Co.	Fredericktown, Md.
James F. Purvis & Co.	Baltimore.
Thomas M. Jones	Easton, Eastern Shore of Md.

Or, to the subscribers, at their residence in Alexandria.

Persons having likely servants to dispose of, will do well to give us a call, as we at all times will pay higher prices in cash than any other purchaser who is now or may hereafter come into market. All communications promptly attended to.—FRANKLIN & ARMFIELD."—*Nat. Intel.*, July 2, 1833. This was marked " May 9—dtf " and ran far into 1834.

That Birch & Jones were also their agents appears from the facts that the advts. of the two firms repeatedly began on the same day and bore the same directions to the printer as to continuance, and in an advt. for a pair of horses, presumably for the overland trip to Natchez, Armfield requested persons in Washington to apply to Birch & Jones—*Nat. Intel.*, June 23, 1834.

[39] Andrews, 142, 148; Jay, 157.

if the increase in the trade and their facilities for taking advantage of it were any criterion, their business was much larger by 1836.[40] A good judge of conditions in the District believed that the firm had cleared $33,000 in 1829,[41], when their trade was perhaps only one-half or one-third of what it became in 1835-36. About 1834 Armfield was reputed to have made nearly $500,000.[42] Franklin's wealth and fame, in later years at least, much exceeded Armfield's.[43]

The most flourishing slave-pen in the United States in the 'thirties was in direct line both by land and water between the National capital and Mount Vernon. Many curious travelers sought out what had formerly been General Young's house and anxiously knocked at the door over which was the concise but sufficient sign—

> FRANKLIN & ARMFIELD.

Such callers were usually surprised by being received in the parlor by " a man of fine personal appearance and of engaging and graceful manners ".[44] John Armfield was accustomed to have dignified transactions with more or less well bred " planters " and farmers wishing to alter the annoying disproportion between the number of their slaves and their ready money. Like Hope H. Slatter and other successful traders, he felt that his part was not less respectable than theirs, and he knew how much more remunerative it was. Nor did he fear honest and gentlemanly antislavery curiosity. With the good-fellowship of the old South he invited his callers to step to the sideboard and have some refreshments—at least

[40] For an account of their ships etc. see *post* pp. 64, 65, 275-76.

[41] Tremain, *Slavery in the District of Columbia*, 50-51, citing Lundy's *Genius of Universal Emancipation* for Jan. 22, 1830.

[42] 2 Abdy, 180.

[43] See *post* p. 304.

[44] Much the best account is by Andrews, 137 ff., and it supplies most of the details. Abdy, 2 *Journal etc.*, 179-80, and Joseph Sturge, *A Visit to the United States in 1841*, 77-78, agree but are more summary.

a glass of madeira or sherry or, in mid-summer, perhaps
a pungent, frosty julep, which Virginians and others once
rightly doted on. Then he summoned a cicerone with
the keys.

After a grated iron door secured by bolts and padlocks
was opened, the caller was conducted from the yard back
of Armfield's dwelling into another yard or court, covered on one side and surrounded by a high, whitewashed
wall. This was the pen for the male slaves. In July,
1835, Professor Andrews found about 60 of them there—
a few boys from 10 to 15 years of age and nearly all the
others young men. They talked and laughed as they
stood about or amused themselves by some rude sport.
The remnants on a long table where they had been eating indicated an abundance of wholesome, plain food.
The slaves seemed to be fairly clean and well dressed;
the exceptions, as the guide explained, were the negroes
too recently purchased to have benefited by the change.
Near this yard was a similar one containing about forty
female slaves, much like the others as to ages and circumstances. There was only one mother with an infant,
because women with very young children were not easily
disposed of in the Southwest. Except a few, who seemed
to have been weeping, the women also had a general air
of contentment. Convenient to both pens was a clean and
well arranged kitchen. Then there was a tailorshop, where
two suits for each slave were made preparatory for the
long journey and the far-away sale. The clothes were
substantial and those for the women showed some taste.
Outside these slave-quarters, but a distinct part of the
establishment, were to be seen several tents, wagons,
horses and other equipments waiting for the quota of
slaves to be completed before starting overland for
Natchez. Except one or two such caravans each summer,
the slaves were sent all the way by water. In a corner
of one of the yards was a " hospital ", but, as only young

and healthy negroes were bought, it was little used. Next
to both yards was a long two-story building where all the
slaves were locked up at night. They were also chained,
if there was any suspicion of an attempt to escape. Their
blankets were lying in the sun near the grated doors and
windows. The general aspect of the place suggested a
well-conducted prison, for such it was—Franklin & Armfield's receiving-jail.

The guide had no such thoughts. He called attention
to the comfort and good fortune of the slaves: when they
came here, they were ragged, hungry and wretched,—look
at them now! Mr. Armfield was always very careful not
to separate families either in buying or selling, and preferred to obtain married couples. He was so kind-hearted
that he had recently purchased more than fifty negroes
from an estate to prevent the breaking up of families, and
sold them likewise, thus receiving from $1,000 to $2,000
less than if he had disposed of them separately or in lots.
His superior character and methods were highly respected.
Even the negroes, when they learned that they were to
be sold, begged to be taken to him. Without ever having
heard of Dr. Johnson's paradox—that the greatest liar
tells more truth than falsehood, and the worst man does
more good than evil—this employee was confident that a
few good qualities in a trader made a good man. Yet while
he was expatiating on Armfield's alleged virtues and
on the good fortune and happiness of his slaves, one of
the most intelligent of them watched the caller and secretly
showed dissent whenever the eulogist looked away.
" Still, in imagination, I see his countenance, anxiously
and fearfully turning from the keeper to me, with an expression which seemed to say, like the ghost in Hamlet,
' I could a tale unfold '." [45]

Few negroes were, indeed, physically more comfortable

[45] Andrews, 138.

than those clean and neatly dressed captives, resting and
fattening like beeves. It would have been strange if such
attractions had not caused slaves about to be sold to prefer
Armfield (especially if he had some of their kindred or
friends) to a mean-looking, itinerant speculator. It was a
good investment in advertising for a large trader ostenta-
ciously now and then to buy a family and sell it undivided;
for it tended to lessen dread of him on the part of other
slaves and, what was much more important, helped to remove any prejudice against dealing with him. Fortunately
four manifests of shipments to New Orleans, made a few
months before this call, have been preserved and disclose
what we need to know.[46] Of the four cargoes making a
total of 646 slaves, 396 were apparently owned by Franklin
& Armfield. Among these 396 there were only two full
families: the fathers were 21 and 22 years of age, the
mothers 19 and 20 and the children 1 and 1½. There were
20 husbandless mothers with 33 children, of whom one was
2 weeks old, 4 others were less than 1 year old, 19 were
from 1 to 4 years old, and 9 were from 5 to 12 years of age.
The remaining 337 were single and may be grouped thus:

```
  5 were from  6 to  9 years old, both inclusive
 08   "    "   10  " 15   "     "    "      "
145   "    "   16  " 21   "     "    "      "
101   "    "   22  " 30   "     "    "      "
  9   "    "   31  " 39   "     "    "      "
  8   "    "   40  " 50   "     "    "      "
  1   above    50     ,    a man of 60.
```

93 per cent of these 337 were from 10 to 30 years of age.
    Assuming that the manifests are truthful representa-
tions, these conclusions seem obvious: that there had been
neither any disadvantageous purchases of family groups
to prevent separations nor any purchases of families for
the purpose of separations later; and that the ages of the

---

[46] They were dated Dec. 20, 1834, Feb. 5 and 26, and March 26, 1835. All
manifests referred to in this book are in the Library of Congress.

337 single slaves indicated scores of separations. But the separations must have been made by the vendors, either Virginia and Maryland masters or itinerant speculators. Because such speculators were supposed to divide families when advantageous, original owners were likely either to refuse to deal with them or to make the divisions and obtain all possible profit along with the risk of getting a bad name for selling to such persons. Thus, except the improbable assertion of the cicerone, that Franklin & Armfield were careful not to separate families in buying, these manifests give unexpected evidence of a substantial basis for the good name that this firm possessed. Their business was strictly legal, and to establish it firmly and make it highly remunerative, as they had done, they realized that they must conduct it on a plane that would appeal to the farmers and planters from whom they wished to buy, as well as to those to whom they desired to sell.

Late in 1836, Franklin & Armfield sold out their entire business in the District of Columbia. It was from them that " Yellow-House " Williams bought the " Uncas " and the " Tribune " on which those shipments had been made.

Early in the 'thirties a small trader, living near a little ferry on the upper Potomac, was searching for slaves throughout Montgomery and Frederick counties, Maryland. He knew all the country roads, the names and the financial condition of most of the slaveholders. He was regularly at certain taverns and stores in Fredericktown and Rockville to get letters from or to meet persons that had been attracted by reports of his liberal offers. And he promptly inspected all proffered slaves.[47] He displayed

---

[47] *Cash in Market.* I wish to purchase about FIFTY *Likely Young Negroes*, of both sexes, from ten to thirty years of age. Persons wishing to dispose of slaves, would find it to their advantage to give me a call, as I feel disposed to pay the highest market price. Any information left for me at Francis Kidwell's Tavern, Rockville, or at the Union Tavern, Fredericktown, or at my residence, near Nowland's Ferry, will be punctually attended to. GEORGE KEPHART."—Rockville, *Maryland Journal and True American*, Feb. 14, 1832. This ran at least as late as Jan. 8, 1833.

such talent that Franklin & Armfield soon made him one of their agents. He progressed with marvelous rapidity. Imagine his pride in being able to conclude his advertisements in 1837 thus: " Myself or agent can at all times be found at the establishment formerly owned by Armfield, Franklin & Co. at the west end of Duke street, Alexandria."[48] And for his New Orleans trade he also bought that firm's slaver called the " Isaac Franklin ".[49] His name was George Kephart. A traveler was informed at that establishment in 1841 that it sometimes contained 300 or 400 slaves and that in some years from 1,500 to 2,000 were sent South from it.[50] If that was true, Kephart probably surpassed Franklin & Armfield.

" Did you ever hear of a trader named George Kephart?" the author inquired of Fred Fowler,[51] an ex-slave born in Frederick county, Maryland, and employed at the Library of Congress, 1876-1919.—" Ever'body in Frederick knowed Kephart, an' was afeerd of 'im, too. When it was reported that he was about, they trembled. At different times, two years apart, he bought my uncle Lloyd Stewart and my aunt Margaret Stewart. He was supposed to have sent 'em to Georgia, but they was nevah heerd from."[52]

The return of the southwestern part of the District of Columbia to Virginia, in 1846, included the little city of Alexandria. This much reduced the trading in the District. Yet four years elapsed ere the bringing in of slaves for sale was forbidden by the compromise of 1850. More than one-third of a century had been required to stop what was an old disgrace when John Randolph denounced it in 1816. And during all but the last few years of that

[48] *Nat. Intel.*, June 30, 1837.
[49] *Ibid.* Oct. 9, 1840, has an advt. of it.
[50] Sturge, *A Visit to the U. S. in 1841*, 101.
[51] 5 *Journal of Negro History*, 476-80, contains the present author's sketch of Fowler.
[52] See *post* p. 91 for more about Kephart.

3

period one could have occasionally seen chained gangs of slaves from Maryland passing near the Capitol on their way to some jail on Seventh street or in Alexandria, to the Richmond market or to the far South. Slavery and the local slave-trade in the District did not end in 1850: for more than a decade longer the slaves already there might as freely as ever be bought and sold and taken to any part of the South.

CHAPTER IV

THE IMPORTANCE OF SLAVE–REARING

While Rome was conquering and expanding, slaves were cheap, for the captive enemies amply supplied the demand. " But when the principal nations of Europe, Asia and Africa were united under the laws of one sovereign ", says Gibbon, " the source of foreign supplies flowed with much less abundance, and the Romans were reduced to the milder but more tedious method of propagation." The prohibition of the African slave-trade after 1807 limited the future supply of slaves in the United States to virtually the natural increase. When the marvelous expansion of cotton culture caused an insatiable demand for slaves, the need and profit of slave-rearing were obvious and inevitable.

Many a prudent man of family economizes to buy safe bonds or preferred stocks, likely to rise in value, perfectly negotiable and bearing good interest. He hopes to save all the income and to keep the bonds or stocks, but they are purchased less on account of their security than because, in addition to reasonable security, they are most available for cash or as collateral, in an emergency. Slave property was considered to have these qualities, and in the South no other property, not even bonds, so readily served these ends. Where slaves and more slaves were regarded as the highest form and the most respected evidence of wealth, they were seldom reared expressly for the market, ten or fifteen years off; yet the rearing of them was deemed most important where their ordinary labor was least remunerative, as in Maryland, Virginia and Kentucky. And because the sale of at least some of them was likely—either to pay debts, to obtain money or

67

for division between heirs or legatees—that contingency was rarely lost sight of.[1]

But what did Southerners closely associated with slavery say about slave-rearing? It is their evidence that is decisive.

An advertisement in Charleston, South Carolina, in 1796, offering fifty prime negroes for sale contained these sentences: * * * " they are not Negroes selected out of a larger gang for the purpose of a sale, but are prime, their present Owner, with great trouble and expense, selected them out of many for several years past. They were purchased for stock and breeding Negroes, and to any Planter who particularly wanted them for that purpose, they are a very choice and desirable gang."[2] At all times " breeding slaves ", " child bearing women ", " breeding period ", " too old to breed " etc. were familiar terms.

Slave-rearing early became the source of the largest and often the only regular profit of nearly all slaveholding farmers and of many planters in the upper South. Especially in Virginia, as Francis Corbin wrote in 1819, *" miserabile dictu* our principal profit depends " on the increase of our slaves.[3] In a Virginia case in 1848, the Court said that " the scantiness of net profit from slave labor has become proverbial, and that nothing is more common than actual loss, or a benefit merely in the slow increase of capital from propagation."[4] John Ran-

---

[1] If only part of a gang was to be disposed of, it was the young slaves. Here is a good illustration of what very often happened:—The executor of A. T. Goodwyn held a public sale of all the decedent's crops, stock, household furniture and plantation utensils and of some of the negroes—" 20 SLAVES, consisting of men, women, boys and girls, between 14 and 25 years of age, selected out of a lot of more than 100.—TERMS. Cash for the Slaves, and a credit of 12 months for the other property " * * *.—Petersburg, Va., *Republican*, Sept. 29, 1847.

[2] U. B. Phillips (editor), 2 *Plantation and Frontier*, 57.

[3] *Mass. Hist. Soc. Pas.*, Jan., 1910, p. 263.

[4] Catterall, 1 *Judicial Cases Concerning American Slavery and the Negro*, 215.

dolph's oft-quoted remark in the tariff debate of 1824 [5]—
that if the decrease in the value of slave labor [in Vir-
ginia] continued and the slaves did not run away from
their masters, the masters would have to run away from
their slaves—was a serious figure of speech from his point
of view; for he, being an emancipationist, could not think
of selling his negroes, although they were increasing in
value. And in addressing the Kentucky Colonization Society in 1829, Henry Clay said that " nowhere in the
farming portion of the United States would slave labor
be generally employed, if the proprietor were not tempted
to raise slaves by the high price of the Southern market,
which keeps it [the price] up in his own." [6]

After the second decade of the 19th century the decline
in the value of lands and crops, except the best tobacco,
was so great in Virginia that only " The demand for ' Virginia leaf ' and the sale of the surplus negroes [rapidly
increasing in price] to the Southern cotton-planters enabled the inhabitants to keep the wolf from the door and
to maintain a semblance of their former hospitality." [7]
The debate in the Virginia legislature of 1831-32 about
the abolition of slavery was very elucidating. The antago-
nists agreed on two important facts—that slave-rearing
was a common means of profit and that traders and other
buyers annually took thousands of Virginia slaves to distant States.

" The exportation [of slaves to other Southern States,
said Thomas Jefferson Randolph] has averaged 8,500 for
the last twenty years. * * * It is a practice, and an
increasing practice in parts of Virginia, to rear slaves for
market. How can an honorable mind, a patriot, and a
lover of his country, bear to see this ancient dominion,
rendered illustrious by the noble devotion and patriot-
ism of her sons in the cause of liberty, converted into one

[5] Not in 1814 as Prof. Phillips says, *Amer. Negro Slavery*, 391.
[6] 6 *African Repository*, 10.
[7] Ambler, *Sectionalism in Virginia*, 112.

grand menagerie where men are to be reared for market
like oxen for the shambles.[?]'' [8]

Still more light was thrown on these and kindred questions in 1832 by Thomas R. Dew (an able young professor in William and Mary College, of which he was made
president in 1836) in a proslavery dissertation on the
'' Abolition of Negro Slavery '' and by Jesse Burton Harrison in a long antislavery article entitled '' Slavery
Question in Virginia ''.[9]

Dew so effectively analyzed the plans of the antislavery
men and made such a frightful contrast between what he
fancied abolition would mean and what he conceived to
be the great value of Virginia's slaves, that he has been
credited with causing a proslavery reaction. The rising
value of slave property had already brought about a
change of opinion, but Dew was the first both to see the
facts clearly and to proclaim them with matchless skill
and effect. What could more impress needy slaveowners,
as thousands of Virginians were, than to tell them that
their negroes were worth $100,000,000—'' nearly one-third
of the wealth of the whole State ''? And he added with
evident pride: * * * '' from all the information we can
obtain, we have no hesitation in saying, that upwards of

[8] Pamphlet copy of speech of Jan. 21, 1832, in the Virginia House of Delegates, pp. 12, 15. In speeches in the same place on the same subject Henry
Berry estimated the total annual exportations from Virginia at about 9,500
(Speech of Jan. 20, 1832, p. 7) and Thomas Marshall put the number still
higher (Speech of Jan. 14, 1832, p. 8). These figures are cited not with
approval as to accuracy, but as evidence of the contemporary opinion that
thousands of slaves were annually sold from Virginia. For the author's
opinion as to the approximate number sold at this time see post p. 385.

[9] The articles appeared in 12 Amer. Quarterly Review (Sept. and Dec.,
1832), 189-265 and 379-426. Neither was then signed. Dew soon revised,
enlarged and republished his dissertation in pamphlet form under the title,
Review of the Debate in the Virginia Legislature of 1831 and 1832 (Richmond, 1832). Slaughter (Virginia History of African Colonization, p. 64)
says that Harrison was the author of the reply to Dew, which was reprinted
as a pamphlet and widely circulated. It also reappeared in 9 African Repository, pp. 1-15, 33-51.

6,000 are yearly exported to other States. Virginia is, in fact, a *negro* raising State for other States; she produces enough for her own supply, and six thousand for sale."[10] "Many in our State ", he said, "looked forward to an immediate fall in the price of slaves from this cause [the interdictions of Southwestern States against bringing in from other States slaves to be sold]; and what has been the result? Why, wonderful to relate, Virginia slaves are now higher than they have been for many years past; and this rise in price has no doubt been occasioned by the number of Southern purchasers who have visited our State, under the belief that Virginians had been frightened into a determination to get clear of their slaves at all events; * * * and we are, consequently, at this moment exporting slaves more rapidly, through the operation of the internal slave-trade, than for many years past ".[11] In different places he said: * * * " The 6,000 slaves which Virginia annually sends off to the South are a source of wealth to Virginia " * * *.[12] Every legislator in the State " should beware, lest in his zeal for action [in favor of colonization], this efflux, which is now so salutary to the State, and such an abundant source of wealth, be suddenly dried up " * * *.[13] When slavery is destroyed, "no matter how, the deed will be done, and Virginia will be a desert." * * *[14] " For a similar reason [the greater care of negro children and women since the abolition of the foreign slave-trade] now, the slaves in Virginia multiply more rapidly than in most of the Southern States; the Virginians can raise [them] cheaper than they can buy; in fact, it [raising slaves] is one of their greatest sources of profit. In many of the other slaveholding States, this is not the case, and consequently, the same care is not taken to encourage matrimony and

---

[10] *Pro-Slavery Argument*, 357, 359.

[11] *Ibid.*, 361-62.

[12] *Ibid.*, 378.

[13] *Ibid.*, 360.

[14] *Ibid.*, 384.

the rearing of children.'' [15] '' The largest portion of
slaves sent out of Virginia is sent through the operation
of our internal slave-trade; a full equivalent being thus
left in place of the slave, this emigration becomes an advantage to the State, and does not check the black population as much as at first we should imagine, because it
furnishes every inducement to the master to attend to his
negroes, to encourage marriage, and to cause the greatest
possible number to be raised, and thus it affords a powerful stimulus to the *spring* of black population, which, in
a great measure, counteracts [compensates for] the emigration.'' [16] Obviously that was intended to be a frank
and triumphant justification of slave-rearing for the
market.

O Jesse Burton Harrison's condemnation of slavery was
hardly less effective than Dew's defense. '' The only
form in which it can safely be said that slaves on a plantation are profitable in Virginia, is in the multiplication of
their number by births. If the proprietor, beginning with
a certain number of negroes, can but keep them for a
few years from the hands of the sheriff or the slave trader,
though their labour may have yielded him not a farthing
of nett revenue, he finds that gradually but surely, his
capital stock of negroes multiplies itself, and yields, if
nothing else, a palpable interest of young negroes. * * *
The process of multiplication will not in this way advance
the master towards the point of a nett revenue; he is not
the richer in income with the fifty slaves than with twenty.
Yet these young negroes have their value: and what value?
The value of the slaves so added to his number is the cer-

[15] *Ibid.*, 369-70.
[16] *Ibid.*, 473. In the 1832 edition of Dew's pamphlet (*Review* etc., p. 120)
the wording was " encourage building "—evidently a misprint for *encourage
breeding*, and it was so understood at the time and long afterward (*Slavery
As It Is*, 182; Geo. M. Weston, *The Progress of Slavery* (1857), 113); but as
this was a very indiscreet phrase, " marriage " was later substituted for
" building."

tain price for which they will at any time sell to the southern trade. * * * An account, on which we may rely, sets down the annual number of slaves sold to go out of the State at six thousand, or more than half the number of births! * * * *And will ' the aspiring blood of Lancaster' endure it to be said that a Guinea is still to be found in America, and that Guinea is Virginia?* [17] That children are reared with the express object of sale into distant regions, and that in numbers but little less than the whole number of annual births? It may be that there is a small section of Virginia (perhaps we could indicate it) where the theory of population is studied with reference to the yearly income from the sale of slaves. Shall the profits to Virginia, from this contaminated source, be alleged as an economical argument to magnify the sacrifice involved in the abolition of slavery, and this too by statesmen who profess to execrate the African slave trade? For ourselves, we can see but little difference between this form of the internal slave trade and the African trade itself.'' Then evidently wishing to preclude a charge that he was accusing Virginians generally of slave-breeding for the market, and hoping to arouse the resentment of the great majority against the relatively few, so as to obtain support for gradual emancipation, he continued: '' But we have too deep a stake ourselves in the good name of the land of Washington and Jefferson, to be willing to admit that this form of profit from slaves ['' yearly income from the sale of slaves ''] is cherished by any but a very few persons. This is not then an income which Virginia loves to reap.'' And wishing to show confidence that the evils of slavery and slave-rearing for profit could be checked, he added: '' She scorns those who resort to it, and will count lightly of the sacrifice which the extinction of this fountain of impure wealth would involve.

'' Banishing this then out of view, there is no productive

[17] Italics not in the original.

value of slaves in Virginia. Shut up all outlet into the southern and southwestern States, and the price of slaves in Virginia would sink down to a cypher."[18]

Ex-President Madison, who impressed even Harriet Martineau as having a profound hatred of slavery, commented on the licentiousness of the negroes, which he said, stopped short of only the destruction of the race, every slave girl being expected to be a mother by the time she was fifteen.[19] Yet he could not conceal his pride in the fact that the latest count showed that one-third of his slaves were under five years of age—somewhat remote from race-suicide! This natural increase was always put on the profit side of the ledger, no matter how much the master complained of being impoverished by it.

The Charleston *Mercury* of May 16, 1838, contained an advertisement the main features of which were as follows:

" A GIRL about 20 years of age (raised in Virginia, and her two female children, one 4 and the other 2 years old. She is * * * remarkably strong and healthy, never having had a day's sickness, with the exception of the small pox, in her life. The children are fine and healthy. She is very prolific in her generating qualities, and affords a rare opportunity for any person who wishes to raise a family of strong and healthy servants for their [his] own use. Sold for no fault."[20]

A newspaper of high standing would not have accepted such an advertisement if there had been much sentiment against slave-breeding for profit.

[18] 12 *American Quarterly Review* (Dec., 1832), 391-92.

[19] 1 *Retrospect of Western Travel*, 191.

[20] It ended with this sentence: " Any person[s] wishing to purchase will please leave their addresses at the Mercury office, directed to E. J." The author made a careful copy from the file in the Charleston Library. [Weld's] *American Slavery As It Is* (1839), 175, gives a substantially accurate copy, except as to italics and capitals.

In a S. C. case in 1844 it was said: " Mr. Gist * * * did not disguise the fact that he wished to sell [two negro girls] * * * because they had an objectionable habit, that of eating dirt, and which, in his opinion, rendered them unprofitable as breeding women." Accordingly he had sold the two for $1,000 in 1842.—2 Catterall, 392.

The wife of a Georgia planter wrote that " many indirect inducements [are] held out to reckless propagation, which has a sort of premium offered to it in the consideration of less work and more food counterbalanced by none of the sacred responsibilities which hallow and ennoble the relation of parent and child; in short, as their lives are for the most those of mere animals, their increase is literally mere animal breeding, to which every encouragement is given, for it adds to the master's live-stock and the value of his estate." [21]

The most careful planters everywhere considered slave-rearing of prime importance. One in Alabama, who was so liberal-minded that he encouraged his negroes to read the Bible, described his own prosperity by saying that his slaves had been " generally healthy and very prolific, and their increase is no small matter in the item of profits ".[22] Another expressed the common opinion: " Well treated and cared for, and moderately worked, their natural increase becomes a source of great profit to their owner. Whatever therefore tends to promote their health and render them prolific, is worthy his attention." [23] " With us the proprietor's largest source of prosperity is in the negroes he raises ", said Secretary of the Treasury Howell Cobb, in 1858, when also president of the Georgia Cotton Planters' convention.[24]

John C. Reed—also a Georgian, graduated from Princeton in 1854 and afterward a lawyer in his native State—had rare knowledge of social conditions and was clear and frank in his convictions. He wrote: " Although the

[21] Frances Anne Kemble [Mrs. Pierce Butler], *Journal of a Residence on a Ga. Plantation in 1838-39*, 122.

[22] 21 *Southern Quar.*, 213, 216. " Slave property increased rapidly. Child bearing sometimes began at twelve years and frequent births made a heavy per cent of ' profit ' ", wrote Rebecca L. Felton.—*Country Life in Georgia etc.*, 79.

[23] 1 *Amer. Cotton Planter* (n.s.), 295.

[24] 2 *Amer. Cotton Planter* (n. s.), 331.

profits of slave-planting were considerable, the greatest
profit of all was what the master thought of and talked
of all the day long,—the natural increase of his slaves,
as he called it. His negroes were far more to him than
his land." * * * " Really the leading industry of the South
was slave rearing. The profit was in keeping the slaves
healthy and rapidly multiplying. This could be done at
little expense in agriculture where even the light work-
ers were made to support themselves." Accordingly, he
said, "many of these older sections turned, from being
agricultural communities, into nurseries, rearing slaves
for the younger States where virgin soil was abundant." [25]

Other Southerners went much further, saying that in
several States slaves were reared for sale rather than
for their labor. Moncure D. Conway, whose father was a
slaveholder near Fredericksburg, Virginia, wrote: " As a
general thing, the chief pecuniary resource in the border
States is the breeding of slaves; and I grieve to say that
there is too much ground for the charges that general
licentiousness among the slaves, for the purpose of a large
increase, is compelled by some masters and encouraged
by many. The period of maternity is hastened, the average youth of negro mothers being nearly three years ear-

[25] *The Brothers' War*, 49, 156, 432. "While some of the Southern States
were slave-exporting, all of them—even the cotton States—were more inten-
sively employed in slave-rearing than in anything else."—J. C. Reed to the
author, Aug. 15, 1908.

Dr. Ferguson, an old physician whose father and grandfather were large
planters, said to the author in New Orleans in 1902: "My grandfather took
special care of the pregnant women and early put them on lighter work.
As soon as the infants were weaned they were sent off to Mississippi City
to be cared for by some of the old women. When they were strong enough to
be 'water-toters' they were brought back to the plantation to work. As a
rule, the planters down here did not want breeders; but those that did would
encourage their slaves to pair off, would fix them up with a house and tell
them that they would be sold if they did not have a baby in a year. Sometimes my grandfather would buy several women at a time. He had them
carefully examined by a young physician who was his special friend."

lier than that of any free race, and an old maid is utterly unknown among the women.''[26]

The stock-farmer indifferent to enlarging his herd would be no more of an anomaly than was the planter that did not keep close count of his pickaninnies and rejoice in the profit that grew with them. They were his pride and appealed to his imagination. '' All the little darkies by natural increase were net profit!'' exclaimed an old lawyer in Natchez, the son of a rich ante-bellum planter. This was because on a farm or plantation the necessary outlay for their support (from birth until they reached 6 or 8 years of age, when they began to work and were readily salable or hired out)[27] was hardly appreciable. Their food and scant clothing were the simplest and cheapest possible, and an ample average allowance was one-third as much as was given to a fieldhand, whose entire maintenance, according to liberal estimates, cost

[26] *Testimonies Concerning Slavery* (Second edition, London, 1865), 20.

A Southerner wrote to Olmsted: '' In the States of Md., Va., N. C., Ky., Tenn. and Mo., as much attention is paid to the breeding and growth of negroes as to that of horses and mules. Further South, we raise them both for use and for market. Planters command their girls and women (married or unmarried) to have children; and I have known a great many negro girls to be sold off, because they did not have children. A breeding woman is worth from one-sixth to one-fourth more than one that does not breed.'' —*Seaboard* etc., 55.

A Mississippian whom Olmsted met on the James River said: '' But they [the Virginians] did not keep them to make corn * * * , they kept them to breed and raise young ones. It was folly to pretend that they did not.''— Olmsted, *Back Country*, 284. *Ibid.*, 285-86, gives a long quotation from the Brandon, Miss., *Republican* showing that slave-rearing for profit was believed to be common in the border slave States.

Professor Hammond's epigram about conditions in Md. and Va. describes what was true as a rule: '' Henceforth slaves were seldom kept in these States for the sake of raising crops, but crops were often cultivated for the sake of raising slaves.''—M. B. Hammond, *The Cotton Industry*, 54.

[27] 2 Catterall, 509, cites a case in Tenn. in 1839, where a boy about 8 years old was hired out for 12 months for $15 and clothes, and soon was sold by the sheriff for $345. Phillips, ed., 2 *Plantation* etc., 58, quotes an advt. of '' a girl of 5 that sews.''

not more than $30 per year.[28]   In 1823, Madison expressed this opinion: "The annual expense of food and raiment in rearing a child, may be stated at about 8, 9, or 10 dollars; and the age at which it begins to be gainful to its owner, about 9 or 10 years.[29] It was still less on a plantation in the lower South where the children were brooded by an old nurse.[30]

Add to this petty cost the loss because the mother did not work for a month or two on account of child-bearing and there still remained room for an enormous per cent of profit on each child reared under favorable circumstances. Between 1830-1860, according to the year and the region, each babe in arms added from $100 to $200 or more to the value of its slave mother.[31]   It was just the reverse in

[28] Olmsted, 2 *Cotton Kingdom*, 238; *Seaboard* etc., 688; M. B. Hammond, who thinks that $20 per annum was about the average expenditure for slaves of all ages throughout the cotton belt, cites different high authorities, *Cotton Industry*, 91.   See also Reed, *Brothers' War*, 334; Ingle, *Southern Sidelights*, 77.

[29] 9 *Madison Writings*, 133.

[30] 2 Catterall, 407-408, cites a case in South Carolina where it was said that "$9.75 per annum allowed * * * for feeding the young negroes, is extravagant", and that only a little more was paid for the board of a mother and children when put out at public outcry to the lowest bidder, where a profit was expected to be made.

[31] E. A. Andrews, *Slavery* etc., 147; Ingraham (2 *The Southwest*, 244-45) said, about 1834, that an infant added about $100 to the value of its mother, and increased about $100 in value every three years to maturity.   Before 1840, in Mo. "children from 2 to 5 years of age were sold for from $100 to $200."—Trexler, *Slavery in Mo.*, 39.   But interstate traders often objected to them as an encumbrance.—Andrews, 149, 165, and *post* p. 137 n.

2 Catterall, 100, cites a N. C. case where it was held that in 1829 the mother was worth probably $300, but in 1838 the administrator sold her and her four children for $1,487.50.

Two juries in Virginia, in 1822 and 1825, respectively, made these appraisements of the same slaves:

	First jury	Second jury
Amy, the mother	$300	$200
Wilson, about 4 years old . . .	200	200
Washington, about 2 years old . .	150	125
Charlotte, (?) months old . . .	75	90

—1 Catterall, 186.

Massachusetts in colonial days: slavery there being unprofitable, the infants were considered an encumbrance and, when weaned, were given away like puppies.[32] In the 'fifties, average boys or girls from 8 to 12 years old would bring at least $400 or $500; the best sometimes more than twice that much. Crops rarely, if ever, afforded such a ratio of profits, and never one-tenth so easily.[33]

Conservative estimates placed at from four to eight per cent the average net annual value of the natural increase of the slaves on a plantation, apart from the advance in price, which was fully as much more.[34] It was often sev-

---

[32] Moore, *Slavery in Massachusetts*, 57.

[33] " In different parts of the south the following prices were obtained for children in May, 1857:—Jack, 4, $376; Elvina, 5, $400; Bettie 8, $785. In Md.: a girl about 14, $900; a small girl, $880; small girl, $350. In Mo.: girl, 9, $805; boy, 5, $487; boy, 2 1-2, $325."—Weston, *Progress of Slavery*, 116-17, gives details.

Nancy, girl about 10, $765; a boy belonging to Mrs. Durham, about 12, $915.—Chas'n Tri-weekly *Mercury*, Dec. 10, 1859.

" In Petersburg, Va., on the 28th a gang of 39, mostly children, sold for $22,082.50, one of them, a girl of ten years brought $1,151."—Augusta Daily *Chronicle and Sentinel*, Jan. 1, 1859.

A child 11 years old sold for $1,525 in Crawford county in 1860.—*Phillips*, 2 *Plantation* etc., 73.

For many other examples, see chapters IX and XVI.

[34] In S. C. in 1848 it was held that the natural increase was " an item which is always prominent in the planter's calculation, and which would unquestionably amount to 5 or 6 per cent per annum upon their original cost."— De Bow, 1 *Industrial Resources of the Southern and Western States*, 163.

" Mr. X [a rice-planter] boasts a steady increase of his negro stock, of five per cent per annum, which is better than is averaged on the plantations of the interior."—Olmsted, 1 *Cotton Kingdom*, 235.

On one of the largest La. sugar plantations the overseer alleged that it was about five per cent.—W. H. Russell, *My Diary North and South*, 274.

Ante-bellum lawyers in Natchez gave the present author similar evidence. The one already quoted said that " the increase of the negroes amounted to at least five per cent of the investment, and where the young women were well taken care of they bore about once a year ". The other, a Confederate general, used these words: " One of the great sources of wealth was the increase of the negroes on the plantation; nothing like it except the increase of the Israelites. It was very common for the girls to have babies at fifteen and I have known cases at fourteen years of age." See *post* p. 83 n., for cases of mothers at 13.

eral times as much as a planter's profit on his crop, when
the value of the slaves, lands and improvements were
counted as capital and the overseer's wages and the factor's commissions for sales, purchases and loans were
deducted. Indeed, the merely agricultural result of planting was more often a loss than a gain. Professor Phillips goes so far as to say that " by the close of the 'fifties
it is fairly certain that no slaveholders but those few
whose plantations lay in the most advantageous parts of
the cotton and sugar districts and whose managerial abil-
ity was exceptionally great were earning anything beyond what would cover their maintenance and carrying
charges." [35]   But planting was a necessary means to the
desired ends—being a planter and having an increasing
number of slaves, who were both reared with great profit
and were continually rising in value.

Men otherwise careless and spendthrift were eager to
multiply their slaves, realizing that by keeping the natural
increase the whole number would rapidly augment like
money at a high rate of compound interest. If the master
could manage to live from the labor of his negroes, the
equivalent of riches was only a matter of time. Ten young
slaves (of whom five or six were girls) worth hardly $5,000
in 1840, might treble their number by 1855, when the value
of the thirty of all ages was fully $20,000—an enormous
gain without counting any surplus from labor and crops.
In two or three decades a small planter, starting in a
fertile region with 15 or 20 young slaves, might, by industry, economy and purchasing girls and boys, easily
become a " large planter ", with a gang of 40 or 50 sturdy
fieldhands and more than that many children. Twice all
that was *possible* in Alabama, Mississippi and Louisiana,
if one gave the closest attention to slave-rearing, raising
crops and buying more negroes to make new plantations
out of cheap and fertile virgin soil;—it was *possible,* but

[35] *Amer. Negro Slavery,* 391-2.

rare, only because enterprise and thrift were rare and extravagance and carelessness common.

Thus, next to the great and quick profit of bringing virgin soil under cultivation, slave-rearing was the surest, most remunerative and most approved means of increasing agricultural capital. It was advised and practised by the wisest rural slaveowners.[36] A young female slave, unless skilled or comely, was, as Olmsted said, most prized for breeding qualities, and he quoted a Virginia planter who was proud of the fact that " his women were uncommonly good breeders; he did not suppose there was a lot of women anywhere that bred faster than his; he never heard of babies coming so fast as they did on his plantation; it was perfectly surprising; and every one of them, in his estimation, was worth two hundred dollars, as negroes were selling now, the moment it drew breath."[37] Fecundity at an early age was considered a great virtue,

---

[36] Planters often had to pay their lawyers in slaves. John C. Reed's grandfather said that Robert Toombs welcomed such payments, usually bought the interests of his associates and sent the negroes to his Chattahoochee plantation; that the associates were likely soon to spend the cash, while Toombs became rich. " 'John, get as many young breeding-women as you can. Hire them out where they will not be abused, and after a while you can collect them on a good plantation of your own. The increase of your negroes will make you rich.' I had talked this all over many times with my sweetheart and that was our plan. The plantation was to be in the Mississippi valley or in Texas, as my grandfather advised ".—J. C. Reed to the author, Aug. 15, 1908.

[37] *Seaboard* etc., 55, 57. " 'I hear you were very unlucky with that girl you bought of me last year?' [said a La. negro-trader to a former client.]— 'Yes, I was; very unlucky. She died with her first child, and the child died, too.' * * *—'Well, it came right hard upon you—just beginning so.'—'Yes, I was foolish, I suppose, to risk so much on the life of a single woman; but I've got a good start again now, for all that. I've got two right likely girls; one of them's got a fine boy, four months old, and the other's with child—and old Pine Knot's as hearty as ever.' "—*Seaboard* etc., 647.

" FANNY MUST GO! — SHE is a No. 1 girl, 18 years old, good house servant and hard to beat. Don't forget the *day*, such girls will *pay*, Saturday 25th, at 10 o'clock. * * *—M. C. CAYCE & SON ".—Memphis *Avalanche*, Feb. 25, 1860.

" For Sale.—A likely NEGRO WOMAN, about 20 years of age, with a fine baby 12 months old. The woman is a first rate cook, washer and ironer and

and actual or prospective infants increased the market value of slave mothers.[38]

A girl of seventeen years that had borne two children was called a " rattlin' good breeder " and commanded an extraordinary price.[39]

Young mothers with several small children were extremely valuable, and buxom girls of from 14 to 18 years were

is sold for no fault. Apply to H. BONZANO, 38 and 40 Tchoupitoulas street."—N. O. *Picayune*, Jan. 5, 1856.

" For Sale.—A NO. 1 Cook, Washer and Ironer—age 24 years—with a likely boy child, between two and three years old. This is truly a No. 1 woman. A bargain can be had by calling soon, on W. E. DYER, Agent."—Memphis *Eagle & Enquirer*, Apr. 6, 1854.

[38] In one Tenn. case the judge spoke of " the slave, so peculiarly valuable for her physical capacity of child-bearing "; and in another it was held that " the value of the slave had become much greater by the birth of a child and the increase of the price of property."—2 Catterall, 579, 543.

A New Orleans auctioneer said when selling Margaret and her infant: " She is between 16 and 17 years of age, and is six months gone in pregnancy of her second child * * *. She'll no doubt be the mother of a great many children * * *; and that is a consideration to a purchaser who wants to raise a fine young stock."—Ebenezer Davies, *American Scenes and Christian Slavery*, 56.

At the end of an advt. and list offering at private sale the negroes belonging to the estate of Col. John H. McIntosh at Burlington Plantation in Florida, was this sentence: " Eight infants born since June ".—Charleston *Courier*, Jan. 4, 1853.

" There are thirty-six of them in number, at present, and prospect of an accession of one or two more, by birth ", wrote a Georgia planter wishing to sell.—Phillips, 1 *Plantation etc.*, 172.

[39] John S. Wise, *End of an Era*, 83. Wise (pp. 85-86) represented a rural politician as saying: " ' You see, I live a long way from here, and I ride down to the legislatur', and, when I get here, I sell my horse and live cheap, and aims to save up enough from my salary to buy another horse and a ' chile-bearin' woman ' when the session's done; and then I takes her home, ridin' behind me on the horse. [1 Catterall, 297, cites a case where the purchaser took his female slave away in the same manner. Calhoun's father returned from a visit to Charleston with a purchased slave riding behind him. —Hunt, *Calhoun*, 129.] Thar ain't no way I could provide for gittin' the man and the young uns home, even if they was given to me ' " * * * " and, as he counted it [his money], said, ' Martha Ann, cheer up; you'll find me a good marster, and I'll get you a new husband.' He might well have added, ' and the more children you have, the better I'll like you.' "

" A young girl who would breed like a cat " could not do heavy plantation work, said a writer in 3 *Amer. Cot. Planter*, (n. s.), 76.

usually at a great premium because of good looks or proved or expected fecundity.[40]

[40] Many more than the following examples might be given of early motherhood, fecundity and girls selling at high prices:—

Names.	Mother when.	Age when sold.	No. of children.	Their ages.	Traders' names.	Chas'n Courier.
Susan	17,	23,	3,	6, 4 & 2.	McCall.	Feb. 21, 1860;
Rose,	22,	40,	8,	18 to 1.	Capers & Heyward.	Jan. 13, 1860;
Nancy,	16,	33,	9,	17 " 1.	J. S. Ryan.	Sept. 18, 1856;
Millie,	13,	25,	3,	12 " 6.	Capers & Heyward.	Feb. 1, 1860;
Sarah,	14,	25,	3,	11 " 4.	J. Russell Baker.	Feb. 23, 1860;
Lucretia,	15,	28,	5,	13 " 1.	R. M. Marshall.	Jan. 24, 1859;
Susan,	16,	22,	2,	6 and 2.	Porcher & Baya.	Jan. 27, 1860;
Woman,	13,	33,	3,	20, 13, 10.	Tardy.—Mobile Advertiser,	
"	17,	37,	6,	20 to 2.		Jan. 5, 1860.
"	15,	27,	4,	12, 10, 5, 3.	T. N. Gadsden, post p. 168.	
"	17,	30,	4,	13, 10, 9, 4.	T. N. Gadsden, post p. 168.	
" & (husband)	13,	25,	4,	12, 10, 8, 5.	T. N. Gadsden, Mercury,	
						Jan. 24, 1833;
Eliza,	15,	21,	2,	6 and 4.	(Thigpen estate) $3050.	
					—Savannah Republican,	
						Feb. 16. 1859.

In La., 1857, Adeline, 20, with 2 children, 3 and 4, brought . . $2,505,
whereas, Silla, 30, with child of 3, brought but 1,610,
and Lucinda, 35, with child of 2, ... 1,325.

—22 De Bow, 439.

In Ga., 1856: two girls, 15 and 14, each sold for 1,280;
another, 14, ... 1,305;
another, 16, ... 1,525;
another girl, 18, (in family way), ... 1,500;
a woman, about 20, with a babe in arms, ... 1,840;
whereas a boy, 18, brought only 1,290;
and a man, 22, only . . . . 1,500.

—Wm. Chambers, American Slavery and Colour, 207.

Where " the best field hand, a boy 21 years old sold for . . . 1,900 ",
a girl, 17, and her baby, nine months, brought 2,150;
another, 18, with a child, 3, more than 2,500;
a woman, 30, with three children, the oldest 6 years . . . . 4,525.
The latter two lots were bought by heirs, which often increased the price.—Phillips, 2 Plantation etc., 73.

In Newberry, S. C., woman with 3 children . . . . 2,700.

—Tri-weekly Charleston Mercury, Dec. 10, 1859.

Griffin sale (Columbia, S. C.) " Nancy and 3 small children, . . 3,560 ",
" Charlotte a girl about 16 for . . . . 1,395 ".

—Mobile Register, Jan. 13, 1859.

Paul E. Tarver [Turner?] sale (post p. 341 n.) " one family, eight in number, with only three [working] hands, sold for . . . . 10,025."

—Augusta, Ga., Chronicle etc., Jan. 8, 1860.

Such facts were matters of common knowledge and daily gossip. In perhaps a large majority of cases it was needless or futile to give attention to the paternity of the children. But on well-conducted plantations, matings—it was misleading to call them marriages when in law there was no such thing—were always favored, usually encouraged and sometimes virtually compelled, because believed to be conducive to order, health and industry as well as to natural increase. Every planter preferred the matings to be between his own slaves, when numbers and ages were suitable, and it was not rare for a large planter to make it a positive restriction. Then each couple was given a cabin and a little plot of ground for a garden. James H. Hammond of South Carolina gave an additional bounty

Harmon sale (*post* p. 356 n.) " Jeff and wife and 4 children (oldest 6 years old) . . . .   5,200 ";
" Mage (18 years old) . . . .   2,045 ";
" Tay and 2 small children . . . .   2,600 ".
—Mobile *Advertiser*, Jan. 18, 1860.

McLemore sale, 1854 (*post* p. 350) woman field-hand, 37, and 6 children, 2 to 7 . . . .   5,000.
" A wench and her infant were sold in Columbia, on Monday for   1,615 and another similar pair for . . . .   1,270 ".
—Charleston *Mercury*, Feb. 9, 1860.

In Charleston:—
J. S. Ryan sold " Lizzy, an excellent house servant and her infant " for . . . .   1,300.
—*Courier*, Dec. 1, 1859.

Oakes sold a " wench ", 14, ...   970.
—*Mercury*, Jan. 11, 1860.

White sold a house servant, 30, and 3 children . . . . . .   2,200.
—*Mercury*, Jan. 20, 1860.

Marshall, " young negress, 18 years old, and her infant, . . .   1,160 ";
—*Mercury*, Feb. 1, 1860.

Ryan & Son, " a woman 25 years old, and her 2 children, 2 and 4 years old, ...   1,470 ".
—*Mercury*, Feb. 15, 1860.

Marshall, " wench, 17 years old, for . . . .   1,400 ";
Capers & Heyward, " wench, 18 years old, for . . . . .   1,165 ";
Ryan & Son, " wench, 20 years old, with an infant, for . . . .   1,180 ".
—*Mercury*, Feb. 22, 1860.

of $5 to first " marriages ", and doubtless many others offered special inducements.[41] After that, if the picka-ninnies were numerous at the quarters, and there were no violent jealousies, no disturbances of the peace, little or no attention was given to the paternity of the children.[42] It was, of course, different with the servants at the " big house ", where ostensible decencies were attempted to be maintained for the sake of the master's family.

The rules for plantation management and the reports of the overseers demonstrate that masters always wished to know about the number of actual and prospective infants. Both sympathy and interest often prompted sending delica-cies from the kitchen and showy, cheap articles of apparel to the mothers. Such special attentions and a long rest were highly appreciated.[43] Some rewards were virtually premiums. Mrs. Roger A. Pryor's uncle gave a small pig to the mother of each new pickaninny.[44] Because field-

---

[41] Augustus B. Longstreet—judge, journalist, minister, small planter, author of *Georgia Scenes*, and at different times president of four colleges in S. C., Ga., Miss. and La.—" did not think it unbecoming to him to complain when negro men and women whom he had more or less forcibly shoved into matri-monial alliances and then settled off in neat houses of their own[?], refused thereafter to live in those houses as they had originally been paired."— Wade, *Longstreet*, 272. See Phillips, *Old South*, 203-05, 243-44, 256, 270, 274, 278, 285 and 317, for matings under various conditions and influences.

[42] When inspecting a large plantation in the Lower Miss. valley, Olmsted asked if the negroes began to have children at a very early age. " ' Some-times at sixteen ', said the manager. ' Yes, and at fourteen ', said the overseer * * * . Women were almost common property, though sometimes the men were not all inclined to acknowledge it; for when I asked: ' Do you not try to discourage this? ' the overseer answered: ' No, not unless they quarrel.' ' They get jealous and quarrel among themselves sometimes about it ', the manager explained, ' or come to the overseer and complain, and he has them punished.' ' Give all hands a damned good hiding ', said the overseer. You punish for adultry, then, but not for fornication? ' Yes ', answered the manager, but ' No ', insisted the overseer, ' we punish them for quarreling; if they don't quarrel I don't mind anything about it, but if it makes a muss, I give all four of 'em a warning.'"—Olmsted, 2 *Cotton Kingdom*, 209-10.

[43] Smedes, *Southern Planter*, 78, gives details of attentions that were cer-tainly exceptional in the case of fieldhands.

[44] *Reminiscences of Peace and War*, 148.

hand mothers were prone to neglect their infants, sometimes with fatal results, James H. Hammond had a plan
that showed practicality worthy of his Yankee father: for
every baby that had been properly attended to, thirteen
months old and in sound health, he rewarded the mother
with a muslin or calico frock.[45] But the most effective
utilitarian generosity was to promise the women their
freedom as soon as they should bear a certain number of
children. There were several such cases in Virginia courts.
When slaves were cheap, one master provided in his will,
in 1761, that if " Jeany[Jenny] brings ten live children "
she should have her liberty. Much later, in 1828, when
slaves were more valuable, the master of another Jenny
offered to reward her likewise when she should bear five
children, one for each of his. And about the same time
it was the dying request of a Mrs. Dejarnet that her slave
Fanny should be manumitted whenever she should bear
five children, one for each of hers.[46]

Was it strange that the slaves understood? " Look,
missis! little niggers for you and massa; plenty little
niggers for you and little missis! " On that plantation
girls of sixteen commonly had children and it was not rare
for women of thirty to have grandchildren.[47]

Reports of prodigious fecundity and profits were always
welcome subjects of conversation. Ruffin estimated that
a gang of slaves on a farm would normally increase four-
fold in thirty or forty years.[48] Mrs. Catterall cites from
court reports many cases of fecundity like these: Nancy
bore 17 children in 18 or 19 years; in an indefinite time
Hannah had borne 14 or 15; another " negro woman had
13 children, three of whom were sold "; another died in
1853, leaving 10 children * * * one sold, and " Sue, giving

[45] Phillips, *Amer. Negro Slavery*, 272.
[46] 1 Catterall, 104, 151, 313.
[47] Kemble, *Ga. Journal*, 58-61.
[48] Quoted by Olmsted, *Seaboard*, 280. Dew (*Pro-Slavery Argument*, 368)
thought that doubling every fifteen years would be possible.

birth to a child every two years.''[49] An ante-bellum physician in Tuskegee, Alabama, mentioned a case to the author where '' a single negro couple brought a $25,000 increase in forty years ''; and an old planter and former Confederate officer met there remarked: '' As soon as a man had the money he bought a girl, and before many years she had a family that was worth $10,000.'' Howell Cobb's slaves multiplied '' like rabbits '' and were expected to double in number every ten or twelve years.[50] On his father's plantation this had been much exceeded by '' an aged woman [that] could call together more than one hundred of her lineal descendants ''.[51] De Bow knew of '' a plantation of fifty or sixty persons * * * from the descendants of a single female in the course of the lifetime of the original purchaser ''.[52] In 1767 some members of Presbyterian churches in Prince Edward county, Virginia, subscribed a sum of money and purchased two slave girls. These and their descendants were annually hired out and '' the hires appropriated to the payment of the salaries of the [common] pastor '', till 1835, when they numbered about seventy. Then the owners, believing that it would be better for the slaves, ordered their sale and the investment of the money obtained.[53] It was a very lucrative religious enterprise. Thus cases of great fecundity and profit were so frequently and so widely recounted that they were believed to be almost the rule. And John C. Reed aptly likened the ease and profit of slave-rearing to having a magical orchard that bore regularly, gathered and cared for its own fruit and steadily enlarged its own area and production.[54]

[49] 2 Catterall, 407, 509, 543, 569, 408. See *post* p. 210, note 26 for a case where a mother had borne 4 children in 4½ years, and then all were offered for sale '' together or separately to suit purchasers ''.

[50] Phillips, 1 *Plantation etc.*, 179.

[51] Thos. R. R. Cobb, *Law of Negro Slavery*, p. ccxviii.

[52] 30 *De Bow*, 74.

[53] 24 *De Bow*, 289-90.

[54] *Brother's War*, 48.

CHAPTER V

VIRGINIA AND THE RICHMOND MARKET

"As a general rule, the slaves only half work, and the masters do not work at all. The masters are prodigal, and the slaves are wasteful", said Henry Berry in the Virginia legislature.[1] "When I came to Fairfax county [in 1836] the farms were very large, but the land was generally poor", wrote the Reverend Joseph Packard. "Negro slaves were numerous, but no one seemed to make money by farming or care much for making it."[2] Virginia's self-complacency was perfectly expressed by her great humorist, George W. Bagby: "Time was abundant in those days. It was made for slaves, and we had the slaves." Of course agriculture did not improve. Henry A. Wise told Virginians during his successful campaign for the governorship in 1855: "You all own plenty of land, but it is poverty added to poverty. Poor land added to poor land, and nothing added to nothing makes nothing; while the owner is talking politics at Richmond, or in Congress, or spending the summer at the White Springs, the lands grow poorer and poorer, and this soon brings land, negroes and all under the hammer."[3] The Virginians that settled elsewhere with their slaves were a complete loss to the State. Only the slaves sold were a source of profit to Virginia; and that but slightly aided agriculture, apart from slave-rearing. Otherwise the high price of slaves was a great agricultural disadvantage, for

[1] Speech of Jan. 20, 1832, on the abolition of slavery, p. 7.
[2] *Recollections of a Long Life*, 106.
[3] He elaborated with a humorous story, the gist of which was as follows:— A stranger riding along the highway and falling in with a planter of the neighborhood asked him who owned this house, and this, and this. Thrice the planter answered: "It is mine, stranger"; then he added, "but don't suppose I'm so darned poor as to own all the *land* about here."—Chase & Sanborn, *The North and the South*, 55.

88

it increased the cost of labor, already nearly twice too much to be remunerative.[4]

Many a Virginia " country gentleman " or " planter " was unable to keep his family in comfort and feed and clothe his negroes decently without ultimately selling some of them or running deeply in debt. The greater his debts, the more he tried to avoid letting the public know of any sale, for it was a proclamation of poverty. Secret sales or further loans with deeds of trust on his best negroes— or mortgages with power of sale, or possession of the slaves as collateral and a bill of sale, to be void if the debt was paid by a certain time—these were the usual alternatives. Postponements and continued carelessness or extravagance made conditions worse. Yet a score or two of slaves were so unquestionable a token of riches that small credits were easily obtained and increased, for merchants were afraid of getting into disfavor in such cases if they forced a settlement. It was almost proverbial that Virginia " planters were not used to paying their debts until they died ".[5] Thus they " never sold any slaves ", but regularly used them as actual or ostensible security until finally some or all must go to reimburse creditors. This was the type known as " the poor, rich Virginians ". And they fancied that they were impoverished by their negroes!

It was more difficult for a small slaveholder needing cash or credit to postpone selling or giving a deed of trust on a negro. Because the creditor was likely to be ruthless, the master often thought it better to dispose of a slave at once.[6] If he needed a considerable amount of cash and

---

[4] Edmund Ruffin wrote in 1859 that no one could afford to buy negroes for any agricultural undertaking in Va., and he had not known of any such case for two years.—26 De Bow's Review, 649-50. Prof. Phillips (Old South, 245) quotes a Va. planter as saying in 1860: " I look upon it as murder [financial suicide] to lay out money in negroes to work in Va."

[5] Packard, Recollections, 108.

[6] " In all parts of the South, it is the custom of village storekeepers to sell goods on a credit of twelve months, at the expiration of which time, if you are rich and influential, you are seldom asked to pay up, but simply to give

wished to avoid the sharp practices of the money-lender or the itinerant speculator, he could obtain nearly a fair market price by leaving his slave or slaves with one of the many commission merchants or auctioneers that promised " liberal advances on consignments ". Settlement of the account would follow sale. Such masters had no prestige of riches and social standing to maintain.

In his philosophical old age a native of the Old Dominion and a Confederate general of cavalry remarked to the author: " In Virginia, negroes were raised and sold; it was a nursery of slavery. Traders went through the country buying up two or three here and there and brought them to the Richmond market." If only one was bought, he or she was mounted behind the trader's saddle or, more often, sat beside him or at his feet in the gig or was carried on some public conveyance. In " The Old Virginia Gentleman " Bagby described what was to be seen on a certain " main, plain road ": " Twice a week the stage rattled along, nobody inside, a negro in the boot, the driver and the negro-trader, both drunk, on top." Near a railroad or navigable water one or many slaves might be shipped to market as easily and in much the same manner as an equal number of calves. Otherwise, if numerous, they were driven as a chain-gang. Shortly after William H. Seward halted at a country tavern in Virginia, in 1835, ten negro boys, between the ages of six and twelve, tied together two and two at their wrists and fastened to a rope, emerged from the dust that they had made as they shuffled along the road. A tall, gaunt white man, with a long whip drove them through the barnyard gate, up to the horse-trough to drink and then to a shed, where they lay down and moaned until they fell asleep. They had

your note for the amount due. If you are in only moderate circumstances, however, and so ' short ' that you can not meet your yearly bills promptly when payday arrives, * * * all he asks is that you too shall give him your note, but secured by *good collaterals*—which means a trust-deed of your land and negroes."—D. R. Hundley, *Social Relation in Our Southern States*, 138.

been bought of different persons and were trudging to the Richmond market.[7] '' Hardly a day passes in which large companies [of slaves] may not be seen traversing the roads of Virginia on their way to the southern frontier '', wrote a Virginia historian in 1847.[8] Joseph Holt Ingraham, who early became a resident of Mississippi and died there in 1860, commented as follows on what he saw and learned in Virginia in the 'fifties: '' So necessary is the annual decimation of slaves by sale to support these old decayed families, that it has become a settled trade for men whose occupation is to buy slaves, to travel through the ' Old Dominion ', from estate to estate * * *. Here he [the trader] gets one, there another, and in a few weeks he enters Lynchburg, Alexandria or Richmond with a hundred or more * * *. As it is, slaves are raised here more as a *marketable* and money-returning commodity than for their productive labor.'' [9]

After the Virginia section of the District of Columbia was returned to the Old Dominion, in 1846, and the bringing of slaves for sale into the District was prohibited, in 1850, Alexandria naturally attracted such trade and traders as had formerly centered in Washington. One of the most notorious of these was Joseph Bruin, who was also well known in New Orleans. In 1859, George Kephart and Wm. H. Birch, two Washington traders in the 'thirties, and J. C. Cook and C. M. Price were conducting the old Franklin & Armfield slave-pen under the style of Price, Birch & Co.[10] Kephart continued there until the spring of 1861, when he hastily left Alexandria just before the United States troops seized it. His slave-pen was soon

---

[7] F. W. Seward, 1 *Wm. H. Seward*, 271.

[8] Howison, 2 *History of Va.*, 520. Of course he did not mean that all had either been purchased or were to be sold.

[9] *The Sunny South or the Southerner at Home*, 523.

[10] This partnership was dissolved in Dec., 1859 (Alexandria *Gazette*, Jan. 1, 1860) but their sign remained much longer. See illustration opp. p. 92.

turned into a prison where captured Confederates brooded over an amazing topsy-turvy.[11]

In the little city of Lynchburg four traders—George Davis, M. Hart, E. Myers and Seth Woodroof—were advertising in the Christmas (1845) and other numbers of the Lynchburg *Republican,* and auctioneer Charles Phelps was selling slaves both privately and publicly.[12] Davis, alone, had previously called for 200 young negroes of the usual ages, had promised fully as high prices as could be obtained in Richmond or in any part of the State, was " determined to be liberal in every instance ", and, of course, was ready to go in any direction to inspect and make offers.[13] Davis and Hart as partners would buy any number of negroes that would suit the Southern market. Myers wished only " a parcel of negroes of both sexes ", but otherwise was not less enterprising. He could be found at this hotel or at that store. Woodroof sought from 75 to 150 between the ages of 10 and 25, later ex-

[11] Moncure D. Conway wrote:—"The firm of Kephart & Co., Alexandria, Va., was, ever since I can remember, the chief slave-dealing firm in that State, and perhaps any where along the border between the free and slave States. * * * Upon the secession of Va., the U. S. made a successful effort to occupy Alexandria. One of the first spots visited by our troops was the shamble of Kephart & Co. The firm had fled, and taken its salable articles with it; but a single one remained—an old man, chained to the middle of the floor by the leg. He was released, and the ring and chain which bound him [were] sent to the Rev. Henry Ward Beecher." Conway also printed interesting excerpts from letters found there. Several were from well known traders, especially Bacon Tait of Richmond, Joseph Bruin (not " Brewan ") of Alexandria and New Orleans, and Thomas Boudar (not " Boudor "), a well-known New Orleans commission merchant in slaves.—*Testimonies Concerning Slavery,* 21-26. Capt. John Cussons, a scout in Longstreet's corps, captured and put in this prison, many years later related his experiences to the present author.

Mrs. Mary G. Powell, an authority on the history of Alexandria, kindly supplies the following information: The Armfield house, which is now (1923) 1315 Duke street, between Payne and West sts., has been remodeled and is called the Norman Apartments. A considerable portion of the old slave-pen has been removed but some of the east wall still remains.

[12] *Republican,* Apr. 17 and Aug. 28, 1845.
[13] *Republican,* June 9, 1845.

The Old Franklin & Armfield Slave-Pen

In Alexandria, Virginia, as it was in 1861

tended to 30.[14] By 1852 he had a newly erected brick building on First or Lynch street, behind the Farmers' Bank,
where he would " board negroes sent to Lynchburg for
sale or otherwise on as moderate terms, and keep them as
secure, as if they were placed in the jail of the Corpora-
tion ".[15] This shows that it was customary for traders to
keep their slaves in the public jail, where they were treated
much like felons.

Toward the end of the 'thirties there were about as
many traders in Petersburg as there were in Lynchburg
in 1845. Overley & Sanders, supposed to be engrossed in
buying in eastern Maryland, were also busy in Petersburg,
where they represented themselves as " particularly anxious to make a shipment of negroes shortly ". Henry
Davis wished to find about 50 young negroes and soon
make " another shipment " to New Orleans. Ansley Davis
sought twice as many and would visit adjacent counties to
inspect those for sale.[16] The trader Davises were so numerous [17]—like the Joneses, Woolfolks, Hills and others
to be noticed—that one can only conjecture as to how many
of them were included in Dr. Gamaliel Bailey's reference
several years later:—" The Davises, in Petersburg, are
the great slave-dealers. They are Jews, who came to that
place many years ago as poor peddlers; and, I am informed, are members of a family which has its representatives in Philadelphia, New York, etc.! These men are
always in the market, giving the highest price for slaves.
During the summer and fall they buy them up at low
prices, trim, shave, wash them, fatten them so that they

[14] *Republican*, June 9 and Dec. 25, 1845.

[15] Stowe, *Key to Uncle Tom's Cabin*, 139, quotes his advt. and also that of
J. B. McLendon, who was buying negroes between the ages of 10 and 30.

[16] Wm. Jay, *Misc. Writings on Slavery*, 266.

[17] Besides George, Henry and Ansley just mentioned, there were Thomas N.
Davis, buying in Washington and Alexandria, in 1838 (Clephane, 3 *Columbia
Hist. Soc. Recs.*, 235), Benjamin Davis, selling, in Hamburg, S. C., 120 he had
brought from Petersburg, Va. (Wm. Jay, 267), and Hector, John B., Robert
H., Benjamin and Solomon in Richmond in the 'fifties.

may look sleek, and sell them to great profit.''[18] Increased facilities for transportation had made it easy for sellers in that neighborhood to send their negroes the short distance to Richmond and get higher prices, yet small traders, auctioneers and, especially, hiring agents were still doing much business in Petersburg.

Norfolk was a port where many slaves were shipped and still more were transshipped. In 1839, James S. Buckingham found the trade there extensively practised and '' without censure or reproach ''. There was a pen so near the hotel where he stopped that he could occasionally hear the shoutings and cries of the negroes whom the traders were collecting for distant markets.[19] The two best known buyers in Norfolk in 1859-60 were John W. Starke and John J. Whitehurst. Both had their offices about opposite the Union Hotel on Union street. Whitehurst's was distinguished by a '' sign of the Red Flag '', and in the rear he had '' a safe and convenient jail ''. Starke promised to pay Richmond prices for young men and women.[20] Such purchases were for the far South. Auctioneers and commission merchants, dealing in miscellaneous articles and produce, as well as slaves, made a large proportion of the sales. Some, perhaps all, were ready to make advancements on consignments.

How different was the Richmond of the 'fifties from the Richmond of today, so ambitious, enterprising, with wide and beautiful streets confidently, triumphantly, reaching out for a great future and a population counted by hundreds of thousands! In 1850 it contained hardly 28,000

---

[18] *Key to Uncle Tom*, 151.

[19] 2 *The Slave States*, 485. A few years later, Seward saw there a sign " James Grey's Private Jail " "ostentatiously spread out in large letters on an ediface as large as the jail in Auburn ", N. Y.—F. W. Seward, 1 *Wm. H. Seward*, 779.

[20] Norfolk *Southern Argus*, Jan. 4, 1860. An advt. in the *Southern Argus* in Jan. 5, 1855, showed that W. W. Hall also had a private jail.

Some of the Cells in the Old Franklin & Armfield Slave-Pen

inhabitants, of whom less than 16,000 were white and more than 12,000 were colored; in 1860, it had not quite 38,000— about 14,000 colored and about 23,000 white. State politics radiated from the capitol, which crowned an imposing hill from which one looked across and far down the James River, over buildings, a few squares away, where most of Richmond's business was done. The Exchange Hotel, the leading inn, on the corner of Franklin and Fourteenth streets, was near the center and contained the city post-office and the offices of numerous agents. In the same neighborhood were several churches, and the City and the St. Charles hotels, at numbers 4 and 8 Fifteenth street, then often called Wall street because banks and brokerages were grouped there. Odd Fellows' Hall was and is midway between 14th and 15th streets, on the northeast corner of Franklin and a little street known as Mayo above and Locust alley below Franklin. This building had " a handsome and commodious hall, well arranged and constantly in demand for concerts and other popular exhibitions." [21]

The rapids of the James had been sufficiently used for water-power to make Richmond look like a manufacturing city to persons coming from the lower South and Southwest, but not to Northerners or Europeans. To these the tobacco industry and the slave-trade seemed strangest. In 1850 more than 17,000 hogsheads of tobacco were inspected in Richmond, and there were 43 tobacco factories with about 2,400 laborers,[22]—eight and one-half per cent of the city's population and largely slaves. But it was the grotesque solecism, the slave-trade, that Northerners and foreigners were most curious to see. Richmond was the best place in the State to sell nearly all kinds of slaves at good prices without publicity as to ownership. Speculators, planters, farmers, urban purchasers of domestic

[21] Montague's *Richmond Directory and Business advertiser for 1850-1851*, 15. Political meetings were also held there.—*Daily Enquirer*, May 25, 1853.
[22] Montague, 14.

servants for their own use all preferred to go to Virginia, especially to Richmond, for negroes, because this indicated a certain social as well as a financial advance.

The selling and hiring of slaves was so fully recognized as a business of general public interest that city directories usually indicated resident traders. But not all traders liked to be so classed, and it was easy to avoid it, if one dealt in other things. Then without disadvantage, if slaves were also mentioned in advertisements, one could pass for a " general agent ", a " broker ", a " commission merchant ", an " auctioneer " etc., according to circumstances. The presence of non-resident traders, planters and other visiting buyers was not often known to the public unless they advertised, which was rare. And there was always much private buying and selling for use or speculation that involved no publicity, no professional trader, no jail. Accordingly the most that could be learned from newspapers, public sales and advertisements was only part.

The *Richmond Directory of 1852* contained the names of 28 persons designated as traders, and surely several other men, classed as auctioneers, general agents or commission merchants, were doing as much slave-trading as any of them.[23] Richmond's slave-trade was much larger at the end of the decade. The *Directory for 1860* separately grouped the names and addresses of 18 " negro traders ", 18 " agents, general collecting ", and 33 " auctioneers ", counting only one person for each " Co.",

[23] Capt. J. Thompson Brown of the Confederate artillery, for nearly half a century a very successful real estate agent and auctioneer in Richmond, remembered 15 of these traders, 4 of the private jailors and 9 of the auctioneers. " I return the list [from the *Directory for 1852*] you sent me with [my] (X) cross-mark opposite the names of those I personally knew were 'nigger-traders', as they were called by the 'vulgar and vulgarly so-called', 'fo' de war'. I personally knew the others, Ed. D. Eacho, Newton M. Lee, E. A. J. Clopton and others ".—Letter of July 30, 1917, to the author.

although there may have been more.[24] Several that were
" traders " in 1852 had become " auctioneers " by 1860,

[24] NEGRO-TRADERS, AGENTS AND AUCTIONEERS IN RICHMOND,
1858–60.

" Negro Traders.

[1]	Davis, B.,	Locust al.
[2]	Davis, Solomon,	Locust al.
[3]	Davis, John B.,	Wall [15th] bt. Franklin & Broad.
[4]	Dupree, Wm.,	head of Marshall.
[5]	Faundron, R.,	cor. 17th & Broad.
[6, 7]	Jones & Slater,	Locust al.
[8]	Lee, N. M.,	Franklin bt. Mayo & 15th.
[9]	Levy, Ash,	Locust al.
[10]	Lumpkin, Ro.,	Wall bt. Franklin & Broad.
[11, 12]	McDaniel & Blackburn,	Wall bt. Franklin & Broad.
[13]	McMurray, Chas.,	h. cor. 17th & Broad.
[14]	Omohundro, O.,	al. nr. Wall.
[15]	Reese, Samuel,	Franklin bt. 15th & 16th.
[16-17]	Smith & Edmonston,	Franklin bt. 15th & 16th.
[18]	Templeman, H. N.,	Locust al."

—*Richmond Directory 1860, business section*, pp. 27-28.

" Agents, General and Collecting.

[Probably all attended to slaves, but not exclusively; some, like
Tabb & Son, sold slaves; agents of other kinds were classed as,
" Agents, Insurance ", " Agents, Real Estate ", " Agents, Ship-
ping " etc.]

[1]	Atkinson, Jno. S., with J. F. Sutton, Jr.	
[2]	Bagby, Thos. J.,	8 Wall [15th].
[3]	Clopton, E. A. J.,	cor. Wall & Franklin.
[4, 5]	Cocke & Close,	14th under Exchange Hotel.
[6]	Eacho, E. D.,	14th & Franklin.

[" Attends to hiring out Negroes, renting out Houses and
collecting claims."—*Business Directory, 1858-9.*

[7]	Hill, Robt.,	Wall bt. Main & Franklin.
[8]	Jewett, Geo. H.,	18th bt. Main & Franklin.
[9]	Jones, Geo. Harris,	14th, Exchange Building.
[10]	Lewis, Lucien,	Metropolitan Hall, Franklin.
[11]	Lyne, Ro. B.,	Metropolitan Hall, Franklin.
[12]	Martin, Jno. K.,	Law Building.
[13]	Phillips, Wm. S.,	12th bt. Main & Bank.
[14, 15]	Richardson A. W., with Wm. Holt Richardson.	
[16, 17]	Tabb, P. M., & Son,	cor. 14th & Franklin.
[18]	Tyler, G. W. H.,	Marshall bt. 6th & 7th."

—*Richmond Directory, 1860*, p. 245.

4

although they had probably doubled or trebled their slave-trading. And not one member of the firms that had the

" Auctioneers.

[Probably some of these did not sell slaves, while others sold them only occasionally; but 8 or 10 of the largest and best known traders are exclusively in this list, for they did an auction and commission business in negroes, and many of them had private jails.]

[1-3]   Browning, Moore & Co.,   Franklin nr. Wall [15th].

        [* * * " will give their undivided attention to the sale of Negroes."—Richmond Semi-Weekly Examiner, Jan. 1, 1861.]

[4]   Cook, Edward B.,   70 Main.

[5, 6]   Dabney & Canthorn,   15th bt. Main & Cary.

[7, 8]   Davenport, J. & G. B.,   15th & Cary.

[9]   Davis, Hector,   Franklin bt. Mayo & 15th.

        [" Auctioneer & commission merchant for the sale of Negroes."—Rchd. Business Directory for 1858-59, p. 54.]

[10]   Davis Ro. H.,   Franklin bt. Mayo & 15th.

[11, 12, 13]   Dickinson, Hill & Co.,   cor. Franklin & Wall.

[14]   Digges, J. H.,   86 Main.

[15, 16, 17]   Dunlop, Moncure & Co.,   cor. 11th & Cary.

[18, 19, 20]   Edmond, Davenport & Co.,   cor. 17th & Dock.

[21, 22]   Goddin & Apperson,   cor. Bank & 11th.

        [" Real Estate Auctioneers."—Business Directory for '58-59, p. 54.]

[23]   Keese, Thos. W.,   cor. Cary & 12th.

        [" Will attend to the sale of Real estate, and every description of mdse."—'58-59, p. 56.]

[24]   Lyne, Ro. B.,   Metropolitan Hall, Franklin.

[25]   Nott, Alex.,   cor. Main & 15th.

[26, 27]   Pulliam & Betts,   Franklin bt. Mayo & 15th.

        [" Auctioneers for the sale of Negroes. Odd-Fellows' Hall." —Business Directory for '58-59.]

[28]   Sheppard, Wm. Y.,   Tobacco Exchange, cor. 13th & Cary.

[29, 30]   Taylor, Jas. & Son,   11th bt. Bank & Main.

        [" Real Est." '58-59, p. 56.]

[31]   Williams, A. D.,   11th bt. Main & Bank.

[32, 33]   Wortham, Chas. T. & Co.,   Dock bt. 26th & 27th."

        —Directory 1860, business section, pp. 3-4.

[34]   Hill, Lewis, who was a produce and commission merchant especially in wheat, flower, corn and tobacco, stated in his advt.: " And continues to hire out Negroes ".—Business Directory for '58 and '59, p. 74.

Not one of these lists is supposed to be complete.

three best known marts [25] was classed as a trader in 1860;
all were " auctioneers "! Not the business, but the name,
was avoided more than formerly. Several others that were
not listed in 1860 as traders, were advertising as doing
some kind of slave-trading. Tabb & Son, who were never
classed as traders, but only as general and collecting
agents, were advertising as far away as Baltimore that
they had " removed their office to the old Postoffice, under
the Exchange Hotel, * * * where they will continue to HIRE
OUT NEGROES and TO SELL THEM, (publicly or privately); to
rent houses " etc. " They have been engaged in the business upwards of thirty years past " * * *.[26] Thus these
" agents, general and collecting ", were not only traders
but also interstate traders. The public announcements of
the persons that on their own accounts or on commission
regularly bought, sold or hired out slaves were apparently
more numerous than those of any other class of advertisers and often appeared close to the advertisements of lawyers, schools and both retail and wholesale merchants of
various kinds.[27] Of 15 advertisements in immediate sequence in the *Enquirer* of January 1, 1859, 14 were about
forthcoming sales of slaves, and all but two of the 14 sales
were in Richmond. But, again, all that and more was only
part.

Let no one suppose that the marts, offices and jails of
these men, however classed, were in secret places. The
capitol square would have been preferred if it had afforded
suitable accommodations. All the requirements were found
in the immediate neighborhood of four churches and the
Exchange Hotel (where not less than five agents dealing
in slaves had their offices) and within or bordering on a
rectangle not so large as that bounded by the National
Capitol, the Senate and the House office buildings and the

[25] See *post* p. 117 for the three mentioned by the *Enquirer*.
[26] Baltimore *Sun*, Jan. 17, 1859.
[27] *Enquirer*, Jan. 1, 1861, supplies good examples.

Library of Congress. The St. Charles and the City hotels were also used by traders, and the Odd Fellows' Hall building—now (1930) occupied by the William Byrd Press and looking very modern, as the photograph shows—had become the busiest of Richmond's many slave-marts.[28] Just below this corner, on Locust alley, there were at least six traders; but they were not of the Odd Fellows' Hall class, yet nearly all such were within two or three squares of it and on or near Franklin or Fifteenth street.[29]

In adjacent streets and alleys were many private jails. Most of them were at the service of any slaveholder; a few were more or less reserved for the business of the trader-proprietors. The charge per day in any part of the South was rarely more than forty or less than twenty-five cents. Hector Davis—perhaps the most prosperous " auctioneer and commission merchant for the sale of ne-groes " in Richmond in 1859-61, and who " pledged his best efforts to obtain the highest market prices "—widely advertised that he had a safe and commodious jail where he would board, at thirty cents a day, all slaves intended for his sales.[30] This small charge was undoubtedly de-

[28] There Pulliam & Betts were holding their auctions in 1859 and 1860; and Pulliam & Co. (A. C. & R. P. Pulliam & D. K. Weisiger), and Davis, Deu-pree & Co. (S. R. Fondren) in 1860-61.—*Enquirer*, Jan. 1, 1859, Jan. 2, 1861.

Soon after the Civil War John T. Trowbridge wrote of Odd Fellows' Hall: " It was interesting, by the light of recent events, and in company with one who knew Richmond of yore, to make the tour of the old negro auction-rooms. Davis & Co.'s Negro Bazaar was fitting up for a concert hall. We entered a grocery store,—a broad basement room, with a low, dark ceiling, supported by two stout wooden pillars. ' I've seen many a black Samson sold, standing between those posts; and many a woman too, as white as you or I.' Now sugar and rice were sold there, but no more human flesh and blood."—*The South* (1866), 183.

[29] " The great slave-mart [neighborhood] of Richmond was around 15th street, [mostly] between Main, Franklin and Broad streets, where there were many private jails and auction ' blocks ' or rooms, Lumpkin's alley being the center. This [section] I frequently visited when a boy."—Capt. J. Thompson Brown, July 30, 1917.

[30] Raleigh, N. C., *Tri-weekly Standard* from May, 1858, to Jan., 1859, and perhaps much longer.

ODD-FELLOWS HALL AS IT LOOKED IN 1922

Richmond's busiest slave-mart was in the basement

signed to attract patronage,—just as Pulliam & Co. laconically advised the public, " Porter always at each depot " [to take charge of slaves sent for sale]. In 1852, Robert Lumpkin, George W. Apperson and G. W. Atkinson each had a slave-jail in Birch Alley.[31] Lumpkin, who also had a livery stable, was so prosperous that this alley took his name. That was, indeed, distinction in the trade. Omohundro's jail fronted on an alley running west of Fifteenth between Franklin and Main streets. Bacon Tait—who was a large interstate trader, shipping to New Orleans as early as 1835, and became very wealthy—had a jail and slave-mart on or near the southeast corner of Cary and Fifteenth streets.[32]

Fredrika Bremer visited several of the private jails in 1851. The door of one of them was opened by an apparently good-tempered slave whose ankles were fettered with heavy irons. His master had hired him out to work in the coal-pits, but after something disagreeable happened the slave refused to continue work there; so he had been sent here to be sold and meantime to have his spirit broken by those fetters. Within sat a strong-limbed negro, silent and gloomy, who had cut off the fingers of his right hand as a strange revenge against his master, for separating him from his wife and children and ordering him sold South, on account of some offense, as was alleged. In another jail she saw a room where the slaves of both sexes were flogged. There were the iron rings in the floor to which

[31] *Richmond Directory for 1852.* This alley seems to have been an irregular and undeveloped passage that later was succeeded, or left to the west, by the extension of 15th [Wall] st. from Franklin to Broad, which would account for Lumpkin's location, in 1860, on " Wall between Franklin and Broad ". Captain Brown first knew the street as " Lumpkin alley " and remembered a slave pen there—" a large building surrounded by tall brick walls ".—Letter of Feb. 9, 1904.

[32] Capt. J. Thompson Brown described the place as having a very high fence around it and being " like a stockade or jail; in fact, it was a jail, not a jail for criminals but a jail for negro slaves to be kept in until sold. * * * Bacon Tait became very wealthy. He resided in the eastern portion of our

they were tied down before they were beaten with that paddle, a broad strip of cowhide, which looked rather harmless. " ' Oh, yes, yes; but ', replied the keeper, grinning with a very significant glance, ' it can cause as much torture as any other instrument, and even more, because one can give as many blows with this strip of hide without its leaving any outward sign; it does not cut into the flesh.' " One jail seemed to make a specialty of " the so-called ' fancy girls ' for fancy purchasers ". We shall see what that meant. In another there was " a pretty little white boy of about seven years of age sitting among some tall negro girls. The child had light hair, the most lovely light brown eyes, and cheeks as red as roses; he was, nevertheless, the child of a slave mother, and was to be sold as a slave." [33]

In most Southern cities there were hotels that had places where slaves of patrons could be locked up at night, but that did not suffice for careful large buyers or sellers desiring secure custody and to be near their negroes. Several Richmond traders offered accommodations that satisfied these needs. Early in the 'fifties a young man from Syracuse, seeing " a professional looking man, neatly dressed and swinging a slender, gold-headed cane ", who had purchased a boy, followed them, to learn where the slave would be taken. " I went far enough in the rear not to be noticed until he turned into an entrance, over which was the sign ' LUMPKIN'S JAIL '. I entered a large open court. Against one of the posts sat a good natured fat man, with his chair tipped back. It was Mr. Lumpkin. I duly introduced myself as from New York, remarking that I had read what the Abolitionists had to say, and that I

city and I sold out his landed estate here, and on it is now a large portion of the city known as Fairmont." And "there was a very large one [slave-mart] on the S. W. corner of 15th & Franklin", Nat. B. Hill's. Capt. Brown also sold a private jail in Locust alley once conducted by one of the Davises.— Letter of Feb. 9, 1904.

[33] Bremer, 2 *Homes of the New World*, 533-35.

had come to Richmond to see for myself. Mr. Lumpkin received me courteously and showed me over his jail. On one side of the open court was a large tank for washing, or lavatory. Opposite was a long, two-story brick house, the lower part fitted up for men and the second story for women. The place, in fact, was a kind of hotel or boardinghouse for negro-traders and their slaves. I was invited to dine at a large table with perhaps twenty traders, who gave me almost no attention, and there was little conversation. They were probably strangers to one another.'' [34]

Private sales, usually made at the slave-pens or at the traders' offices, were an essential feature of the trade, even on the part of auctioneers, and afforded the advantages of approximate secrecy. And buying privately, seeking the best and paying accordingly were supposed to be superior and planterlike.

If slaves were not soon disposed of privately—and paying for their board and custody in idleness was not conducive to gain and patience—they must be sent to the auction-block. Almost daily several auctioneers advertised that they would sell 20, 25 or 50 negroes. These announcements were more or less stereotyped, like those of the buyers for the Southern market: the figures, although occasionally surpassed, usually indicated hopes rather than facts. When specific lots or gangs were to be sold on special days, they were described. Most of the public sales were in long, empty shop-rooms or warehouses, with filthy floors and bare, dirty walls. Near one end were coarse and badly whittled benches or chairs enough to seat forty or fifty persons, a platform from two to four feet high,

[34] MS. recollections of Otis Bigelow, who spent most of his manhood in the District of Columbia and Md., dying in 1919.

E. II. Stokes, who bought out Betts & Gregory, had an almost perfect equipment. He called attention to his " New Auction House for the Sale of Negroes ", located on Franklin street, third door below 15th. He was " prepared to board persons engaged in the trade, and also their servants, having ample accommodations for both ", and would " make liberal advances on all property in hand ".—*Enquirer*, Apr. 18, 1861.

and some sort of a screen. The conditions in Odd Fellows' Hall were much better. Some of the auctions were announced to begin at 9.30, others at 10 o'clock, but as a matter of fact and courtesy those in the same neighborhood usually proceeded in sequence. The audience varied from barely a dozen persons to a hundred or more, according to the number of the slaves or the success of the advertisements. If the sale was at all important, there were sure to be present men dressed to suit the popular notion of a " Southern gentleman "—a man wearing formal chin-whiskers, a large hat, a long black coat, a low-cut waist-coat, heavy gold seals and carrying a gold-headed cane. But more numerous were those that resembled either small farmers or drovers or horse-traders. And there was no such occasion without some unkempt, gaunt white idlers, with much curiosity but no cash, hoping to see and hear something without cost or effort. Numerous members of the motley company languidly talked, swore without cause or effect, smoked, whittled and profusely expectorated. A foreign visitor described what he called the " supernumeraries " in the scene as " ' got up ' in a way worthy of the occasion, wearing as they do hats in every state of decomposition and of every color. Their features are callous; and one gentleman we particularly noticed, who had a cow-hide-looking weapon, which dangled between his legs in such a way as to make one wander whether his feet were cloven or not." [35]

The appearance of the slaves whom the intelligent-looking negro porter brought in was very different from what they presented when on their way to the jail, a week or two earlier. Then most of them wore meager and ragged clothes. If not bareheaded and barefooted, few had anything better than cotton bandannas or shapeless old hats on their heads, or anything better than sprawling tatters of leather on their feet. Near the postoffice Frederick

[35] Eyre Crowe in 29 *Illustrated London News* (Sept. 27, 1856), 314. For a reproduction of his drawing, see opposite p. 110.

Law Olmsted, on a cold and sleety morning, saw a porter leading three handcuffed negroes by a rope—a middle-aged man, a girl of about twenty and a boy considerably younger. All three were dripping wet and thinly clad—the girl having an old handkerchief around her neck, over a common calico dress, and another handkerchief twisted about her head. "What are they? What's he going to do with them?" the traveler asked of a white resident, who had also stopped to look at them.—"Come in a canal boat, I reckon: sent down here to be sold"; and then he added, "That ar's a likely gal."[36] Neither rags nor misery could prevent a "likely" slave, especially a "gal", for sale, from arousing fancies of profits. But three shivering hounds would have elicited as much sympathy. However miserable these or other slaves may once have appeared when they were brought to Richmond, there on the benches near the auction-block, they were clean, alert and not conspicuously sad. All had strong shoes and owned hats or turbans, even if not worn. An English traveler described the male slaves at an auction in Richmond as dressed in gray woolen coats, pants and waistcoats, colored cotton neckcloths, clean shirts, coarse woolen stockings and stout shoes. The man wore a black hat; the boy was bareheaded.[37] The artist Crowe, who accompanied Thackeray on his lecturing trip in 1853, both sketched and described the slaves, sitting there "huddled close together, neatly dressed in gray, young negro girls with white collars fastened by scarlet bows, and in white aprons."[38] They were sometimes overdressed, for it was profitable.

A Jew named Levy, who had a clothing-store for

---

[36] *Seaboard Slave States*, 30.

[37] William Chambers, *Things as They are in America*, 276; Olmsted, *Seaboard* etc., 32 ff., and 2 *Cotton Kingdom*, 372 ff. quotes Chambers's unequalled account of what he saw of Richmond sales one forenoon.

[38] *With Thackeray in America*, 133 ff. See photostat of the *Illustrated London News's* woodcut of his sketch, opposite p. 106.

negroes in the basement of the City Hotel, would gladly have explained how much such outfits enhanced the selling price of slaves. He made a specialty of supplying clothes for just such occasions. He " particularly solicited the attention of traders " and " persons bringing their servants [!] to the city for hire or sale ". Did he prosper? How could it be otherwise when seven leading traders vouched for him![39]

A guarantee of ordinary health and physical, not moral, soundness was a matter of course in every sale, private or public, unless expressly disclaimed or the slave's condition was known to the purchaser. In case of any substantial misrepresentation, the vendor was liable to a suit for a breach of warranty, actual or implied. But what the purchaser wanted was a good slave, not a lawsuit, however good; moreover, purchaser and vendor might soon be too far apart to make reparation feasible. The buyer's only safe rule was: *Caveat emptor;* inspect for yourself; there are risks enough at best. It would have been no more absurd to " buy a pig in a poke " than to purchase a strange, fully-grown slave without thorough scrutiny and inquiry as to his or her antecedents and physical condition. To inspect was a plain matter of business. Purchasers and spectators were about as indifferent to the nudity and the sex of ordinary slaves as everybody is to those of small children. To be otherwise indicated pruriency or hypocrisy rather than virtue.

The most careful buyers kept informed as to new arrivals and went to the jails to inspect them. Then, and when the slaves were brought to the auction-mart, they were plied with such questions as: " How old are you?" " What can you do?" " Who raised you?" " Why are you sold?" " Anything wrong with you?" Hands were opened and shut and looked at inside and out. Arms and legs were felt of as a means of deciding whether they were muscular

[39] *Directory for 1852,* p. 27 of advts.

WAITING TO BE SOLD IN RICHMOND, IN 1853

From a sketch made from life by Eyre Crowe

and regular. Backs and buttocks were scrutinized for the welts that heavy blows with a whip usually left. Necks were rubbed or pinched to detect any soreness or lumps. Jaws were grasped, fingers were run into negroes' mouths, which were widely opened and peered into. Lips were pressed back so that all the teeth and gums could be seen. This performance closely resembled that of an expert reading a horse's age. If there was any suspicion that one eye might not be good, a strange hand was clapped over the other and the slave was asked what object was held before him. The hearing was likewise tested. All such inquiries were made with equal freedom whether the slave was man, woman, boy or girl. The descriptions of many observers substantially agree with what Chambers saw: " About a dozen gentlemen crowded to the spot while the poor fellow was stripping himself, and as soon as he stood on the floor, bare from top to toe, a most rigorous scrutiny of his person was instituted. The clear black skin, back and front, was viewed all over for sores from disease; and there was no part of his body left unexamined." [40] Anybody that was interested,—or merely wished to appear so, as some always did, for they thought it gave them importance,—might join in the inspection. When scars or any irregularities or signs of disease were found, there were significant nods and an exchange of knowing glances.

[40] Chambers, *Things As They Are in America*, 281. C. R. Weld, *A Vacation Tour in the U. S. and Canada* (1855), 299; James Redpath, *The Roving Editor*, 9-10, 247-48, give somewhat similar descriptions of inspections.

A New Yorker traveling in the South happened to visit these marts the same morning as artist Crowe, Mar. 3, 1853. In his account occurs this passage: "I saw full twenty men stripped this morning and not more than three or four of them had what they termed ' clean backs ', and some of them —I should think full one-quarter of them—were scarred with the whip to such an extent as to present a frightful appearance; one in particular was so cut that I am sure you could not lay your finger on any part of his back without coming in contact with a *scar*. These scars were from the whip and were from two inches to one foot in length. These marks damaged his sale; although only about 45 to 50 years old he only brought $460; but for these marks he would have brought $750 to $800."—N. Y. *Tribune*, Mar. 10, 1853, p. 6. See illustration opposite p. 108.

It was both less common and less essential thoroughly to inspect the women and the girls, although it was not rare to do so. In any case, it was considered important to know how many children a young woman had borne and what the probabilities were as to the future. If a girl was more than 18 or 19 years old and had borne none, it lessened her market value. Such perfectly natural and even inevitable incidents of slave-trading were often regarded by travelers as outrageous. Charles R. Weld, an English barrister, illustrated this in describing what he saw: "Personal examination [of the women in public] was confined to the hands, arms, legs, bust and teeth. Searching questions were put respecting their age and whether they had [had] children. If they replied in the negative, their bosoms were generally handled in a repulsive and disgusting manner." [41] A matter-of-fact New Yorker recorded his impressions as follows:—"In those days, all frocks were secured in the back with hooks and eyes, so that it was an easy matter to go to the women and unhook their dresses and examine their backs for any signs of flogging. In fact such signs made a woman unsalable. As all purchases were warranted, if any trader, after a sale, was suspicious of a diseased condition, he took the woman upstairs into a private room where she was subjected to a physical examination." [42]

The slaves calmly submitted without protest, and, if they had no blemishes, with apparent indifference. If you think that strange, it is because you overlook what slavery was. Its first and never-ending lesson was absolute obedience and submission, regardless of right or reason. The slightest sign of resistance or disobedience might bring overbearing punishment. The philosophy of life that mas-

[41] *A Vacation Tour*, 300. For more, see James Redpath's *Roving Editor*, 251-52.

[42] Otis Bigelow, *ante* p. 103. All other evidence known to the author indicates that no one wished to bid until he felt reasonably sure of soundness or of a lack of it. Of course there were often subsequent examinations.

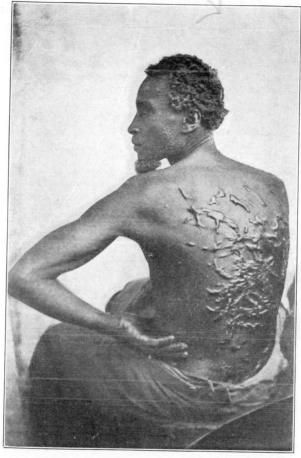

From a Photograph of a Slave with a Back Scarred
by Whipping

ters, mistresses and clergymen tried to instill into the minds of the slaves was, " Servants obey your masters ", which included pleasing them in every way, being as useful and profitable as possible, happy and even proud of the opportunity to serve. This was reënforced by making a dreadful example of the free negro—whom everybody depreciated and discouraged and many persons treated as an outcast, which cruel fortune often compelled him to be, even in the free States. Favors, rewards and much of the legitimate happiness that slaves enjoyed depended on cheerful compliance, real or feigned, with orders and customs. All slaves understood that they were property and likely to be taken for debt or sold in case of special need or whim. As modesty is a cultivated virtue, hardly compatible with slavery, the inspection was one of the least painful features of the sales. But many visitors liked to report how dreadfully they were shocked.

Until the auctioneer mounted his platform and began to speak, one might have thought from his general appearance that he was a rough planter or gambler or saloon-keeper. In fact, he had intimately associated with all of them. His easy self-possession and almost careless mastery of the conditions were soon manifested. He commanded a few jests and trifling remarks, which he employed to enliven the company. The nimbleness of his tongue and the quickness of his glance increased as he warmed to his task. He rattled out figures, sputtered and repeated a small variety of phrases, ejaculations and questions; halted suddenly to crack some broad joke, then as suddenly hastened on, and thus with his ready store of tricks, quips and droll exaggerations compelled close attention.

No two slave-auctioneers nor any two auctions were altogether alike, but some of their common features on important occasions may be represented as follows:—

" Gentlemen, I'm goin' to sell yo' this mornin' some ez

likely niggers ez evah yo' seen put up.[43] They ah sol' fo' no fault, an' ever' one of 'em is wahanted. But look at 'em fo' yo'se'f. *You*-all know good niggers. Yo'll see theah ain't a lot theah what yo' won't want t' own." He paused to look for signs of doubts; he was willing to wait until all were satisfied. Then he continued: " Now Gentlemen, aint yo' foun' 'em ez I tol' yo'? Ah yo' radey t' begin?" Then, as an aside: " Come heah, boy." " Gentlemen, I'm goin' t' give yo' a bahgin. Did *you*-all evah see a finer lot'n this heah boy? No, yo' nevah. He's only twelve yeah ol', an' I wahant him ez soun' ez a dollah. Ain't he a likely nigger ever' ways? In fo' yeah mo' he'll be biggah'n me, an' wo'th mo' 'an a thousand dollahs on yoah *plan-ta-tion* er in any mahket, ef he's wo'th a cent. He kin hoe co'n er cott'n, drive, wait, er run errunds, er learn any trade. *Now*, what do I heah fo' 'im? He's intell'gent and reli'ble,—what'll you *staht* 'im at, sah?"— turning his keen eyes on a prosperous-looking man that was showing special interest. " He'll soon make a good gentleman's sahvant, er a gyahdnah,—how much do yo' bid? See them *han's!* Why yo' could learn 'im,—to *sew,* learn 'im *anything.*" Several persons moved up near the auction-block to take another close look at the boy. " Now who'll say five hundud? Of co'se yo' will, two o' yo'. Theah's two gentlemen what know a good sahvant. Now, Kyonel [Colonel], will yo' make it five fifty? Thank yo', suh. *Fifty* I have; say six; make it six hundud. Why gentlemen, sho' yo' don't expect me to *give* 'im to yo'! Heah, boy, show them gentlemen how yo' kin run ". The boy jumped off the block and ran up and down the room,

---

[43] *Nigger* was the usual word employed in the trade, colloquially and often in newspapers and books. See Wise, *End of an Era,* 81-85; James Redpath, *Roving Editor,* 7; C. R. Weld, 301; Pollard, *Black Diamonds,* pp. ix-xi, 20, 61. 100, 101. Many planters, and persons that wished to imitate them, often meant to say *negro,* but pronounced it *niggrah* or *niggruh,* which could hardly be distinguished from *nigger.* It was an affectation of elegance or humanity to call any except the domestic slaves *servants,* for they were not such; but many, even traders, indulged in it for show, as has been noticed.

while all watched his quick and energetic movements. Even this child felt eager to display his qualities to the best advantage, so as to sell for a high price. " That'll do; come heah, boy. None o' yo' gentlemen don't want no liklier boy'n him. Now, do I heah *six?* Thank yo', Jedge. Six hundud dollahs is bid fo' this prime lot, but he's wo'th three hundud *mo'.* Six; make it six fifty; six say *fifty,* give me *fifty,* go *fifty; fif-ty*—do I—heah? If any of yo' gentlemen wants a body-sahvant er a waiter er a stable-boy, heah's yoah opperchunity." " Six-*thirty* ", someone called out. And the auctioneer again rattled out the figures and sputtered the short phrases, sweeping every face with his rapid glance, sure to detect the slightest nod or expression of assent, and all the while speaking, moving, gesticulating and occasionally clapping his hands with a rhythm that had a fascination. No longer getting large bids, he welcomed ten-dollar offers and then five. With ringing voice and nervously wavering hand, he cried: " *Six hundud an' ninety-five dollahs*—Seven hundud, I have; say seven *five."* And once more he juggled the phrases, then slackened and drawled his speech: " *Seven— hun-dud*—an'—*five*—is—bid; let me have *ten;* do I heah *ten?* Yo'll *lose* 'im! Ah you-all *done?* Seven—hundud— an'—five—dollahs! Once—twice—third—an'—*last*—call; goin', *goin'* "—and as his right hand struck the palm of his left, making a loud crack—" *sold* fo' *seven hundud an' five dollahs* to Mr. Jenks." Unless one owned slaves or was enthusiastic about slavery or was evidently a foreigner, it would have been regarded as very bad form to ask whether Mr. Jenks was a planter from the lower South, or some trader or his agent buying for the Southwestern market. Anything unsympathetic might be resented.

The general method of sale was about the same whether the " lot " was a boy, a girl, a man, or a woman alone or with young children, or a full family. The prerequisites for good bids for male fieldhands were youth and strength; for mechanics and servants, reliability and skill; for young

" wenches ", health and fecundity. Looks counted for
much in the case of mulatto girls. When young women
were on the block the auctioneer often indulged in broad
humor or suggestions that would have been considered
indecent on almost any other public occasion.[44] Women
and children were on the block almost as often as men. A
full, large family, unless the parents were young and strong
fieldhands, rarely sold well at auction, except to a trader
intending to divide it. When reasonably good bids could
not be obtained, the slave or slaves were withdrawn to
avoid a sacrifice, which would injuriously have affected
later bidding. William Chambers saw a woman with three
little girls, respectively about three months, two and three
years old, on the auction-block. The porter was directed
to hold up the " fine, healthy baby ", while the auctioneer
called attention to the " woman, still young, and three
children all for $850." But that was insufficient; because
the bidding was sluggish they were withdrawn. Such
groups were common.

As soon as all the slaves for sale at one mart had been
offered, someone cried out: " This way, *gentlemen!* "
Then nearly the entire company followed him to a neighboring trader's where there was another lot waiting to
be sold. And so the prospective buyers and the spectators
went from place to place until the different supplies for
the day's auctions were disposed of.

When Weld was about to leave one of the Richmond
establishments, a slave-porter entered with a woman followed by two little children three and four years old, and
carrying a third still younger in her arms.

" She was a remarkably handsome mulatto, and her children were nearly,

---

[44] Thomas Hamilton, who saw many slave-auctions in New Orleans, wrote:
" When a woman is sold, he [the auctioneer] usually puts his audience in
good-humor by a few indecent jokes."—*Men and Manners in America* (1843),
347. The auctioneer said: " Show your neck, Betsy! There's a breast for
you; good for a round dozen before she's done child-bearing! "—*7 Galaxy
Magazine*, 120.

if not fully, as white as the fairest Americans. * * * Her story was brief: she was not married, and the man whose passions had made her his mistress as well as slave, willed that she should be sold with *his* children. * * * All attempts at extracting further information were met by a scornful refusal to divulge ought [aught] of her past life, and when her small soft hands and bosom were examined, on which her infant was reposing, her eyes flashed fire * * *. Followed by her two little children, who clung to her dress like scared lambs, shrinking from the gaze of the rough men who pressed round them, she ascended the platform, and the auctioneer recommenced his business. * * * He set a high price on the woman and her children, declaring he expected at least $2500 for the lot. The first bid was $800; languid biddings succeeded, until the amount reached $900. The woman was then ordered down, and followed by her little children, was made to walk up and down the room. On resuming her place on the platform, the biddings became a little brisker; but as no eloquence on the part of the auctioneer could raise them above $1100, the lot was withdrawn. The visitor was told that " the woman alone would have realised more than this amount, but there is a strong aversion against purchasing white children." [45]

They always suggested a very uncomplimentary suspicion; but if they had been girls of 14 or 16 years of age, it would have been different.

Northerners and foreigners were surprised, and sometimes even disappointed, by the usual absence of harrowing scenes, handcuffs and rough treatment, and the presence of tidiness and cheerful looks. But who would have bought negroes looking like filthy, listless vagabonds or vicious characters? There was a purpose in those bright, showy, new clothes, in the promises of good masters and improved conditions, and in giving each slave, according to age and taste, an exhilarating drink of whiskey or gin, some much coveted tobacco, a shining coin, a gaily figured bandanna, a toy that seemed to have life, or a piece of candy. Some members of plantation gangs less well treated were so passive as to seem indifferent, while others showed a lively interest in the bidding. Now and then a happy-go-lucky fellow or an irresponsible buffoon might arouse much mer-

[45] Weld, *A Vacation Tour* etc., 302-304.

riment. As money was the measure of a slave's value, why should he not act on the proverbial saying, "A nigger is worth what he'll fetch",—especially when he was superlatively praised and made important before a crowd? They had long been encouraged to put high estimates on themselves and to boast if they had been sold for large sums. "I'z a seben-TEEN hundud dol-lah niggah, *I iz*," one would say. Another would assume superiority by alleging: "*My* massa done paid *twenty-two hundud* 'n' fifty f' ME!" Between young men there was often keen rivalry to show who could bring the highest price. At the cost of an extra drink and much flattery the contest was very profitable—to the vendor. But the rheumatic, the crippled, the aged and those hoping to buy freedom, not rarely took a more practical view and depreciated themselves as much as they dared to do, so as to prevent sale or to predispose their new master to put them on light tasks or cheaply to sell them to themselves.

The separations were less painful to the slaves than the Abolitionists fancied but more painful than the Southerners would admit. A dignified coachman and his wife, the "mammy", might be as devoted and affectionate as their master and mistress; whereas, at the other extreme, in the hoe-gang or the plow-gang the relations were usually as loose as circumstances permitted. Fortunately, rude slaves did not have fine feelings, but, regardless of morals, they had strong attachments to persons and places and were very gregarious. Consequently they were often ready to risk the severest punishment in attempting to return to old associations, although the stay must be clandestine and brief. Numerous advertisements mentioning where runaways had been reared, had wives, children, brothers or sisters, and were "likely to be lurking", were conclusive evidence that masters understood the strength of these ties;[46] but the desire to get

[46] Of four successive advts. for four runaways, in the Richmond semi-weekly

the largest possible returns from sl
to differ widely from sentiment. Cha
the sorrow the woman with three little
on parting from her husband, two day
not genuine, for soon she was laughing
antics of a trick-dog. Probably the dog
that purpose. Where pains were not ph   , even suffering slaves were so child-like that they resembled the
poet's babe, born

> "To weep, to sleep, and weep again,
> With sunny smiles between * * * ."

The saddest moments were not often at the auctions nor
before strangers, who were usually unsympathetic; but
either on leaving "home", or some hours or days subsequent to the sale and after payment had been arranged—
when the victims were driven away or the train or the boat
started. In any case, slaves knew that a conspicuous
demonstration of sorrow would surely bring punishment
in addition.

Notwithstanding these facts, nearly all persons that
have left accounts of viewing public sales knew of one or
more examples of keen sorrow on account of separations.[47]
Here is a sad vignette from the account of what the New
York *Tribune's* correspondent witnessed:—

"She was a fine looking woman about 25 years old, with three *beautiful*
children. * * * One of these traders asked her what was the matter with
her eyes? Wiping away the tears, she replied, 'I s'pose I have been
crying.'—'Why do you cry?'—'Because I have left my man behind,
and his master won't let him come along.'—'Oh, if I buy you, I will
furnish you with a better husband, or man as you call him, than your

---

Enquirer of March 13, 1857, one was about a young slave that had been reared
and bought in North Carolina, whither he was supposed to have returned.
Each of the other runaways was said to have a wife in another county and
was presumed to have gone to her. For others see *post* p. 206, note 13.

[47] For exceptional exhibitions of sorrow, see 2 Bremer, 533; the Turnbulls',
2 *American Photographs*, 51; R. Russell, *North America*, 255; J. B. Cobb,
Mississippi Scenes, 81-93.

e.'—' I don't want any *better* and won't have any *other* as long as
lives.'—' Oh, but you will though, if I buy you.'—' *No, Massa, God
helping me I never will.'* * * * The most indecent questions were put to
her, all of which, after a little hesitation, she answered. But when asked,
if she could turn out a *child a year?* she replied, ' *No, Massa, I never
have any more and I sorry I got these.' "* [48]

John S. Wise, a son of the Governor, found that at an
auction he attended the slaves "brought good prices.
'Niggers is high' was the general comment". "Damn it,
how niggers has riz!" exclaimed a stranger at James
Redpath's side on a like occasion in Richmond.[49] "Who
bought them, where they went, whether they were separated from father, mother, brother or sister, God knows ",
added Wise. All that most visitors knew was about the
same as what Crowe witnessed—"the usual exodus of
negro slaves, marched under escort of their owners across
the town to the railway station, where they took their
places, and 'went South'. They held scanty bundles of
clothing, their only possession."

Popular curiosity about sales and prices was so great
that the traders found it easy to obtain much free advertising. When the editor of the Warrenton *Whig* was in
Richmond in January, 1857, Dickinson, Hill & Co. told
him " that the gross amount of their sales of negroes
last year [1856] reached the enormous sum of two millions! The entire sales of other houses of a similar kind
in Richmond would make the amount go over four millions,
and still the business is increasing. We ourselves (wrote
the [editor of the] *Whig*), witnessed the sale of 35 servants at an average of $700. Negro girls, not 10 years of
age, sold for $800." Under the title of " RICHMOND NEGRO
MARKET " this was copied by one or more Richmond

[48] See *ante* p. 82, note 39, for a similar case of " I'll get you a new husband ".
When Arfwedson was going from Charleston to Savannah, a trader brought
on board the steamer at Beaufort, a handsome young woman purchased from
a planter in whose family she had been reared. Her separation from her
husband and others was most distressing.—1 *U. S. and Canada*, 1832-34, 403.
[49] Wise, 83; Redpath, *Roving Editor*, 250.

newspapers and then widely recopied in the lower South.[50] No one seemed to question the "over four millions". The only fear—very common in the lower South—was that this amazing amount of slave-trading would before many years make Virginia a free State.

The Richmond *Enquirer* was a newspaper of exceptional dignity; it had the reputation of being relatively almost antislavery,[51] and another son of Governor Wise was one of its editors. An editorial article, July 29, 1859, about "OUR SLAVE MARKET" gave, "for the benefit of our country and Southern readers", a list of "the average prices brought by slaves in Richmond", and remarked with complacency: "In looking round at the slave sales in Richmond, made at the well-known marts of Dickinson, Hill & Co., Pulliam, Betts & Co., Hector Davis, and others, we find that active negroes, likely families, as well as boys and girls, command high prices, and there are several gentlemen in the market who are purchasing for their own plantations in the South." [52]

[50] Between the Turnbulls', 2 *American Photographs*, 239-40, and the Baton Rouge *Weekly Advocate*, Feb. 8, 1857, slight errors are corrected and all is made clear.

[51] C. R. Wold, *A Vacation Tour*, 288-89; Wise, *End of an Era*, 87.

[52] The average prices "for the best class of slaves" were:

"No. 1 men,	20	to 26,	from	$1,450	to	$1,500.
Best plough boys,	17	" 20,	"	1,350	"	1,425.
Boys from	15	" 17,	"	1,250	"	1,375.
Boys "	12	" 15,	"	1,100	"	1,200.
Best grown girls,	17	" 20,	"	1,275	"	1,325.
Girls from	15	" 17,	"	1,150	"	1,250.
Girls "	12	" 15,	"	1,000	"	1,100.

Of course the quotations only represent the rates offered for the best class of slaves. The inferior grades are numerous and command prices in accordance with the quality."

About Dec., 1853, Chambers obtained from a leading Richmond trader the following price-list, anomalous because slaves *under 18 were classed according to height*. Presumably this was to avoid mentioning that young children were regularly marketable. Chambers noticed that the preparation of the list re-

The men that conducted these " well-known marts " were not called traders either here or in the city *Directory*, and the buyers were referred to as if all were gentlemen planters. " Our slave market " was evidently a source of pride. And why not, according to Virginia laws and customs? Since Professor Dew foretold the profit of slave-selling at least thirty or forty million dollars must have been received by Virginians for slaves reared, sold and taken to the lower South, apart from what had been gained by slave-trading for use in the Old Dominion.

Yet few Virginians ever thought of themselves as rearing slaves for the market. They were always dreaming that somehow they and their children were to become large planters. All visions of prosperity and social prominence had a rural setting, in which slaves were abundant and immediate financial returns were little considered. Slave property was incomparably desirable, for it could be used either to adorn riches or to screen poverty. The owner of even a small gang of slaves, unless he was a notorious spendthrift, could maintain an outward air of prosperity. If he sought office or needed a new carriage, if he wished to send his son to " the University " or his family to " the Springs ", he considered it quite proper to sell any valuable but sometimes troublesome slave or to give a deed of trust on one or more of the best. When the usual consequences happened, he felt regret, but no self-reproaches, for the results were wholly contrary to his *wishes* and *intentions*. He had not *reared slaves to sell* nor *preferred*

quired much consideration. An ordinary list could have been written off promptly.

" 'Best Men, 18-25,			$1200 to $1300	Young Women,		$800 to $1000
Fair	do.	do.	950 " 1050	Girls, 5 feet,		750 " 850
Boys, 5 feet,			850 " 950	Do., 4 " 9 ins.		700 " 750
Do.,	4 "	8 ins.	700 " 800	Do., 4 "		350 " 452 ' "
Do.,	4 "	5 "	500 " 600			
Do.,	4 "		375 " 450		—Chambers, 277.' "	

to sell them, and he had fancied that he could somehow repay the loan for which he had given his best as collateral. So the easy-going, unlogical, complacent Virginian was unperturbed. But what he called necessities had enabled the trader—the "hated trader"—to obtain what he desired.

CHAPTER VI

HERE AND THERE IN MARYLAND, KENTUCKY AND MISSOURI

There seems to have been less slave-trading in Maryland during the 'fifties than during the 'thirties but somewhat more than during the 'forties. The scouring of all agricultural counties continued. The pride of possessing slaves was lessening and the profit of selling them was increasing. With each year new traders came and some of the old were lost sight of. William Harker was a remarkable exception, for he was " in the market " for a quarter of a century— 1835-59, and he bought " all likely negroes from 8 to 40 years of age ".[1]

The suppression of the interstate trade in the District of Columbia benefited Baltimore as well as Alexandria. But not one of the traders conspicuous in Baltimore in 1835 was conspicuous there twenty years later.[2] The best known resident traders in the 'fifties were John N. Denning, B. M. & W. L. Campbell, Joseph S. Donovan and Jonathan M. Wilson. All were, at one time or another, dealers of the first class.

By advertising for 5,000 negroes, Denning posed as the largest of slave-speculators. He seemed ready to buy all that were marketable, whether " slaves for life or a term of years, in large or small families, or single negroes ", and even those restricted to remain in the State, if they " sustained good characters ",—but nothing was said about

[1] Cambridge *Chronicle*, Aug. 22, 1835; Easton *Star*, Mar. 8, Nov. 8, 1853, Jan. 11, 1859.

[2] The firm of James F. Purvis & Co. survived, but as " stock-brokers " doing an " exchange and collection " business.—Woods's *Directory for 1856-57*, 213; Matchett's *Director* [*sic*] *for 1855-56*, 275. These designations may have indicated prosperity and social ambition rather than abandoning the trade.

120

reselling them to persons of good character. To enlist assistants, he would pay "liberal commissions" to anyone that would aid him. And whatever others might do, his motto was, "Families never separated"! Great as he wished to be as a trader, he must have been still greater as a magician, if he could conduct such a business without dividing hundreds of families.[3]

The height of the success of the Campbells was near the end of the decade. Early in the 'fifties they were walking in the footsteps of Hope H. Slatter, whose good-will they endeavored to enjoy by advertising that they occupied "Slatter's old stand".[4] Manifests preserved in the Library of Congress show that between April 3, 1851, and November 20, 1852, they shipped 339 slaves from Baltimore, all but a few of whom went to New Orleans. A closer acquaintance with the Campbells may be postponed until we meet them in New Orleans, where they were the best known of all Maryland traders.

Joseph S. Donovan, who appealed to slaveholders for 500 negroes, put special stress on the facts that his office and yard adjoined the Baltimore and Ohio station and were close to the steamboat landings; and, later, that he had built a secure jail where he would "receive negroes for safe-keeping, at the southwest corner of Eutaw and Camden streets, opposite" the west side of that station.[5] Extant manifests tell of his shipments of 144 slaves from Baltimore to New Orleans between April 3, 1851, and December 2, 1852. Publicity, convenience and safety were

[3] His office and jail were at 18 S. Frederick st., between Baltimore and Second sts. "Trees in front of the house."—*Sun*, Nov. 20, 1852.

[4] "SLAVES WANTED.—We are at all time purchasing SLAVES, paying the highest CASH prices. Persons wishing to sell will please call at 242 Pratt St. (Slatter's old stand). Communications attended to. B. M. & W. L. Campbell."—*Sun*, Nov. 20, 1852. In different *Directories* and years the number changed, perhaps due to a renumbering rather than a change of place.

[5] *Sun*, Feb. 11, 1851; Nov. 20, 1852; Jan. 25, 1859. The site is now (1930) occupied by Swift & Co., packers.

winning features. He must have acquired a considerable
fortune from the traffic, for his widow endowed a chair
of English literature.

Jonathan M. Wilson was active in both Baltimore and
New Orleans as early as 1848 and as late as 1859, having
at least three different partners during that period.[6]

Notwithstanding incompleteness, the so-called *Director
for 1855-56* gave the names and addresses of at least 14
resident traders.[7] Among about 20 resident traders known
to be there in the latter half of the 'fifties there were as
many as three Kings (" King & Bros., traders "), two
Warehams and two Warfields.[8] Most of the 20 must have
had assistants. The general auctioneers, almost as numerous as the traders, also sold slaves, at least occasionally. Some of the general commission merchants, less
often than in Virginia and most of the other Southern
States, incidentally dealt in them as they did in agricultural produce of different kinds. Besides all these, there
were " agents ", also known as " general agents ", who

[6] Stowe, *Key to Uncle Tom's Cabin*, 160-61; *Sun*, Mar. 20, 1856; Jan. 25,
1859. He was a resident at Donovan's old stand, 11 Camden street, according
to the *Directory for 1856-57*, and his advts. showed that he kept his slaves
there; but neither this nor the previous *Directory*, which mentioned a
different place of residence, indicated his business.

[7]

Name	Address
" Allen John,	241 Gough "
" Campbell B. M. & W. L.	office 284 w Pratt "
" Casey Thomas	255 e Lombard "
" Donovan Joseph S.	11 Camden "
" Goman George	Penn. avenue extended "
" King Samuel H.	36 Thames "
" Mitchell John S.	105 William "
" Ritz John Z.	118 Harford avenue "
" Robinson Joseph	287 e Pratt "
" Thompson Edward	Cambridge "
" Wareham James	127 Orleans "
" Warfield Caleb	242 Conway "
" Warfield Thomas	4 McHenry "

John N. Denning was still represented as living at his old address, but his
business was not indicated.

[8] Wood's *Directory for 1856-57*, pp. 146, 275.

welcomed all sorts of commissions in regard to slaves, real estate and almost any kind of personal property.

Kentucky was the offspring of Virginia in population, traditions and agricultural methods only less than in territory. The predominant influences were established when slaves were cheap and thousands of acres of fertile land could be had " for a song "—as bounty for military service, by settling on them and making slight improvements or by complying with other easy requirements.[9] Pioneering under such conditions could be made very profitable. From the beginning of statehood the interests of slavery and of what was at least nominally a plantation system were supreme, although only a very small fraction of the settlers were directly concerned with either. How little the antislavery movement there gained in practical results after a long agitation was demonstrated by the declaration in the constitution of 1850 that " the right of the owner of a slave to such slave, and its increase, is the same, and is as inviolable as the right of the owner of any property whatever ".[10] The phrase " *and its increase* ", denoted consciousness of the profit of slave-rearing and determination that slavery should be permanent.

The soil and climate of Kentucky are unsuited to a plantation system. The tobacco crop, which notoriously exhausts the soil, was the only large one on which slave labor could be used with any considerable advantage over free labor. Yet, as in all new slave States, an energetic and thrifty farmer, after he had saved a few thousand dollars or possessed the equivalent in slaves, could in a decade or two acquire a relatively large fortune by employing his increasing gang in bringing fertile wild land under cultivation and then selling or renting the farms.

[9] I. E. McDougle, *Slavery in Kentucky* (3 *Journal of Negro History*), 214-16, gives a good account of them.

[10] Poole, 1 *Federal and State Constitutions*, etc., 684.

When he halted and fancied himself a " planter " or a landholding " aristocrat " and idled and spent accordingly, the tide of fortune soon began to recede. If he could limit himself to the products of his lands and the labor of his slaves—and it was much easier to do so than in Virginia—the natural increase and the advancing money value of his negroes were sure to make him well off. But, to a less degree than in the older slave States, carelessness or extravagance was the rule.

Kentucky early began to export slaves and also continued to import them,[11] even after the law of 1833 forbade it.[12] Before 1820 different travelers reported seeing at Natchez and New Orleans evidences of considerable trading in negroes gathered in the border States and brought down from Kentucky on flat-boats. A firm of traders in Paris, Kentucky, was said to have 100 slaves on hand in 1822. And Joseph Holt Ingraham wrote, about 1834, that, although Kentucky was contributing only a small proportion of the slaves brought into Mississippi, its quota was yearly increasing.[13]

A somewhat recent Southern writer on slavery in Kentucky says:

(1) " There is no mention in the newspapers of any dealers there [Louisville] before the year 1845."

(2) " It is noticeable that none of the Louisville directories for this period [the 'forties and the 'fifties] mention any slave dealers."

(3) " It is very difficult to find out how many slave dealers there were in the State, for few of them ever came out in the open and advertised their trade." [14]

---

[11] The words *export* and *import*, although generally implying foreign commerce, were commonly used in reference to the interstate slave-trade and are so employed in this book, because there are no facile substitutes.

[12] See *post* p. 272.

[13] On the different points see John Rankin, *Letters on Amer. Slavery*, 45-47; Asa Earl Martin, *The Anti-Slavery Movement in Kentucky*, 88-89; [Ingraham], 2 *The Southwest etc.*, 237.

[14] McDougle, *Slavery in Kentucky* (3 *Journal of Negro History*), 230, 231.

All these assertions are "important, if true". Let us put them to the test of facts.

1. Slave-trading in Louisville was, indeed, more conspicuous after than before 1845. The annexation of Texas was the general explanation. In the 'twenties, 'thirties and early 'forties much of the business was conducted by small traders, who did comparatively little advertising. Other persons, with more enterprise and better standing, combined slave-trading of different kinds with real estate transactions, lending money or handling divers sorts of merchandise, and regularly so advertised. According to circumstances, they were called agents, general agents, general commission merchants or auctioneers. Consequently it has often been assumed that they were not also traders. The illogic of this may be illustrated thus:—A. and B. separately conducted wholesale businesses and each annually sold liquors to the amount of $100,000. A. dealt in nothing else. Because B.'s sales of liquors were a part of his wholesale grocery business, he was also a grocer. But was he any less a liquor-dealer because he also sold dry groceries? So with agents, general commission merchants and auctioneers that dealt in slaves: they were slave-traders whatever else they may have been or been called. Before as well as after 1845 they were numerous in Louisville and elsewhere in Kentucky, and they publicly announced their business. Occasionally one finds an advertisement of a man that seemed to be dealing exclusively in negroes.[15]

[15] It would be easy to multiply the following examples of *slave-dealers advertising prior to 1845:*—

"J. G. BARCLAY & Co. called themselves "Commission Merchants * * * prepared to attend to receiving, storing and forwarding all kinds of merchandise in any direction, by land or water. They keep constantly for sale, a general assortment of groceries, iron and western produce."— Louisville, Ky., *Public Advertiser*, Feb. 10, 1827. Neither by word nor by association was there any suggestion in this general advt. that they also dealt in slaves. But in the same column they also advertised:

"*FOR SALE.*—A NEGRO WOMAN about twenty-five years old, and

2. When Professor McDougle says, " It is noticeable that none of the Louisville directories of this period mention any slave dealers ", that is equivalent to an assurance that he has carefully examined the *Directories*. We know that numerous agents, general agents, commission

two children, the eldest a girl five years old, the other a boy about four years old, not to be separated, but will sell them low for cash in hand. The character and terms can be made known by applying to J. G. BARCLAY & CO."

" Gray & Stewart, who were also general commission merchants, were likewise dealing in slaves:—

" NEGRO GIRL FOR SALE.—A Negro girl, 13 years old, stout and healthy, for sale by Gray & Stewart."—*Ibid.*, Dec. 29, 1827.

" NEGRO WOMAN FOR SALE.—A NEGRO woman, 35 years old, who is a good cook and washer " * * * —*Ibid.*, Jan. 7, 1829.

" *WANTED TO PURCHASE.*—A NEGRO GIRL, from 15 to 25 years of age, acquainted with cooking and washing, and who can be well recommended " * * * *Ibid.*, Aug. 29, 1829.

In 1827 J. C. BUCKLES and DAVID HERAN were conducting " a general Agency and Commission Business ". " They solicit the Agency of a few Steam Boats, above and below the Falls, assuring owners that they will attend to their business strictly ", said their public announcement.—*Ibid.*, Feb. 10, 1827. No hint of slave-trading. But beware of making any assumptions. Two weeks later this appeared:

" THREE or four likely young negroes for sale, inquire of BUCKLES & HERAN.—*Ibid.*, Feb. 24, 1827. Heran soon dropped out of the firm, and Buckles vigorously continued the various branches of such a miscellaneous business and, of course, did not neglect slave-trading:—

" FOR SALE.—A Likely negro girl, 18 years of age, well acquainted with house work, cooking, &c. Apply to J. C. BUCKLES."—*Ibid.*, Sept. 17, 1828.

" FOR SALE.—A LIKELY negro girl, about 18 years of age, sound and healthy."—*Ibid.*, Mar. 14, 1829.

" WANTED.—A Likely girl, from 15 to 18 years of age, accustomed to house work, and of good character."—*Ibid.*, Mar. 14, 1829.

Strictly speaking, an auctioneer is a person that sells things by competitive, public bidding. But Southern auctioneers commonly sold slaves privately also. Muir, Ormsby & Co. had:

" FOR SALE.—A LIKELY negro girl, about 18 years old—a good cook and washer."—*Ibid.*, Mar. 14, 1828.

" Joshua Lee, Auc'r " had what he called the " LOUISVILLE HORSE MARKET AND AUCTION AND LIVERY STABLE ", where, as he said, horses would be " received and particularly attended to " and where he would " also sell on commission, at public or private sale, HORSES, SLAVES,

merchants, auctioneers and others making
part of their living out of slave-trading wer
designated by one of those general terms an
ers or dealers in slaves, and that the names o
traders and visiting buyers for private use were not given
in the *Directories*. Moreover, in all cities the many residents that traded secretly were not designated as traders,
nor was anyone else unless he chose to be or was notor-

CARRIAGES, WAGGONS, &c."—*Ibid.*, Jan. 13, 1827. Would anyone deny
that Lee was a horse-trader as well as an auctioneer, and *vice versa?* He
was no less a slave-trader, according to his opportunities.

The following advt. betokens the regular trader that dealt in negroes only:

"Cash for Negroes.

"CASH will be given for likely young NEGROES, from 12 to 25 years
old. Appply to THO. KELLY, Union Hall, Louisville."—*Ibid.*, Dec. 19, 1829.

Apart from each having one or more advts. about slave-hirings, J. M.
Hewett and J. H. Bagby, respectively in the winters of 1840-41 and 1841-42,
showed that they were traders. These three notices by J. M. Hewett, "Gen'l
Ag't", appeared in the *Public Advertiser*, Jan. 5, 1841, and many other
days:—

"FOR SALE.—Several servants, both male and female, at No. 7, 3d street,
below postoffice."

"NEGROES FOR SALE.—2 MEN, first rate bagging hands."

"FOR SALE.—A NEGRO GIRL in her 11th year."

The Louisville *Daily Kentuckian*, Jan. 1, 1842, and many other days
contained the two following advts, by Bagby:—

"NEGROES WANTED.—I HAVE orders to purchase 3 or 4 good Women
or Girls, from 15 to 25 years of age, who understand cooking and washing.
For such as will suit fair prices will be paid in cash, if application be
made soon to J. H. BAGBY, Gen'l Agent, No. 7, 3d street. Also, 2 or 3
likely boys, from 12 to 15 years old, all of which [sic] are wanted for
persons in this city."

"Negroes Wanted.—I AM authorized to purchase 2 or 3 negro women from
18 to 25 years of age, of good character, and good house servants; also 2
or 3 girls from 12 to 14 years old; for such as will suit fair prices in
cash will be paid. Apply to" * * * etc.

A firm classed in the *Directory for 1843-44* as "grocers and commission
merchants", advertised in the same and many other numbers of the
Kentuckian:—

"NEGROES WANTED.—WE will give *cash* for six or eight young healthy
slaves of good character, for the use of a farm in the western country.—
AND'R. & ROBT. BUCHANAN."

ious as such; and some enumerators were careless about mentioning occupations. Notwithstanding these facts, *each of the five Louisville Directories* between 1836 and 1860 that the author has found *mentions from 7 to 81 traders, or, in a few instances, employs a synonym.*[16]

3. Whether or not more than a few slave-dealers in Kentucky " ever came out in the open and advertised their trade " will be sufficiently demonstrated by what is to be shown of the trade in two Kentucky cities. Professor McDougle's assertion seems still stranger when we consider that he followed it, in the same paragraph, with details about six large traders in Louisville between 1845 and 1850. He knew of them only because they were " out in the open ", calling for slaves with all possible publicity.[17] Merely one of these was among the 44 traders designated in the *Directory for 1848*. And there was at least one more, John S. Young, " out in the open ".[18]

Slave-trading flourished in Louisville until the Civil War. The fact that the *Directory for 1859-60* designated but 15 traders etc., probably indicates a lack of thoroughness on the part of the enumerators or a shunning of the words *trader* and *slave-dealer*, rather than a decline in the trade.[19] Matthew Garrison and Tarlton Arterburn had

[16] The *Directory for 1836* (by Collins) names at least 28 traders; that for 1843-44 (Collins), 81; that for 1845-46 (Jegli), 7; that for 1848 (Jegli), 44; that for 1859-60 (Tanner), 15. In each case the present author has copied the names and addresses. A few may have been overlooked.

McDougle, 231, correctly uses *traders* and *slave-dealers* as synonyms and so does the Lexington *Directory* for 1859-60.

[17] Prof. McDougle, p. 230, names William Kelly, T. & J. Arterburn, William F. Talbott, Thomas Powell and John Mattingly.

[18] " Wanted to Purchase.—I WILL pay fair Cash prices for some 30 or 40 NEGROES, from the ages of 10 to 25 years old, male and female, for farming purposes. JOHN S. YOUNG, No. 74, 5th st., Louisville, Ky."— Frankfort *Commonwealth*, Dec. 11, 1849, and often.

The *Directory for 1848* listed him thus: " Young J S, real estate agent, office 5th, bt Main and Mrkt, bds Exchange hotel."

[19] The following are the entries found:—

" Arterburn T. & J., (Talton & Jordon Arterburn,) slave dealers, e s 1st bet Market and Jefferson."

been active traders in Louisville for nearly two decades.[20]
The Arterburn brothers aspired to leadership and with
flaring advertisements called first for 100 and then for
250 negroes. Such purchasers usually shipped directly to
the Southern markets. The Arterburns announced: "Negroes always on hand for sale". This indicated that they
kept a slave-depot for residents and for visiting planters
and traders.[21] John Clark, another trader, was at the same
time and in the same place also offering the highest cash
prices. His office—and presumably his slave pen—was at
his home.[22] There were doubtless many others, less prosperous, that exclusively engaged in the trade.

Then the divers agents, the commission merchants and
the auctioneers. E. R. Dean advertised as an "agent"
and was classed as a "real estate agent", both of which
he was. None the less he had, without any affectations,
the traits of a very enterprising "nigger-trader", for
he was that also. Few traders anywhere were so active
in as many kinds of slave-trading. He would purchase

"Cassell Jacob T., trader, h w s Floyd bet Chestnut and Gray."

"Clark John, slave dealer, s s Market bet 5th and 9th."

"Ernwine George, trader, h e s 12th bet Walnut and Madison."

"Foster Hugh L., trader, bds n s Gray bet 1st and 2d."

"Garrison Matthew, slave dealer, s w 0th bet Main and Market, h e s
2d bet Market and Main."

"Gibbons Austin, trader, h n s Market bet Clay and Shelby"

"Reed Gabriel, trader, h s s Madison bet 14th and 15th."

"Slaughter Austin H., trader, h Portland av s w cor 2d cross."

"Stringer John, trader, h n s Green bet Campbell and Wenzel."

"White Robert K., speculator, h n s Broadway bet 3d and 4th."

"Wolfe Emanuel, trader, h n s Main bet Preston and Jackson."

"Wood Heaman, trader, h s s Chestnut bet Clay and Shelby."

"Woolford Charles H., trader, bds Neel house."

[20] The *Directory* for 1843-44, p. 52, has the entry "Garrison and Artibon,
traders". The designation of Tarlton Artibon also as a trader makes
identification certain, despite the misspelling. One advt. spelt Arterburn
with a final *e*.

[21] Louisville *Democrat*, Jan. 1, 1859 (see photostat) and *Courier*, Dec.
12, 1859.

[22] Louisville *Courier*, Dec. 12, 1859.

slaves " of every description, age and sex, for city customers " and was " daily selling and hiring negroes for
the ensuing year " [23] and especially desired one boy and
4 girls, each 14 years old, and 4 women, each 20 years
old.[24]   Also in 1859 three auctioneers announced their
eagerness to sell real estate, negroes, etc.; and their notices
of forthcoming vendues of slaves showed the scope of their
business.[25] Accordingly, they, too, were traders.

Apparently not Louisville but Lexington had the best
equipped slave-markets in the State, although its inhabitants in 1860 numbered less than 10,000, of whom about
one-third were colored. The slave population of Fayette
county, in which Lexington is situated, was rivaled by only
two counties in the State: Jefferson county, in which
Louisville is located, contained a few more slaves and
Christian county, near the southwestern corner, had a few
less. Fayette and neighboring counties of central Kentucky supplied most of the slaves that were gathered in
Lexington pens for the " Southern markets ".

Orville H. Browning, a Kentuckian who became a citizen
of Illinois, succeeded Stephen A. Douglas in the United
States Senate and was Secretary of the Interior in Johnson's Cabinet, revisited his native State in 1854.   In Lexington he went to see " a negro jail—a very large brick
building with all the conveniences of comfortable life, including hospital. 'Tis a place where negroes are kept for
sale. Outer doors and windows all protected with iron
grates, but inside the appointments are not only comfortable, but in many respects luxurious. Many of the rooms

[23] Louisville *Democrat*, Jan. 1 and 2, 1859. See photostat of former advt.
[24] Louisville *Democrat*, Mar. 24, 1859.
[25] Advertisements of C. C. Green & Co. and of W. A. Holland, in the
Louisville *Courier*, Jan. 5, 1859. On that date Green & Co. advertised that
three days later they would sell, at their auction-rooms, a boy of 19, " a
good hand in a tobacco factory, a No. 1 house and diningroom servant.
Also a negro woman, 24 years old, a good cook and washer, with her three
children, aged respectively 6, 4 and 2 years. Terms cash."

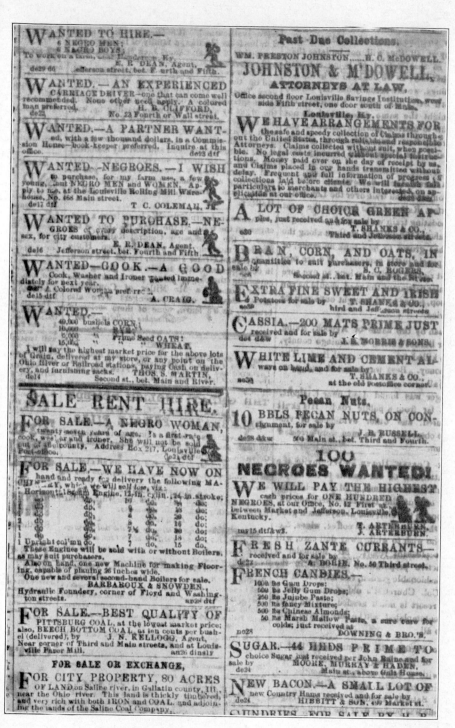

ADVERTISEMENTS OF LOUISVILLE SLAVE-TRADERS

From the Louisville *Democrat*, January 1, 1859

are well carpeted and furnished, and very neat, and the
inmates whilst here are treated with great indulgence and
humanity, but I confess it impressed me with the idea of
decorating the ox for the sacrifice. In several of the
rooms I found very handsome mulatto women, of fine
persons and easy genteel manners, sitting at their needle
work awaiting a purchaser. The proprietor made them get
up and turn around to show to advantage their finely
developed and graceful forms.'' $1,600 was the price of
one of the girls.[26]

Do you wonder why the trader did not have them display their needle-work instead of their '' finely developed
and graceful forms ''? Obviously they were of the class
everywhere known as '' fancy girls '', prospective con-
cubines—common in all large markets, but rarely so advantageously displayed. Except New Orleans, Lexington
was perhaps the best place in all the South to specialize in
them; for it was a great center or a favorite resort for
prosperous horse-breeders, reckless turfmen, spendthrift
planters, gamblers and profligates, whose libertinism was
without race prejudice.

An English traveler found five slave-pens there in 1858.
The one visited was described as '' very clean and comfortable ''; it contained 40 slaves; and from it about 100
had recently been sold and '' had traveled by railway
chained together ''. [27]

The Lexington *Directory for 1859-60* had a department
called the '' Business Mirror '', where men of respectable
occupations were grouped under such words as attorneys,
auctioneers, banks and bankers, barbers etc., etc., but there
was no reference to bars, saloonkeepers etc., for obvious
reasons. Yet four firms of '' slave dealers '', composed
of at least seven principals, were reflected in that representative mirror; and eleven traders were designated in

[26] 1 *Diary*, 138-39.
[27] Trotter, *First Impressions of the New World*, 252.

the body of the *Directory,* apart from silent partners. At least three firms were large interstate traders.[28]

R. H. Thompson, formerly a buyer and agent, had been so successful that he had bought and " just opened and refitted the old and well known Mart previously occupied by Bolton, Dickins & Co.", his former employers. He would give the usual superlative prices in cash " for all kinds of sound and likely negroes "; he would also buy and sell on commission and generously reward anyone that furnished him with information " as to where I can purchase negroes ". " My house is the largest and most secure jail in the State ", he boasted. That enabled him to " take care of the negroes of traders and others " safely and on liberal terms and was indicative of the relative extent of the traffic in Lexington.[29] Unmirrored but hardly less conspicuous were several other prosperous traders:—Joseph H. Northcutt, who ceased to employ two well-known slave-trading agents named Robard and took two partners, Silas and George S. Marshall. The Robards were promptly engaged by R. W. Lucas, who throughout the year would purchase a large number of negroes.[30] He had a roomy pen, conveniently opposite the county jail, and kept it well-stocked with a good assortment of house

[28] In the following list, the result of a search through the *Directory,* the names mentioned in the " Business Mirror " (123) are italicized and the men whose names have a * before them had branch offices in Natchez and probably elsewhere in the Southwest.

* " *Blackwell, Murphy & Ferguson,* (A. B., Felix G. M. & Geo. F.) slave dealers, office w s Broadway b Front and 2d."

" Cleary John R. trader, s s main opp. Jefferson."

" Collons H. slave dealer, n e c Upper and Pine."

" Colwell A. B. slave dealer, n s Main b Mulberry and Walnut."

" Lawrence Hiram, trader, n w c Upper and Bolivar."

" *Marshall Silas,* slave dealer, n s Main b Walnut and Back."

* " Pullum Wm. A. trader, s s High b Broadway and Mill."

" *Thompson R. H.* slave dealer, office s s Short b Spring and Jefferson, h s s 3d b Mulberry and Walnut."

* " *White W. F. & Co.* slave dealers, s s Short b Broadway and Spring."

[29] Lexington Semi-Weekly *Kentucky Statesman,* Feb. 21, 1860.

[30] See photostat of advts. by Northcutt, Marshall and Co. and of Lucas.

ADVERTISEMENTS OF LEXINGTON SLAVE-TRADERS

From the Lexington Semi-weekly *Kentucky Statesman,*
January 13, 1860

servants, field-hands and mechanics, so as to supply all comers. He advertised as far away as Nashville, and made a specialty of selling " low for cash ",[31] to attract the farmers and planters of the near or remote Southwest, who could buy slaves in Kentucky more conveniently than in Virginia and almost as cheaply. Of these six traders only Silas Marshall was noticed in the *Directory.*

How did all these sixteen or more traders, and perhaps several times as many petty traders in Fayette and neighboring counties, find slaves for their traffickings? Exactly like their fellows in Maryland and Virginia. Scores of original owners, eager for high prices and cash, responded to the traders' advertisements and oral solicitations. In every county slave-holding estates of decedents were put up at auction for the usual reasons. Overdue loans, secured by deeds of trust or mortgages with power of sale, were almost automatically bringing slaves into the market. Opportunities were all about. The regular and volunteer assistants, to whom all large traders promised generous rewards, knew how to find them. And the leading newspapers were always helping.[32]

Does all that evidence indicate that slave-traders were numerous and notorious in Louisville and elsewhere in

---

[31] Nashville *Republican Banner,* Jan. 6, 1860.

[32] Apart from advertisements about hirings, the following (the first three of which appeared in the Lexington Semi-weekly *Kentucky Statesman* of Feb. 6, 1855) will serve as specimens:—

Some anonymous person, using " Apply to the Editor ", wished to sell privately 2 negro men, a negro woman and her two children.

M. B. Morrison, apparently an auctioneer, would sell at the courthouse door, on a February " county court day ", a good seamstress, washer and ironer and a tolerable cook, who was stout and healthy.

Hanson and Woolley, " attorneys of the owner " offered, at private sale, three young women, one with a girl of 3 years.

On Feb. 8, 1855, " the heirs of Haldeman " would hold a vendue at the court-house door—the official auction-block in every county—where, " without reserve for the purpose of a division of property ", they would dispose of " one woman, about 45 years of age, with her boy child, 3 years old; one boy, about 10 years of age, and two girls, one about 11 and the other about 7

Kentucky for decades, or that they were " few " and did not come " out in the open " and advertise their trade?

Hierocles preserved in the amber of his *Facetiae* a little dialogue humorously illustrating fundamental incapacity to weigh evidence and draw rational conclusions:—" I heard you were dead ", said one.—" And yet ", replied the other, " you see that I am still alive."—" Well ", said the first in perplexity, " I don't know what to believe, for he who told me is much more deserving of confidence than you." Professor McDougle is equally perplexed. There was hardly anything more obvious about slave-trading than the fact that slaves, no two being alike, could not be standardized and quoted in market reports like stocks, bonds, hogs, poultry, potatoes, hides or sugar. Personal and physical elements, ever-varying but hardly perceptible to strangers, were often very important, and chance entered into nearly every purchase. Yet Professor McDougle—after giving many examples of slave-trading, stating on his own account that " Kentucky furnished many slaves for the Southern market ", and approvingly quoting George D. Prentice as saying that Kentucky slaves were sent South in large numbers and that any one could purchase them in Louisville [33]—nevertheless feels such profound respect for the tradition that slave-trading was a very small, insignificant and wholly despised matter, that he finds himself in this deep quandary: " If there was a trade in slaves which was regarded purely as a commercial enterprise, as some would have us think [!], then it is very hard to understand why these splendid

years of age."—*Ibid.*, Jan. 2, 1855. The wording clearly indicates that the three year old child was to be sold with his mother, but that the children of 7, 10 and " about 11 " years were for sale separately.

In the Christmas and other numbers of 1855 the executor of one Nancy McClelland announced that on New Year's Day he would " expose at public sale to the highest bidder, in front of the court house, Lexington ", a man about 30 or 33 years old, " a likely negro girl about 10 or 12 years of age; and a horse and buggy ".

[33] McDougle, 227-232.

trade papers [the Louisville *Prices Current* etc.] did not contain any account of the business.''[34]   Had Professor McDougle known of the New Orleans *Price-Current*—many times more important than the Louisville publication— and found that it did not contain either the word *slave* or *negro,* his logic would have compelled him to doubt the existence of the slave-trade, slavery and even the negro in Louisiana. The obvious explanation in each case is that neither publication cared to notice either the slave-trade or slavery any more than scores of other subjects.

In its tendencies, Missouri, except in the northern counties and the city of St. Louis, was not much less Southern than Maryland or Kentucky. Where, as a certain captain said, '' every decent Missouri family had at least one slave, and usually from two to four, as house servants '',[35] slaveholding must have been a *sine qua non* of social standing. Cotton flourished in only the southern counties. The chief staple crops were tobacco and hemp. Persons accustomed to slave labor thought it necessary, especially for these crops; it was at least convenient and mobile. And a flourishing, expanding South without slavery was inconceivable to them.

Missouri's 25,000 slaves to a white population of 115,000 in 1830 showed that there had been an abnormally large immigration of slaveowners, for Mississippi and Alabama offered planters vastly greater advantages. Presumably the number had been swelled by propaganda about the political and economic importance to the South of getting all possible slave territory out of the Louisiana purchase. In some sections of Missouri, in the early days, slaves were so much more plentiful than money that they were often used as a medium of exchange in the purchase of land.[36] For large sums they were almost as exchangeable

[34] McDougle, 231.

[35] Trexler, *Slavery in Missouri*, 1804-65, 19.

[36] Trexler, 50. 1 Catterall, 428, cites a case even in a Ky. court, in 1857,

as gold. In Maryland and Virginia thousands of slave-holding farmers were working nearly exhausted fields. West of the mountains the route to Missouri was easy and nearly all by water. If prospective settlers could sell their farms and stock for enough cash to pay their debts and meet the expenses of the journey, they knew that the increased value of their slaves in Missouri would enable them to get established there on much better land, and still have slave property worth more than it was at home. As elsewhere in the border slave States, it was soon learned that it was more profitable to sell slaves than to keep them for their ordinary labor. Consequently many were early shipped to the far South. About 1834 it was at least believed in Natchez, Mississippi, that $200,000 was to be invested in Missouri slaves for that market alone, and that one trader had recently left with $100,000 for that purpose.[37]

Let trader Walker illustrate what was occurring in Missouri even in the ' thirties. He scoured the State for his supplies and kept them on his farm near St. Louis until he had enough for a cargo for the lower Mississippi River markets. On one of his round-about searches he went from St. Louis by steamboat to Jefferson City and then by stage into the interior of the State. After purchasing a score or so as he passed the farms and villages, he returned with them to the Missouri River at St. Charles, where a woman with a babe four or five weeks old was added to the gang. Not finding transportation by river, he bought two horses, started the slaves, chained together, while he rode ahead and his mounted porter, William W. Brown, a very intelligent mulatto slave, brought up the rear. Soon the baby began

where " the consideration paid [for the land] was a negro boy at the price of $300 ".

[37] [Ingraham], 2 *The Southwest*, 237-38. Ingraham had intimate personal knowledge of conditions in Natchez, as we shall see.

to cry and continued to do so throughout much of the day. Walker's angry complaints and the mother's efforts were useless. The next morning, as the march was about to be continued, the infant again began to cry. Walker then " took the child by one arm, as you would a cat by the leg, walked into the house [where he had stopped the previous night] and said to the lady: ' Madam, I will make you a present of this little nigger; it keeps [up] such a noise I can't bear it.'—' Thank you, sir,' said the lady." [38] The mother's frantic appeals were not only in vain but caused her to be chained with the gang, as she had not previously been. On his farm Walker worked the slaves during the day and kept them in his private jail at night. Among a gang of 100, all chained and manacled, whom he took down the river, a few years later, there was a preacher named Solomon, who had been sold from his wife and children. [39]

Professor Trexler gives this excellent general description of the trade in Missouri:—" In addition to the vicious, the runaway, and the slave of the financially depressed owner, there was a surplus from the natural increase, and consequently a considerable amount of business in the local exchange of negroes existed. Besides this there was the itinerant buyer for the Southern mar-

---

[38] *Narrative of Wm. W. Brown* (Boston, 1847), 48-49. Many years later, John Doy witnessed a similar incident:—

"In the afternoon, before one of these gangs was sent off, a very dark woman was brought [in] with quite a light-colored baby. One of the traders asked the owner, likewise a trader, what he was going to do with that brat. ' D—d if I know ', was the reply. ' I'm bothered to know what to do with it.'—' We can't take it in the wagons and have it squalling all the way! '—' Here ', said the owner to an inhabitant of Platte City, who just then came in with a boy for sale, ' don't you want this thing? You may have it for twenty-five dollars. D—n it ', he continued, snatching the babe from its mother's arms by the shoulder and hefting it, ' it weighs twenty-five pounds! Will you take it? '—' Yes.'—' Take it now.'—And the child was carried off amid the heart-rending shrieks and pleadings of the agonized mother."—*Narrative of John Doy*, 61-62.

[39] Wm. W. Brown, 51-52, 81.

kets.   The smaller towns seem to have been regularly
visited, while the larger centers had prominent dealers.''
Lexington had two—one of whom '' was a wealthy planter
of good repute '', making a hotel his city headquarters
and having a three-story building as a slave-pen.   Platte
City had a thriving trade, St. Joseph had at least one
firm of slave-dealers, and Columbia and Marshall were
not neglected by the traders.[40]   And the advertisements
and the movements of the traders conclusively show a
very active traffic in slaves because of the prices they
would bring in the lower South.

Missouri's slave population in 1860 was not quite
115,000—a little more than one-half that of Kentucky and
a little less than one-fourth that of Virginia.   The whole
of St. Louis county contained not quite 4,400 slaves.
Nevertheless, a very large traffic in slaves was carried
on in the city of St. Louis even before 1850.   How does
one know this?   Because Green's *Directory for 1851* put
the word *trader* after the names of at least 30 residents.
Undoubtedly many others escaped that designation.[41]

[40] Trexler, 47.
[41] Incomplete list of Traders in St. Louis, 1851:
  1   " Beck Henry, trader, ns Carr bet Seventeenth and Eighteenth."
  2-3   " Blakely and McAfee, traders, 93 Olive."
  4   " Bridgford William T., trader, 219 Carr."
  5   " Brindley Thomas, trader, ss Elm on alley bet Main and 2d."
  6   " Clayton David, trader, 129 n Fifth."
  7   " Donovan Michael, trader, 272 n Eighth."
  8   " Farley John, trader, 250 n Fifth."
  9   " Fawcett Thomas, trader, ws Fourteenth, n of Carr."
  10   " Foley Patrick, trader, es Centre, s of Market."
  11   " Frederick Francis, trader, es Buel, s of Soulard."
  12   " Hart Philip, trader, 129 Market."
  13   " Kennedy Curtis, trader, ws Ninth, n of Franklin av."
  14   " Kennedy Riley S., trader, ws Ninth, s of Wash."
  15   " Lynch B. M., negro trader, 104 Locust."
  16   " Lynch John, trader, ss Pine, w of Fifteenth."
 (above)   " McAfee Alfred B., (Blakey & M.) 93 Olive."
  17   " McDonald John, trader, 94 Walnut."
  18   " Maguire James, trader, es Sixth, n of O'Fallon."

Apart from these were the general agents, auctioneers, commission merchants and secret speculators, besides many visiting traders. So many could not have engaged in this business where the resident slave population was sparse, if St. Louis had not been the center of the trade in Missouri and a point from which slaves were shipped to the far South—thus closely resembling the District of Columbia before 1850. While the white population of the city rose from 73,000 in 1850 to 157,000 in 1860, its slave population declined from 2,656 to 1,542, and its free negroes increased from 1,398 to only 1,755, which was not much more than the natural increase. Evidently many resident slaves were sold down the River. And St. Louis was, indeed, one of the five or six cities that sent the most negroes to the insatiable " Southern market ".

The traders and the newspapers of St. Louis displayed exceptional enterprise and boldness in the quest for slaves. Advertisements to buy, sell, " hire-out " or " hire-in " slaves or for the recovery of runaways were accompanied by one or more black figures representing a negro in flight—the man bearing a pack supported by a staff over his shoulder and the woman, bareheaded or wearing a bandanna, carrying a small store of supplies rolled up in a bag or mere cloth. These pathetic figures seemed to stand out from the printed page and attracted attention at the first glance. That is why they were used.

19   " Mattingly John, trader, boards at City Hotel."
20   " Meyer Henry A., trader, sw cor Fifteenth and Biddle."
21   " Miller Charles, trader, 216 n Ninth."
22   " Mispal Henry, trader, ws Thirteenth, bet Davis and Cass av."
23   " Norton Thomas, trader, rear 84 Chesnut."
24   " Novey Peter, trader, ne cor Ninth and Broadway."
25   " Peter Herman, trader, es Ninth, bet Wash and Carr."
26   " Smith Asa B., trader, ss Morgan w of Eighteenth."
27   " Smith William, trader, 35 s Eighth."
28   " Tuthill Patrick, trader, 110 s Fourth."
29   " Wells Samuel, trader, es Broadway, n. of Chambers."
30   " White William, trader, sw cor Sixth and Washington av."

This bit of sign language represented slavery, and the negro's as well as the public's attitude toward it, and was a perfect symbol of the avariciousness of traders and slave-selling masters, of the servility of the press and of the indifference of the public.

In the winter of 1851-52 John Mattingly, who for several years did much business in Louisville, Kentucky,[42] was so anxious to get 100 negroes " of every description " as soon as possible that he promised to " pay at all times from $50 to $100 on the head more money than any other trading man in the city of St. Louis or the State of Missouri ". And he could " at all times be found at Barnum's City Hotel ".[43]

Blakey (often spelt Blakely) & McAfee seem to have done the most extensive business in Missouri. They offered to " pay cash for all sound negroes aged from 8 to 45 years " and would " visit persons wanting to sell in any part of the State ". Willingness to go anywhere in a large State to buy all sound slaves from 8 to 45 years of age was conclusive evidence of extreme eagerness. The nearest approaches to it were Harker's advertisement in Maryland and Richard's in the District of Columbia offering to purchase those between 8 and 40 years old.[44] McAfee was in charge of the St. Louis office, Blakey of that in Palmyra, and they had regular agents at Frederickstown, Hannibal and Columbia. And all that implied many special agents and assistants also in other places. At 93 Olive street, St. Louis, the firm had " a good yard and jail, suitable for boarding " all slaves that came into their possession.[45] Thus Blakey & McAfee were prepared to extend the benefits of the trade to any Missouri slave-owner.

[42] McDougle, 230.
[43] *Key*, 146, quotes one of his advts. See photostat of St. Louis *Mo. Republican*, Jan. 23, 1852.
[44] *Ante* p. 120.
[45] See photostat of the *Mo. Republican*, Jan. 23, 1852.

Reuben Bartlett, the St. Louis agent of the Memphis firm of Bolton, Dickins (often misspelt *Dickens*) & Co., wished to buy for the Memphis and New Orleans markets and advertised, like Blakey & McAfee, that '' persons having negroes for sale can be waited on at their homes, anywhere in the State ''.[46] Soon this firm established a main office in St. Louis and '' our Mr. Dickins '', one of the partners, took charge. It was on Chestnut street between Sixth and Seventh, and had the important advantage of being near the city jail. Dickins was direct and plain-spoken. He had cash for all good negroes that might be offered; and as he was buying for the Memphis and Louisiana markets, where the prices were notoriously high, he added with convincing simplicity: I '' can afford to pay, and will pay, as high as any trading man in this State ''.[47] Later he wanted '' *One Thousand Negroes* '' and, willing to pay most, he gave sellers this advice: '' Test the market by giving every buyer a *chance,* and not rely upon advertisements that profess to pay more than others.'' Dickins seemed to be a trader without shams. The firm's place was then at No. 52 Second street, between Pine and Olive. Above the door was the appropriate sign:

| NEGROES BOUGHT HERE. | [48]

For several years late in the 'fifties, Corbin Thompson was one of the largest slave-merchants in St. Louis. In his pen at No. 3 South Sixth street, '' one square south of the county jail '', he promised to keep securely all negroes entrusted to him for sale. He claimed to have '' a high and healthy location with ample room '', where he would '' board, buy and sell on commission as low as any other dealer in the State of Missouri ''. He was also ready to '' take pains to select good homes for those sold in this

[46] *Mo. Republican*, Jan. 23, 1852.
[47] *Mo. Republican*, Dec. 24, 1852.
[48] *Mo. Democrat*, Feb. 1, 1855.

State if required ''! But what he was confident of was that buyers and sellers alike ought to call on him '' before closing elsewhere ''; for, as he said, '' I pledge myself to give satisfaction to all '',[49]—all but the slaves.

Bernard M. Lynch may have been no worse than his fellows, but more is known about him. He was very active throughout the ' fifties. Between 1851 and 1861 his business was in turn at three different places: first, at '' 104 Locust street, between Third and Fourth ''; then at '' 100 Locust street, between Fourth and Fifth '', and, finally, at '' his large, airy, new quarters, No. 57 South Fifth street, corner of Myrtle,'' now Broadway and Clark avenue.[50] He assured the public that he paid the highest cash prices, bought and sold on commission, furnished board to all slaves left with him, had '' a good yard for their accommodation '' and '' comfortable quarters, under secure fastenings ''. He also knew how to attract patrons by less common means. While all sellers naturally desired the highest prices, some of them earnestly wished to prevent their slaves from getting into the hands of bad masters, and many more were content if they could plausibly allege that they had made such provision. Accordingly Lynch, although openly buying for the Southern markets, advertised: '' Particular attention paid to the selecting of homes for polite servants.'' That was one of the most knowing tricks of the trade, for it was sure to attract buyers as well as sellers and thus be doubly profitable to Lynch. His rules also showed peculiar shrewdness and slave-trading wisdom. The first of them, placarded in his office, was: '' No charge less than one dollar '', although the price for a slave's board was thirty-seven and one-half cents a day. When selling or buying

[49] *Mo. Republican*, Feb. 3, 1858.

[50] *Mo. Republican*, Jan. 23, 1852; *Mo. Democrat*, Feb. 1, 1855; *Mo. Republican*, Feb. 3, 1858; Trexler, 48, 49; *Mo. Republican*, Aug. 3, 1860; *3 Cyc. of the Hist. of St. Louis*, 1333.

ADVERTISEMENTS OF ST. LOUIS SLAVE-TRADERS

From the St. Louis *Missouri Republican*, January 23, 1852

ADVERTISEMENTS OF SLAVE-TRADERS IN THE ST. LOUIS
Missouri Democrat, FEBRUARY 1, 1855

for others, his commission was two and one-half per cent.
If he could adjust orders for sales to those for purchases,
one hand washed the other and he made two commissions.
Because his jail was so safe and he took the same care
of the slaves of others as of his own, he assumed custody
only at the risk of the *masters!* [51]

Lynch, Thompson and many others, like their fellows
in Kentucky, Virginia and Maryland, obtained most of
their supplies by a thorough combing of town and country.
Dr. John Doy, a free soil settler in Kansas and for months
confined in Platte City and St. Joseph jails, vividly described one phase of the process:—"Every few days we
would have a fresh arrival [at the St. Joseph jail] in the
shape of slaves sent in for sale, or a prisoner for trial.
Wright, the trader, who lived in town, was always ready
for a bargain, and would generally buy any one who was
sent to be sold for a trifling fault, as was sometimes the
case, but the trade was by no means so brisk as at Platte
City.   There they were brought in numbers, and as many
as five coffles were once sent off in a week, while from St.
Joseph they were shipped by twos and threes to the
agents at St. Louis—one named Lynch, and the other
Thompson—who kept slave-pens in that city." [52]

A clergyman whose church was but half a square from
Lynch's pen at 100 Locust street took some clerical visitors to see it in 1859.   They found Lynch sitting in front
of his establishment.   Although a lawyer in the party gave
a jocose warning against this "pack of abolitionists",
Lynch bade them welcome, led them to the entrance to
the jail, drew out a great iron key, inserted it in the lock,
turned back the bolt, swung open the door and expressed
regret that his stock on hand was small.   Like a careful
jailor, he locked the door behind the visitors and remained

---

[51] Trexler, 49-50, prints the office rules and shows how many, or rather,
how few, slaves Lynch kept on hand at tax-paying time.

[52] *Narrative of John Doy*, 98.

on the outside. The room had but one small window, which was near the ceiling. The floor was the bare earth, and the furniture was three wooden benches without backs. The negroes within numbered but seven, and both sexes were herded together without any arrangement for privacy. " Secure fastenings ", indeed; but hardly " comfortable quarters ".   " One fairly good-looking woman of 40 tearfully entreated " the visitors to buy her, repeatedly promising to be faithful and good.[53]

Outgrowing this place, Lynch in 1859 moved to 57 South Fifth street on the corner of Myrtle, now Broadway and Clark avenue, where a two-and-one-half story brick house with barred windows, strong bolts and locks, was his jail.[54] His immediate predecessor there had made a specialty of dealing in children of from 5 to 16 years of age. Mothers with their broods were often bought and later sold separately.[55]   Lynch advertised that he purchased and kept " on hand for sale at all times " " all descriptions of negroes suited to the Southern markets ".   Like many another in the trade, he graciously advertised his thankfulness for past favors and solicited " a continuance of public patronage ".[56] This " public patronage " was not to be continued long.   Soon after the outbreak of the Civil War the United States Government seized this place and filled it with persons charged with disloyalty.[57]   As in Alexandria, Virginia, what had recently been a prosperous slave-pen was crowded with Confederate soldiers or sympathizers.   No cup could have been more bitter.

[53] Rev. Galusha Anderson, *A Border City During the Civil War*, 182-84.

[54] 3 *Cyc. Hist. St. Louis*, 1333.   About 1898 there was a drug store on that corner.—*Ibid.*

[55] Rev. Galusha Anderson, 185-86.   See also *post* p. 210.

[56] *Mo. Republican*, Aug. 3, 1860.

[57] 3 *Cyc. Hist. St. Louis*, 1333.   Anderson (186), forgetting that Lynch moved to the corner of Fifth and Myrtle sts., supposed that the trader in children continued there until the Civil War ended his business.   Trexler (p. 49), not noticing the location of Lynch's last pen, assumes that the one taken for a military prison was at 100 Locust street, and, overlooking the fact that Fifth and Myrtle sts. were the earlier names for Broadway and Clark ave., mentions two slave-pens as being on what was the same site.

CHAPTER VII

SLAVE-HIRING

Slave-hiring was a restricted kind of slave-trading and was common in all Southern States. It concerned not the title to the slave, but only his or her labor for a definite period or purpose and usually at a specific price. The influences that most often induced the hiring out of slaves were profit, a dislike to sell (lest it should be inferred that the owner had met with reverses or was speculating) or a wish to retain control over the slave for the slave's good or the master's prestige. Prestige of some degree went with the ownership and the hiring of slaves and was an important factor, but has been much ignored historically. The hirer's interest began with expectations of benefit from the slave's services and naturally terminated with them.[1] Self-interest prompted the owner to try to prevent his human property from suffering any physical injury; it was hardly possible to do much more. To the slave, the hiring was less objectionable than sale to a bad master, but more objectionable than sale to a good master, for this brought a comfortable home and lasting associations.

Many thousands of slaves were annually hired as household servants for private families, boarding-houses and hotels. Mrs. Roger A. Pryor was a very rare exception in preferring free negroes.[2] Still more numerous were the slaves hired to work in fields, forests and (in a few States) factories and mines, to dig canals and build rail-

---

[1] Chancellor Johnston said in a South Carolina case in 1839: "Hired slaves are commonly treated more harshly, or with less care and attention, than those in possession of their owner. Their health is less attended to; they are less likely to increase, and their moral qualities are almost always deteriorated."—2 Catterall, 374. A similar opinion was expressed in a Tenn. case.—*Ibid*, 563.

[2] *Reminiscences in Peace and War*, 43.

145

roads and highways. Before small farmers were able to
buy a slave they commonly felt that they must hire one,
at least a girl or a boy. Merchants, mechanics, contractors,
drovers and liverystable men required helpers. Most persons hired because purchase was beyond their means or
the demand for the labor was temporary. The fact that
the hirer as well as the owner was popularly considered
as belonging to the slaveholding class was often influential, and all the more so because if one neither owned nor
hired a slave, one might be called a "poor-white."

The market value of fieldhands and some other crude
slave laborers normally began to decline by the time they
were about 35 or 40 years of age. But long after mechanics, coachmen, cooks and most kinds of skilled servants
were too old for the " Southern market " they could be
let out for more than double a good interest on what they
would sell for.) That meant much to needy or improvident
owners, not likely to discount the risk of a slave's death.
And an income from hirings was preferred to one from
real estate, stocks or loans because, without the care of
management, it gave the appearance of having superfluous
slaves. In all Southern cities numerous residents, especially children, widows and maiden ladies, were partly
or wholly dependent on what came from hiring out slaves.[3]

---

[3] A North Carolina father let his son, living in Ala., take 12 slaves, hire
them out for $1200 and have half of it to pay for board and schooling.—2
Catterall, 169. A North Carolina will read:—" I wish Nathan and Jerry to
be hired out to support and school my three youngest children * * * .—2
Catterall, 224. Similar, *ibid.*, 60. Another North Carolina will gave hires
for the benefit of the testator's grandchild.—*Ibid.*, 108.

Susan W. Baker paid a $3. tax on each of 36 slaves, Josephine M. Douglass
on 14, Mrs. Sarah Frazer on 16, Miss S. R. Hort on 25, without owning
any other taxable property in Charleston.—*List of Tax-Payers of Charleston
for 1860.*

"Negroes are a kind of capital which is loaned out at a high rate, and
[in Savannah] one often meets with people who have no plantation, but who
keep negroes to let and receive very handsome sums for them every month."—
Das Ausland, quoted by N. Y. *Tribune*, Apr. 28, 1860.

After keeping a lunatic at the public expense for five years, the commis-

A large proportion of the rough workmen and of the house-servants for hire were remnants of the estates of deceased or impoverished masters. When slave property was in probate, or possessed by a life-tenant unable to employ it, or belonged to orphan children or other wards in chancery, it was usually necessary to hire out the slaves.

As payment in advance, like house-rent today, was not customary, the rule, except between trusted friends, was to require security and a bond giving the details of the contract. Otherwise there was much danger of a misunderstanding and consequent loss.

Hirings might be made publicly or privately, at almost any time or place and for any period. But in most cases the period began just after New Year's day and ended just before Christmas. In rural districts the hirings might take place on a farm or a plantation, in front of the cross-roads store or tavern or on the steps of the little court-house, and were often to the highest bidder at public out-cry. For sales, there was no special time: the itinerant trader, with cash in hand, might appear and reappear any day; and the large markets were always open. Most of the hirings in a whole county occurred on one or a few days and, except in a large city, in relatively few places.

In numerous Virginia villages the hirings on a single day must have outnumbered the sales there during the whole year, for the same slaves might be hired out annually many years in succession. Moreover, masters in distant counties not rarely sent their slaves to Richmond to be hired out. "Friday last, January 1st, [1858] was hiring day in Warrenton. * * * At least 500 servants were for hire." [4] That could hardly have been more than half or one-third of the whole number thus disposed of in Fauquier county, where the slave population in 1860 was 10,455.

sioners of the S. C. Asylum for the Insane were much surprised when they discovered that he owned three slaves whose annual hire was worth more than enough to support him.—1 Catterall, 373.

[4] Alexandria *Gazette* and *Va. Advertiser*, Jan. 6, 1858.

This indicates that from 1,000 to 1,200 or from 10 to 12% of its slaves were hired out. At Catt's Tavern, West End, in Fairfax county, near Alexandria, about 450 were offered, January 2, 1860, and that was less than the usual number.[5] Each of several other villages in that county had a special day for public hirings and there were private hirings of considerable numbers elsewhere.[6] As the slave population of the county was only 3,116, it looks as if fully 25% of them may have been hired out. If the owners and the prospective hirers near Fairfax Court House did not make satisfactory arrangements there, they continued their efforts in Dranesville and perhaps in Centerville or West End. When the weather was favorable, large crowds gathered, for to many slaveholders and would-be slave-holders and to inquisitive rustics generally these were considered very important occasions. Because there were also public sales of slaves and estates, it was not beneath the dignity of " planters " and large traders to be present. The plain farmer, mechanic or country storekeeper that led away his first hired slave was proud of having risen into the slaveholding class.

The slaves, wherever taken, continued to speak of the place where they had been reared as " home ". Early in December many agents, executors or administrators inserted notices in the leading newspaper of their respective counties saying that a strict compliance with the terms of the hirers' bonds would be required, especially the agreement that the negroes should be " delivered well clothed ". If any of the master's or mistress's family still lived at the old " home ", holiday cheer might be enjoyed there with relatives and former associates; but if the place had been sold or rented, the slaves lost all that and went

[5] *Ibid.*, Jan. 3, 1860.
[6] *Ibid.*, Dec. 25, 1860, announced that the public hirings for Fairfax county would take place at Fairfax C. H., Saturday, Dec. 29th; Dranesville, Monday, Dec. 31st; Centerville and West End, Tuesday, Jan. 1, 1861. It also advertised a private hiring of 18 slaves for Dec. 31st.

from hirer to hirer, unless a few days were spent in some agent's or public slave-jail.[7]

When the main purpose of hiring out slaves was to get a good income without labor or care, it was needful to employ someone to prepare the papers, to judge the security, to collect the money and to look after the welfare of the negroes. Such persons, called "general agents" or merely "agents", conducted a business that resembled what in a free society would be a combination of an employment bureau and a real estate and collecting agency; and in rural districts they went from place to place at stipulated times. They were numerous in all Southern cities; for, with a little capital and enterprise, with agreeable manners and a large acquaintance with slave-holders, they could easily make a living. They differed from the regular traders, brokers, auctioneers and commission merchants dealing in slaves, as small real estate agents differ from brokers, auctioneers and speculators in real estate—mainly in degree. There was no positive line between them: some general agents, having sufficient money, bought and sold slaves, and some of the large traders and slave-auctioneers did not scorn to keep up the less remunerative feature of attending to hirings.

The evidences of hirings were most conspicuous in Rich-

[7] Here are advts. that well illustrate different features of rural hirings:—

"THE PUBLIC HIRING of the SERVANTS belonging to the estate of Mrs. Susan R. Page, deceased, will take place at Millwood, on Monday, 31st day of December, 1860. All persons who hired servants belonging to this estate, for the present year, will be required to comply strictly with the requisitions of the bond, in every particular. The servants must be sent home the day before Christmas. ROBT. C. RANDOLPH, M. D., Executor of Susan R. Page, deceased. Millwood, Clarke county, Dec. 6."—Alexandria *Gazette*, Dec. 25, 1860.

"PUBLIC HIRING.—Will be hired out at the Half-way House, in the county of Chesterfield, on Saturday, the 1st of January, 1842, for the ensuing year, a large number of valuable hands, consisting of men, women, boys and girls, belonging to the estate of John Stratton and others. The persons who hired hands of me the present year, will please direct them there on that day, clothed agreeable to the conditions of their bonds.—RICHARD BOOTH, Ex'or of John Stratton, dec'd."—Richmond *Whig*, Dec. 28, 1841.

mond. The *Directory for 1860* gave a list of 18 agents.[8]
Probably all these and many more, besides some of the
regular traders, auctioneers and commission merchants,
attended to hirings.[9] Their offices were close to those of
the leading traders and in or near the hotels. Sometimes
as many as seven of their very wordy advertisements appeared in a row, nearly filling a long column of a newspaper.[10]

These agents seemed to find a special charm as well as
profit in this kind of slave-trading, for it brought them
into close relations with slaveholders of the best social
standing. Their advertisements expressed their thanks
to " friends and patrons for their favors during the past
year ",[11] promised " good prices [to the owners] and good
homes to the negroes ", and to supply the slaves with
" ample and comfortable accommodations * * * till hired
out, and every attention, personal and medical, * * * during the year ".[12] The respectability of this business was
shown by the advertised names of persons designated as
patrons [13] and sometimes as references, which obviously
meant about the same thing. One Richmond agent's list
of references named 49 persons living in 20 different
places; [14] another's list, published in Alexandria, about
110 miles away, named almost as many persons, living in
ten different counties; [15] and still other Richmond agents,
advertising in Baltimore, about 160 miles away, must have

[8] See *ante* p. 97 n.

[9] Such were Pulliam & Slade, *Directory*, 1850-51, p. 175; Pulliam & Davis,
Directory, 1852, p. 54 of the advts.

[10] Semi-Weekly *Enquirer*, Jan. 11, 1861.

[11] Clopton's advt. in Richmond *Enquirer*, Dec. 14, 1858.

[12] Edgar Macon of Richmond in the Alexandria, Va., *Evening Sentinel*,
Dec. 23, 1858.

[13] James Moore's advt. read: " He takes the liberty to refer to the following gentlemen, for whom he has done business of this kind, some of them for
many years."—Richmond *Enquirer*, Dec. 31, 1859.

[14] Lyne in Semi-Weekly *Enquirer*, Jan. 11, 1861.

[15] Cocke in Alexandria *Gazette* etc., Dec. 25, 1860.

had a much wider circle of patrons.[16]   Among the names
thus spread before the public were those of one or more
judges, generals, colonels, physicians, clergymen, "Hon-
orables ", elders and many others, including Pendletons,
Barbours, Dabneys, Fitzhughs, Custises, etc.   This indicates the scope and standing of the business and shows
that the Richmond market was much used by hirers, as
well as by sellers, all over the State.

One agent incidentally told what numerous slaves had
to endure while waiting to be hired, in contrast with the
advantages he offered: He had large office-rooms where
negroes would " not suffer by exposure to the weather,
as many do during the hiring season, who are sent to the
city for hire, and who are not thus provided with good
and sufficient shelter."   He could also supply ample accommodations at night, with board at a moderate cost,
until the slaves were hired out.[17]   Another put stress on
having " a large comfortable apartment connected with
his office, where those servants * * * not provided with
places to stay at night during the hiring, may remain, with
a good fire, FREE OF CHARGE ".[18]   Such remarks would have
been suicidal for an agent if it had not been common for
masters to neglect their slaves when the weather was often
stormy and the temperature much below freezing.

A Richmond agent mentioned as his " usual terms, 7½
per cent for hiring out, bonding, collecting the same, and
attention during the year in cases of sickness.   Medical
attention can be had at $3 each—medicine gratis." [19]

Persons with slaves to let out were advised to provide
lists of them and to send forward the negroes as soon as
possible after Christmas, so that they should be ready
for inspection and the hirings.   The lists, often printed
so as to be handed or sent to applicants, contained brief

16 P. M. Tabb & Son (who were also interstate slavetraders) in Baltimore
Sun, Jan. 17, 1859.

17 Tabb & Son's advt. in Richmond *Enquirer*, Jan. 2, 1861.

18 Clopton's advt.   Semi-Weekly *Enquirer*, Jan. 11, 1861.

19 Robert Hill, Richmond *Whig*, Dec. 24, 1841.

but highly commendatory descriptions of the personal qualities and the work of the negroes and mentioned the price asked by the year or the month, unless the hiring was to be by auction. At such a time, the owner and the agent fully appreciated and praised the merits of the slaves.[20]

Olmsted described a gang that had just arrived in Richmond and the agent to whom they were delivered:— " They were all men and boys, and each carried a coarse, white blanket, drawn together at the corners so as to hold some articles; probably, extra clothes. They stood in a row, in lounging attitudes, and some of them, again, were quarreling, or reproving one another. A villainous-looking white man stood in front of them. Presently, a stout, respectable man, dressed in black according to the custom, and without any overcoat or umbrella, but with a large, golden-headed walking-stick, came out of the door of an office, and, without saying a word, walked briskly up the street; the negroes immediately followed, in file, the other white man bringing up the rear. They were slaves that had been sent into the town to be hired out as servants or factory hands. The gentleman in black was, probably, the broker in the business." [21]

City residents with one or a few superfluous slave servants were less dependent on the agents; hirers were often found by advertisement, oral report or by letting the slave, if trustworthy, seek them. In this case the slave was given a brief memorandum, stating the terms of the bearer's hire and requesting any one interested to apply to the undersigned. For nearly a week the streets and alleys about the trading quarter swarmed with negroes of va-

[20] One E. P. Nash of Petersburg, in offering several valuable men for hire, described them as follows: " HENRY, well and favorably known as an experienced drayman and good hand with horses; ANTHONY, a likely young man, favorably known as a dining-room servant, store boy, or gardener. In all these different occupations he has had considerable experience and is well tried. ANDREW, an experienced and cleanly whitewasher, plasterer, &c., also well known."—Petersburg *Republican*, Jan. 5, 1846.

[21] *Seaboard, etc.*, 30-31.

rious ages and either sex, with shining faces and in holiday attire. Any benevolent looking white person with a well-to-do air was likely to be addressed in turn by many smiling, bowing slaves: "Massah, please, sah, hiah me." Because the slaves that were looking for hirers naturally tried to please the prepossessing and repel others, it was often said that they chose their own temporary masters. There were obvious advantages to the slave and the hirer in starting with mutual predilections; and the owner was sure to profit by it if these favorable impressions continued, for they connoted good treatment and contentment. Thus the slave might choose his hirer, save his master all expense and be, in these respects, a free agent. Young and untried negroes for hire had to be watched or kept close to the agencies or the jails.

Slaves of almost any kind could be found for hire. A Petersburg, Virginia, agent advertised, "Servants of every description for hire by Joseph E. Cox".[22] The Louisville, Kentucky, real estate and general agent that kept himself most before the public made this announcement:

"Wanted to Hire.—FIVE HUNDRED NEGROES, OF ALL AGES, sizes and sex, for the ensuing year. Persons having Negroes to hire will do well to address E. H. DEAN, Agent."[23]

Yet some persons never dreamed that slave-hiring was even akin to slave-trading. Fieldhands, washers and ironers, cooks, porters, waiters, house-maids, plain mechanics of various kinds and half-grown boys and girls were numerous in nearly all hiring markets. In Richmond, Lynchburg, Petersburg, Louisville, Nashville and many other cities considerable numbers of slave boys were regularly hired in tobacco or other factories. /Sturdy and reliable draymen were to be had in any city, but only at high prices, for they could earn much by doing odd jobs.\ In special regions one could find excellent tanners. In parts

[22] Petersburg *Republican*, Jan. 12, 1846.
[23] Louisville *Democrat*, Dec. 29, 1859.

of North Carolina ordinary turpentine-hands were numerous, and coopers and distillers of turpentine were not rare.

The Virginia coal mines were worked mainly by slaves, some of whom were owned by the proprietors of the mines and others hired at from $120 to $200, about 1855.[24] " This ' coal pit nigger ', as other negroes called them, [wrote one of the author's old friends, who as a boy was familiar with conditions in a county where there were many mines] was considered the lowest caste among slaves. Some children, both negroes and whites, imbibed this impression and thought they were related to the Devil and would actually run away from them." To the slaves, coal-mining must have been very disagreeable work, but hirers and owners took a cheerful view of it. A mineowner offering " full prices " said: " During the past four years not a single serious accident to life or limb has occurred in our underground operations. All hires will be paid punctually, in quarterly payments, at my office in this city." [25]

How different was the fortune of slaves hired by hotels, especially at the numerous " Springs "! [26] Waiters and chambermaids were decently dressed, had an abundance of food, by artful servility and flattery ingratiated themselves with guests so as to obtain tips, imitated the airs of belles and beaux and without difficulty secured liquor that temporarily heightened merriment, but often kindled jealousies and resulted in tragedies with knives or razors.

The slave wet-nurse was a peculiar but not rare commodity, almost exclusively in the hiring-market, because the need and the capacity were temporary. Although having an infant of her own, she could, if buxom, spare one ample breast for the profit of her owner; and, if of good character and appearance, she was at a premium. There

[24] Olmsted Seaboard etc., 47.

[25] JOHN J. WERTH, Richmond Semi-Weekly Enquirer, Jan. 16, 1857.

[26] " FIFTY SERVANTS WANTED for the Springs, viz. Dining Room Servants, Chambermaids, &c., Persons having such for hire will call immediately.— TOLER & COOK."—Richmond Daily Enquirer, May 13, 1853.

was no prejudice against having one'[...] a slave, but the nourishing of white an[...] fountain seemed like race equality a[...] parents. Accordingly a still more v[...] without a child " was often demande[...]

Some cases of hirings seem almost incredible. [...] Norfolk, Olmsted met a slave who was the property of a church and was hired out by its trustees to a lumberman in the swamps.[28] That was a small enterprise in comparison with that of the several Presbyterian churches in Prince Edward county, Virginia, that in common owned and hired out nearly seventy slaves in the course of as many years—all resulting from the original purchase of two prolific slave girls.[29]

In 1859, there was for hire in Alexandria, Virginia, a very intelligent and experienced slave pilot, worthy to be trusted with precious lives and valuable cargoes in any storm, for he had been " on the Potomac River, as boy and man, all his life, as pilot, captain of vessel, &c; [was] regarded as one of the best in the country, in that capacity ", and was called " honest, capable and perfectly reliable ". He usually hired for $175 annually.[30]

A Richmond firm of general agents advertised:

" FOR HIRE, either for the remainder of the year, or by the month, week, or job, the celebrated musician and fiddler, GEORGE WALKER. All persons desiring the services of George, are notified that they must

---

[27] " To Hire, a Wet Nurse, with her young child; she is warranted perfectly sound and of very good character. Apply at this office."—Charleston *Courier*, Aug. 24, 1830.

" WET NURSE WANTED.—*A Colored Wet Nurse* without a child. She must be well recommended. None other need apply. Apply at 20 Meeting St."—*Courier*, Dec. 24, 1859.

The custom was immemorial:

" To be Hired as a Wet Nurse, A HEALTHY YOUNG NEGRO WOMAN, With a good breast of milk and no child. Enquire at No. 106, King-street."—Chas'n, S. C., *Royal Gazette*, May 1, 1782.

[28] 1 *Cotton Kingdom*, 154.

[29] See *ante* p. 87.   [30] Alexandria *Gazette etc.*, Jan. 11, 1859.

t for them with us, and in no case pay to him or any other person,
amount of his hire, without a written order from us.—George Walker
admitted, by common consent, to be the best leader of a band in all
eastern and middle Virginia." [31]

A still more peculiar kind of slave-hiring—if it may be
so classed—was that of one of the most famous of musical prodigies, " Blind Tom ". He was a babe when, about
1850, a Georgia planter bought him and his fieldhand
mother from a trader. Before Tom was ten years old,
although blind and semi-idiotic, he was attracting large
and enthusiastic audiences, but only in the Southern cities,
for he could not safely be taken out of the slave States.
He gave no less than five concerts in Charleston early in
1860. The master gained much money exhibiting the wonderful performances of this boy, while, it was said, the
mother continued her labor in the field.[32]

As a rule, with many exceptions, including mechanics,
male cooks, coachmen, barbers, tailors etc. past middle
age, the prices for hirings or " hires " were in proportion
to what the slaves would sell for. Like selling prices, they
varied widely according to circumstances of time, place,
ownership, reputed qualities of the individual slaves etc.
Accordingly there could be no precise standard, even in
one region, but only averages of relatively few specific
cases. It was the highest prices that were most talked
about. Thomas Jefferson Randolph said in 1832: " The
interest on money is 4 to 6 per cent. The hires of male
slaves is [sic] about 15 per cent upon their value: in ten
years or less, you have returned your principal with interest." [33] In the 'fifties the hiring price commonly
ranged from 10 to 20 per cent. of the market value of the
slave, apparently averaging from 12 to 15 per cent, with
numerous exceptions outside the extremes. When com-
pared with a slave's original cost, the percentage for the

[31] TOLER & COOK in Daily *Enquirer*, June 27, 1853.
[32] 8 *All the Year Round*, 126-29, gives many details about Tom.
[33] Speech of Jan. 21, 1832, p. 16.

hiring was often fully 25 per cent.[34]   There were two main reasons for great variations and high rates: first, an irrational and uneconomic demand for slaves, often much in excess of the value of their labor; and, secondly, the risk of losing both principal and interest if a slave died, unless there was a life-insurance, which was very rare.   For a woman with one or more little children only one-half, or less, the average price for hire might be obtained, for the children required much of her attention, must be fed by the hirer and would in other respects make the mother less desirable.   If a mother and three or four little children were properly cared for, her labor might be amply paid for by merely the increase in the value of the children during the year.   The prices for hirings, much more than for sales, depended on local or not distant conditions, for their range was seldom beyond 50 or 100 miles, except for boathands and laborers constructing railroads and canals.[35]

[34] Mrs. Catterall cites a large number of cases where the prices for hirings are given, but as important details are lacking, it would be absurd to try to draw precise conclusions from them.   Jack, worth at least $1,000, was hired out for $200 annually, i. e. for about 20 per cent. of what he would probably have sold for.—2 Catterall, 392.   A negro worth from $200 to $400 had been hired out for $100 per year, or from 50 per cent to 25; another, worth $200, hired for $8 per month, $96 per year, or 48 per cent; and still another, worth $350 hired for $120 or about 34 per cent.—2 Catterall, 524, 552, 488. All were exceptionally high.   It was estimated in a S. C. case that a cake-baker worth about $1500 would hire for about $20 per month, $240 per year, or 16 per cent.—2 Catterall, 446.   In cases cited 1 Catterall, 220 and 223, the percentages were 12 and 12½, respectively.   Numerous estimated or actual hires are cited, 2 Catterall, 374 and 460-61, and many more can be found by using the indexes.

[35] The Bureau of Agriculture at Washington made an investigation as to the average price paid for agricultural slave labor in 1860 from Virginia to Texas and reported as follows:—

	Men	Women	Youths: either sex, not under 14		Men	Women	Youths: either sex, not under 14
Va.	$105	$46	$39	Miss.	$166	$100	$71
N. C.	110	49	50	La.	171	120	72
S. C.	103	55	43	Texas	166	109	80
Ga.	124	75	57	Ark.	170	108	80
Fla.	139	80	65	Tenn.	121	63	60
Ala.	138	89	66	—Hammond, *The Cotton Industry*, 90.			

On account of financial depression, many of the hires for 1857, in northern Virginia, were said to have gone unpaid. The prices there for 1858 were somewhat lower and the demand for slaves was less.[36] Contemporary local reports about the hirings in Warrenton, West End, Fairfax, Centerville and Brentville show great variations during the three years 1858-60: male fieldhands were let out by the year for from about $80 to $140; women for from about $40 to $80; boys and girls for from about $25 to $75; railroadhands for about $150, and mechanics for from $150 to $175.[37] In 1859, Edmund Ruffin thought $1,200 " about the highest present price for young and able men ", in Virginia, and that they would hire for $130.[38] In Lynchburg in 1859, women, for cooks, etc. commanded from $50 to $75, and boys and girls from $25 to $50.[39]

Prices were called " unusually high " when, in the neighborhood of Lancaster, South Carolina, in 1860, "prime fieldhands, fellows, ranged from $150 to $175; women from $80 to $120 ",[40] which were about 12 to 15 per cent of what they would have sold for.

To report the prices of hirings among one's neighbors was like giving personal news, but to quote those paid in other States showed an intense public interest. If prices rose in Richmond, it was sure to be announced far and wide, because it was significant and important.[41] The hir-

[36] Alexandria *Virginia Sentinel*, Jan. 5, 1858.

[37] These statements are based on numerous reports from those places appearing in the Alexandria *Gazette* during the first week in January of 1858, 1859 and 1860.

[38] 26 *De Bow*, 657, 656. This showed that in his opinion the hire was about 11 per cent of the market value.

[39] Charleston *Tri-Weekly Mercury*, Jan. 4, 1859.

Trexler, *Slavery in Mo.*, 30-33, gives many interesting details about prices at different times in that State.

[40] Charleston, Daily *Mercury*, Jan. 7, 1860.

[41] " Hiring in Virginia.—The Richmond *Index* says owners and agents for the hiring of negroes in that city, are asking an advance of from 10 to 15 per cent. on last year's prices, and many are really taken at the advance."— Montgomery *Confederation*, Jan. 17, 1860.

ing of tobaccohands, as such, did not appreciably concern South Carolina, but the Charleston *Mercury* knew that its readers would be especially glad to learn that in Lynchburg they commanded from $130 to $180 annually.[42] And its quoting a lengthy article about hirings in North Carolina indicated that they were both common and that there was general curiosity about them.[43]

Because the work required of slaves hired for constructing railroads, canals etc. was severe and demoralizing, especially high prices must be paid. In 1859, even in Warrenton, Virginia, they commanded $150 annually, the employer having to take out an insurance on them and also give each slave one dollar a month for pocket-money.[44] In Lynchburg, railroad contractors were offering as high as $200 each for all able-bodied men they could procure.[45] The most vigorous and of the " prime fieldhand " class were sought at that price. In 1860, one firm

---

[42] *Tri-Weekly Mercury*, Jan. 4, 1859.

[43] " HIGH PRICES FOR TURPENTINE HANDS.—On Tuesday last six negro men were hired out for this year by J. P. McLean, guardian of the minor heirs of C. Hargrove, deceased, for $1326, being an average of $221 each. These are higher prices than have ever been known to be paid for turpentine hands in this country. Negroes generally hired unusually high this season.

Of the hiring at Raleigh, the *Standard* says: ' Negro men for ordinary farm and railroad work, hired from $100 to $125 per annum. Good cooks ranged from $75 to $100; house servants at from $60 to $75 and $80. Girls and boys in proportion. Turpentine hands were bringing $100 to $175. We learn that turpentine hands in some of the adjoining counties are hiring for from $200 to $225.'

At Goldsborough, the *Independent* says: ' Negro[e]s appeared to be in great demand, and hired at exorbitant rates. We saw some bring $300 and upward; field hands brought from $100 to $150; good cooks $100 and upwards, and small boys and girls from $40 to $75.'

At Wadesborough, the *Argus* says that ' field hands hired, for [from] a girl aged 14, at $44, to an able bodied man at $130. Good cooks went off as high as $75.'—Fayetteville *Observer*."—Charleston, S. C., *Mercury*, Jan. 12, 1860.

[44] Alexandria, Va., *Gazette*, Jan. 4, 1859.

[45] Charleston Tri-Weekly *Mercury*, Jan. 4, 1859.

of contractors in Georgia offered the same; [46] another offered $180, payable quarterly, and promised a weekly ration of " five pounds of bacon, one peck of meal, one quart of molasses, a quarter of a pound of soap and a quarter of a pound of tobacco ", and, as clothing for the year, " four shirts, four pair of shoes, two pair of summer pants, two pair of winter pants, a heavy well-lined coat, blanket and hat ". [47]

For firemen and deckhands the Memphis and New Orleans Packet Line in 1858 was paying $40 a month because of the hard work and risks. [48] This was presumably fully 30 per cent. of their market value. If they were insured, the master received the financial protection without lessening the physical danger to the slaves.

For obvious reasons hiring prices were highest in Mississippi, Louisiana and Texas. The Polks owned a faithful and profitable blacksmith, named Harry, who, reared a family of eleven children for them, was sent from Tennessee to Mississippi to be hired out, and remained many years. When he must have passed three-score his master received $487.00 annually for his hire. [49] A little later Thomas Dabney, in Mississippi, received $500.00 annually for the services of a young blacksmith. [50] In Louisiana a gang of 25 of all ages hired for $5,165.50. Most of them seem to have commanded from 15 to 20 per cent. of what they might have sold for. [51] At a public hiring in Colum-

[46] Augusta *Chronicle and Sentinel*, Jan. 7, 1860.

[47] *Chronicle and Sentinel*, Jan. 1, 1860. In Jan., 1858, the Nashville and Chattanooga Railroad was offering only from $125 to $150 per year for from 150 to 200 slaves.—Nashville *Repub. Banner*, Jan. 3, 1858.

[48] Memphis *Eagle and Enquirer*, Jan. 5, 1858.

[49] J. S. Bassett, ed., *The Plantation Overseer*, 161-63.

[50] Smedes, *A Southern Planter*, 104. Augustine Smith, a Mobile trader advertised a carpenter, 50 years old, for sale and added that he had been "hiring for $50 per month".—*Advertiser*, Jan. 12, 1860.

[51] "NEGROES RISING—HIGH PRICES. The following named slaves, belonging to the minor child of J. T. Shelton, deceased, were hired out at

bia, Texas, 31 negroes including men, women and children, brought a total of $7,650 for the year. One commanded $600, " and nearly half of them were bid off as high as $300 ", each.[52]

The hirer temporarily succeeded to the owner's authority over and obligations to the slave. He must supply food and clothing, but this meant little more than providing for the barest physical necessities—two suits of clothes, including a hat, shoes and a blanket for a man and corresponding clothing for a woman. It was made part of the contract in hiring by the year that the slaves should be returned well clothed, so as to make a favorable impression for a new engagement. The hirer was not bound to furnish a bed, but often did so.[53] The temporary master might punish the slave or cause him to be punished, but if the punishment was excessive and injury resulted, the hirer was liable for damages—to the owner,

Homer, Claiborne Parish, La., recently, for the year 1860, at the following high prices:

Harvey, blacksmith	$430 00	Bias, plow boy	$240 00
His wife	269 00	Wash, 12 years	161 00
Abe, field hand	330 50	Jim, old man	260 00
Iverson, "	360 00	Mitchell, field hand	327 00
Tom, "	315 00	Juda, old woman	171 00
Henry, "	302 00	Betsey, " and one child	336 00
Frank, "	340 00	Margaret, young woman	260 00
Bill, lame negro	246 00	Lucinda and 3 children	250 00
John, plow boy	201 00	Jand, old woman and 2 chil-	
Harrison, "	189 00	dren	178 00."

—29 De Bow's Review, 374.

[52] Memphis Weekly Avalanche, Jan. 31, 1860.

[53] The Misses Turnbull (2 American Photographs, 238) give details about the requirements in Richmond, which seem to be about the average for domestic servants.

"Today [Oct. 28, 1835, at Columbia, S. C., wrote Prof. Lieber] Tom, as we call him, entered our service. He is about fourteen years old, and we pay his master $4.50 a month. The little boy brings with him a blanket, which is all he ever had to sleep upon. He has but one shirt. Slavery is abominable in every respect.—Oct. 29. Last night Matilda and Abby (the nurse) made a mattress and pillow for little Tom ".—Perry, Life and Letters of Francis Lieber, 109.

6

of course. To prevent the neglect of slaves when ill, the most careful owners made a small extra payment to the agent. One Richmond firm advertised that " in case of sickness they see that every attention is paid, employing their own family physician, except when some other is preferred by the owner ". [54] Another, as has been mentioned, thought $3 for each slave enough for " medical attention "—" medicine gratis ". Almost any guarantee, prohibition or requirement might be made a part of the contract. [55] To change the slave from an understood and safe to a dangerous employment was at the hirer's risk. Unless otherwise stipulated, it was the hirer's loss if the slave shirked, became ill or ran away; but if he died, without fault of the hirer, the owner lost both the slave and the hire thereafter. [56]

There was an increasing practice of virtually hiring certain kinds of slaves to themselves—especially supposedly trustworthy and resourceful carpenters, blacksmiths, barbers, draymen, truck-gardeners etc.—by allowing them to earn and retain money according to their opportunities, on condition that they gave their masters stipulated sums or percentages of earnings each week or month. This, being in direct conflict with the spirit of slavery, was forbidden in all the slave States; but it was freely practiced, and prosecutions for violations of the laws were so rare as to be almost curiosities. [57] To the slaves it seemed

[54] Tabb & Son's Advt.

[55] It was provided in the case of several slaves belonging to the estate of Wm. Oswald, deceased, and hired out by auction by A. Brooks, that they were " not to be taken out of the county of Mobile; not to be employed on any water craft; no deduction will be made for lost time, but in case of death the hire will cease; the Administrator to furnish clothing and medical attendance."—Mobile *Advertiser*, Jan. 1, 1860.

[56] Anyone interested in the details of liability in hirings should read Wheeler's *Law of Slavery*, 152-64; Trexler, 34-35, for the law in Missouri; Catterall, *Judicial Cases* etc., indexes under " Hire of slaves ".

[57] Hurd, *Freedom and Bondage*, 798, gives references to the laws. Prof. H. M. Henry (*Police Control of the Slave in S. C.*, 100) could find only two cases of prosecutions in nine counties of S. C.

like attaining semi-freedom, and was accordingly much sought after. It was a great incentive to thrifty slaves to work with zest and save as much as possible, in the hope of being able to buy their entire freedom. Although this kind of hiring out was not usually financially disadvantageous to the masters, it gave them a complacent feeling of generosity.[58] But the great majority of slaves that wished to make such an arrangement fared like Polk's blacksmith: "Harry's efforts to hire his own time did not succeed. Polk was receiving too fine a return by the existing method."[59]

In tobacco factories and in lumber-camps, the hirers of slaves often gave them regular tasks, which were counted as the temporary master's minimum return for the price of the hire, and then the laborer was paid on his own account for all that he did in addition. Apart from the strict control, this was almost equivalent to a partial subletting of the slave to himself, and had a similar effect.[60]

All those privileges were *pro tanto* a refutation of the main excuse for slavery—that negroes would not work except under compulsion—and belied what the Laureate of Slavery sang:

> " The negro freeman—thrifty while a slave,
> Freed from restraint, becomes a drone or knave,
> Each effort to improve his nature foils,

---

[58] " One large, old woman I remember so well—maum Eva. She served as monthly nurse to the ladies over the town, and would pay my mother so much each month; ' Hiring her time ' she termed it. In this way she made considerable money and lived well, always having something nice to eat in her house."—Mrs. V. V. Clayton, *White and Black under the Old Regime*, 24-25.

R. Q. Mallard described one of his father's slaves as follows: " Harry Stevens was a very valuable slave, for he was a carpenter, pursuing his trade in Liberty [county, Ga.] and the adjoining counties, and paying his master a sure monthly and handsome wage, while laying by something for himself and the family."—*Plantation Life Before Emancipation*, 48.

[59] Bassett's comment in *The Plantation Overseer*, 162.

[60] Olmsted, *Seaboard etc.*, 102, 103, 153 ff.; Robert Russell, *North America*, 151-52.

Begs, steals, or sleeps and starves, but never toils,
For savage sloth, mistakes the freedom won,
And ends, the mere barbarian he begun." [61]

Those privileges were also the best means of developing and demonstrating skill, intelligence, self-reliance—the true stepping-stones to freedom.   For these reasons there was a popular radical outcry against them, which was well expressed in one sentence by Edward A. Pollard: " What we want especially in the South, is that the negro shall be brought down from those false steps which he has been allowed to take in civilization, and reduced to his proper condition as a slave." [62]   And it then passed for a wise observation to say that self-hiring was half freedom and half slavery and combined the evils of both. With different purposes, the only persons in each section who could look into the future agreed that " it must be all one thing or all the other ".

[61] Grayson, *The Hireling and the Slave*, 27.
[62] *Black Diamonds*, 55.

CHAPTER VIII

THE HEIGHT OF THE SLAVE-TRADE IN CHARLESTON

Charleston had an ancient, quaint and foreign appearance. In a few neighborhoods it was even brilliant and impressive. It had several churches and public buildings of pleasing architecture. Here and there were imposing, detached houses, with high ceilings, wide hallways, and on each floor a great verandah looking out on a luxuriant garden of beautiful semi-tropical trees, shrubs and flowers. The narrow streets were much more numerous than the broad, and were often lined with rude, ill-shapen, neglected structures, showing that comfortable living, neatness and thrift were virtues not generally practised by a large portion of the white inhabitants and were unknown to the colored. Happy-go-lucky negroes, slave or free, swarmed in alleys and side-streets. Only a little more than half of the city's population of about 40,000 in 1860 were white—a decline of about 2,500 since 1850.[1]

Parallel with the Cooper River are East Bay, State, Church and Meeting streets, in succession. Lower Broad street ends at East Bay street, and to the north of Broad are Chalmers and Queen streets. Within or close to the few blocks bounded by Broad, East Bay, Queen and Meeting streets, were the " Old Exchange or Customhouse ", the City-hall, the *Courier* and the *Mercury* buildings, the Charleston Library, nearly all the leading churches and banks, the offices of many lawyers, factors, brokers, commission merchants and of agents of railroad, steamboat and telegraph companies. Virtually all the buying, selling and hiring of slaves in Charleston was done in this small section.

[1] *Preliminary Rept. on U. S. Census 1860*, 242; *U. S. Census 1870, Population*, 258.

The " Old Exchange or Customhouse " at the foot of Broad street, on East Bay, is the most historic building in perhaps all the South. The Sons of the Revolution in South Carolina have placed on it a bronze tablet with an eloquent inscription saying that on this site was the guard-post of the early colonists of South Carolina; here Stede Bonnet and other pirates were imprisoned; this building was erected in 1767 as an exchange and customhouse; here the first independent government in America was set up; here Revolutionary patriots were incarcerated; from here Isaac Hayne was led to execution; here George Washington in 1791 was entertained by his grateful countrymen. With no less historical importance they might have added: From colonial days until after the middle of the nineteenth century from several hundred to many thousand slaves were annually sold to the highest bidders, in front or just north of this building. As the postoffice was long in the Exchange, visitors as well as residents called there daily for their mail, and, after about 10 A. M. on sale-days, were sure to notice the crowd that gathered about the slaves.

With both pen and pencil Eyre Crowe made vivid pictures of what he saw there March 10, 1853, when the red banner of the slave-broker and auctioneer Alonzo J. White was waving over a gang of 96.[2] In contrast with those dark and filthy salesrooms in Richmond, here all was in the balmy air under blue skies. The negroes, dressed in bright, clean, winter clothes, wearing striped, cotton caps or turbans, and crowded on platforms, were very conspicuous against the background of brick walls. Grouped about them were planters, traders and curious on-lookers, wearing long coats, high hats and beards of formal cut, listening to the auctioneer, questioning and inspecting the negroes, exchanging opinions and viewing the familiar

[2] Jan. 25, 1859, White elsewhere sold to Stephen D. Doar 33 negroes " as the property of Hon. R. B. Rhett ".—Robertson, Blacklock & Co. in acct. with S. D. Doar, MS.

THE OLD EXCHANGE OR CUSTOMHOUSE IN CHARLESTON

The bronze tablet is shown at the extreme right

THE AUCTION-PLACE JUST NORTH OF THE OLD EXCHANGE

but, to them, ever-interesting show. Just then the auctioneer was appealing for higher bids on a buxom negress standing by him on the auction-block and holding her infant. Near the outskirts of the crowd two slave pickaninnies, evidently forgotten for the moment, were crawling about. White's slave porter, a " blacksnake " whip in hand, sat on a horse, watching the gang and waiting to drive to the jail all slaves not taken in charge by their purchasers. On one side was a carefully shielded palmetto, emblem of the State. In the foreground was a howitzer, point down and half embedded like a hitching-post. It still impressively marks this truly historic spot.[3]

When, on January 7, 1852, a member of the French Academy witnessed a public sale of negroes there and, but a few steps away, of a horse and an ass, he called this common occurrence " *une scène hideuse* " and was astonished to learn that the auctioneer moved in good society.[4]

Undoubtedly this auctioneer was Thomas Norman Gadsden.[5] He was a grandson of Thomas Gadsden (a brother of General Christopher Gadsden of the Revolution) and a second-cousin of Christopher's three eminent Gadsden grandsons—John, a lawyer; Christopher E., a bishop and long the rector of St. Philip's Church; and James, soldier,

[3] Crowe, *With Thackeray in America*, 151-52; *Illustrated London News*, Nov. 29, 1856, pp. 555-56. About 1018, part of a building on the east side was torn down to make room for an automobile supply-station.

[4] J. J. Ampère, 2 *Promenade en Amérique*, 113.

[5] He held the only slave-auction the *Courier* mentioned for that day. It was of a gang of 42, belonging to the estate of John Vinyard and averaged $400. each, which was thought to indicate that slave property was increasing in value in S. C., for several aged and infirm negroes were among the number sold.—*Courier*, Jan. 8, 1852.

R. L. Carpenter, an English clergyman, witnessed sales there Apr. 9, 1850, " by a [slave] merchant I met the evening before. * * * Of course my acquaintance did not officiate in person, any more than the high-sheriff would act as hangman; meaner men are found ready to do the work."—*Observations on American Slavery*, 28. Probably this reference is also to Gadsden, for of all the persons mentioned by the traveler and the *Courier* as selling slaves that day, Gadsden is the only one likely to have been met at any social gathering.

planter in Florida and South Carolina, president of the South Carolina Railroad, Minister to Mexico and negotiator of the Gadsden Purchase,[6] living at " Pimlico ", his large rice plantation, about thirty miles up the Cooper River. These and one other brother were graduates of Yale and, besides many other Gadsdens, lived in or near Charleston. In a community where old families of high character were numerous, few stood higher than the Gadsdens. For about a quarter of a century Thomas Norman Gadsden—often called Norman Gadsden to distinguish him from numerous other Thomases in the family—was better known and probably sold more negroes (scrupulously spelt *negros* by Charlestonians for decades) than any other South Carolina trader.[7] He made what for that

[6] J. G. Bulloch, *Families of Bellinger and De Veaux* (Savannah, 1895), 100-101.

[7] Advts. in the *Courier* in Jan., 1833, indicate that, next to Hugh McDonald, who was shipping many slaves to New Orleans, Gadsden was already the largest trader. The scope and variety of his business 20 years later are partly shown by seven advts. which appeared in the *Courier* of Jan. 4, 1853. After the first advt. unimportant details and repetitions are omitted:—

1. " By THOMAS N. GADSDEN.
At private sale, forty prime NEGROS, consisting of prime young field men, waitingmen, waiting and house servants, plough boys, well grown families, one tight cask cooper, one blacksmith, two young women, field hands. Apply as above at N. W. COR. STATE & CHALMERS-STS., Broker, Auctioneer and General Commission Agent."

2. " TO HIRE, two prime young men, BRICKLAYERS and PLASTERERS."

3. " THIS DAY, the 4th inst., will be sold at the North side of the Exchange, at 11 o'clock, ROBERT, a first rate House Servant and Waitingman, about 24 years old, warranted sound. Terms cash, purchaser to pay me for bill of sale."

4. " *VIRGINIA NEGROS.* [Same time and place.] One uncommonly prime WOMAN, 27 years old, a good cook, washer, ironer, and general good house-servant, under a warranted character, with her 4 children, 12, 10, 5 and 3 years old. ALSO, A very prime WOMAN, 30 years old, and a complete cook, washer and ironer, under warranted character; with her 4 children, 13, 10, 9 and 4 years old."

5. " *FIELD NEGROS.* [Same time and place.] July, an elderly Man, but stout and able bodied. EVE, his wife, 45 years old, a good field hand. MESSIC, a very likely Boy, 13 years old, a field hand. MARY, a likely GIRL, about 8 years old, and ROBERT, a likely BOY, about 4 years old."

A Slave-Auction at the N

From a drawing from life made by Eyre C

Exchange, March 10, 1853

rated London News of November 29, 1856

time and place was a very large fortune.[8] Early in the 'fifties he purchased the spacious, handsome house (116 Broad street, next east of St. Andrew's Hall) built by the " Dictator " John Rutledge, and employed the most artistic ironworker in the State to ornament its front door and balconies. They still compel admiration.[9] Christopher Gadsden and John Rutledge were the leading spirits in South Carolina in 1765 and represented their State in the Stamp Act Congress at New York City. In the 1850's, a slave-trading grand-nephew of one was flourishing in the quondam mansion of the other. This was much less inappropriate than it may seem, for it was John Rutledge that said of the foreign slave-trade: " Religion and humanity have nothing to do with this question." The African slave-trade did not damage Henry Laurens and his contemporaries that engaged in it. Why should the domestic slave-trade, much less brutal, seriously injure Thomas Norman Gadsden, if he possessed education and sociability to match his wealth and kinships?

Good as slavery seemed, and necessary and profitable as was the trade, there were grave practical objections to continuing the slave-auctions there by the Exchange: the

6. "*COMPLETE SEAMSTRESS.* [Same time and place.] A very prime WOMAN, about 32 years old, a most complete seamstress, washer, ironer and clear starcher, to be sent out of city, but not to go out of the State."

7. "An able bodied MAN named Jack; to be sold [Jan. 5th, north of the Exchange] without any warrantee of soundness whatever."

For some choice bits from his slave-trading correspondence, and his bill for advertising, boarding and selling a slave, see 2 Catterall, 406-07 and 444-45.

[8] In 1859 he paid taxes on Charleston real estate valued at $134,700. There were only four persons, two estates and a company paying taxes on higher valuations: Wm. Aiken on $290,600, Thomas Bennett on $252,000, Otis Mills on $165,000, and Miss H. Pinckney on $148,600. The estate of Isaac Barrett paid taxes on $149,500 and that of R. F. Henry on $146,100. Otis Mills & Co. had $227,000 in real estate.—*Tax Payers of Charleston for 1859.*

[9] "The heavy iron balconies and fence * * * were added by Mr. Thomas Norman Gadsden, who bought it in 1853."—The Huger Smiths' *Dwelling Houses of Charleston,* 255. A later writer has carefully dissociated the old slave-trader's name with this house. See Mrs. Leiding's *Historic Houses of S. C.,* 9.

crowd often overflowed into East Bay street and obstructed traffic; it was sure to attract the attention and excite the condemnation of Northern and foreign travelers. This naturally irritated the better class of Charlestonians, who were highly intelligent, well-bred, hospitable, and rightly wished to be judged by their best qualities and not by the worst phase of slavery. Finally a city ordinance forbade the sale of negroes, horses, carriages etc. near the Exchange, after July 1, 1856. For several months subsequently the traders held public as well as private sales in or just outside of their offices—Capers & Heyward, on the south side of Adger's wharf, Thomas N. Gadsden on the northwest corner of Chalmers and State streets, Wilbur, Oakes and others at their respective places in State street. As early as July, 1856, Thomas Ryan & Son had both a salesroom—which was described as " the Auction Mart in Chalmers-street, next to [and east of] the German Engine House "—and also a " lot " or " yard ", " immediately in the rear " of it.[10] They were very convenient and soon met with general favor. Before the end of the 'fifties virtually all public sales of negroes, except some by legal process, were held at what was variously called " Ryan's Mart ", " the Mart in Chalmers street " and, finally, " the Slave Mart ". Its exterior appearance and that of the immediate neighborhood changed but slightly during the next sixty years. The building was originally 44 by 20 feet, and there was a 22 by 18 foot yard in the rear. The façade resembles nothing seen elsewhere. On either side is an octagonal pillar more than 20 feet high, with a graceful arch between them. The Mart, a salesroom with a 20-foot ceiling, was light and airy, for the space below the arch was open, so

[10] These facts are gathered from numerous advts. of slave-auctions. According to the *Census of the City of Charleston, 1861*, it was No. 8. It and No. 6, also a brick building east of it, were owned by Ziba B. Oakes, the trader. Nos. 4 (brick) and 2 (wood, on the n. w. cor. of State and occupied by T. N. Gadsden) were owned by Theo. A. Whitney.

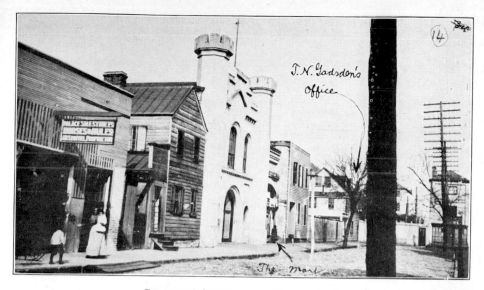

T. N. Gadsden's Office

The Mart

CHALMERS STREET AS IT WAS IN 1907

THE SLAVE-MART BUILDING AS IT WAS IN 1907

Negro tenements had been built inside

that the auction table, about 10 feet long and 3 feet high, might be placed lengthwise near it and allow ample room for the spectators to pass in and out and stand either inside of the building or in the street, according to the weather.[11]

Just back of the Mart and the engine-house, but facing Queen street, and only a few rods east of the Huguenot church, was " Ryan's nigger-jail ". The jail proper was a detached double-house—four stories high, with barred windows, and bolts and locks on every door—in a lot 60 feet wide and 175 feet deep. Brick walls, about 20 feet high, helped to make, out of what had probably been some rich man's residence, an exceptionally large and complete slave-jail and slave-pen.[12] Between the lot of the Mart and that of the jail a heavy gate, with iron bars and a brass padlock, opened on stone steps.

In March, 1858, Charles Mackay, then writing his *Life and Liberty in America,* spent many days in and near Charleston. Like all distinguished travelers he was beset with adroit and confident arguments in defense of slavery. If he would not yield to arguments, he should at least visit a plantation, see the conditions and learn how erroneous his preconceptions were. He accepted an invitation from General James Gadsden to visit " Pimlico ". Thus South Carolina's perhaps best known planter was to demonstrate one way what her best known trader for a quarter of a century had demonstrated the other way. How strange and yet how typical of the old South! The

[11] Not long after the Civil War a two-story negro tenement was built within the Mart, leaving a passageway on the east side, through the right-hand door, shown in the photograph taken by the author in 1907. Before 1922 the tenements had been removed, the rear walls had been extended, covering most of the lot, the Mart had been repaired and turned into an automobile salesroom.

[12] The cooking was done in what originally was probably the kitchen and servants' quarters—a two-story brick building, a little back of the jail but on the east side of the lot. In the southwest corner of the yard was a small structure called the " dead-house ", the morgue. It was there when the premises were first inspected, in 1902, but all except a few bricks and other slight signs of it had disappeared by 1922. The jail and the kitchen were still there in 1922.

host was cordial, frank, attentive, and the talk, food and drink perfected mental and physical enjoyments. The guest was appreciative, open-minded, eager to see and understand the strange phenomena of slavery and of rice culture. He learned how the rice-fields were plowed and flooded; why the mules were often worked in boots and the slaves went barefooted. He saw the not uncomfortable slave cabins, the hospital where the sick were cared for, the chapel where a missionary twice on Sunday discoursed of God's grace and of the duties of slaves to their masters, and the nursery where about seventy children were watched and fed while their mothers were working in the rice swamps. These swarming little "hominy-eaters"—as the General called them, for eating hominy was, as yet, their only serious occupation—were so fat and shiny that the guest doubted if it would be possible to collect a plumper and merrier set of children in any country under the sun. They grinned, chuckled, ran about like playful puppies, broke out in childish guffaws and finally sang some religious hymns in that quaint and musical half-moan peculiar to negroes. A little later the visitor was amazed by suddenly being implored, in broken English, by hale old "Uncle Tom", who had been on this plantation for nearly half a century, to be allowed to remain where he was instead of being taken to Africa. The visitor's amazement and the slave's fear disappeared when the merry General explained that it was all a joke: Dr. Mackay had not come to carry the old African back to his native jungles. Tom considered a cigar and a glass of whiskey ample compensation for his temporary distress. Although the visitor still had some lingering misgivings about "the peculiar institution", he concluded: "On this plantation I have no doubt, from what I saw, that the slaves are kindly treated, and that the patriarchal relation in all its best aspects exists between the master and his poor dependents."[13]

[13] Charles Mackay, 1 *Life and Liberty in America*, 319 ff.

RYAN'S "NIGGER JAIL"

Showing the rear, the kitchen (on the right) and part of the yard, as they looked in 1907

" Pimlico " was and was to be more typical than the guest supposed.

Dr. Mackay was evidently kept so busy with social attentions that he quite forgot the importance of investigating Charleston's slave-trade. He seems not even to have heard of the Mart, although every number of Charleston's newspapers contained many advertisements of sales there, pocketed on a side-street. In all the South there was not another city where the traffic in negroes could have been so easily and advantageously studied. But that was a fact which the courteous and amiable Charlestonians very naturally did not mention, a study they did not encourage.

In Charleston, even more than in Richmond, the words *trader* and *negro-trader* had come to be shunned, except colloquially: as the business increased, the precise designation was avoided. Most of the men dealing in slaves advertised as " brokers, auctioneers, and commission agents " for the purchase and sale of real estate, negroes (in Charleston carefully spelt " negros " and in South Carolina legally meaning slaves),[13a] stocks, bonds, etc. Their business cards daily appeared in the newspapers along with those of lawyers and physicians and the advertisements of merchants and of various kinds of enterprises. And in the *Courier's* column of " city intelligence " brief notices of an exhibition of Rosa Bonheur's paintings, of a theatrical benefit, of the digging up of human bones in a tidal drain, of the annual meeting of the Carolina Art Association and of the organization of a Robert Burns Club, were accompanied by the following:

" *Negros Arrived.*—The [220] Negros belonging to the estate of Colonel J. E. McPherson, advertised to be sold tomorrow, the 16th inst., by J. W. Gray, Master in Equity, have arrived and may be seen at the Jail." [14]

[13a] " The word ' negroes ' has a fixed meaning (slaves) ."—Quoted, 2 Catterall, 311.

[14] *Courier*, Feb. 15, 1860. The sale continued two days and the slaves brought an average of $600.—*Courier*, Feb. 17, and *Mercury*, Feb. 18, 1860.

That looked as if slave-trading was highly respectable. By persistently calling themselves " brokers ", the traders compelled brokers of other kinds to describe themselves as stock-, cotton-, insurance-, ship-, or exchange-brokers etc. They disposed of slaves both privately and by public outcry, and as readily took orders to buy as to sell. As brokers they received two and one-half per cent, while the local and visiting " nigger-speculators " bought outright and ran the possible risks for the probable profits. Doubtless some of them originally intended not to deal in slaves; but Charleston had a sluggish market for stocks, real estate (except plantations) and general merchandise, especially during the months when slave-trading was most active and profitable.

When Mrs. Stowe printed a table showing that during two weeks in November, 1852, 64 newspapers in eight States offered 4,100 slaves for sale, it was considered incredible.[15] Yet two issues of the Charleston *Courier*, twenty-four years apart, give more amazing information. That of February 23, 1836, contained 29 slave advertisements: four were about four runaways, and 25 related to buying, selling or hiring about 900 negroes. In the same issue three bookdealers advertised for sale *The South Vindicated from the Treason and Fanaticism of Northern Abolitionists*. " This is a most triumphant vindication of the outraged South, and should be in the family circle of every friend of the country ", said one of the advertisements.

The *Courier* of January 2, 1860, contained 38 slave advertisements: three referred to three runaways, six to hiring six slaves, and 29 pertained to 1914 slaves then for sale privately or soon to be put on the block. All but 366 of these were in the Charleston market. The *Mercury* of the same date had 32 slave advertisements about 1936

[15] *Key to Uncle Tom's Cabin*, 142-43. The disclosure still seemed remarkable to Mr. Rhodes, 40 years later.—1 *Hist. U. S.*, 324.

slaves: four to recover runaways, and one by an anonymous " planter " in New Orleans desiring to buy " 50 to 100 " (say 75), and 27 called attention to 1857 negroes for sale at once or in the near future—1521 in Charleston and 336 elsewhere. The *Courier's* advertisements mentioned 191 slaves that were not in the *Mercury's*. Thus two newspapers in Charleston on the same day advertised 2048 slaves for sale in the near future, or half as many as Mrs. Stowe found offered in eight States by 64 newspapers during two weeks. That is why Charleston had so many " brokers ".

Before the end of the 'fifties Charleston had perhaps outstripped Richmond as a selling-market. Yet few persons except interstate traders suspected, as a Mississippi newspaper said, that South Carolina had " for the last eight or ten years thrown upon us [Mississippi] more slaves than any one of the old slave States ". [16] Without an exhaustive search in the *Directory for 1859* and in the *Courier* and the *Mercury* for 1859-60, it has been found that more than fifty residents were engaged in buying or selling slaves as at least a part of their business. [17] Not many of these—not even Thomas Ryan

[16] Olmsted, *Back Country*, 285.

[17] **TRADERS, AUCTIONEERS OR BROKERS IN SLAVES, 1859-60:**
All but a few of the persons whose names follow have been found advertising slaves for sale in 1860, as a part of their business. The few and nearly all the others were designated as brokers or auctioneers in the *Directory for 1859*.

Alexander, Thomas, [1859], broker, house 11 Horlbeck alley.

Austin, Robert, [1859],	broker, 10 State st.
Baker, J. Russell,	17 State st.
Bennett & Rhett,	28 Broad st.
Bowers, J. E.,	5 State st.
Capers & Heyward,	S. side Adger's whf.
Cohen, Jacob & Sons,	24 Broad st.

DeLeon, H. H., [1859] broker & auc'r, 119 E. Bay.

DeSaussure, Louis D.,	23 Broad st.
DeWitt, G.,	17½ State st.
Drayton, Charles E. R.,	W. side State st., four doors north of Chalmers.
Faber, Joseph W.,	67 Meeting st.

& Son—dealt exclusively in slaves; some annually specu-
lated in, or obtained commissions on, only a small number,
while others, in one way or another, dealt in many hundred. Certainly a score or two more—among the factors,
the brokers, the auctioneers and the commission merchants,
nominally selling only cotton, rice, real estate etc.—incidentally accepted opportunities likewise to increase their
incomes.

Crowded were the public and the private jails, the
yards and the rear buildings of the " brokers ", and the
otherwise vacant warehouses and stables. But the supply did not exceed the demand. Knowing all about the

Ford, J. Drayton,	24 Broad st.
Gadsden, Thomas N.,	N. W. corner Chalmers & State sts. [Listed as still active in 1859.]
Gilchrist, J. M., [1859]	broker & com. mcht., 11 State st.
Gourdin, Wm. Allston,	Meeting st., opposite S. C. Institute Hall.
Hume, Thomas M.,	29 Broad st.
Laborde, J. P.,	4 Chalmers st.
Lee, Hutson,	51 Broad st.
Lockwood, P. L.,	No address found. In the *Mercury*, Dec. 7, 1860, under " Auctioneers' Private Sales ", he adver- tised " a fine plantation carpenter ".
McBride, M.,	1 Chalmers st.
McCall, B.,	1 State st.
Marshall, R. M.,	33 Broad st.
Mordecai, B.,	5 State st.
Nipson, Francis,	No address found. He advertised sales at the Mart, Apr. 12, 1860, and other days.
Oakes, Z. B.,	7 State st.
Olsen, C. M.,	19 State st.
Ottolengui, J., [1859]	broker, 20 Broad st.
Porcher & Baya,	25 Broad st.
Rhett & Fitzsimons,	40 Broad st.
Riggs, J. S.,	4 State st.
Rodgers, T. L., [1859]	broker & auc'r, 6 State st.
Ryan, J. S.,	22 Broad st.
Ryan, Thomas & Son,	12 State st.
Salinas, A. J.,	6 State st.
Shingler Bros.,	7 Broad st.
Simons, Wm.,	No address found. Under " Auctioneers' Private Sales " he advertised " a complete house- servant ", in the *Mercury*, Dec. 7, 1860.

resources of this market, two firms of interstate traders were each advertising for the purchase of 500 slaves,[18] and many other Southwestern traders had regular buyers here. The *Courier* alone during January, 1860, shows that the Charleston " brokers " disposed of more than 2,200 negroes that month. Probably there were a few hundred others, enough to make a total of about 2,500. As many were superior slaves, commanding from $1,000 to $1,200 or more, each, the whole number must have brought more than $1,500,000, perhaps nearly $2,000,000. January was the busiest month of the season—November to March, both inclusive. During the other seven months the trading was comparatively slight. $4,000,000 is a conservative estimate of Charleston's slave-trading for the exceptional year after October, 1859,—about the same as Richmond's in 1856.

Whence came these slaves for the market? From Virginia and the border States, or were they natives of South Carolina? What were their qualities? Why were they sold? And whither did they go?

During about a fortnight, more than a thousand were driven to the jails or the pens. A gang of 102 came from a rice plantation on the Peedee and were taken to the Jail for custody and inspection pending sale at the Mart on January 5th. There were 100 from the Colleton district, 120 from St. Thomas Parish, 164 from the Santee River, 36 from James Island, 235 from up the Cooper River, and numerous other gangs, families or individuals from

Spencer, Seth,   10 State st.
White, Alonzo J.,   27 Broad st.
Whitney, T. A.,   No address given in his advts.
Wilbur & Son,   S. W. corner State and Chalmers.
Willis, Henry, [1859] broker & auc'r, 83 Church st.
Willis, Henry, Jr., [1859] broker, 19 State st. He was called an " exchange broker ", as were Shingler Bros., who often sold gangs of slaves.

[18] Forrest, Jones & Co. of Memphis, and G. A. Robinson at 90 Church st., Charleston.—*Courier*, Jan. 23, Feb. 20, 1860. See *post* p. 263 n.

various neighborhoods not far from Charleston. Most
of them were brought by coast or river packets. If not
locked up in one of the many warehouses near the
wharves, they were most often driven up Queen street
to Ryan's " nigger jail " or on to the somber and still
impressive Charleston Jail, there in Magazine street.[19]
Almost daily large troops in faded, dirty clothes were
seen shuffling along in loose, irregular file, in the dusty
streets,—never on the sidewalks. At a distance, a
stranger in the South might have mistaken them for
weary, herded families of vagabonds. That was when
they were arriving. Like others elsewhere, they presented
a very different appearance when moving in the opposite
direction—to the Mart.

Anyone in Charleston on January 9, 1860, and at all
curious about the slave-trade, would have found the Mart
and Ryan's jail the most interesting places to visit. The
leading newspapers from Charleston to Galveston had
advertised the " remarkably prime gang " about to be
sold.[20] Traders and planters from many parts of the South
had responded in person or with orders. It was hardly
less an advantage than a pleasure for local traders, " brokers ", auctioneers, factors and, not rarely, lawyers to
attend such great sales, for accurate knowledge of the value
of slave property was important to all of them. Numerous
others were never absent on such occasions—those idle
persons that went where the attractions of the day were

---

[19] " NOTICE.—NEGROS (either singly or in gangs), will be received in
the Charleston Jail on as favorable terms as elsewhere, for safe keeping.
Accommodations roomy.—JOSEPH POULNOT, Jailor ".—*Courier*, Jan. 7,
1852.

Not many years previously the Work House was much used for the same
purpose, and until after the ordinance of September 25, 1849, slaves put there
for custody and sale were not kept apart from the negro criminals.

[20] Advts. of this sale in both the *Courier* and the *Mercury* since the middle
of Nov. had requested the New Orleans *Picayune* and *Delta*, the Memphis
Eagle and Enquirer, the Mobile *Register* and the Galveston *News* to copy
three times and send their bills to Shingler Bros.

greatest, and snobs that fancied themselves of the aristocracy because they followed and could gossip familiarly about planters and cite the high prices slaves were commanding. A great planter's death and funeral were of much less extensive popular interest than the public sale of his negroes.

For nearly a week this gang had been subject to inspection at the Mart,[21] but that did not preclude more of it at the sale. To facilitate this, the slaves were arranged as much as possible in a row around the yard of the jail with their backs to the wall. Each slave or mother and infant wore a number that corresponded with one in a printed descriptive " list " or " catalogue ", giving the age, habitual occupation and any other important fact. In ancient Rome, a scroll hanging from the neck of a slave for sale served the same purpose. Some were stripping and others were dressing, and still others were all but naked, while prospective buyers satisfied themselves that there were no serious whip-scars, no signs of rheumatism or of more serious diseases, which at first were hard to detect but might make a slave almost as much to be shunned as a mad-dog. Yes, those nearly 250 were all to be sold that day, if long enough. And many others, soon to be sold, were there in the jail, where barred windows were filled with the woolly heads and the shiny faces of temporary prisoners, eager to see what to them was the most interesting of spectacles. And they were wondering if, when their day came and they could put on their carefully guarded new clothes, they would sell for a high price and go to a " quality " planter near Georgetown or Beaufort or the Savannah River—or whether some mean but prosperous overseer or some meaner trader would bid them in and take them to a hopelessly remote region.

[21] The *Mercury* of Jan. 4, 1860, had announced that they had " arrived, and can be seen at the Mart ", which indicates that at this time Ryan's jail was a part of the Mart.

As St. Michael's musical bells sounded one quarter-hour after another from ten o'clock, through State and Church streets to the Mart there was a leisurely movement of men from Broad street, where lawyers, brokers, traders, factors, merchants and planters casually exchanged courtesies, when going to or returning from the postoffice or on some other errand. When eleven o'clock sounded, the inspections were still going on. Soon the slave porter ordered about a score of those to be sold first to prepare to move. He led them through the gateway into the yard of the Mart. They all seemed passive, almost indifferent, except that the whites of their wide-open and rolling eyes disclosed anxiety and made a strange contrast with their ebony faces. There was no haste, no impatience. Finally the auctioneer mounted a long table-like platform extending lengthwise of the Mart, and, with mingled dignity and deference slowly spoke in about these words:—" Gentlemen, ah you radey? *You*-all bein' heah shows that this is an important sale. Ez you know, two-hundud an' thirty-odd niggrahs ah to be sol '. The notice of the sale has tol' you they ah a very prime an' valu'ble gang, 'customed to the culchah o' rice an' provisions, an' among 'em ah valu'ble coopahs, kyahpentahs, blacksmiths, boathan's, drivahs, an' so fo'th an' so fo'th. The whole plantation o' twenty-three hundud acahs whah they wah raised an' worked, has been offered at private sale. An' now you ah heah to buy this prime an' likely gang o' two hundud an' thirty-odd head o' niggrahs, which ah sol' fo' no fault, but, ez you know, to close out all o' this kind o' property belongin' to the late Gen'al Gadsden's Pimlico plantation."

What a surprising change since those merry days at Pimlico! Were the negroes of one planter in a hundred thus sold? Yes, it was a common occurrence, but, like death, all such cases seemed exceptional to the persons concerned. The slaves were usually worth much more than all the rest of a good plantation, including the real estate, livestock, equipments, produce, etc., and were readily both mortgageable and salable at good prices. Therefore part or all of them were put on the market when a planter died leaving considerable debts or several heirs. Scores of such cases could be cited; thousands of them might easily be found in Southern newspapers and probate records. And it was typical of the frequency with which both small and large plantations and gangs of slaves were sold that the *Mercury* of January 2, 1860, advertised for sale 21 gangs of 10 or more slaves each and 25 plantations.

James Gadsden completed his three score and ten years in the spring of 1858, shortly after Charles Mackay's visit, and died the following Christmas. Pimlico's great live-oaks, draped in funereal hanging-moss, seemed to weep and moan; and scores of his slaves did, indeed, weep and moan, for " Ol' Mawsa " was dear to them. They could not imagine that anyone else outside of Bible history had ever been so great and powerful. And they considered that his greatness and distinction were also their personal possessions. When the body was removed to St. Philip's church for the last ceremonies and burial in the churchyard, December 27, 1858, none more than old " Uncle Tom " could have envied the favorite servants that accompanied the mourning family. Presumably few of the fieldhands born on the plantation had ever seen or expected to see Charleston. But there " at the Mart in Chalmers street ", under the hammer of the auctioneer and " goin '—*goin* ',—GONE " to whomsoever bid highest for each individual, small group or " family ", were the Pimlico slaves of one of the best of South Carolina's many good " patriarchs "—General Gadsden.

And that was about what General Gadsden must have expected to happen. He was heavily in debt on his own account and still more so for notes given by J. Gadsden & Company. There was a mortgage on his slaves for $9,000, which had to be paid off before they could be sold. And

shortly before his death he had sent a slave to a Broad
street " broker ".[22]   Where there were many legatees
of a planter's estate much encumbered by debt,[23] they
were likely to insist on an early sale for division so as
to escape the risks and consuming expense of adminis-
tration and probable mismanagement.   Ere a year's crop
had been disposed of, it was decided to put the Pimlico
estate on the market.   It was hoped that the slaves might
be purchased by one person, to prevent the separation of
families and friends.   They were at first offered exclusively at private sale,[24] then " at private sale as an entire
gang, up to the fifth of January ".[25]   At that time of inflated prices it was probably expected that the 235 negroes
would sell privately for nearly or quite $200,000—half
cash and the rest in a year with interest.   No satisfactory
offer came.   Few planters in all the South could arrange
for such a purchase.   The factors, the bankers and the
interstate traders that had ample resources for it knew
how and when to buy more advantageously.   General
Gadsden must have foreseen that it was only a little more

[22] The item in the administrator's account reads: " July 30, 1859, Nett
proceeds of Man April No. 229 on appraisement appraised at $500, sold
by R. M. Marshall, Broker, this Negro having been placed in his hands
for sale previous to the death of Genl. Gadsden. $516.24 ".

[23] In his last will and testament, made in 1853, he bequeathed all his
property to his wife with power to dispose of it as she might choose.   But
he directed that, in case she should not avail herself of her rights, the
property should be divided into eleven parts and be distributed among his
four living brothers (Thomas, Philip, Alexander and Octavus), one sister
and the children of those deceased.

[24] *Courier*, Nov. 15, 1859.   This was a common practice and, with large
plantation gangs, likely to result as this offer did.   It was so with the Cabell
estate, sold for division by E. C. Cabell of Tallahassee, Fla., and H. C.
Cabell of Richmond, comprising 4,500 acres of land, 118 Negroes, 36 mules
and horses, plantation stock, implements and produce.   " The Negroes are
likely family Negroes. originally from Va.   Among them are plantation
carpenters, a good plantation blacksmith, a good family cook, and house
servants * * * The Negroes will be sold for cash " * * * .—Savannah *Republican*,
Dec. 25, 1858.

[25] *Mercury*, Jan. 6, 1860, and many previous days.

certain that his funeral would be in St. Philip's church, where one of his brothers was long rector, than that his slaves would be sold at the Mart, hardly 100 feet from the office of his second-cousin Thomas Norman Gadsden. But the General was a " patriarch " and Thomas N. was a slave-trader.

As only 174 of the Pimlico slaves were disposed of on January 9th, at an average of $700,[26] the auction was continued on the 10th, when many of the most valuable were sold. The 235 brought nearly $176,000, or an average of almost $750 for all ages.[27]

Stephen D. Doar, a very thrifty and prosperous planter near the South Santee River, paid not quite $13,000 for 19, and S. E. Habersham, presumably a Georgia planter, nearly $20,000 for about 25. But what of the traders, especially those in Charleston we know so well? Five of them bought a total of probably about 40 slaves, paying over $31,000—Z. B. Oakes $3,880, A. J. Salinas $2,200, Robert Austin $6,540, Thomas Ryan $7,000, B. Mordecai $12,000. If they had been acting as agents, the names of their principals, or at least some of them, would have appeared in the administrator's account.[28] Thus many of the Pimlico slaves must have been resold publicly or privately in Charleston and other markets.

On January 10th, other gangs besides the Gadsden remnant of 61 were brought into the Mart—one of 65 and another of 25.[29] The sale of a gang of 100 and of another

[26] *Mercury*, Jan. 10, 1860.

[27] Shingler Bros., the auctioneers, on June 30, 1860, turned over to the administrator $87,922.32 as the cash half-payment. The rest was due in Jan., 1861.

[28] The first half-payments were in cash, directly or indirectly, and the second in bonds or notes, which were readily cashed by banks and commission merchants.

Mrs. Gadsden's sister, Miss S. R. Hort, cashed the bonds of two of the most thoroughgoing State-street traders, Mordecai and Oakes, for about $8,000, and of two other purchasers for nearly half as much.

[29] The gang of 65 sold at an average of $625 and that of 25 [the 26

of 124, originally set for that day, had to be postponed. Small lots were occasionally sent to the Mart with little, if any, previous notice. Z. B. Oakes sold three girls there that day: Emma, an excellent cook and washer, 18 years old, because unsound was resold " on account and risk of former owner ", for $910; " Sarah, a likely girl, seamstress and lady's maid, 16 years old ", for $1,000, and " Juliet, a likely brown girl, 14 years old ", for $970.[30] That was a fair sample of what " likely " girls brought in Charleston. Both Sarah and Juliet were servants of " good character and sold for no fault whatever ", but only " to change investment "—a euphemism commonly employed to obtain the highest price, to preclude the inference (and perhaps to conceal the fact) that the seller was either in financial straits or was a speculator. They were announced as for sale only to residents of Charleston, but this did not bar local traders from buying.[31] Also on that day J. Russell Baker put on the block an unnamed " single-boy, about eight years of age ", who was " warranted sound ", and said to be " very smart ".[32]

These 329, sold at the Mart on January 9th and 10th, 1860, must have brought nearly a quarter of a million dollars. And that was only a part of the trading during those two days.

In the busiest season there were rarely less than from 25 or 50 slaves advertised for sale privately; sometimes there were hundreds—on January 17, 1860, the *Courier* alone announced as many as 234. There were many others, not advertised but merely listed at the offices of the " brokers "; and secret and direct buying and selling for speculation or use were common. Of course not all offered

mentioned in the report was presumably due to a birth] at an average of $665.—*Mercury*, Jan. 11, 1860.

[30] *Mercury*, Jan. 10, 11, 1860.

[31] Such and other restrictions will be noticed in the next chapter.

[32] All these advts. were in both the *Courier* and the *Mercury* of Jan. 10, 1860.

at private sale were so disposed of; many had to be sold
at auction. By quitting the sights and talk at the Mart,
on the second day of the Gadsden sale, January 10, 1860,
and walking a few hundred yards, one could have learned
much that was interesting about this private trading. At
29 Broad street " broker " Hume was welcoming inquiries
about a gang of 72 " very prime " negroes accustomed to
the culture of cotton and provisions. For custody and
inspection this gang had been sent to the Mart and Ryan's
jail, in time to witness some of the outdoor proceedings
there on the 9th and 10th. As no satisfactory private
offer for them had been received, Hume was expecting to
sell them publicly on the 12th, but on the 11th the whole
gang was sold privately " at an average of $665 each ".
After like expectations, Capers & Heyward privately obtained an average of $750 for a gang of 30. At 25 Broad
street a member of a distinguished Huguenot family, the
head of the busy slave-selling firm of P. J. Porcher &
Baya, was calling attention to " a remarkably likely
woman of good character, about 25 years of age, a first-rate
seamstress, and a good washer and ironer and cook "—a
perfect house-servant, in fact—named Ellen, with her son
March, a " likely and sprightly boy, about eight years
old ". Another of Huguenot origin, Wm. Allston Gourdin,
was ready to explain to anyone that called at his " brok-
erage, auction and commission rooms ", on Meeting street
opposite Institute Hall, where many important public as-
semblies were held, the advantages of buying Emma, a
cook 26 years old, and her child. Joseph W. Faber, at
67 Meeting street, just south of Hibernian Hall, where
Thackeray gave a course of lectures in 1853, was making
a specialty of " several families of servants [presumably
15 or 20 persons] accustomed to the city, who are not sold
for fault ". This chanced to be a poor day to visit State
street, where traders McCall, Baker, Bowers, Mordecai,
Oakes, Olsen, Riggs, Thomas Ryan & Son, Salinas,
Spencer, Wilbur & Son and others had their offices. Only

McCall, of this State-street group ,was advertising any one
for sale privately—" Ann, about 30 years old, a good cook,
washer, ironer, and general servant." [33]

The best place to go was 23 Broad street. There one
could have found Louis D. DeSaussure.[34] The DeSaussures
were intellectually equal and socially not inferior to the
Gadsdens. Louis was the grandson of Chancellor Henry
William De Saussure, called the Chesterfield of South
Carolina, and the Chancellor's son Henry A. was Louis's
father. Both, father and grandfather, bravely stood with
the best of the Unionists in the days of nullification.
Only South Carolinians could appreciate the social distinction of being a member of the St. Cecilia Society; to
them it meant more than membership in the Society of
the Cincinnati. Louis's father (Henry A.) and brother
(Wilmot G.) were each, in turn, president of the St.
Cecilia and also held high office in the State branch of
the Cincinnati. Louis was a member of both societies.
On July 4, 1846, he was host to the Society of the Cincinnati. Moreover, he was long president of the Cotillion
Club. At the end of the 'fifties he was also probably the
most prosperous slave-trader in South Carolina. As
Thomas N. Gadsden's fortunes were in decline in 1856,
when Louis D. DeSaussure's were in the ascendant, how
fitting that Louis, the liberty-loving host of the Cincinnati,
should hold the last slave-auction on the historic spot by
the Exchange![35] It was like the rising sun of the Arctic
summer greeting the setting.

[33] The Wilburs had four slaves for hire.

On the 17th, J. S. Riggs offered 28 privately—5 mothers, each with one
child, and 18 single slaves. As usual there was no mention of fathers or
husbands. On the 25th, A. J. Salinas advertised 42 slaves besides " several
other families ".—*Courier* of those dates.

[34] That was the usual spelling at this time, but earlier the name was
often written De Saussure, Desaussure and de Saussure. The last was
undoubtedly the original form, for ancestors once owned a borough in
Lorraine, France, called Saussure.—Wm. Harper, *Memoir etc. Henry Wm.
De Saussure*, 6-7.

[35] It consisted of this typical "family": Eveline, a washer, about 27,

On January 10, 1860, DeSaussure was calling public attention to his lead in mechanics: Stephen, Scipio, Jack and Jacob, respectively 35, 45, 25 and 21 years of age, were all " good carpenters ", except Jacob, who was only " a plantation carpenter ". DeSaussure also had a large supply of female " single " negroes. A " single negro " might be treated as if as devoid of family ties as a mule or a steer is. Such were Kumba, 20 years old, a plain cook; Sarah 18, a seamstress; Jane 30, seamstress; Phillis 35, plain cook; Charlotte 50, a fair cook; Judy 16, a fieldhand; Hannah 42, a fieldhand. None of them had legal husbands, for no such thing as legal marriage between slaves existed; but that Jane, Phillis, Charlotte and Hannah were without children somewhere is wholly improbable. If you had preferred only ordinary and male " single negros " you could have chosen from Will, Andrew, James, Ben, Warley, Hercules, Adam, Billy, David, Primus, Joe and John, whose ages ranged from 20 to 40 years. Except John, a laborer, and Joe, a coachman, they were fieldhands. On the morrow he had two other lots for sale privately: one of 7 house-servants, and the other an exceptional family of husband, wife and four children. On February 9, 1860, he had 7 lots of negroes for private sale, totaling 280 slaves.

His public sales were not less worthy of notice. The *Courier*, February 7, 1860, in its column headed " City Intelligence " announced:

" Special attention is called to the sale, at auction, by Mr. Louis D. De-Saussure, of TWO PRIME GANGS OF NEGROS, accustomed to the culture of Sea Island Cotton and Provisions, to take place tomorrow, the 8th inst., at 11 o'clock, at the Mart, in Chalmers-street."

Besides these gangs of 64 and 26, he also sold two small lots at the Mart that day, making 95 in all. In its column of city news the *Mercury* regularly mentioned the note-

and her children Bellesames 9, Clara 7, Emma 4, and an infant.—*Courier*, June 27, 1856.

worthy prices that the different auctioneers had obtained
at the Mart the previous day. This was a much coveted
free advertisement and financial benefit. On February
17th Louis received an average of $703 for one gang of
34 sea-island cotton negroes and an average of $795 for
another of 20. On February 21st " Mr. L. D. DeSaussure
sold a boy, 21 years old, for $1205; and a disabled wench
for $485." His fortunes rose still higher on the 23d, when
he disposed of " two prime negros at $1,300 and $1,350 ".

And the " brokers " often sold peculiarly different
things at about the same time. Louis, in adjoining advertisements announced these forthcoming sales: first, at the
north side of the Exchange, pew 18 in Grace church;
second, at his office, 147 dozen bottles of Madeira, imported between 1827 and 1847, 12 dozen sherry and 21
dozen sauterne—" all selected with care by the late ———
for his private use "; and third, " at the Mart, in Chalmers
street ", a prime gang of 36 negroes from the James
Island plantation of the late Rawlins Rivers.[36]

DeSaussure's reputation, like that of all great traders,
extended to many States. He advertised in the leading
newspapers of the Southwest and took pains to send them
his lists so as to attract buyers to Charleston or to obtain
their orders.[37] Traces of his activities have been found
in unexpected places. The planter that obtained 19 of the
Gadsden slaves, at least thrice purchased slaves from
DeSaussure, for his own or others' plantations.[38] An old

[36] *Courier*, Dec. 28, 1859. Previously he had offered in adjoining advts.
and at private sale, a pew in Grace church and a gang of 55 negroes.—
Courier, Dec. 31, 1856. Both Capers & Heyward (*Courier*, Jan. 5, 1855 and
Mar. 6, 1860) and Hume (*Courier*, Dec. 12, 1859) had pews and slaves to sell
at the same time.

[37] The Montgomery, Ala. *Daily Confederation* of Jan. 15, 1859, contained
his advt. of the sale of 67 negroes "at Ryan & Son's Mart in Chalmers
street, Charleston, from the estate of Mr. and Mrs. Wm. Barnwell", and
added: "Lists of the negroes can be had by application at the *Confederation*
office."

[38] Doar's acct. with Robertson, Blacklock & Co. MS.

" colonel " of an aristocratic family told the author: " I myself bought from Louis negroes of the Prioleau estate ". And an ex-slave found idling in State street in 1902, said: " I was sol' by DeSaussure for my firs' mawsa to my secon' mawsa." A count of DeSaussure's advertisements in the *Courier* alone, carefully excluding *repetitions* and transfers from private to public sales, shows that he obtained commissions on not less than 193 slaves in January, 1860, and on more than 259 in February.

His gains from sales of slaves and various other kinds of property were almost princely, for that time. The income of no other " broker ", of no professional man, and of few, if any, merchants, equaled his.[39] The lawyer with the most remunerative practice in 1860 was C. G. Memminger—the young Unionist that in 1832 burlesqued the leading Nullifiers in an effective satire in Biblical form, and about three decades later became the Secretary of the Confederate Treasury—yet it amounted to only $8,700. The law firm of James L. Petigru, Henry King and J. Johnston Pettigrew had a professional income of only $14,721 and that of Edward McCrady & Son (the latter became the historian) had $6,800. DeSaussure's commissions alone for 1860 were $10,983. Not all, but most of it, came from slave-trading.[40] The next prosperous " broker " earned a little more than three-fourths as much, and none of the others exceeded $5,000, which was a large business income for that time and place; half of it sufficed for a generously comfortable living.[41] Besides

[39] The factors and the commission merchants made the most money. Nine firms each had incomes or commissions in excess of $20,000, and one, Adams & Frost, had $31,108. But it seems likely that in all but a few cases, the division between several partners reduced the profits of each to $10,000 or less. The *List of Taxpayers of Charleston* naturally does not notice incomes derived from plantations.

[40] Besides that he had " interest on bonds etc.", $2,718. All the figures as to incomes etc. are taken from the *List of Taxpayers of Charleston for 1860*.

[41] After DeSaussure, the thirteen most prosperous slave-selling " brokers " were:

the names of the members of the prosperous law-firm of
DeSaussure & DeSaussure, those of two others of that
family appeared in the tax-list—one a much respected
physician with a good practice and the other an insurance
agent. The total fees, commissions and taxable income in
Charleston of these four DeSaussures lacked more than
$1,600 of equaling the commissions of Louis alone!

Of the large and beautiful residences in Charleston
perhaps the most attractive and commanding was No. 1
East Bay street or East Battery, at the angle made by
rows of houses, with luxuriant gardens, on one side facing
the Cooper River and on the other the Ashley, and occupied by many of Charleston's best families.[42] Its outlook
on the bay was unsurpassed. Forts Sumter and Moultrie
were in clear view. During the long duel between these
forts, April 12, 1861, its spacious rooms and wide ver-
andahs were crowded with anxious spectators. Among
them was a young physician's wife, who was the daughter
of a planter on the Savannah River. In her old age she
described the beauties of slavery as represented in the
most colorful tradition. She quite forgot the essential
feature of slavery that made possible such a cash income
as that of the owner and occupant of this stately mansion,
her "cousin Louis", Louis D. DeSaussure.[43] She had, of
course, seen hundreds of his advertisements of the thousands of slaves he sold at his office or the jails or the
Mart, and she may have known that Louis's great-

J. S. Riggs,	commissions	$8,707	Wm. A. Gourdin,	commissions	$3,028
Capers & Heyward,	"	5,000	Jacob Cohen & Son,	"	2,500
Z. B. Oakes,	income	5,000	A. J. White,	"	2,500
Bennett & Rhett,	commissions	4,000	Thomas M. Hume,	"	2,000
Thos. Ryan & Son,	"	4,000	A. J. Salinas,	"	2,000
R. M. Marshall,	"	3,800	Wilbur & Son,	"	2,000
Porcher & Baya,	"	3,500			

[42] Those of four Ravenels, James G. Holmes, Charles Alston, Daniel Heyward, Francis J. Porcher, Wilmot G. DeSaussure, Charles T. Lowndes and
others.—*Census of Charleston for 1861*, 79.

[43] Mrs. N. B. De Saussure, *Old Plantation Days*, 65 *et passim*.

LOUIS D. DESAUSSURE'S RESIDENCE

The guns point toward Ft. Sumter

EAST BAY JUST NORTH OF L. D. DESAUSSURE'S
RESIDENCE

grandfather, Daniel, the father of the Chancellor, had engaged in both the African and the domestic slave-trade in connection with his commission-merchant business;[44] but such things were easily blinked and forgotten.

There were so many Charlestonians of highly respected families whose comfortable living depended on what they earned from some phase of slave-trading that there was need of a means of differentiating them from others doing the same things. It would have been no offense to persons of social standing to speak of J. S. Riggs, Thomas Ryan (both of whom were aldermen of superior qualities),[45] Oakes, Mordecai, McCall, Salinas, Olsen and others on State street as traders or even as slave-traders, although they were classed in the *Directory* as " brokers ". It was quite different as to DeSaussure, Capers, Porcher, Heyward, Rhett and some others with distinguished family names. They had their offices either on Broad or on Meeting street or on Adger's wharf, and they were of the aristocracy and in close association with the city's most respectable residents—planters, lawyers, editors, physicians, bankers and factors. Did not estates have to be settled in the South as well as elsewhere? Would you have liberated and ruined the helpless slaves, impoverished the heirs and been faithless with the creditors? If not, slaves must be sold. If one refused to handle the slaves, one could not handle the other property. And, remember, they were brokers, usually acting only as agents, auctioneers etc., and were compensated accordingly and not as slave-traders. Such was the common view and is a sacred tradition.

Yet if State and Chalmers streets suggested the possibility of a trader, if Broad street implied the probability of a gentleman and a broker, what of J. Russell Baker on State street, Laborde on Chalmers street, T. N. Gadsden

---

[44] See *post* p. 376 n.-77 n.

[45] *Charleston Ordinances, 1854-59,* p. iv; *Census of Charleston for 1861,* pp. 3, 4.

on the corner of both streets, and the Cohens (Jacob Cohen & Co. were slave-traders as early as 1807), Hume, White, Marshall and other large slave-brokers on Broad street? And how about one of such good Huguenot antecedents as P. J. Porcher, who in 1842 was in " Nigger-Traders row " and at public outcry sold four prime slaves " in the yard back of my office, 10 State street ", [46] but later prospered, moved to Broad street and became a member of a very successful firm of " brokers "? What appreciable difference between the business of a DeSaussure or a Capers or a Rhett or a Gourdin and that of an Oakes or a McBride or a Salinas or a Mordecai, between a slave-selling Ryan on Broad street and two Ryans doing likewise on State street—when " brokers " were traders and traders were " brokers ", all doing the same kind of advertising about the same kinds of slaves, coming from the same variety of masters or speculators and gladly disposed of to the same variety of buyers or their agents? What was the difference when all welcomed inquiries about the slaves assigned to them and, like regular " nigger-speculators ", even had them on view at their offices and in their yards, where they could be fully inspected,[47] sold them

[46] Charleston *News*, Feb. 8, 1842.

[47] Capers & Heyward said of a valuable " family " of a mother and three children: They " may be seen at our office ".—*Courier*, Jan. 13, 1860.

Gourdin's advt. of a gang also of nine advised the public: " The above negros can be seen upon application at the above rooms ", meaning his auction and commission rooms.—*Courier*, Jan. 16, 1860.

Jacob Ottolengui: " The above [six] negros can be seen at my office, 22 Broad street, and can be treated for at private sale, previous to the day of sale."—*Courier*, Jan 1, 1857.

J. S. Ryan: " N. B.   These Negros [a lot of 16] will be at my office [22 Broad st.] daily from 9 to 12 o'clock until sold.   Persons desirous of purchasing, are requested to examine them ".—*Courier*, Sept. 18, 1856.

In an advt. of a prospective auction of a coachman and of a " single girl ", " about 10 years old ", Z. B. Oakes said: " These servants may be seen at my office until the day of sale ".—*Courier*, Mar. 10, 1853.

McBride, at 1 Chalmers st., had an excellent cook etc. and her child of 6 years, who could be " seen at my office until sold ".—*Courier*, Jan. 18, 1860. J. Russell Baker, said the same as to Sarah about 25 and her three children of 11, 6 and 4 years.—*Courier*, Feb. 23, 1860.

privately there or at any jail or publicly at the Mart, received the same commission and deposited their gains in the same banks? With democratic justice, the *Mercury*, in making its announcements, recognized no difference, except in numbers sold and prices obtained. The most perceptible difference was not in the methods but in the profits. Here the " brokers " had a great advantage over the traders: in January, 1860, Porcher & Baya obtained commissions on, at least, 363 slaves, DeSaussure on 193, Capers & Heyward on 106; whereas Riggs earned commissions on only 64, Wilbur & Son on 35, Thomas Ryan & Son on 27, Seth Spencer on 20, Oakes on 15 and McCall on 10.[48] Voltaire would have exclaimed, *Ah, quelle différence!*

The Charleston market also contained slaves of many varieties and of excellent qualities. They supplied conclusive evidence that negroes, if given fitting instruction, could become very intelligent and trustworthy skilled laborers and be of special economic value. This, like many other facts, was both notorious and commonly denied. There was Nick, " a first-rate silversmith and good jeweler ", sold at auction by the Wilburs as part of a sheriff's sale of the property of a King street jeweler.[49] At different times they had a " first-rate house-painter and grainer ", a " good confectioner and cake baker ",[50] " a good drayman, coachman and laborer, sober, industrious and intelligent ", who, " for the last year [had been paying his master] $2 per day, clear profit ".[51] Capers &

[48] Only a few of Salinas's large stock were sold during Jan. These are all minimum figures, gathered from the advts. in the *Courier* alone. Other sales may have been advertised in the *Mercury* or elsewhere, and still others may not have been advertised at all.

In Feb., Capers & Heyward sold 302, DeSaussure 259 and Porcher and Baya 121. These, too, are all minimum figures.

[49] *Courier*, Dec. 5, 1859.

[50] *Courier*, Jan. 17 and Feb. 3, 1860.

[51] Wilbur & Son, *Courier*, Feb. 21, 1860.

7

Heyward had " 5 intelligent and competent boot and shoe-
makers of the most unexceptional character ".[52]   A little
earlier, J. S. Ryan—the Broad street " broker ", not
Thomas Ryan the alderman and State street trader—had
on sale at his office, together with many others, " a first-
rate blacksmith, a prime young fellow ", who had " run
an engine for nearly a year ", and was " a very competent mechanic ";[53] and, a little later, he sold at the
Mart what was still rarer—" a first-rate engineer and
millwright, with his wife ".[54]   McCall had " Abraham, an
elderly man, an excellent gardner * * * , active and intelligent, sound and healthy ", and " Shaderick, an experienced coachman and trusty house servant of unexception-
able character, civil and of industrious habits, * * * sound
and healthy; "[55]   On days not far apart, Thomas Ryan &
Son sold at their Mart two saddlers and harnessmakers
belonging to the estate of B. Fitzsimons, deceased; three
boathands and three firemen, and " a first-rate sailor and
pilot ".[56]   Ship-carpenters, ship-blacksmiths and calkers
were not rare.[57]   Excellent mantuamakers and skilful
tailors, could occasionally be bought.[58]   Seamstresses and
lady's-maids were so numerous that one with any shade of
color might have been supplied.   And the Wilburs had

[52] Courier, Jan. 26, 1860.

[53] Courier, Jan. 6, 1857.

[54] Mercury, Feb. 11, 1860.

[55] Courier, Jan. 27, 1860.

[56] Courier, Jan. 4, 17, 24, 1860.   Soon thereafter, Marshall offered privately
" Isaac, aged about 60 years, a pilot, well acquainted with the coast adjacent
to Charleston ".—Courier, Feb. 1, 1860.   For other pilots, see ante p. 155,
post p. 219 n. and Key to Uncle Tom's Cabin, 13.

[57] DeSaussure offered at private sale " Bristol, 22, a ship-carpenter and good
calker, and Prince, 21 a ship-blacksmith ".—Courier, Mar. 3, 1857.   On Jan.
25, 1859, he sold two ship-carpenters at the Mart, and Thos. Ryan & Son sold
four, one of whom was also a house-carpenter and three were also calkers.
At the same place a year later Hume sold " an excellent ship-carpenter."—
Courier, Jan. 25, 1859; Jan. 24, 1860.

[58] Jacob Cohen & Son had Rebecca, mantuamaker, and her three children.—
Courier, Apr. 28, 1857.   See post p. 218, note 41, for another.   " A master

" a good French cook ", " of good character, warranted
sound ", who would be sold on accommodating terms to
a city resident.[59]

Had the artist Crowe been at the Mart on the last day
of January, 1860, he would have found more subjects
worthy of his clever pen and his wonderful pencil—10 lots
of negroes, about 180, ready to be sold by public outcry
by the Wilburs, Marshall, DeSaussure, and Porcher &
Baya, all of whom, except the Wilburs, were from Broad
street. Several " families " of mothers with their small
children were put on the block that day. While some of
them were huddled together within the Mart, waiting their
turns, or perhaps while " Minda, a likely girl aged 18,
with her infant, aged 7 months ", was selling for $1160,
or little Tenah, a " single " girl of 9 years, was going
for $700 and swelling the commissions of a gentleman
" broker ",[60] in the street, just in front, " a four year old
Durham Bull of Col. Hampton's stock ", with a ring in
his nose, his head proudly uplifted as if to boast of his
pedigree, was led to and fro before " breeders and others "
who had been invited to be present.[61]

Yet it was all natural, inevitable, where slavery was
considered providential and a political, a social and an
economic good. After emancipation it was, perhaps,
equally natural to blink the old facts and opinions and to
create a roseate tradition of slavery as experienced by
only the most fortunate of the domestic servants and to
ignore the semi-bestial life of the plantation fieldhand and
the extent and the inhumanity of the slave-trade. One

tailor " was advertised to be sold, under decree in equity, at the Mart, Feb.
9, 1860.—*Courier*, Feb. 6, 1860.
    [59] *Courier*, Jan. 24, 1860. " Broker " White advertised Adam, " a first-rate
cook, regularly brought up to the business ", of very uncommon qualities for
that market.—*Courier*, Jan. 26, 1860.
    [60] Marshall's advts., *Courier*, Jan. 31, 1860, and report of that day's auction,
Mercury, Feb. 1, 1860.
    [61] Hume's advt., *Courier*, Jan. 31, 1860.

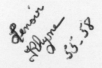

needs only to turn back to the Southern newspapers of the 'fifties to see the great contrast between this Southern tradition and the ante-bellum conditions. The Charleston *Mercury* of April 19, 1859, supplies a general characterization of the commerce in slaves, that well illustrates this difference and explains how it could not otherwise have been possible for the good and the bad to be so closely associated. In the summer of 1858 the United States sloop " Dolphin " captured the slaver " Echo " with a cargo of 300 Africans, probably intended for Cuba. All were brought to Charleston. When the crew was tried for violating the law against the foreign slave-trade, the jury brought in a verdict of " not guilty ". The editor of the *Mercury* theorized about the attitude of the jury by saying that if they had brought in a verdict of " guilty ", it would have been " not only inconsistent, but cruel and hypocritical for them, as members of a community where slaves are bought and sold every day, and are as much and as frequently articles of commerce as the sugar and molasses which they produce " * * * .

CHAPTER IX

DIVIDING FAMILIES AND SELLING CHILDREN SEPARATELY.—RESTRICTIONS

Virtually everybody preferred to be humane, according to Southern standards, when it was not financially disadvantageous or inconvenient to be so. Persons whose interests led them to be otherwise naturally wished to conceal the fact or tried to place the blame elsewhere, for there was no respectability without at least the appearance of being humane. But slavery maintained as a profitable and convenient institution was essentially ruthless in general and inhumane in some of its main features.

Neither marriage nor fatherhood among slaves was legally recognized because recognition would have gravely interfered with property rights; and the legal prohibitions against dividing families were very slight. Whatever recognition family relations received was, with few exceptions, voluntary.

Louisiana, least American of the Southern States, was least inhuman. In becoming Americanized it lost many a liberal feature of the old French *code noir,* but it forbade sale of mothers from their children less than ten years of age (and *vice versa*) and bringing into the State any slave child under ten years of age without its mother, if living. The penalty for violating either prohibition was from $1,000 to $2,000 and the forfeiture of the slave. That would have meant much if it had been strictly enforced. As a rule, the dividing line between children that were worth more with their mothers and those that were worth more without them was at about eight years of age. Thus there was some possible sacrifice of property rights from the eighth to the end of the ninth year. But orphans, however young, and all slaves ten or more years old had no ties that anyone was bound to respect, and they were fre-

197

quently disregarded. A law, without any penalty for ignoring it, gave this pathetic injunction about the aged: " If at a public sale of slaves, there happen to be some who are disabled through old age, or otherwise, and who have children, they shall be sold with such one of their children as they may choose to go with." [1]

At first blush, the Alabama law seems to have had some substantial humanity in it. It forbade levying any execution on a child under ten years of age without including the mother, if living, (and *vice versa*) ; and they must be sold together *unless* a party in interest made affidavit that his interest would be materially prejudiced. In this case they might be sold separately, unless the child was under five years of age. And " in all sales of slaves under any decree, or order of the chancery or probate court, or under any deed of trust, or power of sale in a mortgage, the slaves must be offered, and, if practicable, sold in families [i. e. the mother and her young offspring] ; unless " some party in interest made affidavit that selling them together would be to his material disadvantage.[2] Thus not humanity but expectation of profit or loss was the criterion.

Mississippi provided, as part of its law to exempt from seizure under execution or attachment certain kinds of property supposed to be required for the owner's welfare, that if a debtor should elect to retain a female slave, then she and also her children while under six years of age should be exempt.[3] This latter provision, much like the exemption of a growing crop, was evidently to prevent a sacrifice of the debtor-master's interest—not to give special protection to the slaves.

In Georgia, administrators, executors, guardians and other trustees for the purpose of sale or distribution were

---

[1] *La. Rev. Stats.*, 1856, pp. 60, 58, secs. 74, 75, 67.

[2] *Code of Ala.*, 1852, secs. 2056-57. How careful the parties in interest were to reach purchasers in Southern States far apart was shown by simultaneous advts. of large sales in leading newspapers.

[3] Miss. *Rev. Code*, 1857, 529.

forbidden to separate children not above eight years from
their mothers, or to sell separately husband and wife, recognized as such by the deceased master when both belonged
to his estate.[4] / These provisions were advantageous to the
slaves concerned, but did not affect a living *master's* property rights: it remained entirely legal for him to sell separately any slave of any age whatsoever.

Not one of these prohibitions, save those of Louisiana,
and they but slightly, in any way referred to or hampered
the *owner of unencumbered* slave property: he might sell
or pawn or mortgage or give it away according to profit
or whim, regardless of age or kinship.

Elsewhere in the typical South—in Virginia, North
Carolina, South Carolina, Tennessee,[5] Arkansas and Texas
there seems to have been no restriction of any sort against
separating mothers and children or husbands and wives
or selling children of any age.) Slavery was, indeed, a
" peculiar institution ".

When it was expected to be markedly advantageous, the
everyday practice in selling slaves to pay debts and settle
estates was to divide families, often excepting mothers and
young children. The fact that the law did not prohibit such
separations, but sanctioned and even compelled them when
parties in interest demanded them; that the interstate
traders were suspected of intending to divide families when
they advertised for them; that all but a small percentage
of the slaves they had for sale were " single ", or young
mothers with small children, and that the slaves in the
markets, unless in gangs from estates, were almost exclusively of the same kind—these and many other facts, to be
duly noticed, are conclusive evidence that it was common
to divide families. This was much deplored by many of
the best Southerners and denied by few, except as to their

---

[4] Ga. *Code*, 1861, p. 483, sec. 2523.

[5] " The master or owner [in Tenn.] had unlimited power of sale, and power
over the person of the slave, not extending however to the taking of life or
limbs."—Judge O. P. Temple to the author, Feb. 8, 1904.

own practice.[6]   Probably not one " family " out of fifty
or one hundred in the ordinary market (not of plantation
gangs) comprised more than the mother and the small
children and often only part of these.[7]   At table in a
Richmond hotel Olmsted overheard this matter-of-fact
dialogue showing that a mother with an infant had been
separated from four children between about four and
13 years of age:—" Niggers are going high now, aint

[6] J. B. O'Neall, Chief Justice of S. C., wrote that " slaves are subjected to
continual change: they are sold and given by their masters without writing;
they are sold by administrators and executors, and by the sheriff, (and may
even be sold by constables) "; and that " this continual change of relation of master and slave, with the consequent rending of family ties among
them ", had convinced him that they ought to " be sold with the freehold,
and not otherwise."—De Bow's 2 *Resources of the South and West*, 276.

Thos. Jefferson Randolph said in the Va. House of Delegates, Jan. 21, 1832:
" But here, sir, individuals, whom the master has known from infancy, whom
he has seen sporting in the innocent gambols of childhood, who have been
accustomed to look to him for protection, he tears from the mother's arms,
and sells into a strange country among strange people, subject to cruel task-
masters."—Pamphlet copy, p. 16.

Four days later Philip A. Bolling said there: " High-minded men ought to
disdain to hold their fellow creatures as articles of traffic—disregarding all
the ties of blood and affection—tearing asunder all those sympathies dear to
man—dividing husbands and wives, parents and children, as they would cut
asunder a piece of cotton cloth."—Pamphlet copy, p. 14.

Daniel R. Goodloe, an antislavery North Carolinian, wrote in 1852: " I
have often heard the practice of separating husband and wife, parent and
child, defended, apologized for, palliated in a thousand ways, but have never
heard it denied. * * * In separating husband and wife, or parent and child,
the trader or owner violates no law of the state—neither statute nor common
law."—*Key to Uncle Tom's Cabin*, 64-65, prints his long letter.

In the Southern Commercial Convention at Savannah, 1856, Goulden of Ga.
said that it was an everyday occurrence to go to Va. and take a negro from
his home and family and bring him to work cotton and rice fields.—22
De Bow's Review, 224.

[7] McDougle, *Slavery in Ky.* (3 *Journal of Negro History*, 234-35), reports
the results of sales of 46 slaves of both sexes and all ages. All but ten slaves
were sold in settlement of estates of deceased masters, and the individual
prices show that the men, women and children were sold singly, except one
mother with children six months, four and six years old, respectively.

Trader-agents W. McRea and M. C. Folkes separately advertised in the
Vicksburg, Miss., *Weekly Sentinel* of Jan. 3 and 10, 1855, a total of 35 per-

they? "—" Yes, sir."—" What would you consider a fair price for a woman 30 years old, with a young-one two years old? "—" Depends altogether on her physical condition, you know. Has she any other children? "—" *Yes; four.*"—" Well—I reckon about seven to eight hundred."—" I bought one yesterday—gave six hundred and fifty."—" Well, sir, if she's tolerable likely, you did well." [8]

Of course all single negroes in market did not betoken separations: a considerable proportion of the men under 25 and of the women under 20 had no serious attachments; so-called husbands and wives were often owned by different masters, and selling either for distant use was not called separation, although hardly less painful to the slaves concerned than if they had lived at the same place; a small percentage of the slave women never had children or their children died or were soon left orphans; and many mothers never had husbands but only temporary and changing " friends ", as the shades and features of

sons. There was not one mention of a father, nor of a married couple nor of a full family; those not single were mothers with small children.

See Phillips, 2 *Plantation* etc., 58, for a typical illustration—seven lots making a total of 19 slaves, of whom four lots were mothers with children, but there was no suggestion of a husband or a father.

See Darrington sale, *post* pp. 299, 299 n.-200 n.

Greeley, 1 *Amer. Conflict*, 70, quotes an English visitor who saw many sales in Richmond and New Orleans but there were no married couples among them. That might have been one's experience at public sales in Richmond, Charleston or Louisville, but it must have been exceptional in New Orleans.

[8] 1 *Cotton Kingdom*, 51-52. The following advt. needs no explanation and illustrates what the best newspaper in Va. was willing to print:

" TWENTY FIVE DOLLARS REWARD. ABSCONDED from my jail, on Friday, the 20th inst., a negro woman named ANGELINE. She is of black color, 4 feet 11 inches or 5 feet high. Her forehead is bare of hair. She has uncommon large limbs; is between 22 and 24 years of age, and four months gone in pregnancy. She says she has had six children, and was raised in Greenbrier, Augusta county, Va. She speaks a brogue different from Negroes raised in Eastern Virginia, and is quite intelligent. Said woman will endeavor to go back to Augusta where she was raised, either by the Canal or Central Rail Road. I will give the above reward for her deliverance to my jail or to Messrs. N. B. & C. B. Hill, Richmond. May 28. Geo. W. ATKINSON."— Richmond *Daily Enquirer*, June 18, 1853. All three were well-known traders.

the children indicated. But when women of 35 or 40 were in market without any children or with only those of tender age, it was almost certain that there had been separations. Removals beyond 40 or 50 miles ended all associations almost as completely as death, for it was extremely rare for fieldhands to know how to read and write.

To this rule of separations when a positive advantage was expected, there were many generously humane exceptions, especially in wills. When feasible, servants were treated very differently from fieldhands, for they had been almost like members of the master's household. Only a speculator at heart would altogether voluntarily separate a family of good domestic servants—husband and wife with small children—any more than one would sell a favorite horse or dog, although broken down, to anyone likely to mistreat or underfeed him. Not infrequently neighbors or relatives owning different members of a family would unite them, one master selling to the other for a moderate price. There was usually an advantage in this and also in buying a complete young family, because if kept together it would be less discontented, more manageable and more productive. And it was said to be profitable to buy even the whole gang of a sugar plantation along with the land, buildings and equipment, for each was like a part of a large machine.[9]

Few persons of good standing and not traders ever admitted that they had sold slaves, except "involuntarily"; virtually none admitted that they had divided families. The separate sale of a boy or a girl more than about 12 years old was not usually called a separation, for the child was already considered single. As used,

[9] When the slaves were kept together, remarkable evidence was sometimes given as to the extent of family ties. Auctioneer Beard (*post* p. 324) sold a gang of 124 slaves, *en bloc*, among whom about 19 "families" were listed.— New Orleans *Picayune*, Feb. 28, 1856.

this word *involuntarily* had great flexibility. Sales were " voluntary " in case they were for speculation, but not if " to change the investment " or because " having no further use for the negroes ". They were still more " involuntary " if one ran in debt or borrowed money when a slave was the actual or the prospective security. When the unfortunate time for settlement came it was too late to avoid separation. And even the victims were sometimes so chameleon-like that they regarded their misfortunes as if they had been unavoidable.[10] Almost any one of many excuses sufficed, if the master wished to conceal his poverty or financial misfortune. If a slave was called troublesome or disobedient or thought more of freedom than of work or was vicious or had a bad influence on the other slaves—these or similar " causes " fully justified sale, which was " involuntary ". It was hard to avoid all these " causes " when the master was in need of money.

Without any excuse it was easy, anonymously and secret-

---

[10] The author met a very quaint and pathetic illustration of this at Camak, Ga. While one train was waiting for another, some passengers had bought " chicken lunches " of an old negress who paid for her privileges by dusting the car. The greasy, sodden, chickenless luncheons were so grossly wretched that a wag concluded to complete the burlesque by superlative praise of her " wonderful ' old time ' cooking ", etc. She was elated. " Swish, swish, swish ", whispered her duster from seat to seat, while she talked to herself. As she drew nearer these words could be distinguished: " Yes, sah, dat's what I iz. I'ze one o' dese o-l-e *time slav'ry* niggahs. I cooks like dey done in de ole time. I'ze a reglar No'th Kyli-ny niggah. Dem was good ole times "—"Auntie ", interrupted the author, " did you like the old times better than these?" " *Yas, sah!* I did'n' have to bothah 'bout myself; had evahting I wants; dey *cares* for me."—" Where were you ' raised '? "—" Who? me? I was raised in No'th Kyli-ny ".—" Who brought you out here ".—" *Oh,* I was *sol'*; my mahsa got in debt an' had to 'spoze o' me."—" Did you have children?"—" Yas, *sah,* I did dat; I had two, two small chilluns, one 'bout dat high [indicating a child of 8 to 10 years] an' de uddah a baby, like diss heah chile " [3 or 4 years old].—" Did they sell your children? "—" No, mahsa, I was de onliest one sol'."—" What became of the children? "—" *Nuthin,* dess leff dah, bofe uv 'em."—" Did you ever hear from them again? "—" No, sah, nevah *heahd* f'um 'em no mo'."

ly, to obtain liberal cash advances and early payment in full for slaves of all kinds put into the custody of an auctioneer or a commission merchant. The " broker " attended to everything without advertising either the owner's or the slave's name.[11] One could avoid employing a regular trader by placing the slaves in a public or a private jail, advertising them and requesting interested persons to apply to the printer, the editor, or the jailor, who referred applicants to the owner for particulars. The screens were equal to the needs.

In an advertisement of a forthcoming sale, to call a group of slaves a " family " did not of itself mean that they

[11] Alderman-trader Riggs in Charleston, the least brutal of the large markets, had these at private sale: Charlotte, 30, a likely woman, a good cook, washer and ironer; Phoeby, 26, a likely woman, a good cook, washer and ironer, with her son Frank, 7; Maria, 22, with her child, a cook and washer, and general house servant; Pamelia, 30, said to be a good cook and washer, with her daughter, Sarah, 5; Louisa, 40, represented as being a No. 1 cook, washer and ironer, with her son William, 5; Rachel, 40, cook, washer and ironer, with her son Olney, 6; and the following fieldhands: Henry, 35; Cyrus, 28; Smith, 35; Green, 35; Jack, 30; Charles, 19; Milley, 17; Diannah, 18; Reanna, 19; Amelia, 17; Sally, 17; Frances, 16; Maria, 19; Flora, 18; Matilda, 17; Isabella, 18; Cynthia, 19.—*Courier*, Jan. 18, 1860.

" Negroes for Sale.—A MIDDLE-AGED negro woman, a good washer, ironer and cook, and a very capable servant in every respect; and also her son, a goodlooking and remarkably sprightly mulatto boy of ten years old, are offered for sale. They will not be sold separately. Enquire at the office of the STATESMAN."—Lexington, Ky., Semi-Weekly *Statesman*, Dec. 14, 1860.

Alderman-trader Thos. Ryan had " at private sale, a likely Negro woman, good cook, washer and ironer, with her Child, 2 years old. Two likely young women fieldhands. A very likely woman, fieldhand, with her two Children, 4 and 2 years old. Two elderly women, fieldhands. One elderly woman, good cook and washer. A likely boy, 12 years old. Three likely girls, aged 11, 10 and 9 years."—Charleston *Courier*, Jan. 24, 1853.

Capers and Heyward advertised that they would sell at auction singly and for cash each person in these two groups:

1. Lucy, 30, and Diana, 40, both prime fieldhands; Nanny, 60, poultry-minder and nurse; Peggy, 40, prime fieldhand; Stephen, 21, first rate shoe-maker and servant; Sam, 20, prime ploughman; Shorum, 16, smart boy; Prince, 19, prime; Lewis, 30, laborer; Martha, 23, lady's-maid and child's nurse; Johnny, 12, smart boy.

2. John, 30, fieldhand; Molly, 30, plain cook; Mary Ann, fieldhand;

were to be disposed of together; it was indicative of kinship, and sale collectively was preferred to sale singly if it promised to be equally remunerative. Merely to offer slaves privately as a whole gang or in families, made a favorable impression, although it was notorious that large traders were always looking for opportunities to purchase gangs cheaply and to sell individual slaves or small groups at high prices in the markets of the Southwest. If no satisfactory responses were received and the slaves were sold at auction in such a manner as to realize the largest amount, the original effort was still much to one's credit. The Charleston *Mercury* regularly, and other newspapers occasionally, contained local news-items giving the '' average price '' received the previous day for each gang or group sold publicly or privately. This was the only summary method of describing the general result, and virtually all large sales were so reported. The '' average price '' was usually, but not always, only an average of the many separate prices. And it was not very significant unless one knew the ages, occupations, etc. of the slaves.[12]

Betsy, fieldhand; Sammy, 20, house-servant, coachman, painter, &c.; Hannibal, 17, prime boy; Robert, 22, prime fieldhand; Martha, 21, child's nurse and house servant; Stephen, 21, shoemaker and house servant [2d appearance]; George, 35, coachman and house servant; Lewis, 30 [2d appearance.]—Charleston *Mercury*, Feb. 9 and 29, 1860, respectively.

In different advts., McCall offered two "elderly" men for whom their unnamed owners demanded cash: Ansel, "an experienced meat cook" was "sold for no fault, but to change the investment"; the other was "a carpenter and farmhand", "a confidential and trusty servant, healthy, active and well-disposed", whose name was carefully omitted.—*Courier*, Jan. 17, 1860.

J. Russell Baker had on exhibition at his office and for sale privately "a good coachman, house-servant and cook", all in one (*Mercury*, July 2, 1860), but neither the slave's nor the master's name was mentioned.

[12] Here is an extreme example: "Messrs. WILBUR and SON sold sixty-eight long cotton negroes, at an average of $586, the highest bringing $1375 and the lowest $1."—Charleston *Mercury*, Feb. 3, 1860. If the two extremes had not been mentioned, many persons might have inferred that the gang was sold collectively.

Interested persons easily satisfied themselves that slaves were almost indifferent to separations. This was refuted by the use of handcuffs by new purchasers, by the chain-gangs of the interstate traders and by thousands of advertisements telling that runaways were supposed to have returned to their old homes or gone to kindred from whom they had been parted.[13] And because separations were too notorious to be denied, it was often undertaken to palliate them by saying that they were no worse than those among white persons.[14] White persons left home from choice or at least in their own interest, moved about as they pleased, continued to communicate with kindred and friends and returned to or sent for them at will, when sufficient money could be obtained. Slaves were taken away by force and in most cases all communications with the " old home " were cut off instanter and forever. But any favorable sophistry or sanctimonious mummery was welcomed and hailed as a complete defense. " The question was put to the Savannah River Baptist Association ", says Rhodes,

[13] Many of the advertisements were very significant:— A bright yellow boy, Sam, 16 years old, who five years previously had been purchased of one Robert Jones, was thought to be lurking " at General Williams's, who owns his mother and others of his family ".—Wilmington, N. C., *Journal*, Jan. 3, 1860. Thus Sam had been sold at the age of 11 and after a separation of five years was supposed to be so eager to see his mother that he risked incurring a severe punishment.

One Thomas Davis, offering $50 for the recovery of his slave Paul, said: " I understand Gen. R. Y. Hayne has purchased his wife and children from H. L. Pinckney, Esq., and has them on his plantation on Goose Creek, where, no doubt, the fellow is frequently lurking, and may be most of the time in the City, or sometimes in the neighborhood of Georgetown."—Charleston *Courier,* Jan. 5, 1836.

Isabella, who ran away from W. J. Worsham, had belonged to Robert B. Corbin of Caroline county, Va., and was thought to be " lurking about his farm, where she had a child ".—[Catherine Cooper Hopley] 1 *Life in the South* by A Blockaded British Subject, 147.

[Weld], *American Slavery As It Is,* 164-67, gives about 30 quotations from newspapers of 1837-39 showing similar separations.

[14] Robert Toombs, lecture in Boston, Stephens's 1 *War Between the States,* 643; 25 *S. Lit. Messenger,* 87; 27 *Ibid.,* 91.

" whether in the case that slaves were separated, they should be allowed to marry again. The answer was in the affirmative, because the separation was civilly equivalent to death, and the ministers believed ' that in the sight of God it would be so viewed.' " [15] Yet it did not occur to these facile casuists that a separation " civilly equivalent to death " might be a serious offense " in the sight of God ".

The regular traders also had methods and reasoning to suit their interests. After closely studying Neal's coffle, [16] Professor Andrews asked: " Do you often buy the wife without the husband? "—" Yes, very often ", answered the trader, " and frequently, too, they sell me the mother while they keep the children. I have often known them [to] take away the infant from its mother's breast and keep it, while they sold her." [17]—" When husbands and wives are separated, do they seem to care much about it?"—" Sometimes they don't mind it a great while, but at other times they take on *right smart*, for a long time." Andrews concluded that " in almost every case, family ties have been broken in the purchase of these slaves. Husbands are here whose wives remain in the District, and wives are now looking back upon the dome of the Capitol, which is still in sight, and near which their husbands reside, whom they are never more to meet." Was it less Neal's business to sell than to buy according to opportunities and profits? Yet he assured Andrews that he never divided families! [18] Nor did

[15] 1 *Hist. U. S.*, 317-18.

[16] *Ante* pp. 54-55.

[17] Andrews, 147; *Ibid.*, 165 and 106 for cases in Fredericksburg, Va., and Baltimore. About this time a Tenn. case illustrated both such a separation and the supposed value of a boy three months old: In " 1837, Gambling sold Read, Hannah, a female slave for $1,200, * * * Hannah had a young child, [a boy, three months old,] and her distress at the separation from it induced Read to propose to purchase it; * * * agreed that he should have it for $150." —2 Catterall, 507. Happily this resulted in being just the reverse of the cases in Mo., *ante* p. 137.

[18] Andrews, 148, 147.

the impeccable Hope H. Slatter nor John Armfield nor any other clever trader,—according to their declarations or those of their employees. Such pretenses, if credited, were valuable assets; for there were always many persons willing or compelled to part with their slaves, but unwilling openly to assume any responsibility for dividing families or selling to a trader likely to do so. Yet in all cases where there were voluntary separations in original private sales to a trader, those separations, which were certainly legion, were made by the masters.

Professor Phillips says that " the prices of young children are rarely ascertainable from the bills [of sale], since they were hardly ever sold separately ". [19] " Hardly ever sold separately "! On the contrary, they were hardly less than a staple in the trade. The selling singly of young children privately and publicly was frequent and notorious. Virtually all traders dealt in those from 10 or 12 years of age and many advertised for those from 6, 7, 8 and 9, as already cited examples prove. And the prices obtained for small children [20] demonstrate that the sales were very numerous. But it may be worth while to heap to overflowing the measure of indisputable facts. [21]

[19] *American Negro Slavery*, 369.

[20] For a grouping of the many references to advertisements for and sales and prices of young children the reader should turn to the index.

[21] Benj. Davis advertised that in a lot of 120 which he had brought from Petersburg, Va., to Hamburg, S. C., he had " several women with small children, small girls, suitable for nurses, and several small boys without their mothers ".—Wm. Jay, *Misc. Writings*, etc. 267.

The following may be cited as samples of the many sales of small children, singly, in all markets:—

At private sale in Charleston, Oakes had " a single girl ", Martha, about 10 years old, very likely and handy about the house " (*Courier*, Mar. 10, 1853); Caroline and Linda, both 13, Manda and Lucy, both 12, all four " single "; and " 4 single boys, 10 to 12 years, 3 single girls 10 to 12 years ".— *Courier*, Feb. 9, 1857.

McCall had Ben, a very active, smart and intelligent house-boy, about 11 years old (*Courier*, Jan. 23, 1860); Bennett & Rhett had Patty, 14, and

It was said in a Kentucky case in 1835, where a boy was declared to be worth $350.00 at least, that " a young boy slave * * * , it is well known, will readily command in cash, at all times, his intrinsic value ".[22]   William Chambers, who spent a morning at several of the Richmond slave-auctions, saw four " lots "—a mother with three small girls, then three men singly—taken down because the bidding was low. Then a young woman sold for $710 and a boy of 7 years brought $630.[23]

The Virginia trader with a gang of little boys roped together, whom Seward chanced to meet, had his counterpart in other places. Here is a North Carolina Colonel calling exclusively for children from 8 to 12 years of age:

"NEGROES WANTED.   Fair prices and cash will be given for YOUNG NEGROES from 8 to 12 years old. Apply to Col. Allen Rogers, sen'r, in Wake, or to Joseph A. Whitaker, at Rosehill, Franklin county." [24]

We shall find a trader in Columbia, South Carolina, also making a specialty of little children. Professor Trexler says that in Missouri " Children were at times wrung from their parents. Professor Peter H. Clark of St. Louis re-

Lot, 9, both " raised in the country " (Tri-Weekly *Mercury*, Feb. 15, 1859) ; Marshall had Henry, about 10 and Aaron about 11.—*Mercury*, Jan. 4, 1860.

In Augusta, auctioneer Griffin had two " very likely " girls—Bina, 11, and Emily, 9 years of age.—Daily *Constitutionalist*, Jan. 1, 1860.

In Memphis, A. Wallace, " agent, auctioneer, negro and real estate broker ", had several likely girls from 8 years up and a boy of 9 (*Appeal*, Oct. 11, 1857) ; and J. C. Holland, city auctioneer, made this announcement: " I will sell this day at ten o'clock at Hill & Ware's Negro Mart on Adams street, one likely Negro woman 28 years old, with a girl child 15 months old. Also one No. 1 Boy, 7 years old. This property is sold for no fault, but to close out a lot. Property sound, sale positive and without reserve."—*Avalanche*, Mar. 1, 1860.

A Savannah trader, A. Bryan (*post* p. 223 n.), had for sale singly a " likely intelligent yellow girl child, 5 years, country raised " and " 2 likely girls, 8 and 11 years old ".

[22] 1 Catterall, 329.

[23] *Things As They Are in America*, 278-83.

[24] Raleigh, N. C., *Standard*, Aug. 4, 1836. Mrs. Catteral, II, 77, cites a N. C. case where " Charlotte. then about 2 years of age ", was sold.

members a house on the southwest corner of Morgan and Garrison streets in which lived a woman who bought up infants from their mothers' arms at the slave-markets of St. Louis and raised them for profit." [25]

It seems almost incredible that any one should *advertise* willingness to separate husband from wife, and a mother from her little children, " to suit purchasers ", yet this was sometimes done.[26] Without suiting the purchaser the highest price could never be obtained.

At sales by order or with the permission of the proper court, obtaining as much as possible was the chief concern. In a South Carolina case in 1857 a guardian, who at public sale had disposed of Daphna and her infant child for $350, and " Hannah a small girl child " of Daphna for $160, defended his course by saying that he " must sell so as to git the most ". The chancellor took him to task not for the separation but for selling under such conditions that it was impossible to realize a fair value for the slaves.[27]

[25] Trexler, *Slavery in Missouri*, 52. If the address is correct, this was a second establishment of that kind in that city. *Ante* p. 144.

[26] " As valuable a family ∗ ∗ ∗ as ever was offered for sale ", consisting of a cook, about 35 years of age, and her daughter about 14 and son about 8. " The whole will be sold together or a part of them, as may suit a purchaser." —Charleston *Courier*, Apr. 12, 1828.

" I wish to sell a negro woman and four children. The woman is 22 years old, of good character, a good cook and washer. The children are very likely, from 6 years down to 1½. I will sell them separately to suit purchasers.— J. T. Underwood."—Louisville Weekly *Journal*, May 2, 1849. Prof. McDougle (3 *Journal of Negro Hist.*, 228) cites this and an advt. offering to sell separately a negro man and woman, each about 24 years old, and two children. Only a few lines before citing these advts., Prof. McDougle assures us " that public opinion [in Ky.] would not tolerate any suspicion of a heartless traffic in slaves "!

[27] 2 Catterall, 455. Chief Justice Ruffin of N. C. expressed this opinion: " The Court does not favor sales by executors in large masses ∗ ∗ ∗ Sometimes, indeed, as much, or more can be had, when the property is disposed of in one, than in more parcels, as in the instance of a *family* of slaves, when the children are *all* of tender years. But he, who conducts such a sale, does it at his peril, and must answer for the true value. ∗ ∗ ∗ It would certainly have been harsh to separate these four boys, and sever ties which bind even slaves together. True, it must be done, if the executor discovers that the

In front of the courthouse door at Eatonton, Georgia, the sheriff in April, 1852, sold singly to the highest bidder " George about 20 years old; Olly, about 11; Elizabeth, about 6; Nancy about 6; Francis about 2 ", all of whom had been " levied on to satisfy three mortgage fi fas." [28] Such sales were both common and necessary in all the Southern States; for, as we know, it was customary to borrow money and use slaves as security, either giving a deed of trust on them, or a mortgage with a power of sale, or putting the slaves in the possession of the lender and supplying a bill of sale, to be void in case the debt was paid by a certain time.   For a small sum it sufficed to pledge a small child, as was done in a Tennessee case.[29]

interest of the estate requires it; for he is not to indulge his charities at the expense of others." * * *—2 Catterall, 59.

[28] Milledgeville, Ga., *Southern Recorder*, Feb. 10, 1852. On a single page of the number of Jan. 7, 1851, were 46 notices of prospective sales by order or permission of some court. Several were about little children without their mothers, and of course without their fathers. Two sales were of slaves of Burwell Moss: "Three negroes—John, a boy about 18 years old; Ann, about 4, and Riley, about 3; all levied on " etc. etc. "Also three negroes—Rose, a woman about 16 years old; Nancy, about 8 years old; and Milly, about 6 years old; all levied on " etc. An advt. of an administrator's sale for the benefit of the legatees announced the forthcoming auction of Ann and Lucy, 13 and 9 years old, at the courthouse door in Troupville, Ga.

About 100 negroes of the late Col. John G. Lumsden were also disposed of to the highest bidders at the courthouse door in Eatonton, Ga., "for the benefit of his heirs. These negroes were nearly all raised in the State of Georgia, by the said deceased; amongst them will be found a large number of healthy fine children, boys and girls, young men and young women, a house carpenter, a plantation blacksmith and a miller; almost every description of servants can be had out of the above negroes."—*Ibid.*, Jan. 7, 1851. Many more examples might be given. Hundreds of others can easily be found in the same Georgia newspaper; and the conditions were similar in other Southern States.

Under decree in equity, Sam 5 and Billy 2 years old were advertised to be sold at the Charleston Mart, May 2, 1860. They were at the end of a list of 13 slaves, with three other single slaves ahead of them.—*Courier*, Apr. 18, 1860.

In Tenn., December, 1860, an execution was levied on " Carter, aged 12 years, value $800; Nimrod, aged 7 years, value $400; and Jim, aged 4 years, value $300; * * * to be sold at the market house "[.]—2 Catterall, 596.

[29] 2 Catterall, 516.

For the payment of unsecured debts, it was an everyday occurrence to bring suit for the seizure and sale of slaves, including little children.

Slave property was such a token of aristocracy and riches that many persons made presents of little slaves to favorite children, godchildren, grandchildren, to newborns, and in rare instances the unborn were devised to the unborn.[30] When someone without a tiny slave wished to give one away, there was no alternative but to buy, as did certain Dillards: William and Merritt agreed to bid in a mother with two small children for $360, of which Merritt paid $100 and took Caroline, 4 years old, then gave her to his 5-year-old daughter and removed to Mississippi with them.[31]

According to conditions and sentiment, there was no serious objection to selling orphan children singly. Hundreds of domestic slaves, each belonging to some urban resident of modest means, must have died annually, leaving one or more small children. To help buy another servant or for some other reason, it often seemed best to sell the children, for without the mother it was troublesome for urban owners to rear them. Merely the little orphans that were thus put on the market were too numerous to be described as " hardly ever sold ". Outside of Louisiana, the announcements seldom mentioned that the little slaves

[30] 1 Catterall, 311, cites a case where a certain grandfather was " in the habit of advancing his children in slaves, and of presenting a slave to each of his grand children ".

The will of a North Carolinian read: " I * * * bequeath to my child that is not born * * * the first child that the negro wench Sive does have, if she should have any ".—2 Catterall, 108. A very similar case, *Ibid.*, 112. For references to gifts of children reported in printed records of the courts, see Mrs. Catterall's indexes under " Gift of slaves " etc.

[31] 2 Catterall, 514. In a Va. case a woman having only a life-interest in (and therefore no right to dispose of) Peg and her little Elijah, nevertheless sold him when he was 2 years old to one Martiney, who in the same year resold him to one Johnson, who gave him to his daughter, who took him to Arkansas.—1 Catterall, 227.

were orphans.[32]   This indicated either that in the other
cases they were not orphans or that the vendors were
indifferent as to what one might think.   Here are a few of
the rare exceptions.   Three orphan boys—May [sic],
Charles and Louis, respectively 5, 7 and 11 years old—were
sold at the Charleston Mart, February 14, 1860.   They were
" restricted to the city ".[33]   A week later, two more little
orphans, Charles, 7, and Mary, 5, were sold at the same
place.[34]   Such sales were good opportunities to get a slave
" Little Orphan Annie " to

> " come to our house to stay,
> An' wash the cups an' saucers up, an' brush the crumbs away,
> An' shoo the chickens off the porch, an' dust the hearth, an' sweep."

Although orphans were sometimes mentioned in sales, no
instance is known where a would-be purchaser of children
asked expressly for orphans.   That would have been considered a ludicrous absurdity.

Only four pages after Professor Phillips asserts that
young children were " hardly ever sold separately ", he
quotes the Lake Providence, Louisiana, *Herald's* report of
the sale of General L. C. Polk's slaves at auction, which
said that " men ranged from $1,500 to $1,635, women and
girls from $1,250 to $1,550, children in proportion—all
cash ".[35]   " Children in proportion " obviously implied
that the public was so familiar with the relative prices paid
for children that they could be inferred from prices ob-

[32] In La. it was essential to do so if they were under 10 years of age.   Thus
C. Pitts & Gardner Smith advertised " Two A No. 1 Orphan Children " for
sale privately—Tom, 8, and Rose 5.—New Orleans *Picayune*, Mar. 10, 1860.
Vignie sold at public sale, singly, Reville, " an orphan boy aged 9 years "
and two other boys of 13 and a girl of 12; on another day, Ellen, aged 12, and
Washington, 11, in a lot of 50, among whom there was only one couple, husband and wife, each 50 years of age, without any children, but ten mothers
with one or more children.—New Orleans *Picayune*, Feb. 16, 1856, gives details.

[33] *Courier*, Feb. 14, 1860.

[34] By J. S. Riggs, *Courier*, Feb. 21, 1860.

[35] *American Negro Slavery*, 373.

tained for men, women and girls. And such must have
been the case if the public then knew half as much about
the selling of young children separately as the reader
knows now.

But for expected financial advantages, there would
have been few divisions of families except among heirs or
legatees, and few sales of children singly except orphans.
To protect a vendor's good name or to soften the lot of
a slave, it was not rare to place or to appear to place restrictions on the purchaser's right to separate families,
to sell children before they reached a certain age or to
remove slaves from a specified region. In proportion as
these restrictions put important limitations on the purchaser's rights and were safeguarded, they lessened the
slaves's salability. It would have been easy to follow the
everyday practice of demanding a bond with approved
security when a slave was hired out to a stranger or sold
wholly or partly on credit, or to require a written agreement that if the restrictions should be violated, the sale
should be void.[36] But either plan would have made the
arrangement so undesirable as to reduce the slave's
market value by half or more. And the prospective vendor would not have been pleased any more than the prospective vendee, for the sale of slaves, except in the settlement of estates, commonly waited on special profit or
special need of money. The greater the restriction, the
more requisite was security and the smaller was the price
obtainable. There was the obstacle to, as well as the criterion of, a generous and effective restriction.

In 1835, an administratrix in Maryland, with due author-

[36] This case occurred in Virginia in 1807: " Garland sold a negro woman
with her two children to Bugg who, ' by his deed in writing, * * * did agree
that the sale * * * should be void * * * if the said plaintiff [Bugg] should
sell, hire, convey away, or otherwise divide the said slave from her two
children, until they should respectively attain the age of ten years.' "—
1 Catterall, 114.

ity of the orphans' court, advertised her intention to sell at auction, on a credit of six months, a woman to serve a term of years and her two infants to serve for life. They would be sold only to " a resident or residents of the county " and " the purchaser or purchasers " would be required to give bond not to dispose of the slaves to a foreign [non-resident?] purchaser or even remove them from the county. Although it was obviously contemplated that the children and the mother might be sold separately, probably the restriction as to removal from the county was expected to keep them within reach of one another. Presumably the allowance of six months' credit and the failure to require security were both due to a desire to obtain as much as possible for the benefit of the orphan or orphans, but lack of security left the welfare of the slaves precarious. The outcome is unknown.[37]

A citizen of Madison county, Kentucky, needing money sold for $325 a family slave, supposed to be worth about $400, to another resident of the county, who said that he wished her for his own use there, but soon disposed of her to a trader for the Southern market. The original owner brought suit for having been " deceived and defrauded * * * and caused great distress and anxiety of mind in him and his family ", and obtained judgment for $100 as damages.[38] Because no security, and perhaps no written contract, had been required, the defrauder fancied that he could violate the understanding with impunity.

[37] " *Negroes for Sale.*—By virtue of an order from the orphans' Court of Dorchester County, will be sold at public sale, at Hicksburg, on Thursday, the 12th of February next, on a credit of six months, a negro woman named Silvia, to serve a term of years and her two children, one and two years old, for life. They will not be sold to any but a resident or residents of the county, and the purchaser or purchasers will moreover be required to give bond that they shall not be disposed of to a foreign [non-resident of the county?] purchaser or even removed from the county.—Elizabeth H. Vane, Adm'x. of Mary S. J. B. Vane, dec'd."—Cambridge, Md., *Chronicle*, Jan. 24, 1835.

[38] 1 Catterall, 374-75.

The master saved his good name, suffered only in his feelings, without losing a dollar, but the family slave was in the far South and could not be recovered.

Another case in Kentucky resulted similarly for all parties concerned.[39] The owner of a slave, needing to raise a sum of money, agreed to sell him for $500 less than he was worth, on condition that the purchaser should keep him in the county and not separate him from his wife, but, if compelled to dispose of him, to let the original owner have the refusal at cost price. This was all disregarded and this slave also was " sold South ". The original master brought suit for damages and obtained enough to make up the full value of his property. He preserved his good name, lost nothing; but the slave lost in all respects and forever—an obvious danger not guarded against.

In such cases, to have required a bond with ample security to protect the slave, might have either prevented his sale or so reduced his market value that the master would have been unwilling to make the sacrifice. Except for special reasons, it was incompatible with the prestige of slaveholding to have one's rights restricted, and law and custom were against encroachments on the master's absolute control of his slave. Accordingly few persons cared to buy limited ownership in a slave, unless there was prospect of a large percentage of gain, either from purchase at a very low price or by violating the restrictions.

In many instances the restrictions contained a strong suggestion, even a clear and positive pledge, of readiness to reduce the price or give some other advantage in order to secure some benefit to the slave. But where a marked sacrifice was required, the master rarely provided for due safeguards against a dishonest purchaser.[40]

[39] 1 Catterall, 344.

[40] The following advertisements are considered fair illustrations of this class of cases:—

" FIRST RATE Negro Man, about 27 years old, for sale very low, on

Because shapely and prepossessing young mulattresses
were likely to be bought for an immoral purpose in addition to their work—and quadroons and octoroons were
still more likely to be—conscientious vendors would sometimes attempt to protect them for a time by a restriction

condition he is not to be taken out of this State. Warranted sound in every
particular, a good farm hand, and a first rate teamster. Apply to DICKER-
SON & AUSTIN, Auctioneers."—St. Louis *Daily Missouri Republican*, April
25, 1852.

John Donovan, presumably an agent in Cambridge, Md., advertised: "I
will sell one or more or all of three Negro Men, to persons in the county that
they will consent to live with, as slaves for life. One is aged about 40 years,
one about 28 years, and the other about 40 years or more. Two of them live
now, and have done, in the neighborhood of Vienna, and have hired for a
number of years; the other is now hired on Fishing Creek. They are not sold
for any fault; but their master living at a distance, would prefer selling
them to good homes, and thereby relieve himself of further trouble."—Cambridge *Chronicle*, Dec. 14, 1833.

James Houston offered at private sale: "A young negro man, of good
character, living in the neighborhood of Cambridge—Also, a negro woman,
about thirty-two or thirty-three years old, with a girl child five or six years
old, residing in the neighborhood of Vienna. They will not be sold to go out
of the county; and [are to] have a choice of masters."—Cambridge, *Chronicle*, Oct. 25, 1834.

One B. W. Belsches, living in Sussex county, Va., had "for sale twenty-five
or thirty likely young negroes, consisting of men, women, and children. They
will be sold low if they can be disposed of in families, as it is not my purpose to separate them. Farmers and planters in want of such property are
invited to call on" or address the subscriber.—Petersburg, Va., *Republican*,
Dec. 30, 1846.

Auctioneers Ferguson and Wilkinson, of Norfolk, Va., would sell on the
morrow at a promiscuous sale "one negro girl 10 years old with a likely boy
child [of] 18 months, sold for no fault whatever, an excellent house servant,
properly honest, can wash and iron, sold not to be carried out of the city or
Portsmouth. The owner being in want of money".—Norfolk *Southern Argus*,
Jan. 18, 1855. In this and the Fitten advt. (below) no special advantage was
offered.

Nashville traders, H. H. Haynes & Co., had "a NEGRO MAN of excellent
character for sale, not to be taken out of the county, and in order to secure a
good home, he can be bought on time."—*Republican Banner*, Dec. 31, 1858.

An offer to sell a farm and other real estate, because the owner was going
"to settle a plantation in Cherokee, Ga.", ends thus:

"A FEW SERVANTS. These consist chiefly of cooks, washers and ironers,
and house servants. They are negroes of excellent character; and as the
object of the owner in selling, is to avoid the necessity of separating husbands

like this: " A remarkably likely mulatto girl, 14 years of age, of good character; to be sold only to a responsible city resident." [41]

Some so-called restrictions were specious—were for the sake of appearances or merely expressed a preference or were only advertising devices to deceive the unsophisticated into believing that slaves thus nominally protected must have rare qualities.[42]   Others made general offers or sug-

and wives, they will not be sold out of the city or its immediate neighborhood. For other particulars, apply to JOHN H. FITTEN ", an Augusta slave-agent etc.—*Chronicle & Sentinel*, Apr. 5, 1859.

[41] The owner, undoubtedly wishing to keep his name as nearly secret as possible, gave the commission to trader Salinas.—Charleston *Mercury*, Jan. 31, 1860. Salinas previously advertised similar restrictions as to " a remarkably likely and intelligent mulatto GIRL, about 20 years of age, an excellent seamstress and mantuamaker, warranted as to character, capacity and soundness, and to be sold only to a resident of the city ".—*Courier*, Jan. 5, 1857.

[42] One week, trader Marshall of Charleston had " at private sale, Frank a first rate drayman, well acquainted with the city, and of good character, aged about 34 years, and warranted sound. He will be sold only to a city resident." The next week he advertised: " To-morrow, the 24th inst., at half-past 10 o'clock, will be sold at the Mart in Chalmers-street, Frank, a drayman and porter. He is remarkably intelligent and is well acquainted with the city, and of good character, and warranted sound.—Conditions—One-half cash; balance in one year, with interest, secured by bond and mortgage, with good personal security."—*Courier*, respectively, Jan. 16 and 23, 1860. All restrictions had vanished, if indeed there had ever been any except to deceive the public into believing that the owner of this " first rate drayman " " of good character " was specially kind to his faithful slave; but ample security for the unpaid half of the price was carefully provided for.

At another time Marshall announced, that " by order of the Administrator and with permission of the Ordinary ", he would sell " a family " at the Charleston Mart: Lucretia, aged 28 and a first-rate seamstress and her five children, ranging from one to 13 years of age. " They are sold only to close the estate, and are limited to the State ".—*Courier*, Jan. 24, 1859. Obviously this was to show that the sale was necessary, and to make it appear that the heirs or legatees were guarding the welfare of the slaves. But the highest bidder, even any S. C. trader, would obtain them; nothing was said against separating the family; and " limited to the State ", unless guarded by a well secured bond, was no more likely to be lastingly effective than restrictions about food, clothing and Sunday privileges would have been.

Trader J. Russell Baker offered at private sale, " to a city resident, a family of good and well behaved [house] servants, to remain in the city, as

gestions of some reduction to certain purchasers, but covered everything with secrecy and imposed no positive restraints.[43]

they are sold for no fault": Sarah, 25, James, 11, Eugenia, 6, Fortune, 4. They were "all sound and healthy" and could be seen at his office.—*Courier*, Feb. 23, 1860. Nothing was said about not dividing the family (if left in Charleston) nor about any reduction in price. This would certainly have been required if there had been binding restrictions in the interest of the slaves.

"Broker" J. S. Ryan had for sale privately at his office [22 Broad st.] "William, a very capable and industrious fellow, a ship-carpenter" and also his mother, "an elderly woman, said to be a cook". And he added: "It is the wish of the owner that they be sold together, and to a city resident."— *Courier*, June 23, 1857. This was only a wish. The mother might have been bought and given away the following day.

The Charleston *Courier* of Nov. 25, 1836, contained the following: "Valuable seaman at private sale—has been brought up to the coasting business, and can take a vessel as pilot or cockswain to any part of the country, which he has been accustomed to do, and is now in steady employ, is stout and healthy, and of warranted character, and makes no use of ardent spirits of any kind. To the owner of a coaster, would be invaluable; is sold only to change the property, and not to be carried out of the State. Can be seen at my house at any time this day, or on Monday next. A. Whitney, No. 9 Cumberland St." To have made effective, by a well secured bond, the restriction "not to be carried out of the State", would have reduced by a very large percentage the market value of that model seaman and capable pilot.

"Broker" Hume offered a coachman and ostler, who was "sound, sober and honest" and would be "invaluable to a family". But the sentence, "A purchaser in the city preferred", expressed all the generosity the unnamed master felt for the slave's invaluable services.—*Mercury*, Aug. 1, 1860.

"FOR SALE, A STOUT, healthy YOUNG NEGRO MAN of superior character—not sold for a single fault. He will be sold at a reasonable price,— the purchaser restricted from selling him out of the District of Columbia without his own consent. *Apply at this office."*—Alexandria *Phenix Gazette*, Jan. 6, 1827. A master's right in a slave limited by that slave's consent!

"Auctioneer Dyer of Washington had "for sale [privately] a very valuable and likely negro boy, aged about 15 years, brought up to house-work, an excellent waiter—slave for life. A preference will be given to gentlemen residents of the District or State of Maryland, who want for their own family use."—*National Intelligencer*, Dec. 5, 1836. A mere "preference" did not imply either a reduction or a restriction.

The *Key to Uncle Tom's Cabin*, 141, quotes this absurdly frank sentence from an advertisement in Weston, Mo., in 1852: "I wish to sell her in the neighborhood of Camden Point; if not sold there in a short time, I will hunt the best market; or I will trade her for two small ones, a boy and girl."

[43] In one number of the Charleston *Courier* (Jan. 17, 1860) McCall adver-

Between kindred, neighbors or friends, efforts to prevent separations or removals in the near future were numerous and were easily successful. At private sales one could often judge whether a prospective buyer would, during his life, conform with the conditions; if there was doubt, he could be rejected, but sometimes was not, as the Kentucky cases prove. At public sales it was virtually impossible to prevent anyone with money from buying, directly or indirectly, and then disposing of the slaves as he pleased, unless a bond with ample security was required, which was rarely done. In proportion as the restrictions were positive and important, yet without security, conscientious persons could not afford to pay so much as unscrupulous persons that intended to disregard them.[44] Accordingly such restrictions must often have

tised at private sale: (1) "Lucinda, about thirty-five years old, a good cook, washer and ironer, also a good house servant, of mild disposition, civil, honest, and of industrious habits, sound and healthy. To a city resident she will be sold at a moderate price." (2) "Shad, an experienced Coachman, trusty and confidential House Servant, of unexceptional character, thirty-five years old; healthy, civil, and of sober and industrious habits. To a City purchaser he will be sold reasonable."

At the same time and in the same place Wilbur & Son likewise offered "Toby, about forty years old, a valuable Painter. Will be sold on very easy terms to an approved purchaser."

The Norfolk *Southern Argus* of Jan. 2, 1855, acting as agent, with " Apply at this office ", contained these two advts.: (1) "A likely man servant aged 24 years, brought up in a house in this city, and if sold to remain here, a moderate price will be taken." (2) "A valuable and healthy man, accustomed to wait in the house or store. A purchaser in the city will be preferred so as to enable him to remain with his family."

"CAPERS & HEYWARD, on Jan. 13, 1860, publicly sold for cash at the Charleston Mart a "prime family of [9] plantation negroes ": Rose 40, and her 8 children—Ellen, 18, Anthony, 16, Abram, 14; Chance, 10; Billy, 6; twins Adam and Eve, 4; Charlotte, 1, for an average price of $450 [a total of $4,050].—*Courier*, Jan. 13, *Mercury*, Jan. 14, 1860. Evidently the owner needed cash at once. That all were sold together is conclusively shown by the fact that all had to be resold, Jan. 26, 1860, when they brought an average price of only $400 [a total of $3,600]—*Mercury*, Jan. 26 and 27, 1860. There was no sign of any further restriction. A trader could probably soon have resold the five elder children singly for nearly as much as the " family "

given an advantage to speculators—exactly the persons from whom good masters wished to save their slaves. Could such a sham have been in vogue decade after decade? It seems more probable that the alleged restrictions at auctions, and often at private sales, were chiefly pretenses to attract buyers or to pose as humane and not selling on account of financial reverses or to speculate. These social considerations were regarded as of prime importance and worth moderate sacrifices. But what was vital to the slaves and was represented as a sacrifice and an act of benevolence on the part of the master, was usually left without sufficient protection and was likely to be forgotten or disregarded after a few years; for creditors, legatees and most heirs insist on obtaining their full rights. In most cases there was enough of a contract to enable the master to recover financial losses, but it was virtually impossible to restore the slave to his favored status. Thus, for the master, either a preventive or compensation for financial loss sufficed; for the slave, only a preventive availed.

Of course it was not rare for wills to contain provisions for emancipations and benevolent restrictions. They became matters of record and were rigidly carried out by the proper court. But the motives that prompted such last-opportunity generosities were very different from those prevalent in slave-trading, and were sometimes as much concerned with the final good name of the testator as with the welfare of the slave.

of nine cost, and the mother's work would have sufficed to maintain the others until she and they were worth half as much more.

CHAPTER X

SAVANNAH'S LEADING TRADER AND HIS LARGEST SALE

A South Carolinian who had represented his State in the Philadelphia Constitutional Convention of 1787 and later in the United States Senate, died early in the eighteen twenties, leaving to two grandsons his hundreds of slaves and thousands of acres of very fertile land in Georgia, long used for the culture of rice and sea-island cotton. Many years later an English actress of rare talent, beauty and human sympathy married one of these heirs. When, near the end of the 'thirties, she visited these plantations she was distressed to find what miserable lives the negroes led; but there was some balm for her heartaches in the fact that the worst features of slavery did not exist there, for, as she wrote, " the slaves on this estate are not bought and sold, nor let out to hire to other masters; • • • and • • • members of one family are not parted from each other for life, and sent to distant plantations in other States,—all which liabilities • • • belong of right, or rather of wrong, to their condition as slaves, and are commonly practised throughout the Southern half of this free country " • • •.

Georgians suffered less than South Carolinians on account of the competition and superior advantages offered by the cheap and fertile land in the Southwest. They were also less prone to lead the easy-going, extravagant life of the typical planter. Consequently not so many of their negroes were sold. While Charleston was the center of the very extensive trading in South Carolina, Savannah, with little more than half the population of her rival seaport, had to share Georgia's slave-trading with Augusta, Atlanta, Milledgeville, Macon, Columbus and smaller places.

Savannah shared Georgia's slave-trade with other cities, but Joseph Bryan had almost a monopoly of Savannah's and also had much of that of northern Florida.[1] In December, 1859, he wished to sell " an orderly and well reared gang of 138 negroes, accustomed to the culture of rice ", and to buy " 100 young and likely single negroes " and " 200 negroes in gangs or families ".[2] Such wholesale purchases must have been for remote markets. But he did not reject the smallest and worst features of the trade.[3] From large sales for Georgians and Floridians and large purchases for distant planters Joseph Bryan must have derived an enormous income for that time. In a single number of a newspaper his offerings included six gangs of various sizes and a few odd lots, making a total of 381 slaves.[4] The name of the owner of not one of those gangs was mentioned.

[1] Wm. Wright sometimes had even more small lots of slaves for sale than Joseph Bryan (see Savannah *Republican*, Dec. 18, 1858), but neither he nor one A. Bryan, who did considerable trading, was of the first class. In the *Republican* of Dec. 30, 1859, this A. Bryan had:

" FOR SALE. LIKELY country raised girl, 17 years old, capable servant; likely intelligent yellow girl child, 5 years, country raised; one man and his wife, and 2 girl children, 8 and 4 years old, fieldhands; middle aged woman, good plain cook, washer and house servant; 2 likely girls, 8 and 11 years old; 2 boys, capable to saddle and harness, making intelligent good workmen; 2 men, 24 and 26 years old; several old men and women; 1 woman and 2 girl children, woman good cook; several other families. A. BRYAN, Market Square."

And two Macon traders, J. B. Allgood and C. F. Stubbs, advertised for 200.

In 1860 Joseph Bryan bought 53 slaves of George N. Jones, a large Florida planter, paying a net price of $44,200. Jones said that he was " desirous of investing the proceeds in other similar property ".—Phillips and Glunt, editors, *Florida Plantation Records*, 558-60.

[2] Savannah *Republican*, Dec. 30, 1859.

[3] Charles A. L. Lamar who had caused more than 400 negroes to be brought from Africa to Georgia on the " Wanderer " (see *post* p. 360) had sore trials in disposing of some of them. In July, 1859, he wrote: " I told you Tucker returned one of the boys sold in Columbus—sent him to Akin's for my account!!! He is in Joe Bryan's [slave-pen] and has had a number of fits. He has the itch, and Joe wants him removed. I don't know what to do with him. No one will take him."—143 *North Amer. Review*, 459.

[4] *Republican*, Jan. 28, 1860.

Only a gang of 140 rice-field negroes was, as yet, for sale at auction. The leading newspaper editorially served the leading trader thus:—

"LARGE SALE OF NEGROES.—We would remind all interested of the large sale of negroes, to take place today, at Laroche's Brickyard, one mile east of the city, on the Thunderbolt Road, under the direction of Capt. Bryan. It is seldom such an opportunity is offered to those who have money to invest in that species of property. Good prices to the Captain and good homes to the negroes!"[5]

Two days later it was likewise reported that the average price obtained was but $625—" less than at any sale that has recently come to our knowledge ". " The lot, however, was very far from being a prime one ".[6] After all, the rare " opportunity " was for sellers and advertising purposes, not for buyers, and the matter of " good homes for the negroes " was of no further interest.

The title of captain was not generous for the prosperous and famous interstate trader that in March, 1859, had held a public sale of a gang of about 450 " long cotton and rice negroes ". A paid advertisement of this great slave-auction, in at least ten of the leading Southern newspapers from Richmond to New Orleans indicated where the purchasers were expected to come from and the slaves to go.[7] But no hint was given as to who the master was,

---

[5] *Republican*, Feb. 2, 1860.

[6] *Republican*, Feb. 4. 1860.

[7] " FOR SALE. LONG COTTON AND RICE NEGROES.

A GANG OF 460 NEGROES, accustomed to the culture of Rice and Provisions; among whom are a number of good mechanics, and house servants. Will be sold on the 2d and 3d of March next, at Savannah, by

JOSEPH BRYAN

TERMS OF SALE.—One-third cash; remainder by bond, bearing interest from day of sale, payable in two equal instalments, to be secured by mortgage on the negroes, and approved personal security, or for approved city acceptance on Savannah or Charleston. Purchasers paying for papers.

The negroes will be sold in families, and can be seen on the premises of JOSEPH BRYAN, in Savannah, three days prior to the day of sale, when catalogues will be furnished.

* * * The Charleston *Courier* (daily and tri-weekly); *Christian Index*,

why he was selling so many or where they came from. Bryan must have had very large premises, for it was announced that three days before the sale the negroes could be seen there. But finally it was decided that only the grounds of the Race Course, three miles from the city, could afford satisfactory facilities.

Before the end of February numerous strangers, mainly of an unpolished type, dressed like rough planters and showing some of the qualities of hard-drinking overseers, gamblers or traders, appeared at the Savannah hotels. In the corridors and barrooms, filled with dense tobacco smoke, there was much serious talk, generously interspersed with profanity, " Yes, sah ", " No, sah ", accentuated by military titles in the solemn vocative, and punctuated with frequent expectorations. The talk was, of course, almost entirely about " niggrahs " or " niggers "—what prices some had brought recently; whose had made large crops or been especially prolific, had run away or been recovered; whether the successful trip of the " Wanderer " meant that a reopening of the foreign slave-trade was possible, and if so, what effect this would have on the value of " home-raised niggers ". On these latter questions opinions varied according to supposed interests. But the practical question with all the visitors was to obtain news about the forthcoming sale. Another editorial item supplied the following:

"*LARGE SALE OF NEGROES.*—Upwards of four hundred negroes, of both sexes and all ages, are now quartered at the Race Course, in charge of Capt. J. Bryan, of this city. The sale will commence Wednes-

---

Macon, Ga.; Albany *Patriot*, Augusta *Constitutionalist*, Mobile *Register*, New Orleans *Picayune*, Memphis *Appeal*, Vicksburg *Southron*, and Richmond *Whig*, will publish till day of sale and send bills to this office."—*Savannah Republican*, Feb. 28, 1859.

Mortimer Thomson, a special correspondent of the New York *Tribune*, published in it, Mar. 9, 1859, a long account of this sale. He attended incognito and even joined in the bidding, the better to conceal his identity. The American Anti-Slavery Society reprinted the article in a little pamphlet of 28 pages. It supplies many of the details used in the following narrative.

8

day next, and probably continue for some days. This is probably one of the largest lots of negroes ever offered in the State, and it therefore presents many inducements to purchasers." [8]

This great gang had been brought to Savannah in freight cars [9] and were soon driven out to the Race Course. In sheds built for use during the races, the slaves were " huddled pell-mell " with bundles and boxes containing extra clothing, tin dishes and supplies of food—rice, beans, bacon and corn-meal. Without benches or tables, they sat, ate and slept on the bare floor, except when they could use their baggage as seats or pillows. " On the faces of all was an expression of heavy grief ", wrote the New York *Tribune's* correspondent; " some appeared to be resigned to the hard stroke of Fortune that had torn them from their homes, and were sadly trying to make the best of it; some sat brooding moodily over their sorrows, their chins resting on their hands, their eyes staring vacantly, and their bodies rocking to and fro, with a restless motion that was never stilled; few wept, the place was too public and the drivers too near, though some occasionally turned aside to give way to a few quiet tears. They were dressed in every possible variety of uncouth and fantastic garb, in every style and of every imaginable color; the texture of the garments was in all cases coarse, most of the men being clothed in the rough cloth that is made expressly for the slaves." Gay-colored, cotton handkerchiefs fashioned into turbans were the coverings, if any, that the women wore on their heads. Their dresses were also of cheap and sometimes gaudy stuff. The little children—of all sizes and ages, the youngest only fifteen days old—were noticeably less poorly dressed than their elders. There were " some 30 babies in the lot ".

For several days prior to the sale anyone might inspect

[8] *Republican*, Feb. 28, 1859.

[9] A son of a neighboring planter many years later told the author that, when a boy, he saw the slaves put on the train.

the slaves between 10 A. M. and 2 P. M.[10] Bryan's catalogue of 16 pages supplied only meager descriptions—a numerical list giving the usually one-word name of each slave, followed by figures indicating his or her age, the kind and quality of the work performed, and any physical defects, thus:

> "99—Kate's John, aged 30; rice, prime man.
> 118—Pompey, 31; rice—lame in one foot.
> 345—Dorcas, 17; cotton, prime woman.
> 346—Joe [Dorcas's babe and the only member of her 'family' present] 3 months."

Other information was obtainable only by inquiry and inspection. Each negro conspicuously bore a number. Slaves in gangs just from their plantation work were usually examined much less rigorously than the miscellaneous collections by traders, for wilful deception was quite unlikely. But, *caveat emptor*. And most buyers were fond of showing by inspection that they "knew all about niggers". "The negroes were examined with as little consideration as if they had been brutes indeed", wrote our witness; "the buyers pulling their mouths open to see their teeth, pinching their limbs to find how muscular they were, walking them up and down to detect any signs of lameness, making them stoop and bend in different ways that they might be certain there was no concealed rupture or wound; and in addition to all this treatment, asking them scores of questions relative to their qualifications and accomplishments."

The negroes themselves were but little less eager to look for a good master and to make a favorable impression on any kindly inquirer. Here is a pathetic illustration:—
"'Elisha', chattel No. 5 in the catalogue, had taken a fancy to a benevolent-looking middle-aged gentleman, who

[10] "SALE OF 440 NEGROES!—Persons desiring to inspect these Negroes, will find them at the Race Course, where they can be seen from 10 A. M. to 2 P. M., until day of sale. J. BRYAN, Johnson's square, Feb. 26."—*Republican*, Feb. 28, 1859.

was inspecting the stock, and thus used his powers of persuasion to induce the benevolent man to purchase him, with his wife, boy and girl, Molly, Israel and Sevanda, chattels Nos. 6, 7 and 8. The earnestness with which the poor fellow pressed his suit, knowing, as he did, that perhaps the happiness of his whole life depended on his success, was touching, and the arguments he used most pathetic. He made no appeal to the feelings of the buyer; he rested no hope on his charity and kindness, but only strove to show how well worth his dollars were the bone and blood he was entreating him to buy. ' Look at me, Mas'r; am prime rice planter; sho' you won't find a better man den me; no better on de whole plantation; not a bit old yet; do mo' work den ever; do carpenter work, too, little; better buy me, Mas'r; I'se de good sarvant, Mas'r. Molly, too, my wife, Sa, fus' rate rice hand; mos as good as me. Stan' out yer, Molly, and let the gen'lm'n see.' Molly advances, with her hands crossed on her bosom, and makes a quick short curtsy, and stands mute, looking appealingly in the benevolent man's face. But Elisha talks all the faster. ' Show Mas'r yer arm, Molly—good arm dat, Mas'r—she do a heap of work mo' with dat arm yet. Let good Mas'r see yer teeth, Molly—see dat, Mas'r, teeth all regular, all good—she'm young gal yet. Come out yer, Israel, walk aroun' an' let the gen'lm see how spry you be '. Then, pointing to the three-year-old girl who stood with her chubby hand to her mouth, holding on to her mother's dress and uncertain what to make of the strange scene, said: ' Little Vardy's only a chile yet; make prime gal by-and-by. Better buy us, Mas'r, we'm fus' rate bargain '—and so on. But the benevolent gentleman found where he could drive a closer bargain, and so bought somebody else.''

If the questioner was rough, the slave was likely to depreciate himself by acts and words. The personal-service slaves often exercised much influence at such times, for appearance and disposition were important factors;

but the fieldhands were judged mainly according to age and strength and, if young women, actual or probable fecundity. The vital importance of that quality was well illustrated by a characteristic dialogue overheard at this inspection:

" Well, Colonel, I seen you looking sharp at shoemaker Bill's Sally. Going to buy her ? "

" Well, Major, I think not. Sally's a good, big, strapping gal, and can do a heap o' work; but it's five years since she had any children. *She's done breeding, I reckon.*"

Although heavy and prolonged rain and the expense of hiring special conveyances barred numerous idle curious persons, " the attendance was very large and from all portions of the State and of the States adjoining ".[11] Before 10 o'clock on March 2, 1859, the slaves with much of their baggage were crowded into the grand-stand of the Race Course, a room about one hundred feet long and twenty wide. The auction was held in an adjoining room, which on one side was open to the storm. There was a platform two and one-half feet high and large enough for the desks of clerks and to leave ample space for the auctioneer to stand and slaves to be exhibited. The spectators and prospective bidders crowded about the platform, but the negroes that were not high on the list " gathered into sad groups in the background to watch the progress of the selling in which they were so sorrowfully interested. The wind howled outside, and through the open side of the building the driving rain came pouring in; the bar down stairs ceased for a short time its brisk trade; the buyers lit fresh cigars, got ready their catalogues and pencils, and the first lot of human chattels was led upon the stand, not by a white man, but by a sleek mulatto, himself a slave, and who seems to regard the selling of his brethren, in which he so glibly assists, as a capital joke."

Captain Bryan, described as a prim, officious, slender,

[11] *Republican,* Mar. 3, 1859.

little man with an almost fierce air, was, of course, in
supreme command, but he merely supervised the sale and
took care that the slaves were exhibited to the best advantage. His representative for the vocal and laborious part
was T. J. Walsh, one of the best auctioneers of slaves in all
Georgia, and cited as a reference by commission merchants
as far away as Macon. He had sold thousands, perhaps
tens of thousands and had the prestige of being a large
trader in his own right. Unlike the Captain, Walsh was
carelessly dressed, fat, large, good natured, had a florid
complexion and was " a rollicking old boy, with an eye on
the lookout ", never letting a nod escape, always having
" a hearty word for every bidder ", " and plenty of jokes
to let off " to enliven the company. He was fully equipped
for his part, and it did not handicap him in the least that
the redness of his face was varied by peely spots, probably
the results of blisters, which, it was said, caused him to look
as if he had been boiled in a pot with a red cabbage.

Good auctioneers go straight to the main points. Here
was an exceptionally prime gang—several of them, in fact,
all from one estate—fresh from work and under perfect
discipline. Because there had been relatively few outside
attachments, not many family ties needed to be broken;
and there was an exceptionally large proportion of full
groups, each with parents and children and sometimes with
other kindred. In such cases, sales by families were advantageous. The bidding was by an average price per person.
Thus if a family of five estimated to be worth about $4,000
—the father $1,200, the mother $950 and the children $725,
$650 and $475—were on the block, the first offer might be
$300 or $400 and the sale nominally at $775, but really
at $3,875. This neither usual nor very rare method was
doubtless adopted because skilful auctioneers could get
better prices by it; for the bids tossed about always
remained in seemingly small figures, whereas the value of
the best slave in the group was likely to be uppermost in
the bidder's mind. It prevented dividing families then

and there, but not later; it restricted the buying to persons with large resources, which gave rich traders the advantage, for, having cash, they could afford to outbid planters, who were dependent on their factors or bankers and had to pay a high rate of interest.

All but the small children realized that the old home had been seen for the last time and that past ties, except between persons sold in one group, were soon to be broken. Some manifested distressful anxiety, others appeared stolid. " Blighted homes, crushed hopes and broken hearts was the sad story to be read in all the anxious faces. Some of them regarded the sale with perfect indifference, never making a motion save to turn from one side to the other at the word of the dapper Mr. Bryan, that all the crowd might have a fair view of their proportions, and then, when the sale was accomplished, stepped down from the block without caring to cast even a look at the buyer, who now held all their happiness in his hands." No order of any court, no grasping heirs nor legatees, made it peremptory to obtain the largest amount possible for these slaves, and the sale seems to have been conducted with decent humanity, according to the notions of the best slave-selling planters. There were, indeed, pathetic and sorrowful incidents, but they were not by any fault of the alert Captain nor of the merry auctioneer nor of the owner, whoever he was; they almost necessarily inhered in the brutal business. Our witness supplied several examples.

" The family of Primus, plantation carpenter, consisting of Daphney his wife, with her young babe, and Dido, a girl of three years old, were reached in due course of time. Daphney had a large shawl, which she kept carefully wrapped round her infant and herself. This unusual proceeding attracted much attention, and provoked many remarks, such as these:

' What do you keep your nigger covered up for? Pull off her blanket.'
' What's the matter with the gal? Has she got the headache? '

'What's the fault of the gal? Ain't she sound? Pull off her rags and let us see her.'

'Who's going to bid on that nigger, if you keep her covered up. Let's see her face.' * * *

At last the auctioneer obtained a hearing long enough to explain that there was no attempt to practise any deception in the case—the parties were not to be wronged in any way; he had no desire to palm off on them an inferior article; but the truth of the matter was that Daphney had been confined only fifteen days ago, and he thought that on that account she was entitled to the slight indulgence of a blanket, to keep from herself and child the chill air and the driving rain.''

The vendue continued two days. All but about 20 or 30 (accounts disagree) of the 460 originally advertised were thus disposed of—a few had been left on the plantation on account of illness, and a few others had been sold privately. It was said that 126 were under ten years of age, 182 were over ten and under thirty-one, 88 over thirty and under fifty, and 40 over fifty years of age. There were also several crippled and superannuated slaves. The 436 sold there brought '' an average of a little over $716 a head ''.[12] The highest price received for a single man, a fair carpenter and calker, was $1750; the most for a single woman, a cotton-hand and house-servant, $1250. '' Prime young men generally brought from $1250 to $1350. A family [apparently of brothers and sisters, who in most sales would have been disposed of separately] consisting of a woman 24 years of age, boy 21, girl 17, girl 15 and boy 12—five in number, brought $6025, or an average of $1205 each. A plain plantation blacksmith and his wife brought $2,900.'' [13] '' Anson and Violet, chattels Nos. 111 and 112, were sold for $250 each, both being old, and Anson being down in the catalogue as ' ruptured and as having

[12] Savannah News, quoted by tri-weekly Charleston Mercury, Mar. 5, 1859.
[13] Republican, Mar. 3, 1859.

one eye.' Violet was sold as being sick. Her disease was probably consumption, which supposition gave rise to the following feeling conversation between two buyers:

'Cheap gal that, Major.'

'Don't think so. They may talk about her being sick; it's no easy sickness she's got. She's got consumption, and the man that buys her'll have to be doctorin' her all the time, and she'll die in less than three months. I won't have anything to do with her—don't want any half-dead niggers about me.' "

The aggregate received from the whole auction was variously mentioned as from $300,205 to $307,000. This was somewhat less than was expected, and the average of $716 was much below those of numerous phenomenal sales that were trumpeted throughout the South in 1859 and 1860.

However, Captain Bryan cheerfully contemplated the result. His two and one-half per cent for sale alone and the charges for advertising, custody, food and incidentals must have amounted to about eight thousand dollars. And he knew how to treat his patrons and admirers—whether planters, traders, prosperous recent overseers or merely curious idlers—and they were not without expectations. It was a time for a bibulous expression of mutual good-will fitting so happy an occasion. Baskets of champagne were produced and there was a rapid popping of corks. The company enthusiastically drank congratulations to the dapper Captain and the dappled auctioneer on their great success; and the Captain, like a generous host, drank to the health and the prosperity of all who had favored the occasion with their presence. How perfect a climax to an ever-memorable event!

But who was this prosperous and gentlemanly slave-trader Captain Bryan? Nearly seventy years previously, when Edmund Randolph was Attorney-General of the United States, two youths were at least supposed to be reading law in his office. One was his second cousin, to be famous as John Randolph of Roanoke, and the other was Joseph Bryan, a son of a Georgia planter. In staid old Philadelphia these pampered youths, born in 1773 and still in their reckless teens, easily found and readily yielded to temptations, and soon realized that they had like taste for dissipation and like distaste for the law. One good resulted—an intimate, fraternal and life-long friendship. Within about a decade each was a Representative in Congress from his native State. Bryan married a daughter of General Forman of the Eastern Shore of Maryland. Of their five children the second and fourth were girls; the first became the namesake, the godson, and married a niece of John Randolph; the third was Thomas; the fifth was Joseph, born in 1812, the year of his father's death. Randolph loved and treated John like a son; and, in 1816, when Joseph was too young to leave his mother, John and Thomas were taken to Roanoke, where they passed four years and were often called "my dear children".[14] When only twenty-four years old, Joseph was appointed a purser in the United States Navy, where he remained eighteen years, resigning in 1854. Soon thereafter he turned to slave-trading, and being of an excellent family, like Thomas Norman Gadsden, Louis D. DeSaussure and many other aristocratic traders, he easily prospered.[15]

And who was the recent master of these slaves? Even before the sale he was reported to have appeared in a kindly manner among them. After the festivities were ended it was noticed that the negroes were swarming about a man then known to be Pierce Butler. It was he and his

[14] Bruce, 2 *John Randolph*, 458, 463, 470, 565, 569.

[15] Prof. Phillips (*Life and Labor in the Old South*, 363-64) devotes a sentimental page to the love affairs of Joseph Bryan, senior, and to Randolph's eulogy of him, but gives no hint that the son, to whom he refers (*Ibid.*, 272) as "Joseph Bryan, a slave dealer at Savannah", was in any way related to Randolph's old friend. To have mentioned the relationship would have made a startling anti-climax. And the index contains no reference to the slave-trader: the identical names put together there, even without *Sr.* and *Jr.*, would have suggested a kinship.

brother who inherited from their grandfather, Major Pierce Butler,[16] that great Georgia estate near the mouth of the Altamaha River, where the brilliant young wife, famous as Fanny Kemble, saw the distressing condition of the slaves, yet had the comforting thought—that not one of them had ever been sold or even hired out! But Pierce Butler was a luxurious, romantic absentee (as his marriage betokened), living in Philadelphia and willing neither to devote himself to this great inheritance nor to restrict himself to the returns from it. Finally, unfortunate ventures and the financial crash of 1857-58 compelled him to dispose of his half of the estate. He had come to the sale, bringing from the United States Mint bags of bright new quarters, and was giving each adult negro four shining pieces of silver as a farewell consolation. "Not much; barely one-tenth of one per cent, or one dollar in a thousand", would you say? In fact, it was a rare kindness; for it came not before the sale, when it might have made the slaves look cheerful and sell for more, but after it, when the former master was no longer rich and had nothing to gain except the satisfaction of being kind to the unfortunate.[17]

The slaves became the property of many new masters, undoubtedly including numerous traders, living in several different States. For a week hardly a boat or train left Savannah without taking some of them to their future homes—or other markets. That was the time when the

[16] Kemble, *Journal of a Georgia Plantation*, 43.

[17] Prof. Phillips quotes as if true what one of Butler's slaves alleged, in 1866, his master said to him before the sale: " Bram, I am in great trouble; I have no money and I have to sell some [460!] of the people, but I know where you are all going to. and will buy you back as soon as I can."—*Old South*, 265. The advertisements of the sale in ten newspapers from Richmond to New Orleans indicated where purchasers were sought. Butler could no more have known where all his slaves were going than he could have known how long they were to live; and no sane man, to say nothing of one near bankruptcy, could ever have expected to repurchase 400 slaves scattered over a broad region perhaps 1000 miles long.

slaves realized that they were parting forever from kindred and acquaintances, unless some had been bought with them, and that all might at any time be scattered.

> " The play is over, the farewells said,
> The curtain dropped and the actors fled;
> And the stars shine out and the breeze goes by
> Sweet with the bloom of the fruit-trees nigh.
> A hundred cabins are dark and still,
> And the wind and the moonlight may work their will,
> For those who sat by the open door
> Will never return to its shelter more! "

CHAPTER XI

MINOR TRADING IN THE CAROLINAS, GEORGIA AND TENNESSEE.

In the markets of the Southwest, dealers made a specialty of slaves from Virginia and South Carolina, or " Carolina ", but much less often did they advertise slaves from North Carolina.[1] Few persons boasted of birth in that State unless, according to the variations of the old story, " up near the Virginia line " or " down near the border of South Carolina ". In the Southwest, socially ambitious persons wished to pass as related to or closely associated with well-known Virginia or South Carolina families, and the standing of the former owner of one's negroes could so easily be exploited that slaves from those States were usually preferred. The traders profited by this, much as they did by the humanitarian pretenses of Southern border State sellers. North Carolina slaves bought in either Richmond or Charleston were readily resold as natives of Virginia or South Carolina. And the ease with which they could be sent from Raleigh to Richmond and from Wilmington to Charleston was favorable to these markets.[2] Presumably because of this outward flow of

[1] See index under VIRGINIA, slaves from etc.

[2] As has been noticed, Hector Davis, the Richmond trader, regularly advertised in Raleigh.

In February, 1856, a traveler saw 30 or 40 slaves on a ferryboat crossing the Cape Fear River at Wilmington, " chained together in gangs, and accompanied by their owner or overseer. They were being taken to the slave-mart in this city [Charleston], to be sold at auction to the highest bidder. It was a sad yet novel sight to me, as it was the first time that I had ever seen these human chattels fettered, and driven like so many animals to market. The women were sad-looking creatures, who seemed to realize to some extent their debased and degraded condition; but the men had a stolid look, as if devoid of sensibility, and were, to all appearance, as unconcerned and indifferent to their fate as a flock of sheep on their way to the butcher's shambles."—[Carlton H. Rogers,] *Incidents of Travel*, etc., 44-45.

North Carolina slaves and the fact that her cities, unlike Richmond and Charleston, had few social attractions to planters in other States, she possessed no first-class slave-markets.

But Wilmington had a few interstate dealers that were at least ambitious to do a large business with the South-west;[3] and it was not without regular traders, auctioneers, general agents, brokers, commission merchants, etc., buying and selling, hiring out and looking after slaves for profit, like their brethren in the business elsewhere, yet for some reason they did not display much enterprise. The Wilmington *Journal* was not less ready than other leading newspapers of the South, to use " Apply at this office " for the convenience or secrecy of anyone that wished to buy, sell or hire slaves.[4]

By 1850 many of the upper cotton regions of South Carolina, Georgia and Tennessee were doing much more slave-selling than slave-buying. The large traders still usually found it more profitable to gather their harvests in the border States or in such markets as Charleston's

[3] " CO-PARTNERSHIP NOTICE. THE UNDERSIGNED have entered into Co-partnership in the town of Wilmington, N. C., under the firm of SOUTHERLAND & COLEMAN, for the purpose of buying and selling NEGRO SLAVES, where the highest cash prices will be paid.

They also have a house in Mobile, Alabama, where they will receive and sell slaves on commission. Liberal advances made upon slaves left with them for sale. D. J. SOUTHERLAND, JAMES C. COLEMAN."—Wilmington *Journal*, Jan. 3, 1860.

[4] Nearly all these and still other features can be seen in its numbers of Jan. 3, 1859 and Jan. 3, 1860.

D. Pigott, broker and auctioneer, held his public sales at Exchange Corner.—*Journal*, Jan. 3, 1859, Jan. 3, 1860.

James T. Petteway, a general agent and broker of all sorts of things, did an active business in buying, selling and hiring slaves apparently on commission.—*Journal*, Jan. 3, 1859. Before the end of the year he prospered and took a partner and returned thanks to friends for the liberal patronage they had given him.—*Journal*, Jan. 3, 1860.

F. J. Moore, 34 Market st., was evidently the most popular agent for hiring out slaves.—*Journal*, Dec. 31, 1859.

or Savannah's; but the small traders carefully gleaned these upper cotton and lower grain regions directly or indirectly to help replenish the markets of the Southwest.

Columbia, the capital of the State and the seat of South Carolina College, was the political, social, educational and slave-trading center for all above the coastal regions. The latest available file of an ante-bellum Columbia newspaper shows that in 1851-52 Allen and Phillips, nominally auctioneers and commission merchants, were annually buying or selling for themselves or others at least several hundred slaves. They held public sales of groups of from a few to a few score negroes, and offered at private sale a " likely, intelligent and smart boy about 12 years old, to remain in Columbia ", a similar one without any restrictions, and a mother of 32 years and her five children, the eldest a girl of 15 and the youngest an infant.[5] Where purchasers were expected to come from was shown by a request that Charleston, Chester, Newberry and Fairfield newspapers copy the advertisement.[6] The firm also put on the block " two likely boys, aged 11 and 6 years ", who were " warranted sound and titles indisputable ".[7] Excellent opportunities for speculators in small children! And after the manner of regular traders they were seeking to buy " 5 or 6 likely girls from 11 to 20 years of age " and " 3 or 4 boys from 14 to 20 years old ".[8] J. and L. T. Levin also were disposing of many gangs that had belonged to deceased planters, whose estates were commonly sold for debt or for division among heirs.[9] And as a rule, sales of all kinds were increasing from year to year. South Carolina's slaves were rising in value but otherwise the State was rapidly declining in agricultural competition with the Southwest.

[5] *South Carolinian*, Jan. 31, 1852; Feb. 19, 1851; Dec. 30, 1851.
[6] *Ibid.*, Dec. 27, 1851.
[7] *Ibid.*, Jan. 31, 1852.
[8] *Ibid.*, Aug. 27, 1852.
[9] *Ibid.*, Feb. 19, 1851; Jan. 31, 1852; *Key to Uncle Tom's Cabin*, 134-36.

In 1902, the author stopped at the country market in Columbia to question some weather-beaten remnants of the days of slavery. After one of the most intelligent had told about his experiences in the Civil War, which he, as " cook fo' my young mastah ", had gone through " fum A ter izzahd ", the author gravely asked, as if entirely ignorant on the subject: " Did they sell many slaves here in the ' old time '? "—Bending forward to give emphasis to his surprise that anyone should put such a question, he slowly answered: " Did—dey *sell* 'em? Dey sol' 'em jess like yo' see 'em drive hosses er hogs."—" Er like dey sell chickens er tu'keys! " interjected an old " uncle " with hair as white as cotton.—" Dey sol' thousands of 'em," continued the quondam army-cook, " an de speki-latahs driv 'em off an' dey nevah seed deir folks no mo'. Why, dah was old Cha'ley Logan, he done buy niggahs like dey was hosses er mules, and make heaps o' money." Most of the slaves were supposed to have been taken to "Alleybamy an' de Red Rivah ". A moment later one of our little group broke into the conversation with the ex-clamation: " *Dah ee is now!* "—" Who? ", asked the author.—" Ole Cha'ley Logan! *Dat's him,* walkin' long dah now! " Across the street was a well-dressed, sturdy old man of apparently about seventy-five years, looking much like a neat, thrifty, retired merchant.

All was confirmed by a quaint old printer, Julian A. Selby—" a mine of information, very chatty and entirely reliable ", as he was described by Judge Haskell, who re-ferred the author to him. The printer had known Logan for more than half a century, and they were still in very friendly relations. Logan came to Columbia from Ireland in the 'forties, when he was about twenty-three years old. He was a practical shoemaker. At first he followed his trade, and for a considerable time was superintendent of a shoe-store.[10] He was popular with mechanics, laborers

---

[10] Julian A. Selby's *Memorabilia*, 83.

and shopkeepers and was soon able to speculate in a slave or two and then several at a time. He enlarged his stock, advertised, became known throughout his own and other counties, ventured into neighboring markets, and when his capital, credit and notoriety were sufficient, he began long-range and more profitable deals. Thus he prospered and was supposed to have made a small fortune. He did not rise to the class of a great trader, although his old friend said: " I think that he must have dealt in as many as 1,000 slaves in the years before the war. His purchases were made in South Carolina and most of his negroes were sold here; but he latterly took the best to New Orleans. I remember that on one occasion he left here for Louisiana with eighty-odd, one of them a pretty mulatto girl named Violetta." [11] Logan was still living in the house he occupied in trading days. When his negroes were not too numerous he kept them temporarily in the rear of his dwelling. Any room with barred windows might serve as a jail; unruly slaves were fettered. After the War, Logan took up horse-trading, but subsequently became a prosperous broker.

Among the slaves Logan took to the New Orleans market were undoubtedly some he bought from the estate of John Singleton, a son of Colonel Richard Singleton and a brother of Angelica Singleton, who in 1838 married President Van Buren's son Abraham and became mistress of the White House for the remainder of her father-in-law's term. Colonel Singleton was one of the richest of the South Carolina cotton-planter aristocracy. His slaves were counted by hundreds and his plantations by thousands of acres, which were in a region about 30 to 40 miles east and southeast of Columbia. He gave a plantation to each of his four children, two sons and two daughters. Some of the fieldhands of one plantation were occasionally sent to work on another. Thus two Stroyer sisters, belonging to M. R. Singleton, mated with two men belonging to his

[11] See *post* p. 330.

brother John, who soon acquired the sisters. Before long a great freshet wrought such destruction to John Singleton's slave cabins, barns, race horses and other stock that grief on account of it was supposed to have occasioned his early death. The usual thing followed: his slaves had to be sold to pay his debts. A trader named Manning bought a portion of them, including the Stroyer sisters, " and Charles Login [Logan] the rest ".

The published recollections of a brother of these girls tell what happened to Manning's purchases; Logan's must have fared in about the same manner, for the circumstances were similar. Slaves regarded Louisiana as a dreadful region from which no one could either return or send back word. Pending departure, Manning put in the Sumterville jail all his men that showed unwillingness to go to Louisiana, but he allowed his other slaves to make brief farewell visits to their relatives and friends in the neighborhood. When it was nearly time to leave, some of the men that had formerly appeared willing to go to Louisiana showed signs of resistance; they were handcuffed and guarded. Along with them, " the women and children were driven to the depot in crowds, like so many cattle, and the sight of them caused great excitement among master's negroes. Imagine a mass of uneducated people shedding tears and yelling at the tops of their voices in anguish and grief. * * * While passing along, many of the negroes left their masters' fields and joined us as we marched to the cars; some were yelling and wringing their hands, while others were singing little hymns that they were accustomed to for the consolation of those that were going away, such as

> ' When we all meet in Heaven
> There is no parting there.' "

These purchases were put on the train that brought the others from the Sumterville jail. " As the cars moved away we heard the weeping and wailing from the slaves as far as human voice could be heard; and from that time to the present I have neither seen nor heard from my two sisters, nor any of those who left Clarkson depot on that memorable day." [12]

" There were four or five regular slave-jails in Columbia ", said Julian A. Selby. " Prospective buyers watched the advertisements and looked over the negroes in the jails. Columbia was the central point in this region from which the slaves were sent out. Certainly as many as 1,000 were taken from here in some years. Slaves were auctioned off as if they were cattle. Children were sometimes sold when not more than six or seven years of age. John Kinsler, a brickmaker here, used to prefer to buy little children, because, as he said, they went home to their mothers daily to be fed, and therefore cost him little or nothing for food while they were growing. Slave-trading was not looked upon with favor, of course, but it was regarded as a necessary evil. So far as buying and selling were concerned, our people were perfectly callous. Slavery was considered necessary and must be defended whether moral or immoral. One would have run great risk in attempting to oppose it." [13]

[12] Jacob Stroyer, *My Life in the South*, 1, 41-44.

[13] The paragraphs about Mr. Selby are mainly from notes of conversations with him both in Columbia, S. C. and in Washington, D. C. The following, passages from his letter of Dec. 1, 1902, are worth preserving: " It would be hard to reply accurately to your question as to the average number of slaves sold during any given time. Many sales were made privately—that is, not ' on the block ', as usually termed. Sometimes a slave dealer would keep a lot on hand waiting for a rise in price; at others, again, he would buy and ship West in large numbers promptly. In addition to Lewis' or Sharp's ' nigger jail ', so called, Mr. C. Logan has one on his premises still in existence, where the ' human cattle ' were kept confined for an unlimited time. Lewis' jail is on Assembly street, between Richland and Sumter [?] east side. Logan's is [on] southwest corner Senate and Assembly. Don't remember the number of either. * * *

" As to the slave dealers, there were numbers of individuals engaged in it ' on the sly '—the dealers generally not standing particularly high. In many cases, the head of a family would die and the slaves and other property would be sold to effect a division. Then there was a heavy demand constantly from the rich fields of the West. I know General Hampton shipped

When Miss Bremer was in Augusta, Georgia, in 1850, she visited what she called the slave-market,—presumably only the main and most public one. Yet she found there " forty or fifty persons of both sexes * * * walking up and down before the house in expectation of purchasers ", and most of them were from Virginia.[14] Such importations indicated that this region had less than it needed. Within a few years, at most, Augusta was supposed to have a surplus, for traders were there ready to buy " any number of young and likely negroes, from 10 to 25 years of age ".[15]

The brutality of the trade in this superior little city was manifested by some ambitious liverymen: they would hire or purchase five or six stable-boys and give the highest cash prices for fifty negroes; they also had for sale at their stable a considerable supply of slaves of different kinds.[16]

on one occasion more than two hundred to his Mississippi plantation—near Skipwith's Landing, where he owned immense tracts of land. And so with many others. Breeding was encouraged and the young blacks were carefully looked after by the old women. You can get more information from the files of the Charleston *Courier* than I could possibly give you—there being, I should say, more sales in Charleston than in the balance of the State—all the business of that nature pertaining to the Sea Islands being conducted in that city. Nearly all the factors and commission merchants doing business for the coast planters residing there.

" While I know there were a good many slave-dealers in and about Columbia, I can think of but one other than those referred to above—an Irishman named Forsythe. I will make some inquiries among some of the ' old stagers '—only a few of whom are left—and if I can get hold of any reliable data, will communicate with you."

[14] " They were singing; they seemed cheerful and thoughtless."—1 *Homes of the New World*, 373.

[15] Wm. M. Thomas and R. D. Glover, in the Augusta *Chronicle and Sentinel*, Apr. 22, 1859.

[16] " WANTED TO BUY OR HIRE, FIVE or Six good BOYS, suitable for Stable business. Apply soon. Fair prices paid for either. W. E. ARCHER & CO."—*Chronicle and Sentinel*, Jan. 12, 1859.

" WANTED TO PURCHASE, 50 NEGROES, FOR which the HIGHEST CASH PRICES will be paid. Also,

Have on hand, some good COOKS, HOUSE SERVANTS, and FIELDHANDS. Can be seen at W. E. Archer & Co.'s Stable. W. E. ARCHER, L. GRAVES."— *Chronicle* etc., Dec. 3, 1859.

Their transition from horse-traders to slave-traders being incomplete, they were still both. In a slave society it was almost a natural evolution and not a rare phenomenon.[17] Having horses and vehicles and a large acquaintance with farmers and planters, they could advantageously scour the country without much extra expense.

What a contrast between such brutal traders and the high degree of mechanical skill of some of the negroes in the Augusta market! One, a mulatto, was a " good gas-fitter by trade "; another had " superintended a grist and saw mill " and was also " a fair carpenter ";[18] still another was a " first-rate ostler and carriage driver, a good painter and bricklayer ".[19] And Luther Roll, a local dealer with a fair variety of slaves on hand, offered " a painter, trimmer, cook, house servants, etc." [20]

In 1859 and 1860 at least five regular traders were advertising. The auctioneers, the commission merchants and the agents doing some slave-trading were each nearly everywhere about as numerous as the regular traders. And then, too, as we know, there were always petty traders, traders' assistants and secret speculators. The numerous public sales were held " at the Lower Market House ".[21]

The Richmond journalist and historian E. A. Pollard called Macon " one of the principal marts for slaves in the South ".[22] It undoubtedly had a larger trade than Augusta, for it was more favorably located; but it was not in the class with Baltimore, Richmond, Charleston, St. Louis and two or three other cities, soon to be noticed. Yet its business was far from small.

William Howard Russell of the London *Times*, who was

---

[17] See *ante* pp. 126 n.-27 n. and *post* pp. 250-51 n., 257.
[18] *Chronicle* etc., Jan. 1 and Apr. 2, 1859.
[19] Augusta *Constitutionalist*, Jan. 1, 1860.
[20] *Chronicle*, etc., Jan. 9, 1859.
[21] *Chronicle*, etc., Jan. 2, 1859, *et passim*.
[22] *Black Diamonds*, 28.

there in May, 1861, wrote: " In the course of the drive I saw two or three signboards and placards announcing that ' Smith & Co. advanced money on slaves, and had constant supplies of Virginian negroes on sale or hire '. These establishments were surrounded by high walls enclosing the slave-pens or large rooms, in which the slaves were kept for inspection." [23]

In 1907 the author found several ante-bellum residents of Macon that were willing to give their recollections. An old journalist and local historian, orally employed about the same words and phrases as were often heard elsewhere: " Here negroes were bought and sold like horses; they were bred in the northeastern part of the Southern States, and men went on regularly to Baltimore, Richmond, Lynchburg, etc., to buy them. One of our traders James Dean [sometimes spelt Deane] had a large house in Vineville [a section of Macon]. Of course, negro-traders were not respected. It was common for planters. after selling their crops, to go to the slave-market to buy more negroes."

A former mayor seemed to find a novel and pleasing sensation in looking into the distant past and describing conditions he was familiar with in his youth. " James Dean had a slave-pen on Cotton Avenue. Like many others elsewhere, he was both a planter and a trader. He trafficked in negroes just as one might traffic in mules, and he made a good profit—a big profit. Another, Rafe Phillips, is still alive at the age of 84 and may any day be seen on the street; for he now buys and sells mules." Unfortunately, Phillips did not, like " Ole Charley " Logan, appear at the opportune moment. " A. J. and D. W. Orr also had a slave-trading place on Cotton Avenue. Charles F. Stubbs was another trader. These were the big dealers. There were still others. Yes, John Jossey and Charles Collins were traders. Collins was also a planter and had considerable bank-stock. The largest dealers, such as Dean, Phillips,

[23] W. H. Russell, *My Diary North and South*, 162.

the Orrs and Stubbs, regularly went to Richmond and brought back slaves; Richmond was the headquarters. The barbarity of that traffic was unconscionable. I was born in Georgia and my father had slaves. For my brother, I once bought of the Orrs a negro girl named Charlotte and paid $575. I have been in Richmond and seen the sales there. Dealers took an order for a particular kind of a slave, just as one would for any kind of goods. The inspection was as close as anyone pleased to make it. Women were often stripped to the waist and the men were examined all over. Both were examind much as a physician would a patient. Everybody in the South who could was engaged in [some phase of] the negro traffic. There was, in *fact*, really no difference between buying and selling." His impromptu generalizations were all frankness and he did not stop to qualify them or to mention such exceptions as must be understood as a matter of course.

A very intelligent former slave, who had worked for a cotton-broker before the Civil War and was highly praised by his employer in 1907, a cotton-factor from South Carolina, named the same and one or two other traders.[24] All three forgot J. B. Allgood, who was the senior partner of one of the busiest firms.[25] And no one of the three remembered to mention that Macon's auctioneers and commission merchants also sold slaves.[26]

[24] He gave the following names and addresses of traders:

> Charles Collins, southwest corner of Poplar and Fourth, was believed to have had a pen in one of the northeastern slave States.
> Jim Dean, Cotton Avenue;
> John Jossey, southeast corner of Fifth and Pine;
> Nowell, Poplar street between First and Second streets;
> Rafe Phillips, southwest corner of Poplar and Third.

[25] " 200 NEGROES WANTED. HIGHEST CASH PRICES will be paid for young and likely Negroes, either in families or in gangs. Persons having negroes to sell, can address either of us at Macon, or one or the other of us may be seen at the Screven or Pulaski Houses, at any time during the week. J. B. ALLGOOD, C. F. STUBBS."—Savannah *Republican*, Dec. 30, 1859.

[26] Miller and Waterman advertised as far away as Savannah that they,

Atlanta, one of Georgia's newest little cities in the 'fifties, was still small in 1860, its white population numbering only 7,615 and its colored 1,939,[27] nearly all slaves, of course. In comparison with Augusta and Macon, it was unfavorably located for slave-trading, but it seems never to have been without a few regular dealers; in some years there were probably many persons engaged in the trade. Clark & Grubb supplied further evidence that slave-trading was not detrimental to a business man's reputation, for, as has been noticed, commission merchants, factors, auctioneers, brokers, real estate agents, grocers, hotel keepers, liverymen, etc., etc., often engaged in it as a helpful and profitable adjunct. To their primary business as wholesale grocers and commission merchants, Clark & Grubb added that of negro brokers and " announced that they kept slaves of all classes constantly on hand and were paying the highest market prices for all that might be offered ".[28] Their establishment was on Whitehall street. A different and older slave-mart on the same street was " on the site of the old George Muse store ", according to a local historian.[29]

When John T. Trowbridge was stopping in a war-damaged and absurdly neglected hotel in Knoxville, in 1866, the landlord apologized thus: " Hotel-keeping a'n't my business. Nigger-dealing is my business. But that's played out. I've bought and sold in my day over six hundred niggers ",—spoken with mournful satisfaction, mingled pride and regret. " Now I don't know what I shall turn my hand to. I'm a Georgian; I came up here from Atlanta

as auctioneers and commission merchants, would publicly and privately sell property of all kinds including slaves. And among the names of persons given as references was that of Capt. Bryan's auctioneer, T. J. Walsh.— Savannah *Republican*, Jan. 28, 1860.

[27] *Census, 1870, Population*, Vol. I, p. 102.

[28] Phillips, *Amer. Negro Slavery*, 190, citing the Atlanta *Intelligencer*, Mar. 7, 1860.

[29] The article and a picture of the place are in the Atlanta *Constitution* of Nov. 30, 1925.

[at the] time it was burned."[30]   That was a traderlike boast of superior antecedents.

Nashville, the capital of Tennessee, and the political, social and business center of the State, was advantageously situated for purchases in Kentucky and sales in northern Alabama and northeastern Mississippi. Simultaneously in the same Nashville newspaper, trader Lucas of Lexington, Kentucky, was advertising to attract Tennessee buyers, and trader Hatcher of New Orleans was advertising to attract Tennesseeans intending to sell slaves in the Louisiana market.[31]   The resident leaders in the interstate traffic, 1859-60, were Webb, Merrill & Co., and Lyles & Hitchings. Both firms " would at all times purchase NEGROES suited to the New Orleans market ", and one of them advised the public: " Other descriptions sold on consignment."[32] Much local and intra-state trading was a matter of course.[33] Yet Nashville's market did not rise above the second class. Tennessee's first-class market and phenomenally large traders were in Memphis.

[30] *The South: A Tour* etc., 238.

[31] *Republican Banner*, Jan. 6, 1860.

[32] *Ibid.*

[33] Mitchell's *Tenn. State Gazetteer* (472, 208, 218, 223, 235) mentioned four establishments of " slave agents and dealers " in Nashville in 1860:

   Will L. Boyd, Jr., 50 Cherry st.

   H. H. Haynes & Co., 16 Cedar st.

   R. J. Lyles, 35 Cedar st.

   Webb, Merrill & Co., 8 South Market.

Besides mentioning most of the foregoing, Campbell's Nashville *Directory*, 1859, designated Thomas G. James, 18 Cedar st., as a " slave dealer ", S. H. Bugg and W. W. Philips as " traders ", four others as " agents ", and eight others as " auctioneers ", some of whom were also general agents and others commission merchants.   One of the " agents " was E. S. Hawkins, whose address was the same as that of " slave dealer " James, and he was advertising: " I have 39 or 40 Negroes for sale, of all ages and descriptions, among them are some family favorites that I am restricted to sell them [sic] to good homes in this or some adjoining county."—*Repub. Banner*, Jan. 6, 1860.   We shall meet James doing a large business in two other markets.

CHAPTER XII

Of the cities in the central South, Memphis had by far the largest slave-trade. Its location was very favorable—on the Mississippi River midway between St. Louis and Natchez and in the midst of a fertile region where cotton-planting was rapidly increasing. Slaves were easily brought by water from Virginia, Kentucky and Missouri. After the completion, in 1857, of the railroad from Charleston, via Augusta, Atlanta, Chattanooga, Huntsville and the northeast corner of Mississippi, it was the best readily accessible market for slaves from the upper Carolinas, upper Georgia and most of Tennessee. It was also the most convenient place for the planters of Arkansas, southwestern Tennessee, northern and western Mississippi and northeastern Louisiana to obtain their slaves. Its white population numbered less than 7,000 in 1850 and less than 19,000 in 1860.

In 1852 one of the first things that a traveler saw from the lower steamboat landing was a large sign on what had been the Herron House:

| BOLTON, DICKINS & CO., SLAVE DEALERS. | [1]

And on a principal street, nearly opposite each other, were these:

| BYRD HILL, SLAVE MARKET |

and

| BEN LITTLE, SLAVE MARKET AND LIVERY STABLE. |

Here, as in Augusta, Louisville and elsewhere, the same man dealt in horses, mules and slaves. The public was

---

[1] These seem to be the correct spellings although one name was sometimes printed "Bolten" and the other "Dickens".

invited to " walk in and *look at the stock* "—men and women, girls and boys, of almost every shade of complexion, ranging in age from ten to forty years, all specially dressed to aid their sales and much better clothed than slaves not in the market, except favored body-servants. Of course, " Some of the best looking young women were attired in beautiful de laine, made in the fashion, too ". The " stock " were quickly arranged on seats on either side of the room. One could examine them—teeth, limbs, backs—and call for any exercises to test agility and health. But the merely curious visitor was not allowed to inspect the place where they were locked up at night, and the prospective buyer was wholly indifferent to it; only the grated windows were seen. Close at hand were horses and mules, also for sale.[2]

These were only the most conspicuous traders. In 1857 more than a dozen were regularly advertising.[3] The extent of their purchases is partially indicated by the fact that W. Bradford, one of the least known, ended his advertisement with a request that the Richmond *Enquirer,* the Raleigh *Register,* the Charleston *Courier,* and the St. Louis

[2] N. Y. *Tribune,* Mar. 10, 1853, quoted the account by the correspondent of the Chicago *Times.*

[3] Neville [Nevil] & Cunningham, "174 Main St., three doors north of Adams ".

N. B. Forrest, " 87 Adams St."

Delap, Witherspoon & Fly, "at their Mart on Adams St." expected to receive fresh supplies from S. C. and Va. every two or three weeks.

Bolton, Dickins & Co.—All were advertising in the *Eagle & Enquirer,* June 2, 1857.

W. Bradford, " Wallace's old stand, south side of Court Sq."—*Appeal,* Aug. 14, 1857.

A. Wallace, agent and auctioneer for Bradford, " south side of Court Sq."—*Appeal,* Oct. 11, 1857.

E. L. Wilie, " Monroe St."—*Morning Bulletin,* June 27, 1857.

Mitchell's *Tenn. State Gazetteer* for 1860 (pp. 472, 146, 168, 162) mentioned four firms of " slave agents and dealers ", composed of at least nine persons, and two auctioneers etc., who sold slaves like other merchandise:—

    M. C. Cayce & Son, 8 Union st.; [In 1852 M. C. Cayce had a sale and livery stable and was an auctioneer.—*Eagle & Enquirer,* Jan. 3, 1852.];

    Delap, A. & N., 58 Adams st.;

Republican, " copy to the amount of $10 and send bill to this [*Appeal*] office "—thus showing how the newspapers were serving the slave-traders. And E. L. Wilie, had " a good lot of Virginia and South Carolina negroes " and had " made arrangements with good and experienced buyers to keep a good supply on hand ".

Bolton, Dickins & Co. were still far in the lead. A Memphis lawyer, John Hallum, well acquainted with the members of this firm—which, at different times comprised at least Isaac, Jefferson, Wade and Washington Bolton and Thomas Dickins, the son-in-law of Isaac Bolton— called them, with some exaggeration, " the most extensive negro-traders in the world ", and, said that " they had negro marts in Memphis, New Orleans, Vicksburg, Mobile, Lexington [Kentucky], Richmond, Charleston and other places, Memphis being the place where they had their chief office ".[4] Yet he overlooked " our Mr. Dickins ", who was at St. Louis trying to obtain a thousand Missouri slaves for Memphis and Louisiana markets. At Lexington, Kentucky, Washington Bolton conducted a large and well-known slave-pen. Isaac Bolton was in charge of the distribution of the slaves on the lower Mississippi, with headquarters at Vicksburg. Wade Bolton looked after the business at the chief office. Jefferson Bolton had died a few years previously.[5] They certainly did not have " marts " in Richmond and Charleston, but they probably had directly or

Hill, Weaver & Co., 87 Adams st.;

Nevil & James, 174 Main st.; and

A. S. Levy & Co. [A. Ephraim Frankland] auction and commission merchants, 10 Madison st.

These were probably only the large dealers and but a fraction of the whole number of traders of various kinds.

On the same page with Cayce and Son's announcement that "FANNY MUST GO!" [to the highest bidder] (*ante* p. 81 n.) two other firms of auctioneers etc., composed of at least 5 or 6 persons, were advertising slaves for sale.

[4] Hallum, *Diary of an Old Lawyer,* 76. "Diary" is a misnomer for his inaccurate recollections.

[5] Hallum, 78.

indirectly bought slaves from or sold them to nearly every city and hundreds of counties from Maryland to Texas, both included.

From the autumn of 1855 they had " one of the best [slave] prisons in the State " and were " receiving daily large supplies of fresh negroes from the buying markets ". Then they gave the slave-buying public this choice bit of advice about the royal road to wealth:

" Call and buy before the present stock is picked over, as some is [sic] of the opinion that the first show at a fresh lot is one hundred dollars the advantage—but we say to you the last will be good. So call and make your purchases to gather your crop—and then call quick again and buy to make another crop.—By those means if you will keep up your purchases for ten years there is no telling how much you may be worth. This is the true Road to wealth and if you neglect the present offer of becoming wealthy its your own fa[u]lt and not ours as the Road is laid out plainly.   BOLTON, DICKINS & CO." [6]

It was a trader's rendering of the common proverb and practice: " Buy more negroes to raise more cotton to buy more negroes to raise more cotton."

In the spring of 1857 they were specializing in " acclimated cotton negroes " from Georgia, and were collecting many slaves purchased in other States.[7] About this time Washington Bolton obtained through James McMillan the unexpired term of a free negro apprentice. McMillan was a well-known trader, who for years had ranged over Kentucky searching for slaves for Lexington and Memphis dealers. The apprentice was promptly sent to Memphis and sold as a slave. This was a crime against the apprentice and a fraud on the purchaser. By some rare, good fortune the negro obtained the aid of a lawyer of integrity and by suit recovered his freedom; and the Boltons were compelled to refund the money they had received for him.[8] That made their double wrong notorious and almost

---

[6] Memphis *Eagle and Enquirer*, Nov. 15, 1855.

[7] See photostat from *Eagle and Enquirer*, June 2, 1857, opposite p. 254.

[8] Memphis *Appeal*, May 24, 1857; Hallum, 76.

suicidal; for how could they defend the selling of a kid-naped free negro when they were boastfully offering " the buyers of this country an opportunity of investing their money in good negroes " ? And what would they not do to escape from such a desperate predicament?

Not long afterward, in May, 1857, when McMillan and his partner, Hill, were in Memphis with ten or twelve slaves for sale, Wade Bolton said that he wished to buy a " fancy boy "—a smart yellow house-boy—for his wife, and he requested McMillan to bring a particular one to the Bolton mart for inspection. After some misgivings, McMillan complied at the appointed time; but he found only an acquaintance named Patrick Duffy, somehow asso-ciated with this mart, and Isaac Bolton, whom he did not know and who had just returned from a long absence in Vicksburg. In violent and unquotable language Isaac Bolton accused McMillan of being a rascal and having sold the free negro to the firm, and threatened to kill him if the price was not at once refunded. McMillan said that he did not have the money and that Washington Bolton knew all about the negro at the time of purchase, " and so did you ", McMillan was reported to have added. Isaac Bolton demanded at least a bank-check. McMillan replied that he had no bank-account; but, evidently realizing that his life was in danger, offered to go to his partner and arrange the matter. Bolton pretended to be all the more outraged. Duffy went into another room, and Isaac Bolton drew a revolver and mortally wounded McMillan. When Duffy returned, Bolton took a bowie-knife from his own pocket, removed its case, threw both on the floor near where McMillan had fallen, and, with the coarsest of oaths, said that there was the knife with which McMillan had tried to kill him. Bolton and Duffy scornfully ignored the dying man's cries for water and a pillow and then left him alone. The reports of the pistol-shots and the running of the yellow slave boy quickly brought many persons to

SLAVE-ADVERTISEMENTS BY BOLTON, DICKINS & CO. AND OTHERS

From the Memphis *Eagle and Enquirer*, April 29, 1857

the Bolton mart. The first to arrive found McMillan alone and bleeding on the floor. He was soon put into a furniture van and taken to the personal quarters of the trader-jailor of his slaves. While painfully waiting for the end, known to be near, he repeatedly told the short story of what had happened, and it was taken down. He died that afternoon.[9] Isaac Bolton fled, but soon returned and gave himself up, realizing that flight was inconsistent with his pretense that he had acted in self-defense. He was promptly indicted and bail was refused. Wade Bolton and Patrick Duffy were taken as accessories. Soon the newspapers reported an attempt to bribe the jailor to let Isaac Bolton escape.[10] At another time it was said that Bolton was resting quietly in jail and not alluding to his case,— " but [he] becomes very animated on the subject of dollars, negroes and cotton ".[11] A change of venue to an adjoining county was obtained. The trial began near the end of March, 1858. Twelve criminal lawyers took part in it— five, including ex-Governor Henry S. Foote of Mississippi, for the prosecution and seven for the defense. The evidence showed that R. H. Thompson, then one of the buyers for Bolton, Dickins and Co. in Kentucky, and later their successor in Lexington, as has been mentioned, paid several witnesses to come from Kentucky and testify against McMillan's character. They suspiciously agreed, in contrast with other witnesses, that McMillan habitually went armed and that they would not believe him under oath. The jury promptly gave a verdict of " Not guilty ". It was publicly charged that the jury was " packed " and that some of its members were bribed.[12]

[9] This summary is made up from McMillan's statements *in articulo mortis* (printed in the *Eagle and Enquirer*, May 30, 1857) and from the evidence given at the trial and reported in the Memphis *Appeal* during the first week in April, 1858.

[10] *Morning Bulletin*, July 1, 1857.

[11] *Appeal*, Dec. 4, 1857.

[12] Hallum, 77. The *Eagle and Enq.* said editorially, April 11, 1858, in commenting on this verdict: "We think it time that the execution of the

Meantime the slave-trading business of Bolton, Dickins & Co. had fallen away almost like water when a dam breaks. It was said that the firm spent nearly $300,000 in defense of the senior partner. He was called on to make reimbursement, but refused, for, as he claimed, it was all a partnership matter, and he had suffered more than his share. This started a family "feud, which ultimately involved the lives of 13 men", according to Hallum, who was counsel in one or more cases that resulted.[13] If Hallum was even approximately correct, as he sometimes was, at least a goodly number of this large slave-trading family came to miserable but well-deserved ends.

The name of the trader-jailor in whose house, above or adjoining his pen, McMillan died was Nathan Bedford Forrest,[14] then usually called Bedford or Bed Forrest. His antecedents were of the plainest. His father was a village or cross-roads blacksmith in Tennessee, who moved to the then newly opened Chicasaw country in northern Mississippi, and died there in 1837. He left a widow with eight sons (including one soon to be born) and three daughters. Bedford, sixteen years old, was the eldest child. They had a hard struggle. Five of them—two sons and all three daughters—were taken off by malignant typhoid fever, common in such newly settled regions. The survivors grew up in ignorance and semi-squalor, like other "poor whites". In the Southwest "fierce border scenes of malice and murder" were common. If one had never

law should be placed in other hands, when such palpable treachery as this is carried on in the face of all laws, both human and divine. Thus again is another instance of the taking of human life, in cold blood, justified by a jury of 12 men, calling themselves honest."

[13] Hallum, 77 ff.

[14] Calvin Jones testified that he helped to put McMillan in a furniture van and "went with him to Forrest's yard".—*Appeal*, Apr. 6, 1858. Forrest testified that after McMillan was wounded "he was brought back to my house" and, later, that he died there.—*Appeal*, Apr. 1 and 7, 1858. The *Directory* for 1859 had this entry: "Forrest, N. B.—Slave dealer, 87 Adams, H[ouse] 85."

engaged in a deadly fight with knives or pistols his life seemed dull and spiritless. Forrest had several such adventures. In all of them he is represented as having taken a fearless part, attracting popular attention and obtaining local distinction. He early turned from farming to trading in horses and cattle, in a small way. With an uncle, he had what in that region must have been a feed-stable rather than a livery-stable.

From such contact with farmers and inchoate planters he learned who would sell and who would buy slaves. "Traffic in the selling and buying of negroes was as common in the cotton-belt of the South at this period as the buying and selling of horses or cattle, or any other merchantable live product", wrote Forrest's biographer, the famous surgeon John A. Wyeth, who was born in northern Alabama, knew this whole region and served in the Confederate cavalry. "Into this business Bedford Forrest had entered on as large a scale as his limited means would permit, while he was engaged in mercantile pursuits [dealing in horses etc.] with his uncle at Hernando [Mississippi]. As his capital accumulated under the energy and tact which he exercised, he closed out the business in Hernando, and, moving to Memphis, settled there,[15] devoting his time as a broker in real estate in this rapidly growing young city, and as a speculator in slaves."[16] Thus, like his fellow-townsmen Ben Little and M. C. Cayce, and scores of others elsewhere, he rose from horse-trading to slave-trading. His real estate business must have been small; for his biographers give no details of it, and the present author has met with but one of his real-estate advertisements.

The rush for Texas was in full flow and there had never been a greater demand for slaves. Ben Little was making a specialty of buying for that great region.[17] Forrest's

[15] Mathes, *Forrest*, 15, says 1849; Wyeth, *Forrest*, 17, 1851; Jordan & Pryor, *Campaigns of Forrest* (1868), 25, 1852.

[16] Wyeth, 20.

[17] *Eagle and Enq.*, Aug. 31, 1853.

9

heroic conduct in a steamboat accident in Texas in the spring of 1852 is described by his biographers, but they are strangely vague about the purpose of his journey. If it had been real estate, they would probably have said so to preclude the supposition that it was to take a coffle of slaves.[18] By January, 1853, he was a typical interstate trader, traveling extensively and scouring Kentucky for slaves. He was already employing James McMillan— Forrest supplying the money and giving McMillan one-fourth of the profits on the slaves he obtained.[19]

Forrest's ambition, if not his progress, was evinced by his use, as early as July, 1853, of the figures and language of the large traders.[20] By 1855 he and his new partner, Maples, claimed to "have the best selected assortment * * * to be found in the city ", and were " daily receiving from Virginia, Kentucky and Missouri fresh supplies of likely young negroes ". The " daily receiving " could not have been literally true; but the firm may have had, as was claimed, a jail with a capacity for three hundred slaves, and for comfort, cleanliness and security the most complete of any in the South.[21] A little later, when nominally without a partner, he advised the public that he was " in the regular receipt of Negroes from North and South Carolina every month." [22]

[18] Jordan & Pryor, 27, say that the purpose was "the adjustment of some business affairs ", and Mathes, 15, " some business ".

[19] Forrest's testimony at the Bolton trial.—*Appeal*, Apr. 1 and 7, 1858.

[20] " FIVE HUNDRED NEGROES WANTED.—WE will pay the highest cash price for all good Negroes offered. We invite all those having Negroes for sale, to call on us, at our Mart, opposite Hill's old stand, on Adams street. We will have a good lot of Virginia Negroes on hand, for sale, in the fall. Negroes bought and sold on commission. HILL & FORREST. July 19-d&wtf."—*Eagle & Enq.*, Jan. 4, 1854.

[21] A facsimile of their advt. in the Memphis *Directory*, 1855-56, can be found in Julian Street's *American Adventures*.

[22] " His Negro Depot [the advt. continued] is one of the most complete and commodious establishments of the kind in the Southern country, and regulations, exact and systematic cleanliness, neatness and comfort being strictly observed and enforced, and his aim is to furnish to customers No. 1

On account of his relations with James McMillan, Forrest was an important witness for the prosecution of Isaac Bolton; but his name has been much more conspicuously associated with another murder. Late in the afternoon of Wednesday, June 24, 1857, about a month after the murder of McMillan, a gambler named John Able (often spelt Abel), the son of Joseph Able, also a gambler and murderer, killed John Everson, a respected citizen, in front of the Worsham House, now the Arlington Hotel, for urging the payment of a debt. Popular indignation was intense. At different times and places the lynching of John Able was called for by angry crowds: first, near the place of the crime and, only a few minutes later, at the jail; that Wednesday evening, at the Exchange building, where an indignation-meeting was held;[23] again at the Exchange

servants and fieldhands, sound and perfect in body and mind."—*Eagle and Enq.*, Jan.-June, 1857.

Throughout the spring of 1858 Forrest and Jones claimed to have just received " 75 likely young negroes " from Virginia, North and South Carolina and Georgia.—*Bulletin*, May 10, 1858.

[23] " In a few moments after he [Able] was arrested, a large and infuriated crowd assembled, first upon the ground where the bloody deed was committed, and then proceeded to the jail with the view of taking and hanging him immediately; and had not the crowd been checked by several gentlemen who took an active part in trying to quiet it, they [the crowd] would most certainly have hung him. The crowd was addressed by Major Douglass, Col. Jno. Martin, Gen. W. T. Haskell, Col. J. H. McMahon and others who urged them to deliberate and consider before proceeding further in such an important move. The crowd was very large, numbering between two and three thousand citizens, who were very greatly excited and much enraged. Finally Mr. Oliver Greenlaw proposed that a committee of fifty persons be appointed to guard the jail, and see that Able did not escape, and that the meeting adjourn to meet at Court Square, at half past 8 o'clock in the evening, which was agreed to * * *."

That evening a crowd of between 4,000 and 5,000 persons assembled in and about the Exchange building. After the meeting was organized, a jury of 36 persons was selected to hear the evidence of the crime and to report. The meeting also authorized the appointment of a committee of three persons to serve notice on Joseph Able, the father, that he must leave the city and the county before noon of the morrow; and the meeting further resolved that all gamblers should leave the city within ten days and that all gambling

building, Friday evening, the 26th; and, later that evening and night, first at the jail, then at the navy yard ropewalk and, finally, again at the jail. Shouts for the execution of Able caused the Friday evening meeting in the Exchange building to melt away soon after it was organized; a mob rushed to the jail, seized and carried Abel to the ropewalk to hang him. But there the crowd, as the *Appeal* reported,

" found his wife, mother and sister, who made such frantic appeals that by a nearly unanimous vote it was resolved to take him back to [the] jail and let the law have its course. Able was taken back and lodged in a cell, for a few minutes all seemed satisfield.

A cry arose, 'Hang him', and soon a crowbar was brought into requisition and the outside door of the jail forced. Several speeches were made, and finally the crowd dispersed, with the understanding that the law would be permitted to have its course.

The rope was placed around Able's neck three times, but he displayed no signs of fear. He addressed the crowd, as did his mother. Able said he desired to settle up his accounts, and in a cool manner, stated he had very nearly got through with his arrangements, so far as his property was concerned.

The matter is now left with the Grand Jury and the Criminal Court.[24]

The only active part that any of the three leading news-

houses should be closed. The committee of 36 soon reported that it was of a divided opinion—24, believing the case one of murder in the first degree, were in favor of leaving it to the regular course at law; whereas 12 were for hanging the prisoner forthwith. About three-fourths of the crowd seemed to agree with the 12. " The crowd was greatly excited, and had they been headed by a *leader*, their purpose would have been summarily carried into effect. But having no leader, the crowd soon after its adjournment, dispersed."—*Morning Bulletin*, June 25, 1857. The shorter accounts in the *Appeal* and the *Eagle and Enquirer* agreed with the *Bulletin* in all material respects.

[24] *Appeal*, June 27, 1857. The *Bulletin* of June 27th said that the mob had made preparations and was resolved to hang Able. " The interposition and agonized entreaties of his *mother*, alone saved him. * * * He was taken back by the same crowd that had taken him out, and was again consigned to the calaboose." The *Eagle and Enquirer* of that date said: " The mother of Able appeared upon the scene [at the navy yard] and implored the crowd not to execute him, and no doubt saved his life. He was reconveyed to prison."

papers mentioned Forrest as taking was as a member of the committee of three, appointed by the meeting Wednesday evening, who served notice on the elder Able that he must leave Memphis and never return: " If you do, in our opinion, your life will be the penalty." [25] Except that Forrest's name was also printed with those of three other vice-presidents of the Friday evening meeting, no reference to him in connection with any phase of these incidents has been found in these newspapers.

Yet, long afterward, his biographers, the chief local historian and others, while ignoring Forrest's part in serving that notice of summary and lawless expulsion on one who had nothing to do with this murder, variously represented Forrest as the sole valiant and compelling champion of law and order against the mob at different times and places—at the Worsham House shortly after the murder, Wednesday, the 24th; at the ropewalk, and later at the jail during the evening and before midnight of Friday, the 26th, which Forrest's eulogists misstated as the 25th, when there was neither meeting nor mob. It is erroneously alleged that Forrest alone by impressive appeals dispersed the mob at the Worsham House; that at another time, which is incorrectly indicated, he hastened to the navy yard, cut the rope as the mob was drawing up its victim, defiantly shouted to the crowd that Able should be taken only " over my dead body "; and that then (after a short intermission, during which he, at great peril and with many bruises and scars, had succeeded in getting the murderer back to the jail, and the mob had rushed there to take vengeance) " this one daring soul " " stepped out onto the jail steps and facing that seething mob of three thousand human beings threatened to shoot the first man who approached. Almost unreasonable as it may seem that one man could stand against three thousand rioters, this hatless, disheveled, torn, cut, determined man did that very thing ". [26]

[25] *Eagle and Enquirer*, June 26, 1857.
[26] Young, *Standard History of Memphis*, etc., 98-100.

Descriptions of merely imaginary acts of that kind would be thrilling and excite admiration and comment. What credulity one must have, then, to believe that such picturesque and valiant deeds could be performed on three different occasions and before thousands of persons *without any newspaper taking the slightest notice* of them when both reporting and commenting on what occurred at each of these three times! But to make a slave-trader look like a superior being, he must be represented as a star, playing a noble, decisive rôle, like Achilles, who " rose, and his thundering voice alone put the Trojans to flight ".[27]

Able's trial, like Bolton's, resulted in a verdict of " Not guilty ".

By 1860, Forrest had demonstrated what success an illiterate,[28] poor but energetic man could achieve in a few years by buying and selling slaves instead of beasts and real estate. Since the decline of Bolton, Dickins & Co. he had become one of the best known and richest slave-traders in all the South. Except possibly the youngest, his five brothers—in sequence John, William, Aaron, Jesse and Jeffrey—engaged in the same business with him.[29] He had

[27] For more about Forrest and his biographers see the note at the end of this chapter.

[28] An ex-Confederate general that knew Forrest well—after the war they had their offices in the same building in Memphis—said to the author: " His handwriting was hardly legible and the best that could be said for his spelling was that it approached the phonetic system without being even that." It demonstrated that he did not know the correct pronunciation of very common words. His mistakes were the occasion of much merriment on the part of his old friends, and were often more ludicrous than the labored efforts of Artemus Ward or Josh Billings. His old friend Gen. James R. Chalmers wrote that Forrest's correspondence during the War was regularly carried on through his adjutant-general, and continued: " A soldier came to him [Forrest] a third time asking for a furlough. Twice it had been refused, for we needed all the men that we could get at that time, and when the application appeared the third time, General Forrest in his own handwriting indorsed upon the back of it, ' I told you twist (twice) Goddammit know,' and the man knew that he meant no ".—See Mathes, 382-83, and, for facsimiles, 26, 336.

[29] An old resident of Memphis and ex-Confederate has written to the

all the self-complacency and airs of the successful trader. His possible clients, whether they were sellers in Missouri, Kentucky or any of the seaboard slave States, or buyers in the lower Southwest, were appealed to as if they were his friends,—which in fact many of them were.[30]

He had acquired what for that time was a great fortune. By purchasing fertile, wild land in Mississippi and Arkansas and cultivating it with slaves bought in the cheapest markets, he was said to be producing 1,000 bales of cotton, on which one of his biographers states that he cleared at least $30,000 annually.[31] This is not at all improbable. For several years his annual profits from slave-trading may well have exceeded $50,000. In 1858-61 the average price for such slaves as he sold was nearly $1,000, but let us count $800. Forrest was one of the

author that until about Jan., 1921, "the houses 87 and 89 Adams street, formerly used by N. B. Forrest and his brothers Jesse A. (Aaron H. in 1855), and William H. Forrest as a slave mart", were still standing. According to references during the Bolton trial, John (a cripple from a wound received in the Mexican War) and William were associated with N. B. F. in slave-trading as early as 1857.

[30] This advertisement in the Charleston *Courier* and elsewhere shows his attitude and his outlook.

"Having associated with me in my old business—that of BUYING AND SELLING NEGROES, both on commission and on private account—Mr. S. S. Jones, of De Soto, Mississippi, and my brother, Wm. H. Forrest, of Memphis, I can tender to my friends better facilities than I have ever been able to offer them.—Our buildings are located at 89 Adams street, next door east of my old Mart; they are spacious, combining convenience, comfort and safety—are superior to any establishment of the kind in the State, and equal to any that I have ever inspected.—I respectfully solicit for our new firm, from my old friends and customers and the public, the patronage which I have largely and liberally received hitherto from them, and will only add, that which we promise or say, we guarantee." The firm would also "board, and sell on commission, and keep constantly on hand, a good assortment of Virginia, Georgia and Carolina negroes. 500 NEGROES WANTED. I WILL PAY MORE THAN ANY OTHER PERSON, for No. 1 NEGROES, suited to the New Orleans market".—*Courier*, Jan. 23, 1860, and many other days; also in the daily and weekly Memphis *Avalanche* in the winter of 1859-60, and in the daily as late as March 14, 1860.

[31] Jordan & Pryor, 26; Mathes, 16; Wyeth, 19, 22.

largest traders of that decade, and after the downfall of
the Boltons he was unmatched in Memphis. It seems conservative to believe that in some of his best years he sold
over 1,000 negroes. A 20 per cent profit on only 600 at
$800 each would be a net gain of $96,000. At that time
this was a fabulous income, yet it was within reach of the
largest traders.

Nearly all prosperous traders, whether honest or not,
naturally wished respectable persons to think them superior
to a business in which innumerable disreputable characters
were engaged. One of Forrest's associates alleged, long
afterward, that Forrest was " overwhelmed with applica-
tions " of slaves begging to be purchased![32] If anything
resembling that had been true, it would have been quite
superflous for him to keep up a constant combing of half
a dozen States to supply negroes for his Memphis market.
And his advertisements were as free from any pretenses
of special humanity as were those of Armfield. He knew
the advantage of a reputation for being perfectly honest,
straightforward and having a safe and sanitary prison.
By such virtues he profited. Most of the rest, in his case
as well as in that of others of his class, was largely a
mixture of imagination and misrepresentation. He and
not many others had slave-pens that were relatively attractive, in comparison with those of the great majority of
traders. In such well regulated places it was customary,
for health and cheerfulness, to cause the inmates, twice
daily, to march and sing, accompanied by instrumental
music. Hearing this, and learning that all were well fed
and given new clothes, a slave outside might suppose that
the captives were as happy as they were physically comfortable, and therefore conclude that it would be better to
go with friends or kindred than to remain lonely and
hungry with a bad master until sold to a worse trader.
In any case, such a preference was a choice of evils.

[32] Wyeth, *Forrest*, 20-21.

However, Forrest must early have had a fancy that slaves *ought* to cleave to him. In May, 1853, he and his partner Hill had in their pen a slave named Nat Mayson. Nat was a carpenter, a good fiddler and claimed to be a barber. Not feeling the alleged charm of Forrest's benevolent humanity and preferring old associates, Nat managed to escape. His attractions to Holly Springs, Mississippi, and to Jackson, Tennessee, were so well known that Hill and Forrest advertised that he had probably gone to one place or the other; yet they also advised the public that he " ran away without a cause "! [33]

Forrest's popularity, like that of many other traders, increased with the number of slaves he bought and sold. In 1858, he was, without opposition, elected alderman of Memphis, as traders J. S. Riggs and Thomas Ryan were in Charleston. He was reëlected in 1859, but resigned on account of being called away. Returning sooner than he expected, he was chosen to fill the vacancy. [34] The Civil War soon came, and emancipation destroyed his chief riches,—yet not until after he had demonstrated that he was perhaps the greatest cavalry genius of that conflict.

Note

What has been said above does not sufficiently explain the ludicrous errors and absurdities of the different writers about Forrest's alleged heroism in slave-trading days.

Jordan & Pryor, who wrote in 1867, with Forrest's coöperation, realized the importance of putting the trader as much as possible in the shadow of a hero. They (*Forrest*, etc., 29-33) trusted to fanciful stories, instead of consulting Memphis newspapers. They represented Forrest as standing on the balcony of the Worsham House (late on Wednesday afternoon, June 24th) and appealing to the mob to wait for a meeting to be held on the " next evening ", Thursday, the 25th. The incidents

---

[33] *Eagle & Enquirer*, July 27, 1853. Nat ran away in May, but these traders seem not to have advertised for him until two months later, presumably hoping to recover him without letting the damaging fact be known that a slave could escape from them.

[34] Wyeth, 22; Mathes, 19.

they described as of Thursday, the 25th (when there was no meeting) occurred, if at all, during the evening and night of Friday, the 26th. They portrayed Forrest as acting a picturesque and decisive part on three critical occasions, and finally rising to such a climax as to take "fully three thousand excited men, as it were, by the throats, and by his own imperious will force them to recognize the plenitude of discarded authority"!

After that, why should anyone hesitate to shape and color his account to suit his own caprice?

Dr. Wyeth (21-22) wisely avoided details as to names, years and the three places, and devised a one-act and one-scene performance, where the picturesque was concentrated. He represented Forrest as hastening directly to the jail on the critical night and making an ample display of heroism there, without going to the ropewalk, where, in fact, the mob had Able with a rope around his neck, and his mother, wife and sister were successfully appealing in his behalf. But Dr. Wyeth preferred Forrest as the hero and the jail as the stage, which in fiction has its advantages. Accordingly Forrest, "interposing himself between the victim and the leaders of the crowd, drew from his pocket a knife, and, holding it on high in that ready left hand which he always used by preference in moments of excitement, declared in earnest tones, which no one who heard him and saw the expression of his face could doubt, that he would kill any man or men that laid a hand upon the prisoner. He then addressed the people and their leaders in an impassioned speech, appealing to their calmer reasoning and better judgment, which with his desperate earnestness so swayed the mob that in half an hour they had left the premises."

Mathes (17-18) largely followed Jordan and Pryor, and likewise displayed original imagination and invention, not only as to details but also as to results. He ventured to assure his readers that "Forrest awoke next day to find himself famous, at least in a local way; the papers were full of the thrilling event, and this man was the hero of the hour. He had vindicated a principle in a time of wild excitement, and set the people to thinking as seldom before"! Mathes was also logical: if what he alleged occurred, the newspapers were sure to be "full of the thrilling event". That is what newspapers are for, as everyone knows. But Mathes unfortunately overlooked the inevitable converse of his logic: What if the newspapers virtually ignored Forrest? They did just that!

Judge Young (*Memphis*, 97-101), writing more than half a century after the murder, accepts numerous errors, fancies and legends as if they were good historical evidence. Taking much that is wholly imaginary, he gives minute details and alleges quotations as if he had contemporaneous and unquestionable documents. He describes Forrest as standing on the balcony of the Worsham House and magically persuading the indignant crowd to wait for "a mass meeting at the Exchange Building tomorrow evening", when a meeting at that time was neither thought of nor held. A balcony is, indeed, a good place for a hero to speak from, if the roaring, half-savage mob will listen and be reasonable. If Forrest appeared on that balcony, it was without appreciable effect, for the mob rushed off to the jail intending to seize Able. It was then at the jail, that a certain general, two colonels, a major and others (with no mention of Forrest), successfully urged an adjournment to an orderly meeting after supper. (*Ante* pp. 259-60). But Tradition long ago took an appeal from these and other facts; insisted that the first act should decisively close with a mastery of the mob from the balcony by Forrest, and that subsequent incidents and stagings should all be for his display, as those in "Hamlet" are for the Prince. And Judge Young, with a brilliant flourish, sustained the appeal.

Hallum, a reminiscent lawyer with a tropical exuberance of words and fancies, merits notice along with these writers because he had so much imagination and so unreliable a memory that, by a sort of mental running-switch, he was able to believe and to assert as a fact, that the mob seized Isaac Bolton, instead of Able, and rushed to the ropewalk to hang him! But at the critical moment "Forrest threw himself head long in the breach, mounted a box, with pistol drawn, after the rope was around Bolton's neck, and told the mob that the man or men who dared to pull on the rope and take Bolton's life, must and should die with him on the spot. This brought the mob to immediately recognize its own danger, and their intended victim was not further molested".— *Diary* etc., 77. Hallum unconsciously burlesqued the inevitable results of such methods as all followed.

There is still another offense. In a proud land where chivalry is counted as the first of manly virtues these writers, over-zealous to adorn a slave-trader with the mantle of a hero, have unwittingly taken it from a poor old mother, who by appeals and tears had wrung it from an angry mob.

These six hero-worshipers, widely disagreeing as to incidents and details, resemble the six blind men that went to "see" the elephant and after a mere touch knew all about him—

> "Each in his own opinion
> Exceeding stiff and strong,
> Though each was partly in the right,
> And all were in the wrong!"

Jordan & Pryor ought to have known the truth. Forrest surely knew that he did not make a speech from the balcony with any such effect as they alleged, and he also knew that most of what they said about him on pages 30-33 was substantially false. Yet on page viii is a foot-note signed by him saying that they had "endeavored to make up a chronicle neither over-wrought nor over-colored, as I can testify. For the greater part of the statements of the narrative I am responsible, and all facts and incidents derived from other sources are properly credited in the foot-notes."

CHAPTER XIII

VARIOUS FEATURES OF THE INTERSTATE TRADE

The gang system of the plantations was so effective in compelling work that youth, health and strength were the only absolute prerequisites in fieldhands of either sex. The original masters reared and they or their estates sold thousands of slaves annually; the interstate traders distributed them advantageously; new masters put them to more productive work. The demands for labor were early so great that it was often possible to palm off inferior and vicious slaves as " prime ". This risk much increased the market for boys and girls, who could not be inveterately vicious and were easily taught special tasks in field or domestic work.

Slave revolts had been numerous in the West Indies, and not so rare in the South but that a mere mention of the " horrors of San Domingo " caused a shudder. States to which immigrants from the West Indies were likely to come, early excluded all slaves old enough to have taken part in any uprising.[1]

As masters were paid for slaves convicted of capital offenses, some of the States, instead of imprisoning or executing such criminals, reimbursed themselves by selling them for deportation. According to Representative Weems

---

[1] For example, N. C. in 1795 forbade immigrants from the West Indies and from French, Dutch and Spanish settlements on the southern coast of America to bring in slaves that were more than 15 years old.—Collins, *Domestic Slave Trade*, 117. In 1803 S. C. prohibited the introduction of negroes from the West Indies, South America and, unless with certificates of good character, from any of the United States. But there were no restrictions against importations from Africa.—Collins, 114. The negroes directly from Africa were not feared. H. M. Henry, *Police Control of the Slave in S. C.*, 105-107, shows S. C.'s attitude 1803-18; and Collins, 115-16, briefly describes the laws from 1823 to 1848.

states sold slaves (criminals)

of Maryland, his State had formerly undertaken to sub-
stitute the penitentiary for the gallows; but in a very short
time it was found necessary to enlarge the penitentiary
tenfold or to exclude and deport many convicts.[2] A Maryland law of 1818 provided that any slave convicted of a
crime, who in the judgment of the court should not be
punished by hanging, might be transported for sale. A law
of 1846 directed that slaves sentenced to the penitentiary
should be sold at auction on the expiration of their terms
and transported.[3] Of the total number of 79 persons whom
the two courts found guilty in connection with the Denmark
Vesey plot for a slave insurrection in Charleston in 1822,
35 were condemned to death and 44 to be sent out of the
State.[4] But it was Virginia that had the largest number
of actual or rumored slave uprisings and is known syste-
matically to have sold most slave criminals for removal
from the State. Between 1800 and 1850 more than 600
were thus disposed of (about two-thirds of all found guilty
of capital offenses), among whom were 4 involved in the
Nat Turner insurrection.[5] Virtually all such sales must
primarily have been to traders, for who else would know-
ingly have bought convicts?

The demand for " cottonhands " was often so great
that planters were glad to spend all their money and
exhaust their credit for such slaves as they could obtain.
This, much like the present-day infatuation for automo-
biles, seriously affected other kinds of business and left
the ordinary creditors in the lurch.[6] Traders naturally

[2] 5 *Register of Debates*, 186.

[3] Collins, 122-123. It is worth noting that Del., although unimportant as a
slave State, in 1827-29 passed laws favoring the exportation of slave criminals.
—Collins, 125.

[4] Jervey, *Robert Y. Hayne*, 132-33.

[5] Prof. Phillips, *Amer. Hist. Review*, Jan., 1915, 337, 339; *Amer. Negro
Slavery*, 459, 481.

[6] The Milledgeville *Southern Recorder*, Feb. 2, 1852, expressed the not
new opinion in saying that slaves had been pouring into the State for two
years, in consequence of the repeal of the law against bringing them in,

paid the least possible for slaves and demanded the most obtainable; and it was notorious that some dealt in the unsound and the vicious. The blame was put on the speculators instead of on the States that officially supplied hundreds of convicts sure to be sold to innocent and distant purchasers. High priced or inferior slaves and the running in debt for them while other debts were blinked, irritated so many persons that it was easy to arouse extra prejudice against interstate traders. At various times, but in most cases for only short periods, all except four Southern States forbade the bringing in of slaves for sale; yet residents, save those of Kentucky, were free to buy and bring in for their own use as many as they pleased. Otherwise the laws could not have been enacted or would have been quickly altered.

Except in a few States, they were early repealed. Renewed excitement brought about the reënactment of some of them,—soon followed by fresh repeal.[7] In Georgia, colony or State, the pendulum very irregularly swung to and fro for more than a century.[8] The futility of the provision in the Mississippi constitution of 1832 against bringing in slaves for sale after May 1, 1833, is explained by the fact that until 1837 no act was passed to enforce the prohibition. As a remedy for the financial crisis of 1837 the Governor successfully urged the passage of a law to exclude slaves as merchandise and thereby stop the heavy expenditures for them; but this law was repealed in 1846.[9] Tennessee

---

and were held at high prices; that the market was over-stocked, and to effect sales, they had been sold on credit. The notes given for them had become due and must be met. The negro-trader, having no popularity to lose, was coercing payment, and the merchant and others were left unpaid.

[7] The Ala. legislature passed a law against interstate traders in 1827 and repealed it in 1829.—Collins, 131-32. The Nat Turner insurrection caused the substance of the law of 1827 to be reënacted in Jan., 1832, but the main feature of this law was repealed before the end of the year.—Birney, *James G. Birney*, 104.

[8] For details, see Du Bois, 7, 8; Collins, 119-20.

[9] Collins, 53, 131.

forbade the regular interstate trade for the exceptionally long period of nearly thirty years, 1826-55.[10] Each of the following nine States, after one or more prohibitions of the interstate traffic in slaves as merchandise, finally took off all restraints, except, of course, as to criminals etc.: Maryland, 1850; Virginia, 1819; North Carolina, about 1818; South Carolina, 1848; Georgia, 1855-56; Tennessee, 1855; Alabama, 1832; Mississippi, 1846; Louisiana, 1834.[11] Missouri and Arkansas were so eager for slaves that they never prohibited the trade except in criminals, the vicious etc.,[12] and Florida and Texas barred criminals only.[13] Kentucky's wholly exceptional law of 1833, prohibiting residents to buy and import slaves even for their own use, allowed bona-fide *immigrants* (called "emigrants to this state") to do so, and it also expressly permitted residents to bring in slaves to whom title was obtained "by will, descent, distribution, or marriage, or gift in consideration of marriage".[14] That the law prohibing residents to buy and import for their own use was much disregarded is evinced by the fact that its repeal in 1849 provided for the absolution of the persons that had violated it.[15]

These various laws, with the exception of Kentucky's, were in the nature of police regulations and mainly to ward off evils attributed to the interstate slave-traders;[16]

[10] Collins, 136.

[11] Collins, 124, 112 ,118, 116, 120, 136, 133, 131, 218. Louisiana's prohibition against bringing in a child under ten years of age without its mother, if living, was not included.

[12] The Missouri constitution of 1820 provided that the legislature might prohibit the introduction of slaves as an article of commerce. "The provision was not taken seriously, and the general assembly never acted upon the suggestion."—Trexler, 45.

[13] Collins, 136-39.

[14] *Acts of Ky.*, 1832-33, 258-59. 1 Catterall, 361-62, 321, 323, 359, 376, cites one conviction with a penalty of $600 for violation of this prohibition, and several indictments for violating this and an earlier law.

[15] *Acts of Ky.*, 1848-49, 21-22, 35-36.

[16] It was a matter of course that criminal slaves should be excluded rather more than criminals of other kinds. And several of the States, at least

they were in no sense antislavery nor even against interstate trading by users, although, of course, whatever antislavery sentiment there was supported the prohibitions.
They temporarily affected the methods and the channels of
the interstate trade and made clear to the interstate traders
the risks of selling on credit. A Mississippi law of 1837
even declared void and of no effect all notes relating to the
forbidden traffic. The lessening of credit must have lessened the traffic, and in turn excited opposition from the
persons that thought they needed more slaves than they
could readily pay for. Many planters with cash or notes
with unquestionable security made their purchases, directly
or through traders, in the Atlantic or the border slave
States and thereby usually obtained better slaves at much
lower prices. But that was none the less interstate trading.
According to Ingraham, it was as common, early in the
'thirties, to hear it said of a Mississippi planter, " He is
gone to Virginia to buy negroes ", as it was in New England to hear it remarked of a country merchant, " He is
gone to Boston to buy goods ".[17]

As these prohibitions did not attempt to prevent the
traders with their gangs from passing through the
" closed " States, there was many a well improved opportunity to sell secretly for cash. And as there was rarely
a " closed " State without having one or more " open "
States as neighbors, the traders easily did business across
forbidden borders. Without violating any law, some
established " plantations " in the " closed " States near
the best markets, collected on them " for their own use "
as many slaves as they pleased and, after employing them
during the few years within which sale was forbidden, disposed of them for maximum prices as " acclimated and
experienced". Such undertakings were probably more

S. Ca., La and Miss., at different times enacted laws requiring that slaves
brought in should be accompanied by certificates of character.—See Collins,
114, 127-28, 129-30.

[17] 2 *The Southwest*, 234, 244; Andrews, 174.

profitable than necessary. The interstate trade carried on in Memphis, and Bolton, Dickins & Company's regular advertisements, in the *Eagle and Enquirer* from October, 1851, and Hill & Forrest's advertisements, in 1854, of having Virginia slaves for sale—these facts conclusively show that Tennessee's prohibition was flouted. In 1845, John D. James, a Natchez trader, treated the Mississippi law likewise by advertising that he had about ninety negroes, just arrived from Richmond, and that he had "made arrangements * * * to have regular shipments every month * * * during the season ".[18] Violations of the laws were certainly numerous, and successful prosecutions on any account were few. As Dew foresaw,[19] the laws were virtually dead letters.

A peculiarly interesting exception was the case of a brazen offender, William H. Williams of " yellow house " fame in Washington. In 1840 he purchased 24 convicts from the State of Virginia for $12,000 and gave bond and security for twice that sum that he would dispose of them beyond the boundary of the United States. Failing to land them near Mobile, he succeeded in getting them into Louisiana, where he was soon detected and, in the third trial, convicted. In addition to very large expenses for counsel, this speculation is supposed to have cost him $48,000: the forfeiture of the $24,000 as bonds; the loss of the 24 slaves,

[18] Sir Charles Lyell, 2 *A Second Visit to the U. S.* (Amer. ed., 1849), 126, prints the advt. in full, which began Oct. 16, 1845.

From a suit against James for a breach of warranty of soundness, it appears that the plaintiff bought a slave of him in Natchez, Feb. 5, 1846, but the bill of sale was dated in Vidalia, La., across the Mississippi River, three days earlier, doubtless so as to pretend that the slave had been brought into Miss. by the prospective user.—12 Smedes and Marshall (Miss.), 337, 341.

At least one trader, in the year after the passage of the law of 1837, was more cautious, as this advt. shows:

"NEGROES FOR SALE. The subscriber has for sale at Vidalia, La., opposite Natchez, between 70 and 80 negroes, among which are field hands, house servants, cooks, washers and ironers, and a first rate blacksmith.— Newton Boley."—*Mississippi Free Trader and Natchez Gazette*, Dec. 20, 1838.

[19] *Pro-Slavery Argument*, 362.

who cost $500 each, $12,000; and a fine of $500 for each importation, $12,000.[20]

Criminal and vicious slaves were, of course, not rare in the trade, and the Southwest was the best region in which to dispose of them. But that they comprised more than a small percentage of all the slaves in the market should not be believed. As was often pointed out at the time, a large proportion, if not fully a majority, of the slaves seen in the possession of the regular interstate dealers were boys and girls in their teens or young and strong men and women but little beyond twenty years of age. And the ages given in the manifests of shipments support this view. Relatively few among them were likely to be really vicious.

There were three methods of taking the slaves to distant markets: by ships, coastwise or down the Ohio, the Mississippi and their tributaries; by overland march, and by railroad.

The largest coastwise cargoes of slaves went from Alexandria, Baltimore, Norfolk, Richmond and Charleston to places farther south or on the Gulf or the Mississippi, especially New Orleans. From about 1828 to 1836 Franklin & Armfield carried not merely their own slaves but also those of others, whether planters or traders. One of their slavers was called the " Tribune " and another the " United States "![21] Of the 371 slaves arriving at the port of New Orleans during a week in November, 1831, they brought 150 on the " United States " from Norfolk and 141 on the " Tribune " from Alexandria.[22] In the winter of 1835-36 their fleet included the brigs " Tribune ", " Isaac Franklin " and " Uncas " and was sufficiently large for a sailing from Alexandria and from New Orleans every fortnight

[20] 60 *Niles's Register*, 189; Phillips, *Amer. Negro Slavery*, 193.

[21] Alexandria *Phenix Gazette*, Dec. 22, 1829.

[22] 41 *Niles's Register*, 239.

during the season. These ships were described as " of the first class, commanded by experienced and accommodating officers ", accustomed " to promote the interest of shippers and [the] comfort of passengers ", and they went up the Mississippi by steam.[23] The best were built expressly for this trade [24] and the others were remodeled to suit it. To the coastwise trade they were what slave-trader hotels and boarding-houses were to the local trade. The captain of the " Tribune " willingly showed his ship to an antislavery clergyman. The hold was appropriated to the slaves and divided into two apartments; the after-hold would carry about 80 women, and the other about 100 men. On either side were two platforms running the whole length; one raised a few inches, and the other half-way up the deck. They were about five or six feet deep. " On these the slaves lie, as close as they can stow away.''[25]

Between January 6, 1851, and November 6, 1852, both inclusive, at least 1,152 slaves were shipped from Baltimore to different Southern ports.[26] A greater portion of

[23] *National Intelligencer*, Mar. 2, 1836. Armfield naturally had charge of this shipping.

[24] Andrews, 142.

[25] Wm. Jay, *Misc. Writings etc.*, 157-58.

According to the extant manifests, the following were among the largest coastwise shippers or consignees in the respective cities in the years named:—

   1834-35:

ALEXANDRIA: John Armfield. NORFOLK: W. T. Foster, R. H. Banks, R. L. Marsh. Banks and Marsh were each masters of their respective ships. RICHMOND: Bacon Tait, Lancaster, Denby & Co., John and Sam Corby & Co. CHARLESTON: Hugh McDonald, who is shown by the manifests to have shipped 145 to New Orleans between Dec. 13, 1834 and Mar. 19, 1835. NEW ORLEANS: Isaac Franklin, Thomas Boudar, Edward Williams, Theophilus Freeman, R. W. Semington, Paul Pascal, Brander & McKenna, Bullitt, Shipp & Co.

[26] The *Key to Uncle Tom's Cabin*, 149, gives the names and destinations of vessels carrying 1,033 of these slaves. Of these shipments, only the manifests of those to New Orleans are preserved in the Library of Congress, and not all of these. Two unlisted cargoes of May 17, 1851, and Oct. 18, 1852, comprising 119 additional slaves were sent from Baltimore to New Orleans. In 1851-52, these traders were most conspicuous as shippers or consignees in the cities named:—

the interstate trade from the old States is supposed to
have gone coastwise in the 'thirties than in the 'fifties.

In that trade a large degree of secrecy was possible.
Austin Woolfolk was not the only trader that embarked
his slaves at night and started before dawn.[27] Many
others also suffered from actual or attempted slave muti-
nies by sea or land, for they were frequent; there was
almost always danger of them.[28] And there were storms
and rocks to increase the risks of the voyages. In 1831 the
brig " Comet ", on a voyage between Alexandria and New
Orleans, with 164 slaves aboard, struck the rocks on the
Bahama Banks and was abandoned; the negroes were
rescued and taken to Nassau, New Providence, where they
were declared free by the colonial authorities.[29] Early in
1835 the " Enterprise ", *en route* between Alexandria and
Charleston, bearing about 75 slaves, valued at $40,000 and
belonging to Joseph W. Neal and others,[30] was driven by
stress of weather to Bermuda, and its cargo of slaves was
freed in consequence. In telling Andrews and others of
this loss, young Neal [31] bitterly complained.—" But why
don't you go there and claim them? " asked a bystander.—
" Because ", said Neal, with lavish profanity and profound

BALTIMORE: B. M. & W. L. Campbell and Joseph Donovan. Manifests
show that between Apr. 3, 1851 and Dec. 2, 1852 the Campbells shipped 339
and Donovan 144. RICHMOND: David Currie, Luther Libby, George Davis
(of Petersburg). CHARLESTON: M. McBride, who shipped 23 small lots,
the largest of 13 slaves. NEW ORLEANS: Thomas G. James, Thomas
Boudar, John Hagan, Wm. F. Talbott, C. M. Rutherford.

[27] Andrews, 80. See *post*, p. 368.

[28] *Niles's Register* (Sept. 5, 1829, pp. 18-19; Dec. 26, p. 277; and Jan. 9,
1830, p. 328), reported at least three attempts in a few months.

[29] Wm. Jay, *Misc. Writings etc.*, 252; Sen. Doc. 24th Cong. 2d Sess. Vol.
2, No. 174, p. 43. The " Comet " and most of the slaves were said to belong
to Franklin & Armfield.—Jay, 158. Except 9 owned by a Mrs. Mudd and 9
by a Col. Tutt, the slaves were insured by three New Orleans companies,
who paid the traders, and accordingly, succeeded to their claims.—House
Doc., 27th Cong., 2d Sess., No. 242, pp. 3-4.

[30] Moore, 1 *International Arbitration*, 219; Andrews, 149; Jay, 253.

[31] *Ante* pp. 54-55.

indignation, " *a nigger is just as free there and stands just as good a chance in their courts as a white man!* " [32]   Such sentiments were not so singular as they now appear.   Then the foreign slave-trade was piracy by our law, but the domestic trade was entirely lawful, even on the high seas. Accordingly, our Government long, and at last successfully, insisted that Great Britain should pay for these and other similar losses of slaves that had been involuntarily brought within British territory.[33]

William H. Seward saw a cargo shipped from Richmond and transshipped at Norfolk, in 1846.   A well-dressed white man led on board into the steerage-cabin a long line of 75 young slaves, men, women and children, each except, the children, carrying a bag, bundle, chest or bandbox, containing all the bearer's worldly possessions.   They were " huddled together on the lower deck, [and] looked with puerile curiosity and gratification at all that surrounded them ".   At the port of entry lay a broad, capacious ship waiting to receive them.   It was bound for New Orleans and already had 125 slaves on board.

" As I stood looking at this strange scene, a gentleman stepped up to my side and said: ' You see the *curse* that our forefathers bequeathed to us. * * * Oh, they don't mind it; they are cheerful; they enjoy this transportation and travel as much as you do.' * * * The lengthened file at last had all reached the deck of the slaver, and we cut loose.   The captain of our boat, seeing me intensely interested, turned to me and said: ' Oh, sir, do not be concerned about them; they are the happiest people in the world!' I looked, and there they were—slaves, ill protected from the cold, fed capriciously on the commonest food—going from all that was dear to all that was terrible, and still they wept not. * * *   And these were ' the happiest people in the world'!   The sable procession was followed by a woman, a white woman, dressed in silk and furs and feathers.   She seemed [to be] the captain's wife.   She carried in her hand a *Bible!* " [34]

It should not be assumed, as it was by some persons, that

[32] Andrews, 146.

[33] Moore, 2 *International Law Digest*, 350, 352, 355-57, names the indemnities paid, etc., etc.

[34] F. W. Seward, 1 *William H. Seward*, 778-79.

there were physical sufferings and fatalities in this trade resembling those in the African trade. The manifests gave the names and ages of the slaves, and the United States inspector at the port of entry verified the lists and noted deaths or births. Of the 646 slaves that made up the first four cargoes arriving at New Orleans from Alexandria in 1835 only one death and one birth were noted—both occurring on the " Uncas ", a ship of 155 tons burden, when it was carrying an exceptionally large cargo of 202 slaves. Two or three years earlier Ingraham saw about 100 landed on the levee at New Orleans " in fine condition, looking as lively and hearty as though the sea voyage agreed with them ".[35]

The Mississippi River was the greatest inland channel

[35] 2 *The Southwest*, 234.

Especially in La. and Miss., in 1902 and 1907, the author questioned many ex-slaves about their sale and transportation, and took shorthand notes of their answers. Out of 15 interviewed in the course of a few hours, at Carrollton, La., near New Orleans, all but 2 or 3 had been brought down by traders, and most of them had been sold at least 3 times.

Nathan Ross, of Donaldsonville, La., was originally owned by John H. Robinson, who, about 1846, sold him to a trader in Richmond named Daniel B. Budder. [Unless a name mentioned was common and easily pronounced, the faulty articulation of the ex-slaves compelled one to guess as to the name and its spelling.] " Budder brought 'bout 50 or 60 all de way by boat to New O'leens. We drifted down de Jeems to Po'tsm'uth an' den we was put on de New O'leens ship. Dere was 30 or 40 uthahs owned by tradahs. On board de ship we was treated well; had plenty to eat. We was allowed to walk on deck. We was not in de hol' 'cep'n' at night er when it sto'med. At New O'leens we was taken to a tradah's office. De yahd was walled up 13 er 14 feet high 'round to de front." Ross was there about three months, except when at times he was hired out as an apprentice blacksmith on trial. Finally he was sold privately at the pen to a Creole, who lived 9 miles from Donaldsonville.

Washington Taylor, 72 years old, and also living in Donaldsonville, was born in Gloucester co., Va., near the York River. In 1853 his master sold him from the plantation to a trader by whom he was handcuffed and taken to Richmond on a sulky. In Richmond he was resold to another trader who shipped him and about 80 other slaves around to New Orleans in a sailing vessel. They were treated all right, except that the food was not good—a doubtful criticism. They were put in a trader's pen on Esplanade st. There Taylor was sold to a man who had a brickyard in New Orleans.

of the trade. Charles Mackay's rhymed account of his journey from St. Louis to New Orleans contains these lines:

"Three days on the river,—nights and mornings three,
Ere we stopped at Memphis, the port of Tennessee,
And wondered why they gave it such name of old renown—
A dreary, dingy, muddy, melancholy town.
But rich in bales of cotton, o'er all the landing spread,
And bound for merry England, to earn the people's bread;—
And here—oh! shame to Freedom, that boasts with tongue and pen!—
We took on board a 'cargo' of miserable men;
A freight of human creatures, bartered, bought and sold
Like hogs, or sheep, or poultry—the living blood for gold ".[36]

Mackay's fellow-traveler was more explicit: a company of ten, mostly girls, had been bought in Richmond for a plantation near Vicksburg, costing, all expenses included, about $1,050 each. A gang of 20, put on at Memphis, " were on their way to the New Orleans market to be sold, all except one, a mulatto girl, who seemed to be the traveling companion of the owner, and would return with him ".[37] The men that Thomas Hamilton saw on a Mississippi River boat were " loaded with chains " and the women had on " scarcely rags enough to serve the purpose of decency ". " The men were in an especially wretched and disgusting condition, for their chains prevented their performing the ordinary functions of cleanliness, and their skin had become covered with a sort of scaly eruption." [38]

One of Walker's gangs shipped down the Mississippi was kept in a large room on the lower deck, the men and women together, but handcuffed and carefully watched lest the shackles should be slippped and escape attempted at some landing or by jumping overboard. Once a woman, not fastened, was so distressed by having been sold away from her husband and children that she sprang into the

[36] Charles Mackay, 1 *Life and Liberty in America*, 249-50. *Key to Uncle Tom's Cabin*, 62-63, describes taking on a cargo of about 30 near Memphis.
[37] [Hiram Fuller] *Belle Brittan On a Tour*, etc., 91-92.
[38] *Men and Manners in America* (1843), 333.

river and was drowned. The slaves were treated so much like beasts that it was hardly possible to keep their part of the ship clean. At Rodney, Mississippi, they were landed, put in a pen in the rear of the village and offered at private sale. To make extra profits, many slaves above the usually marketable age had been bought, fattened, barbered and dressed so as to look as young as possible. Whiskers were shaved off and gray hairs were plucked out or dyed. This process made the negroes look ten or fifteen years younger. They were then instructed as to how old, or rather how young, they were to pretend to be. Only those for whom high prices were offered were sold there. The others were shipped to Natchez, where the same plan was followed. After a few days, the rest were taken to New Orleans. Later, Walker's porter saw his own mother, chained to another woman, started by boat from St. Louis for the New Orleans market.[39]

When the gangs were landed at New Orleans and driven off to the high-walled yards they were amazed by strange sights and sounds—countless ships of many kinds and sizes with flags of various designs and colors—the long, crescent levee crowded with thousands of bales of cotton, casks, barrels, boxes and crates of various sorts of merchandise—the queer houses and the public buildings on ground lower than the surface of the river—negroes and white persons chattering and calling to one another in a language no more understood than the chirping of sparrows.[40]

[39] *Narrative of William W. Brown*, 40-43, 77.

[40] An ex-slave, interviewed in Carrollton, La., in 1902, said that when he was about 15 years old his mistress, the widow of Dr. Mackey of Richmond, sold him to a trader, who took him to Winchester, Va., and put him in a jail to wait until a gang was made up. The gang finally contained 60 or 70 persons. The trader had a wagon to carry the things needed. The gang walked and then took a boat [on the Ohio River] and came down the Mississippi to Baton Rouge. There this boy was disposed of at private sale to speculators named Woods & Fox. After the death of Woods and his wife, this slave was sold in Baton Rouge to a man named Cooper. Later, Cooper

From decade to decade the domestic slave-trade became somewhat less inhuman, less like the foreign trade, but it never became humane. In a gang of 51 Maryland slaves, 32 men and 19 women, taken to South Carolina and Georgia markets, about 1805, the women were tied together with a rope about their necks, like a halter, while the men wore iron collars, fastened to a chain about one hundred feet long, and were also handcuffed.[41] The men in double file went ahead and the women followed in the same order. The drivers rode wherever they could best watch and direct the coffle. At the end of the day all, without being relieved of their collars, handcuffs, chains or ropes, lay down on the bare floor, the men on one side of the room and the women on the other. They were started early on the road, but did not have their breakfast until about nine o'clock. The rule was two meals daily, of about the same kind of food; corn-bread or corn-mush, a boiled herring or a bit of pork, and perhaps sour milk, were most common.

On the highway and in the villages the slaves were stared at with covetous eyes, and often the inquiry was made, " Are any of your niggers for sale? " Near Columbia, South Carolina, a persistent stranger said that he

sold him to Harmon Matie, who in turn sold him to a Dr. Laycock, who both practised medicine and had a sugar plantation. " I was wid 'im when de wah begun.   Den I sol' *myse'f wid a musket* "—which meant that he ran away to the Federal Army.

An old woman in Carrollton said that when she was a girl a trader brought her to New Orleans from St. Louis, Mo., on a boat called the Loyal Hill. "In New O'leens we was put in a big buildin' and yahd, which dey used t' call niggah tradahs' yahds. Dere was a showroom, and gentlemen like you come and bought in 'bout 18 of us and took us to Baton Rouge". Her new master's name was John Bird, who had about " 300 head in de field and 100 head of chillun at de house ".

Mrs. Eliza McCollins, also seen in Carrollton, was "brought down by niggah-tradah Henry Moore from Cooper county, Mo." There were hundreds of slaves in the trader's yard where she was put. Her husband was with her.   Moore had a plantation where he kept those whom he did not sell.   She was not resold.

[41] *Life and Adventures of Charles Ball* (Pittsburgh, 1853), 30.

" wanted a couple of breeding-wenches ", and would pay as much as they would bring in Georgia. He looked the whole gang over, " then turning to the women, asked the prices of the two pregnant ones. Our master replied, that these were two of the best breeding-wenches in all Maryland —that one was twenty-two and the other only nineteen— that the first was already the mother of seven children, and the other of four—that he had himself seen the children at the time he bought their mothers—that each of them had a child every year, and that such wenches would be cheap at a thousand dollars each [although the average slave was then worth hardly one-third that much]; but as they were heavy and not able to keep up with the gang, he would take twelve hundred dollars for the two ". The stranger offered one thousand. Finally the trader agreed to accept it if the buyer would pay a blacksmith for taking off all irons, which were no longer needed.[42] Pleased by his fee and the association with slaveowners, the blacksmith supplied liquor, all drank together and he wished his benefactors " good luck with their niggers ". Then the two " wenches " took a sorrowful leave and followed their proud purchaser to his home, while the gang, unshackled, continued the journey.[43]

James S. Buckingham, in 1839, met a drove of slaves a few miles north of Fredericksburg, Virginia—" the men chained together in pairs, and the women carrying the children and bundles, in [on] their march to the South. The gang was under several white drivers, who rode near them on horseback, with large whips, while the slaves marched on foot beside them; and there was one driver behind, to bring up the rear ".[44] Unless the men in such

---

[42] Although Prof. Phillips (2 *Plantation etc.*, 59 ff., quotes extensively from this book, he leaves out all reference to these " breeding-wenches ".

[43] Ball, 31, 33, 34, 59, 60, 63, 64.

[44] Buckingham, 2 *The Slave States of America*, 553.

coffles were shackled, at least until far from home, some-one was likely to slip away; and there had been so many attempts to kill the drivers and to escape that constant vigilance was required.

At early dawn in September, 1834, another English traveler came upon a trader's caravan of 300 negroes in Southwestern Virginia. They had passed the night on the bank of the New River and were preparing to continue their march toward the Mississippi. Some of the women were sitting on logs, others were standing and many little black children were warming themselves at the bivouac fires. Close at hand were about 200 male slaves, manacled and chained together in pairs. Near the gang were several slave-drivers, laughing and smoking, fairly well dressed and wearing broad-brimmed white hats around some of which black crape was wound. There were nine vehicles of different kinds for the white persons and any of the slaves that could not endure the journey afoot. Presently the caravan prepared to cross the river. A man on horse-back selected a shallow ford for the chain-gang. Then came a four-horse wagon attended by another rider and soon followed by wagons containing the children and others. Most of the women were ferried over on flatboats.

Farther on, the Englishman stopped to make a short visit. When he resumed his journey one of his fellow-passengers, accompanied by a slave body-servant, was " a queer, tall animal about forty years old, with dark black hair, cut round as if he were a Methodist preacher, im-mense black whiskers, a physiognomy not without one or two tolerable features, but singularly sharp and not a little piratical and repulsive; all this was set off with a huge broad-brimmed white hat, adorned with a black crape that covered it almost to the top of the crown. His clothes also were black, so that it was evident he intended people should see he was in mourning." At a tavern beyond Knoxville, President Andrew Jackson, stopping for a meal and a

A Slave Coffle Crossing a Ford above Fredericksburg, Virginia

From Buckingham's *Slave States*

short rest, sat smoking a long pipe and wearing a white hat, also wound with crape. A little later, the queer stranger made an ambitious effort to express to his fellow-travelers his great admiration of Jackson: "The old Gineral is the most greatest and most completest idear of a man what had ever lived. I don't mean to say nothing agin Washington—he was a man too; but Jackson *is* a man, I tell *you;* and when I seed him in his old white hat, with the mourning crape on it, it made me feel a kind of particular curious." [45] After this, the Englishman could not refrain from asking him the occasion of his being in mourning.—"Marcus [Marquis] Layfeeyate."—"Do you mean General Lafayette?"—"I reckon that's what I mean."—Lafayette had died a few months previously. Going into mourning for him had considerable vogue. What on the part of President Jackson and high officials was an appropriate expression of national affection and grief, was, on the part of many imitators, ostentatious affectation, often silly, even grotesque. But who was the queer stranger? He was one of the traders seen at the New River, the owner, or half-owner, of that large coffle and also of a fleet of slavers,—John Armfield of Alexandria. An ignorant, drunken "nigger-trader" affecting mourning for the chivalrous, self-sacrificing apostle of liberty, Lafayette!

Neal said that his coffles averaged 25 miles a day after they became seasoned. [46] That was not excessive for sturdy slaves, and there were always facilities so that the ailing might ride. It was also important to make them as cheer-

---

[45] The tangled, lumbering grandiloquence was probably a result of excessive indulgence in brandy and onions, which this trader's slave valet subsequently explained as follows: Contrary to the physician's orders, "when he sees 'em he can't stand it, and den he eats 'em, and dey makes him sick, and den he carries on jist like a house a fire; and den he drinks brandy upon 'em, and dat makes him better; and den he eats ingeons agin, and so he keeps a carrying on".—G. W. Featherstonhaugh, *Excursion through the Slave States* (Harper & Bros., 1844), 46.

[46] Andrews, 149.

ful as possible. And these grown-up children welcomed every diversion. Whoever could act the clown, sing, play on any musical instrument, tell no matter how extravagant yarns about love-adventures, shirking work, stealing liquor, a suckling pig or poultry, was eagerly listened to. Music was the favorite distraction on the march as well as in the slave-pens. There was rarely a numerous group of negroes without a violin, a guitar, a banjo, an accordion, mouthorgans or jewsharps. At the head of a coffle of about 70 met on the highway near Paris, Kentucky, in the 'twenties, were two slaves vigorously sawing their violins, followed by others wearing cockades, and from the center of the gang floated an American flag.[47] That was only an extreme illustration of how the gangs were encouraged to march through villages and towns, singing in melodious, plaintive chorus, while whoever had a musical instrument lustily played it. They were, if not " the happiest people in the world ", often the most light-hearted, not because they liked slavery or were indifferent to being " sold South ", but in spite of it, as the shackles and whips and constant watching demonstrated.

Lewis Adams, an ex-slave and one of the founders of the Tuskegee Institute, told the author that " Columbus, Georgia, rather than Montgomery, was the center of the trade for Tuskegee, which is midway between the two cities. The speculators brought their slaves through here, camped in the public square [in which stands the courthouse], often sold off some or all, or moved on with them as if they were so many mules ". An ex-Confederate captain said that it was " not at all rare for nigger-traders, with their gangs from Virginia and North Carolina to pass through Tuskegee. I have seen them auction off some on the steps of the courthouse, there ". And an ex-Representative in Congress from Mobile gave a similar account of how as a boy he had often seen traders with companies

<hr/>

[47] John Rankin, *Letters on American Slavery*, 45-46.

of negroes go through his native village of Linden, Marengo county, Alabama, which lies about west of Selma.

John Hill, an old planter who from childhood had lived on the west side of the Mississippi a little above Baton Rouge, told the author, in 1907, that the slaves of his region came mainly from South Carolina and Virginia. " Some planters went on after them, others bought in New Orleans or from traders that were passing or had markets in the cities of their neighborhoods. Of course many planters raised a large proportion of their own slaves." He owned about 50 in 1860, most of whom he purchased in Baton Rouge of traders who brought them from Virginia.

Federick Law Olmsted learned that along the road he was taking in the Yazoo valley it was common for drovers and slave-dealers to pass in the autumn with their stock. Sometimes there were as many as 200 negroes in a gang.[48]

Alfred Wornell [49] described how he came down to Natchez in one of trader Pullum's gangs from Lexington, Kentucky: " Sixty-three hade [head] of us walked. Dere was two wagons an' a amb'lance. Dere was only one little chile; de res' was men an' women. De oldes' man was 'bout 45 and de women 'bout 15 to 25. Dey give us meat an' bread an' coffee. Dere was plenty of it while we was comin'. We started 'fore day an' traveled till three o'clock in de ev'nin. We stopped some days to res' up." The members of the gang were treated well, " 'ceptin' some o' de women was whipped 'cause dey fought one o' de men. Fettahs was kep' on my ankles for a week er two 'cause I had run away." There was, of course, a chain-gang. He and two other ex-slaves illustrated how such gangs were fastened together, but far enough apart to allow room for easy marching. To avoid having too large a gang on one chain, it might be divided.—" Were the women chained? " the author asked.—" De *women* could'n' do nuthin'; had ter

[48] *Back Country*, 152.
[49] *Post* p. 306.

foller de men. When dey got sick, dey put 'em in de wagon.'' [50]

Natchez was a market in which many of the most reliable of the interstate traders liked to sell, and it was there that Armfield was taking his caravan. At all periods a large proportion of the slaves for this market were taken over-land. The journey afoot, if made carefully, hardened and enabled them to endure the climate of lower Mississippi and Louisiana. Those that came by water landed at " Natchez under the Hill ", at the base of a precipitous bluff nearly two hundred feet high, on whose brow was the little planter-city. Led by a trader, they climbed the steep road " in a long straggling line, or sometimes in double files in well-ordered procession ''—each slave carrying a bundle, if heavy, usually on the bearer's head. From the top of the bluff they gazed with surprise and wonder up and down the river and across upon Louisiana, an ocean of green lowland. Still more strange was the sight to those that were ending their long march from Virginia — usually requiring from six to eight weeks.[51] Because Louisiana had a bad name for cruelty and fever, the newcomers hoped to be bought by Mississippi planters, especially

[50] William Lister, met in Vicksburg, Miss., in 1902, said that he was born in Va. " I'm 'bout 70 er 80 year ole. I come wid a man down here an' tuck de lan' 'way fum de Indians, an' de speckilatahs went out and brought de black people to make 'em rich,—dat's what dey done, I'll tell yo' plain. My fadah was a *free* man an' married a slave woman. An dat made de chilluns slaves." The gist of his answers to simple questions was:—A trader came to his master's plantation in Va. and bought him, when about 15 years old, and one of his sisters and other slaves, and put them in a slave-jail in Richmond. His mother and one sister had been sold previously. He and his sister and others were brought to Choctaw, Ala. They came afoot all the way. No chains were put on him, but the men were handcuffed. He took his name from a man named Lister, who bought him at Choctaw for $1,000. Much later he was given to Miss Lister when she got married.

[51] [Ingraham] 2 *Southwest*, 235-47, gives an excellent description of the march, arrival etc. A drove of slaves that trader John D. James (of the firm Cochran & James) bought in Va. marched from Richmond to Natchez in about 44 days—from about Aug. 21st to Oct. 3 or 4, 1845.—12 Smedes and Marshall (Miss.), 341.

those whose houses were in the grand forest along the bluff. The negro's notion of the difference between the two States was well explained by this characteristic bit of folk-lore, reported to the author on that bluff by an ex-slave that had been in one of the coffles: "De ole Debel ast Gawd fer a Chrismus giff, an' he tuck dese heah hills fer his ownse'l an' gib de Debel Louzianny". The long file trudged through the town, staring right and left at every object. Sometimes those that had come by water wore their new clothes, but those whose dreary tramp had not quite ended were usually "in the brown rags in which they left Virginia". Almost any kind of a slave-pen was pleasing after the cramped and filthy quarters on a boat or after the varied exposures to the burning sun, drenching rain, deep mud and suffocating dust.

By the middle of the century it became customary to take many of the groups, especially if not large, to market in freight, baggage or the roughest passenger cars. "In the negro car belonging to the train in which we made this journey", between Fredericksburg and Richmond, wrote Charles Dickens, "were a mother and her children who had just been purchased; the husband and father being left behind with their old owner. The children cried the whole way, and the mother was misery's picture. The champion of Life, Liberty, and the Pursuit of Happiness, who had bought them, rode in the same train; and every time we stopped, got down to see that they were safe." [52]

A train on which Olmsted rode between Richmond and Petersburg in the winter of 1853-54 had two freight cars occupied by about forty negroes, most of whom belonged to traders who were taking them to distant markets. "Such kind of evidence of activity in the slave-trade of Virginia is to be seen every day; but particulars and statistics of it are not to be obtained by a stranger here." [53]

[52] *American Notes*, chap. IX.   [53] Olmsted, *Seaboard* etc., 55.

10

Before turning to theology, Lyman Abbott was a lawyer. In 1856 he made a professional trip to Atlanta. When he was passing through the Old Dominion a gang of slaves was put on board his train. " That is the *bad* thing about slavery ", said a young Virginian to Abbott.—" What? "— " These cursed traders. * * * But it is a necessary evil. Sometimes a nigger won't behave himself, or once in a while a master fails and has to sell his slaves. But no one respects the traders or will have anything to do with them. They can't go into society. Everybody despises them."—At first the Northerner considered himself fortunate to have witnessed so rare a sight; but before long he noticed that " every train going south has just such a crowd of slaves on board, twenty or more, and a ' nigger car ', which is very generally also the smoking-car, and sometimes the baggage-car. You notice also, that these slaves whom you constantly meet going south in the trader's hands are not old men and women or by any means malicious-looking ones, as you would naturally expect from your friend's account, but are for the most part apparently picked slaves, boys and girls or young men and women, eighteen, twenty, twenty-five. * * *—But then [as the Southerner had said] these Negroes do not feel these things as we do! They are an altogether inferior race of beings and have no strong affections! " [54]

William Fletcher King, subsequently president of Cornell College, Iowa, witnessed several slave-auctions in Murfreesboro, Tennessee, on New Year's day, 1854. On the cold morrow he " found huddled together between the piles of cotton bales on the [railroad] platform groups of families that had been broken by the sales of the day before ". He was " attracted by their demonstrations of grief at the prospect of speedy and perpetual separation " and especially " by the deep sorrow of the husband and wife who

[54] 107 *The Outlook*, 196-97.

had been involuntarily divorced the day before in spite of the importunate pleading of the husband. When the train arrived the manifestations became most hysterical."[55]

In the latter part of the 'fifties so many slaves were taken through or from Virginia—by traders, purchasers for use and migrating masters—as to cause much comment throughout the South.[56] "An almost endless outgoing of slaves from Virginia to the South has continued for more than two weeks past", said the Petersburg, Virginia, *Express*, early in 1859.[57] About the same time the Portsmouth, Virginia, *Transcript* reported: " Heavy shipments of negroes for the far South are made almost every day by the Seaboard and Roanoke railroad. Yesterday about a hundred arrived here from the eastern shore of Maryland and passed through, and this morning another carload from Delaware was sent on."[58] Editors in Montgomery and Mobile agreed[59] in saying that the shipments by rail via Augusta, Georgia, had averaged not less than two hundred slaves daily during the past two months. But these were sent by only one of several through lines of railroad transportation and were exclusive of the coastwise, the river and the overland routes.

[55] W. F. King, *Reminiscences*, 101-03.

[56] In the spring of 1857 the Petersburg, Va., *Express* said that there was such an "unusual number of slaves" "constantly passing through Petersburg" that many persons thought that in 10 or 20 years Va. would be cleared of its slave population.—Quoted by the Palestine, Tex., *Trinity Advocate*, May 20, 1857.

In 1855, an engineer on the N. C. Railway told Robert Russell that he had carried as many as 600 slaves on one train.—*North America etc.*, 157.

[57] Quoted by the Austin, Tex., *State Gazette*, Feb. 12, 1859.

[58] Quoted by Montgomery *Confederation*, Jan. 13, 1859.

"LARGE SHIPMENT OF SLAVES.—During November and December [1858], 1,886 slaves were shipped over the Petersburg and Weldon railroad for the cotton and rice fields of the South. Tuesday 107 more were sent upon the road; and 100 more are now in Petersburg in readiness to be forwarded to the same market."—Richmond *Dispatch*.—Quoted by the Austin, Tex., *State Gazette*, Feb. 19, 1859.

[59] *Confederation*, Jan. 13, 1859; *Register*, Jan. 19, 1859.

Additional notes on recollections of former slaves.

Two quaint and pathetic remnants of the olden time were found in solemn conversation in front of the Vicksburg postoffice, in 1902. One was sitting on a tall, lank mule and the other was standing and holding a large, dilapidated basket. Although surprised, they gladly answered questions to the best of their poor abilities.

One was born in Va. in 1838. "I knows de yeah 'cause I keeps it set down in my Bible." He was about 20 years old when his young master took him to Richmond and sold him to traders named John and Ren Fonder [so the name seemed to be pronounced, but he may have meant either S. R. Fondren, who in 1860-61 was the silent partner in the firm of Davis, Deupree & Co., auctioneers, or R. Faundron, a regular negro-trader], who resold him there for $1450 to Alonzo L. Brown, who brought him to a plantation near Edwards Station, Miss. When inspected "every rag was taken off". He was brought from Richmond with "30 hade" and in the plainest sort of a passenger car.

No. 2 was stolen from Md. when he was a boy; was brought to New Orleans in 1840 by a trader named John Wesley Read. He had calculated his age by counting from "when de stahs fell", which he saw. [The remarkable phenomenon called the "falling of the stars" occurred Nov. 13, 1833.] With about 100 others he was sold in New Orleans soon after their arrival. His master, named Ben Roach, owned many plantations and took him to one about 17 miles up the Yazoo River.

Kade McCollins, in 1902 living in Carrollton, La., was brought to New Orleans a few years before the Civil War, in a gang "from N. C. by a nigger-trader named Smith". They came on the cars as far as Mobile and by boat from there to New Orleans. He was kept handcuffed all the way. He was resold from Smith's yard [undoubtedly John B. Smith's, see post p. 315 n.] to a Creole who had a plantation on the Red River.

Joseph Gibson, interviewed with others in the Baton Rouge market-place, said that he was born in Charleston, S. C. His first master sold him when a child to a trader named John Wilson, who resold him to another trader named Mordecai (ante pp. 176, 183), who in turn resold him to a man that took him, presumably by the new railroad, to Memphis, where he was bought by Albert Dunbar, who lived near Natchez.

A wrinkled, yellow old woman, probably beyond four score years, joined a group being quizzed at the Baton Rouge market and was impatient to tell her experiences: "I was born'd in Lexin'ton, Kentucky. Dey give me to my mistiss's daughter fer a present. Dey make presunts o' niggahs in doze days, dey did dat. Mistiss died and dey sol' me to a New O'leens tradah named Tom Powells. [Undoubtedly the notorious Thomas A. Powell. See ante p. 128 n. and post p. 295]. He put me in a yahd neah de

French Mahket ". Here the interview ended, for the author needed to hasten away to take a train.

Dr. Dunbar Rowland informs the author that Alonzo L. Brown, Ben. Roach and Albert Dunbar were the names of well known planters in the counties and at the times mentioned by the ex-slaves. Except pronunciations and jumbled phrases, the recollections of old negroes about such subjects as have been quoted were often accurate.

CHAPTER XIV

SOME ALABAMA AND MISSISSIPPI MARKETS

Montgomery, the capital of Alabama and a good ship-ping-point, attracted politicians, planters and much gen-eral business, although in 1860 its total population was less than 9,000, of whom more than half were slaves and 102 were free colored.[1] Its slave-trade was patronized chiefly by the central part of the State, for northern Ala-bama drew supplies from markets in other States, and Montgomery traders had competitors in Columbus, Georgia, on the east, Selma on the west and Mobile on the south-west. Yet the capital did a thriving trade in slaves. The *City Directory* for 1859 listed four " slave depots " along with the same number of banking establishments, whereas for the joyful visitors to the first capital of the Confed-eracy in February, 1861, there were only four regular hotels.[2]

Where Montgomery's two principal streets met and formed an obtuse angle and another street crossed, there was sufficient space for a public market-place in the busi-ness center of the little city. From there a part of Market street (now Dexter avenue) ran up to the capitol, on a commanding site about three-fourths of a mile to the east, and the other part (now Commerce street) ran down to the railroad and the Alabama River, about half as far to the northwest. The best hotel, the Exchange, faced this market-place, and most of the public buildings, banks and churches were near. When Sir Charles Lyell was in Montgomery in 1846 he was amazed to see slaves paraded

[1]
	White	Colored	Total
1850,	6,511	2,217	8,728
1860,	4,341	4,502	8,843

—U. S. Census 1870, *Population*, p. 81.

[2] Prof. Trexler, *Birmingham-Southern College Bulletin*, Dec., 1928, p. 3.

too and fro and sold at auction in this most frequented spot.[3] He overlooked the fact that slave-trading was considered a sign of enterprise and prosperity. Before the end of the 'fifties a large basin was put there to receive water flowing from an artesian well. Thereafter, virtually all public sales were held " at the Artesian Basin ". In all the South there was not another slave-mart so central and conspicuous, for Charleston's was no longer by its historic old Exchange.

It gives one a realizing sense of what the large traders meant by buying for the " Southern market " to find in one column of a Montgomery newspaper three establishments respectively offering at private sale " 150 LIKELY NEGROES, mostly from Virginia ", " 60 LIKELY YOUNG NEGROES from Virginia and South Carolina " and " 50 likely NEGROES just arrived from the Carolinas ".[4] Such advertisements and those about Kentucky mules indicated where this part of Alabama obtained the largest increase to its working force for raising cotton. Slaves born or long in the State were also numerous in the market, for there were always debts and deaths of masters requiring sales, and owners willing for one reason or another to dispose of a few or many negroes. But these did not half suffice.

Zeal in the trade was illustrated by Thomas A. Powell & Co., auctioneers and commission dealers, who, like the Boltons in Memphis, occupied what had been a hotel. As early as 1848 Thomas Powell was a well-known speculator in Louisville, Kentucky.[5] The Montgomery firm was shouting, as if through a megaphone:

" COME ONE AND ALL WHO WANT NEGROES " to our " depot * * * in the center of the business portion of the city, convenient to all the banking houses ".

---

[3] Lyell, 2 *Second Visit etc.* (Eng. edition), 42-43.

[4] Montgomery *Alabama Journal*, Dec. 23, 1853. The names of these traders were Frisbie & Lee, Mason Harwell, and Brown & Bulger. *Key to Uncle Tom's Cabin*, 141, quotes advts. of three other traders there in 1852.

[5] McDougle, 3 *Journal of Negro History*, 230.

They had constantly on hand a variety of " young likely negroes to suit any purchaser " and also room to " accommodate comfortably any number " that might be brought to them to be sold.[6] Thus they were fully equipped to attend to all important branches of the trade.

Apparently the most active dealer in Montgomery throughout the 'fifties was Mason Harwell. Some persons might hold that he was not a trader because he was a general auctioneer and also a bustling real estate agent, sometimes advertising as far away as Augusta, Georgia.[7] On his own account or on commission he would buy or sell almost anything—even railroad stock and nursery supplies.[8] He also carried on various kinds of slave-trading, including a hiring agency; and, as a representative of the Knickerbocker Life Insurance Company of New York, he was ready to insure slaves " at reasonable rates ".[9] A crowd must have assembled about the Artesian Basin, January 2, 1860, to witness the public sale of 30 horses, which had belonged to a circus, and 165 slaves—two chancery sales of 140 and 10 negroes each and a group of 15. Drygoods boxes were rolled out to serve as the auction-block. Harwell sold at least the gang of 15. Of these there were three single negroes and three " families ", one exhibiting the infrequent phenomenon of father and mother with children.[10]

[6] Montgomery *Confederation*, Dec. 8, 1859. See photostat.

[7] " A very valuable plantation near Montgomery " etc.—Augusta, *Chronicle & Sentinel*, May 3, 1859.

[8] *Confederation*, Dec. 26, 1859, Jan. 31, 1860.

[9] *Confederation*, Jan. 3, 1860. An old resident, Mr. W. C. Fuller, told the author that Harwell was a man of respectable standing and that his place of business was about where 20 Dexter ave. now is.

[10] *Confederation*, Jan. 2, 1860. There was an executor's sale of 23 slaves at the same place Jan. 9th.—*Ibid.*

Later in the month Harwell was offering these:—

" AT PRIVATE SALE.—120 NEGROES, among them there is [*sic*] good cooks, washers and ironers, seamstresses, also one good bricklayer and plasterer. Persons wishing to buy negroes, will please give me a call.—M. HARWELL."—*Confederation*, Jan. 31, 1860.

THOMAS A. POWELL & CO.'S SLAVE-ADVERTISEMENT

From the Montgomery *Confederation*, December 8, 1859

As early as 1852 S. N. Brown spoke of his " old patrons ". He was then located " on Market street, above the Montgomery Hall [hotel], at Lindsay's Old Stand ", where he kept " slaves for sale on his own account, and not on commission ", as previously.[11] In January, 1859, he was advertising that he had just received " a large lot of Virginia and Carolina raised FIELD NEGROES—the likeliest ever offered in this market ".[12] At or about this time, he kept his slaves in a one-story frame house with a wide porch, and exhibited them in a large hallway.[13]

When William Howard Russell visited the capital of the Confederacy in May, 1861, he " looked in at one or two of the slave magazines ", and thought them much like those in Cairo and Smyrna. Some of the slaves were allowed to lounge about the doors, " careless of escape or liberty, knowing too well the difficulties of either ". One morning when he was going to the capitol with Senator Wigfall of Texas they stopped to witness " a slave auction held just outside the [Exchange] hotel, on the steps of the public fountain "—the Artesian Basin.

" The auctioneer, who was an ill-favored, dissipated-looking rascal, had his ' article ' beside him, on, not in, a deal packing-case [a dry-goods box] —a stout young negro badly dressed and ill shod, who stood with all his goods fastened in a small bundle in his hands, looking out at the small and listless gathering of men, who, whittling and chewing, had moved out from the shady side of the street as they saw the man put up. The chattel character of slavery in the States renders it most repulsive. * * * A man in a cart, some volunteers in coarse uniforms, a few Irish laborers in a

---

[11] *Key*, 140. There was a John W. Lindsey [*sic*] who in Nov., 1852, was advertising 100 for sale at his depot on Commerce street next to the Exchange Hotel.—*Key*, 141.

[12] His depot at this time was on the corner of Monroe and Perry streets.— *Confederation*, Jan. 15, 1859. In the autumn of 1859 he moved to three doors above but across the street from Montgonery Hall.—*Confederation*, Dec. 8, 1859.

[13] Apart from what the advts. show, the statements as to the locations etc. are based on the recollections of two residents of that time. The father of one of them in 1859-60 kept a store and bakery next door to the Brown pen, when it was in the middle of the block and on the north side of Market st.

long van, and four or five men in the usual black coat[s], satin waist-
coat[s], and black hat[s], constituted the audience, whom the auctioneer
addressed volubly: ' A prime fieldhand! Just look at him—good-natured,
well-tempered; no marks, nary sign of bad about him! En-i-ne hunthered—
only nine hun-ther-ed and fifty dol'rs for 'em! Why, it's quite rad-aklous!
Nine hundred and fifty dol'rs! I can't raly — — That's good. Thank you,
sir. Twenty-five bid—nine hunthred and seventy-five dol'rs for this most
useful hand. ['] The price rose to one thousand dollars, at which the
useful hand was knocked down to one of the black hats near me. The
auctioneer and the negro and his buyer all walked off together to settle the
transaction, and the crowd moved away.—' That nigger went cheap ', said
one of them to a companion, as he walked towards the shade.—' Yes, *Sirr!*
Niggers is cheap now—that's a fact.' " [14]

Before Montgomery was connected with the Atlantic
States by railroad, southwestern Alabama and southeastern Mississippi were most easily supplied with slaves by
the coastwise trade to Mobile and then up the Alabama or
the Tombigbee River.) Subsequently Mobile's slave-trade
was much weakened by the competition of Montgomery,
Selma and other Alabama markets and of several in eastern Mississippi, especially after the opening of the railroads making direct connections, through western Tennessee, with Kentucky and the eastern point of Missouri.
And Mobile's trade was more and more overshadowed by
that of New Orleans. But the planters that sold their cotton in Mobile naturally purchased their negroes there. It
was certainly not a place where large interstate traders
were flourishing in the 'fifties. Except the Wilmington,
North Carolina, firm that started in Mobile in 1860,[15] it is
not known that there were any other regular interstate
traders there on the eve of the Civil War. Judging from
the usual evidence, Mobile's trade was exceptionally small
and the supplies for its market came mainly from the

[14] W. H. Russell, *My Diary North and South*, 165, 167, 168, 169. To test
Russell's reliability the author when in Montgomery in 1902 read this description to an old Norwegian named Olander, who had lived there since 1859.
Before the reading was finished the listener interjected: " That auctioneer was
undoubtedly a man named Clark—a drunkard and rough Irishman."

[15] *Ante* p. 238 n.

estates of deceased or bankrupt planters in southern Alabama and from small slaveowners selling for profit or from necessity; and auctioneers, commission merchants or general agents attended to most of the sales.

Belthazer Tardy & Co., known as auctioneers and not thought of as traders, were doing a great majority of this business in 1859 60.[16] A news-item and a long-standing advertisement in the *Register* of January 5, 1859, called attention to the fact that on that day a large number of " Col. John Darrington's negroes would be auctioned off in front of the new Custom House ". The slaves, numbering about three score, were " all valuable, likely and raised in the country, where they have been from childhood ". " N. B. A peremptory *Cash Sale* this is to be, and no postponement." The advertised list of 46 slaves indicated not one complete family (but a report of the sale mentioned one) and only two mothers with children. All other slaves, except twin boys of 12 years, were apparently sold singly. It was another case of selling " to git the most ", and was very conspicuously successful.[17]

[16] The *Register* of June 12, 1859, informed its readers: " B. Tardy & Co., will sell tomorrow, in front of the Court House, a very valuable lot of likely negroes." At another time the firm had for sale privately: " A NEGRO BOY, a good Baker, and useful at any other work; and a Negro Boy suited for Errand and Office boy. A prime NEGRO BOY, 19 years old, black, has worked five years at Bakery business, and would also make a No. 1 Field Hand, being willing to go at any occupation ", and also a " Negro Boy, 13 years old, mulatto, a smart, intelligent, capable fellow, good at House Work, or as Waiter.—They belong to resident owners and [are] sold as no use for them."—*Advertiser*, Jan. 8, 1860, Sunday supplement. Tardy & Co. also had five other groups of slaves (about 25 persons) for sale about this time.— *Advertiser*, Jan. 5, 8, 24, 1860.

[17] " LARGE SALE OF NEGROES AT MOBILE.—Messrs. Br. Tardy & Co. sold on Tuesday a large lot of negroes, the greater portion at a very considerable advance in price on any sale this season. Four men, aged 32, 30, 22 and 19 years, sold at $1,300, $1,290, $1,605 and $1,635. Three girls, aged 18, 18 and 8 years, sold at $1,402.50, $1,320 and $855. Twin boys, aged 12 years, brought $2,610. Girl, 8 years old, $800. Boy, 14 years, $1,050.—Woman, 33 years old, $920. Family of five—man 35, woman 32, three boys, 11, 9 and 7

There were several other traders at this time, but no one of them seems to have dealt exclusively in slaves.[18]

From early in the century to 1861, the " Natchez market ", apart from its actual location, changed perhaps less than any other large market in the South, for its patrons were almost exclusively planters. It was there that Andrew Jackson, the future President, sent horses and slaves to be sold, as early as 1801 and, if charges in the campaign of 1828 were true, as late as 1811.[19] Natchez must have become a large and profitable market soon after, if not before, the War of 1812. A case in North Carolina shows that four men, probably about 1815, formed a rather amateurish partnership with a cash capital of $21,000, and by selling slaves at Natchez soon made a net profit of $9,500—about 45 per cent.[20]

Until about 1830 the markets were within the city and negroes were sold in almost every street. At times, many brought from the border States in the spring died of the

years old, brought $5,220. Two boys, aged 13 years, $1,000 each. Woman, 28 years and three children 8, 6 and 4 years old, sold for $2,410. Girl, 15 years old, $1,200. Several women, aged from 30 to 38 years brought from $900 to $1,150. Four men brought $1,350, $1,400, $1,410 and $1,470 each.—*Tribune*, 7th."—Savannah *Republican*, Jan. 12, 1859.

[18] After Tardy & Co., came Augustine Smith. He was a typical general agent, for he collected accounts, sold and hired out slaves, rented houses and transacted " any other business requiring an agent "; and his office was on St. Francis street, " opposite the new Postoffice and next door west of the Old State Branch Bank."—Advts. in the *Advertiser*, Jan. 12, 13, 1860. To the same class belonged Augustus Brooks and M. Boullemet. In an advt. in the *Directory* for 1859 Boullemet promised to give " particular attention to selling real estate, negroes, horses, carriages, furniture, groceries etc."

[19] From Natchez, Wm. C. C. Claiborne, wrote to Andrew Jackson, Dec. 9, 1801: * * * " I will try to find a purchaser for your horses, [;] as for negroes, they are in great demand and will sell well." And again, Dec. 23, 1801: " The negro woman he [Mr. Hutchins] has sold for $500, in cash, and I believe he has, or will in a few days sell the boy, for his own price, to Colo. West."— Jackson MSS., Library of Congress.

[20] 2 Catterall, 61.

fever during the summer.[21] To avoid such losses care was
taken to make the importations late in the autumn, after
the first frost, and to keep them in the country, within easy
distance. The chief market, about 1834, was described as
" a cluster of rough wooden buildings, in the angle of two
roads ", a mile from Natchez. There were also four or
five other pens in the vicinity, " where several hundred
slaves of all ages, colors and conditions, of both sexes,
were exposed for sale ".[22] At that time, Natchez had a
population of about 3,000, a majority of whom were colored; and about as many slaves as the entire white population of the little city were annually sold in or near it.[23]
So important a place as that at the angle of the two roads
could not long continue nameless. For a time is was called
Niggerville,[24] which meant *slaveville*, but was more con-
temptuous. Soon it took and retained the name of " The
Forks of the Road ".

The sights, conditions and methods at the various pens
near Natchez were almost the same in the 'fifties as at
the beginning of the 'thirties. The importations from the
Carolinas, Kentucky and Missouri had much increased
and those from Virginia were relatively less. The slaves
that Ingraham saw in two pens opposite each other on
the road between Natchez and the neighboring village of
Washington were described as " either dancing to the
sound of the violin, played by one of their number, playing at marbles, quoits, practising gymnastics, lounging,
sleeping in the sun, or idling about the door, while their
masters, the ' slave traders ', regardless of them, were
playing at cards or backgammon, smoking or sitting about
the door conversing together, or with a buyer; their pres-

[21] [Ingraham] 2 *The Southwest*, 235-36.
[22] 2 *Southwest*, 192, 201.
[23] 2 *Southwest*, 160, 244.
[24] "NEGROES FOR SALE.—The subscribers offer for sale at Niggerville, ·
one mile from Natchez, six carpenters and three blacksmiths. * * * —EATON
& FREEMAN. Niggerville."—Natchez, *Free Trader*, Feb. 26, 1836.

ence not producing the least restraint upon the noisy merriment around them."[25] Such indulgences helped to make slaves seem cheerful and mild-tempered, qualities that were always at a premium.

There was no better place to see a rich planter or a lady indulge in what was one of the most self-satisfying and luxurious of tasks—the purchase of a slave. Especially if one desired a body-servant, a coachman or a maid, all the buyer's vanity as to superior judgment and special requirements was likely to be manifested. If a lady came, it was in her carriage; if a planter, he rode. The trader or some trusty negro was on the lookout for buyers, who were escorted through a secure, high gate. A bell or a loud call had given the slaves notice quickly to line up in the yard—the women and girls on one side and men and boys on the other, in about the order of their height. When Ingraham accompanied a planter, there were twenty or so on each side. All were, of course, in bright new clothes: each man wore coarse corduroy trousers, a roundabout and vest, strong shoes and a cotton shirt, and held a soft black hat in his hand; the women and girls were dressed in neat calico frocks, white aprons and capes, and had fancy kerchiefs on their heads and " were constantly laughing and chattering with each other in suppressed voices ". Thus, with morning, shining faces, they awaited questions and inspection. This did not need to be so searching as when the buyer and the seller were unacquainted and lived far apart. Along the line of the men and boys the planter passed " with a scrutinizing eye— giving that singular look, peculiar to the buyer of slaves as he glances from head to foot of each individual ",—the actual or affected air of the connoisseur. A coachman was desired.—" George, step out here ", said the trader.— " How old are you?" asked the planter.—" I don't recollect, sir, 'zactly—b'lieve I'm somewhere 'bout twenty-

dree."—" Where were you raised? "—" On master R—'s
farm in Wirginny."—" Then you are a Virginia negro."
—" Yes, master, me full blood Wirginny." * * * Yes,
master, I drove ole missus' carage, more dan four year."—
" Have you a wife?"—" Yes, master, I lef' young wife in
Richmond, but I got new wife here in de lot. I wishy you
buy her, master, if you gwine to buy me." The coachman
was bought for $950, the planter " giving negotiable
paper—the customary way of [planters] buying slaves—
at four months." The wife " in the lot ", a seamstress
and nurse, was taken on approval at $750. (It was early
in the 'thirties or the prices would have been much higher.)
The planter and his guest rode off on their horses and the
slaves walked ahead " with elastic steps ".[26]

Shortly before they left, a " handsome carriage drove
up, from which alighted an elderly lady, who, leaning on
the arm of a youth, entered the court ", the yard of the
slave-pen. " After looking at and questioning in a kind tone
several of the female slaves, she purchased two, a young
mother and her child, and in a few minutes afterward, at
the solicitation of the youth, purchased the husband of the
girl, and all three, with happy faces—happier, that they
were not to be separated—flew to get their little parcels,
and rode away with their mistress,—the wife and child sitting within the carriage on the front seat—and the man
on the coach-box beside the coachman." [27]

As they returned to Natchez with their new slaves—the
planter, with head erect, lightly sitting his nervous, fine
horse and proudly discoursing to his susceptible Northern
friend, and the elderly lady and the youth, leaning back in
their carriage with graceful hauteur—everybody understood what it meant and regarded the purchasers with mingled admiration and envy.

When Franklin and Armfield were at the height of prosperity at Natchez, Ingraham wrote: " Negro traders soon

[26] 2 *Southwest*, 193-201 *passim*.   [27] 2 *Southwest*, 200-201.

accumulate great wealth, from the immense profit they make on their merchandise. * * * One of their number, who is the great Southern slave-merchant, and who, for the last fifteen years, has supplied this country [region] with two-thirds of the slaves brought into it, has amassed a fortune of more than a million of dollars by this traffic alone. He is a bachelor, and a man of gentlemanly address, as are many of these merchants, and not the ferocious, Captain Kidd looking fellows, we Yankees have been apt to imagine them. Their admission into society, however, is not recognized. Planters associate with them freely enough, in the way of business, but notice them no farther. A slave trader is, nevertheless, very much like other men.'' [28] This undoubtedly referred to Isaac Franklin, for it described his circumstances. Then or a little later, he also had a large and beautiful residence in Sumner county, Tennessee, near Gallatin, and a large slave-pen where he assembled the negroes purchased in that region for the Natchez and the New Orleans markets. And he obtained sufficient social standing to marry the daughter of a Presbyterian clergyman in Nashville.

A Kentucky youth, who had supplemented his legal studies with courses in medicine and made a specialty of breach of warranty cases in slave-trading, moved to Natchez, like young John A. Quitman from New York. He was soon district attorney for Adams county, of which Natchez was the countyseat. In one of his first important private cases he won a suit against Ballard & Franklin, successors to Franklin & Armfield. This so favorably impressed the traders at the Forks of the Road that they invited him to be their regular counsel at an annual salary. He gladly consented, for his public duties concerned criminal offenses only. '' This was a great mart '', said General William T. Martin as we sat apart from the unkempt crowd at the Natchez courthouse, more than half a century

[28] 2 *Southwest*, 245.

after he was that rising young attorney. " In some years there were three or four thousand slaves here. I think that I have seen as many as 600 or 800 in the market at one time. There were usually four or five large traders at Natchez every winter. Each had from fifty to several hundred negroes, and most of them received fresh lots during the season. They brought their large gangs late in the fall and sold them out by May. Then they went back for more. They built three large three-story buildings, where several hundred could be accommodated. In their day, Franklin and Armfield had quarters in New Orleans, and perhaps also in Baton Rouge, as well as in Natchez. Franklin died about 1850." [29]

In 1852-53 the best known traders at the Forks of the Road were Matthews, Branton & Co., Griffin & Pullum, R. H. Elam and Thomas G. James.[30] Matthews, Branton & Co. were ready " to furnish to any order any description of Negroes sold in Richmond "! Griffin and Pullum would " keep throughout the entire year a large and well-selected stock of Negroes " of all kinds. " FRESH ARRIVALS WEEKLY." In September, 1852, Elam had returned to his stand " with fifty likely young Negroes "; in January, 1853, he had just received 40.[31] Thomas G. James, who was a resident trader in Nashville in 1859, at least,[32] advertised in October, 1852, that he had a long lease of a stand at the Forks of the Road, had " just arrived from Virginia with a very likely lot " of various kinds of slaves, and intended to keep a large supply on hand throughout the year. His having a fine buggy-horse, a saddle-horse and a carryall for sale indicated that this gang had been

---

[29] The two foregoing paragraphs, except where otherwise indicated, are based on careful shorthand notes of a long interview with Gen. Martin in May, 1902. His recollections of trader Franklin and his wife were corroborated by Judge O. P. Temple of Knoxville, Tenn., and others.

[30] *Key to Uncle Tom's Cabin*, 138, 139, 146, 147, quotes one or more advts. of each.

[31] Natchez *Courier*, Jan. 26, 1853.

[32] *Ante* p. 249 n.

brought overland. At another time he likewise announced
that he had just received a " lot of twenty-five *direct from
Virginia,* two or three good cooks, a carriage-driver, a good
house boy, *a fiddler, a fine seamstress* ", besides fieldhands.
He would sell them at a small profit, for he wished " to
close out and *go on to Virginia after a lot for the fall
trade* ".[33] Seven of the many manifests preserved in the
Library of Congress show that Thomas G. James shipped
at least 98 slaves from Richmond to New Orleans between
May 16, 1851, and November 19, 1852. These are conclusive evidence of his bringing, as he alleged, large numbers
of Virginia slaves to the Natchez market.

In May, 1902, when the author was driving on the outskirts of Natchez he saw two old negroes sitting on the
porch of a comfortable little cottage. They welcomed an
opportunity to talk with some one writing " 'bout de ole
times ". Their names were Benjamin Jordan and Pleasant Jones. Soon another " old timer ", an entire stranger
to all, came along the road, was hailed, gladly joined in the
historical symposium and contributed the largest quota of
recollections and humor. His name was Alfred Wornell.
Here were three typical remnants of the interstate slave-
trade with the Southwest: traders had brought two of
them to the Natchez market, and the other was likewise
sold in both Macon and New Orleans.

Alfred Wornell was born in Bourbon county, Kentucky,
in 1831, he thought. When asked how his name was spelt,
he answered:

" I aint no readin' man an' doan know how to spell." After telling
about two masters and being taken to Missouri, he continued: " Jesse
Hutsell bought me an' tuck me back to Kentucky in 1844. He got in
debt and sol' me to Jake Stone, who lived fo' mile from Lexin'ton. I
run'd away from 'im to Bourbon county. I was caught and brought to
de Lexin'ton jail. Tom Scott he bought me and put me in his jail in
Lexin'ton. Den Billy Pullum he bought me. Him an' Pierce Griffin was
niggah-tradahs, an' put me in his jail in Lexin'ton. Pullum brought me

---

[33] *Key to Uncle Tom's Cabin,* 147.

down t' Griffin's yahd at de Forks o' de Road "—a mile or so from where we four were sitting.[34]

There one R. C. King bought him for a ward named McAllister, who owned a plantation called the " Water Proof Place ", where Wornell was sent.

Benjamin Jordan was born in Northampton county, North Carolina, in 1833. When about 19 or 20 years old his young master, William Cordy Jordan, took him to Richmond and sold him to a regular trader named James Crockham. Jordan and others were sent by ship to New Orleans. " Mr. Jeems [James] met us in New O'leens an' brought us up to his niggah-tradah's yahd at de Forks o' de Road. I was in de yahd 'bout two months. Mr. Jeems he broke up [doubtless only went away to get more negroes] and Sam Adams sol' out dem what Jeems lef'." The time indicates that Jordan may have been one of James's slaves mentioned in the manifests and transported to New Orleans and then up to Natchez, and he may even have been one of the lot whom James wished to " close out ".

Pleasant Jones was born in Buckingham county, Virginia. When about 18, his master, James Miller, sold him to a trader in Richmond named Orr, who brought him to Macon, Georgia, partly by water and partly by the cars. Orr was undoubtedly one of the firm so well remembered by the ex-Mayor and other old residents of Macon. Orr sold him to William Jarvis, who took him to New Orleans. " Jarvis got too drunk; Holmes bought me and later sol' me to Thomas Wadell, who lived in Texas. Wadell later brought me back to New O'leens and sol' me to James Gillespie." Jones was sold six times. During the Civil War he ran away to the Federal Army. This explained his comforts and his wearing part of the uniform of the Grand Army of the Republic.

Many besides imported slaves were sold in the Natchez

[34] For his account of his trip to Natchez see *ante* p. 287.

market. John A. Quitman had been a resident of Natchez less than two years when he wrote: '' And the only drawback to their [the slaves'] happiness is that their owners, sometimes, from extravagance or other bad management, die insolvent, and then they must be sold to the highest bidder, must leave the old homestead and the old family, and pass into the hands of strangers. I have witnessed one of these scenes, and but one, though they occur often, and I never saw such profound grief as the poor creatures manifested.'' [35] Such incidents became more numerous as the population increased.[36]

Between 1832 and 1860, the main changes in the Natchez market were in the increased numbers and the nearly doubled prices. In compliance with the one per cent tax law William H. Fitzgerald made a return in 1833 saying that he had sold in the State of Mississippi 30 slaves for a total of $15,200. The highest price was $1,000 and the lowest $300. The average price was not quite $507. About 1834, Ingraham said that a male fieldhand could not be bought in Natchez for less than $800, and a woman for $600. For body-servants $1,000 was a common price. Good mechanics sometimes sold for as much as $2,000 and rarely for less than $900. Coachmen were high; house-servants were at all times worth from ten to thirty per cent more than fieldhands, and a good seamstress or a nurse

---

[35] Claiborne, 1 *Life of Quitman*, 86.

[36] Advts. like the following were not rare:—

"FOR SALE OR HIRE.—43 ACCLIMATED family NEGROES, of whom 38 are cotton pickers, and have been accustomed to the cultivation of cotton in a swamp plantation. For terms and further particulars apply to ALFRED COCHRAN."—Natchez *Free Trader*, Feb. 26, 1836.

R. H. Dickinson, executor of the estate of B. F. Cochran, offered 96 slaves for sale, at the Forks of the Road, at the end of 1850.—Semi-Weekly Natchez *Courier*, Dec. 24, 1850.

An unsuccessful lawyer-planter, J. S. Yerger, living on Deer Creek, Washington county, Miss., advertised that he would sell at auction "100 acclimated slaves, consisting of men, women, boys and girls" and also "30 mules, 6,000 bushels corn, stock, &c." in order "to pay his debts and resume the practice of his profession"—Natchez *Courier*, Dec. 30, 1851.

usually commanded from $700 to $1,000.[37] These probably somewhat exceeded the average market prices there in 1832. Unfortunately neither Blackwell, Murphy & Ferguson (who claimed to be receiving " fresh lots every few days during the season ")[38] nor W. P. Davis (who was boasting that he was selling Virginia and Kentucky negroes " for less than any other man that is trading at the Forks of the Road ")[39] published their prices; but another Lexington, Kentucky, firm, W. F. White & Co., had at Natchez " a likely lot of Kentucky and Missouri NEGROES " and would " sell No. 1 Men [fieldhands for] from $1,600 to $1,650, No. 1 Women [for] from $1,400 to $1,500 ".[40] These were, of course, minimum prices for slaves of that quality; and Virginia and South Carolina slaves were still more valuable there.

The Natchez market never had any serious competitor in the State, although there was trading in nearly all counties, for it was as common as dealing in any sort of livestock and much more profitable. In the little village of Crystal Springs, in Copiah county, M. N. Robertson & Co. had what they called a permanent slave-depot, well-stocked and to be kept so.[41]

Look at Aberdeen. In 1852, the firm of Adams & Wicks had an agent that for two months had " been purchasing for them in the old States "; one of the firm was leaving to make further purchases in North Carolina and Virginia; and they would keep up their supply during the following autumn and winter.[42] And at this time Saunders & Bradley had on hand a large variety of slaves, who could " be seen at the Ferry or at Clark's corner ".[43]

[37] 2 *Southwest*, 244-45.
[38] New Orleans *Picayune*, Jan. 1, 1859.
[39] Natchez *Daily Courier*, Jan. 4, 1861.
[40] Natchez *Daily Courier*, Jan. 3, 1861.
[41] Jackson Semi-Weekly *Mississippian*, Dec. 1, 1860.
[42] *Key*, 146, quotes the advt.
[43] Aberdeen Weekly *Independent*, Jan. 29, 1853.

Vicksburg must have been a good market or the head of the firm of Bolton, Dickins & Co. would not have sold there, but the lack of all except a short file of a Vicksburg newspaper in the 'fifties precludes an attempt to describe it. Prior to 1855, McRea & Folkes had for seven years been partners in a miscellaneous commission business that included the sale of slaves, real estate etc. Thereafter they were rivals. They seem not to have dealt in slaves from distant regions, but only in those brought to them by local owners or neighboring planters, for such slaves were everywhere sold in competition with those imported.

In Jackson, the capital, several large traders were active late in the 'fifties: R. H. Elam, formerly, at least, of Natchez, but at this time having headquarters in New Orleans, was advertising for patronage; W. A. Shewalter had "a permanent depot for the sale of slaves • • • on State street, one square below the old Mansion House "; and A. H. Forrest & Co. also had a depot, where they had " just received from Virginia, South Carolina and Missouri as likely and healthy a lot of Negroes as ever came from those States ". Forrest could " supply all [patrons] with just such Negroes as they may wish at any time ", for, as he added, " my Brother is constantly making purchases in the border States ".[44] It is supposed that this A. H. Forrest was Aaron H., and that " my Brother " was the well-known Nathan Bedford Forrest, with whom all his brothers, except perhaps Jeffrey, the youngest, were at one time or another associated in slave-trading. It seems hardly within the range of possibility that there could have been two A. H. Forrests, each with a great-trader brother. It is much more likely that this firm, buying and selling in special regions, was only a branch of the main business centered in Memphis. In St. Louis, in the summer of 1860, it was seeking to obtain

---

[44] All three advts. appeared in the Jackson Semi-Weekly *Mississippian*, Dec. 9, 1859, and many other days.

" immediately 150 likely young negroes for the Mississippi and Louisiana market ".[45]

But not one of the Mississippi or the Alabama markets had the variety and bustling aspects of those of Richmond, Charleston or Memphis. Nor could any market compare in these respects with that of New Orleans.

[45] St. Louis, Mo., *Republican*, Aug. 3, 1860.

CHAPTER XV

NEW ORLEANS THE MISTRESS OF THE TRADE

By far the most busy and picturesque slave-emporium was New Orleans—the modern Delos of the trade for the lower Southwest. It was the most populous and foreign city either south or west of Baltimore, having 116,000 inhabitants in 1850 and 168,000 in 1860. Nowhere else, except next to the Exchange in Charleston and in the market-place in Montgomery, was slave-trading on a large scale so conspicuous. In New Orleans it sought public attention: slave-auctions were regularly held in its two grand hotels besides other public places; and in much frequented streets there were slave-depots, show-rooms, show-windows, broad verandas and even neighborhoods where gayly dressed slaves were prominently exhibited. In New Orleans, markets and buyers were most numerous, money was most plentiful, profits were largest. Slave-trading there had a peculiar dash: it rejoiced in its display and prosperity; it felt unashamed, almost proud.

One could buy there so-called negroes of every shade of color and kind of occupation:— native Africans, black as ebony, some of them imported half a century previously,[1] others recently smuggled in and knowing only a few words of any language of civilization; Creole octoroon young women as light as southern Europeans, with straight hair, beautiful figures, regular features, and so bright and intelligent that outside of the South they might have passed as ladies from some French colony or from Central or South America; calkers, masons, butlers, coopers, coachmen, lady's-maids, nurses either wet or dry, waiters, waitresses, accomplished seamstresses, highly expert engi-

[1] An advt. of a sheriff's sale of 151 slaves mentioned 7 " African negroes " and another advt. of an auction of 75 slaves mentioned one.—Both in *Picayune*, Mar. 10, 1860.

neers; preachers, who would work in the field six days a week and on Sunday expound the Bible as they fancied they understood it; even a slater that had " served his time at the trade "; " a first-rate wheelwright and white-smith ", and " a No. 1 confectioner and candymaker "; bakers either French or American; " a sugar kettle set-ter "; " a likely negro boy " that would " be exchanged for dry goods, boots and shoes "; a horse-doctor, a spin-ner, a tiger-man, an ox-driver; a valet that spoke Eng-lish, French, Spanish and German and " would suit any gentleman for traveling "; highly skilful gardeners, some long accustomed to beautifying the yards of American planters, others those of Creoles; Maryland cooks who thought that they could not be equaled in the preparation of terrapin or the frying of chicken; better still, Creole cooks, such masters of the French *cuisine* with Louisiana variations as to make every repast a delight; little chil-dren from jet black to blond, with or without mothers, for " orphans " were numerous; butchers, carpenters, black-smiths, plasterers and whitewashers, barbers and hair-dressers in great numbers, and now and then a foreman capable of managing a rice, a sugar or a cotton plantation; and even an old mammy from Virginia or South Carolina, demure and purring like a cat with kittens, still boasting of the " quality " of " *my* ol' massa ". Indeed, it would not have been difficult to find there slaves from every Southern State,[2] from Cuba or from even several different parts of Africa. There were always in this market many kidnaped free negroes, stolen slaves, unclaimed runaways, vagrants, drunkards and general good-for-nothings, re-cently sold for jail-dues—all gathered, one or a few at a time, by speculators, thieves or cheats and brought here

---

[2] In J. A. Beard & Co.'s advt. of an auction of 16 slaves the native States of only 8 were mentioned and these were Ala., Ga., Ark. and Md.—*Picayune*, Feb. 4, 1858. In the same issue Thomas Foster said that he had 250 of various kinds who had been "bought principally in Va., the Carolinas and Ga., expressly for this market."

where they could best be disposed of and where even the riffraff, infancy and decrepitude had a price. All these and still other varieties, besides, of course, fieldhands, stevedores, washers and ironers by the hundred, were to be found in this gay semi-French metropolis of the Southwest. They were here as if by the law of gravitation as well as by that of trade. Many were here as the result of the death, the spendthrift habits or the misfortunes of masters that lived in or near Louisiana, but many more because interstate traders had purchased them in remote States for this market.

How appropriately might this modern mistress of the trade have emblazoned along her great crescent levee the welcome that Delos gave the slave-trader: "Merchant, come into port, discharge your freight—everything is sold"! New Orleans was the trader's paradise. It promised him success, riches, notoriety, as well as every luxury and indulgence that his coarse nature could appreciate. And all large and many small traders throughout the South were in touch with it.

Until late in the 'forties the aversion to being called a trader was hardly felt in New Orleans. Pitts & Clarke's *Directory for 1842* indicated the occupation of at least 185 men—including the well-known slave-traders B. M. Campbell, Thomas Boudar, Theophilus Freeman and John Hagan—by following each name by the concise term " trader "; and it also designated at least 49 persons as " brokers " and 25 as " auctioneers ", most of whom sold slaves. Others may have been overlooked in this search, and, as in other cities, undoubtedly many traders escaped the notice of the enumerators. Thus more than 200, probably not less than 300, residents were engaged in slave-trading, although the volume of this business was presumably not half what it became by the end of the 'fifties. But before this time the word *trader* had come to be shunned, and accordingly it is impossible even approximately to enumerate the traders. A search through the

Directory for 1856—the latest of the slavery period at
hand—finds only 17 names followed by the words " slave-
depot ", " slaves ", " slave trader " or " slave dealer ",
16 followed by " trader " and 38 by " auctioneer ". Undoubtedly most of these auctioneers sold slaves, and
several of them, as we shall see, like some in Richmond and
Charleston, disposed of more than any regular trader.
Then, too, the brokers, the general agents, the commission merchants and factors welcomed opportunities to
participate in some phase of slave-trading. Furthermore,
sporting and gambling tendencies in the Crescent City
were especially favorable to inconspicuous speculating in
slaves by residents. And very numerous were the non-
resident traders that came to sell here or to buy for western
Louisiana or for Texas. Accordingly it seems safe to
believe that the volume of the New Orleans trade, counted
in transactions and dollars,[3] was larger than that of Richmond and Charleston combined.

Sometimes ten or more of the advertisements of the
largest interstate traders were placed in a row, each having a little black figure or figures representing a man or a
woman running and carrying a parcel. They could not
escape notice; they also gave brief details of the business
and of the source and frequency of the importations.[4]
These conclusively show that Virginia slaves were pre-

[3] See *post*, p. 405.

[4] See (opposite p. 316) a photostatic copy from the *Picayune* of Jan. 4, 1860.

J. M. Wilson, an old Baltimore trader, had recently moved from Esplanade
street, in the French quarter, to Baronne, in the American.

Joseph Bruin, who long boasted in his advt. in the N. O. *True Delta*,
1859-60, that he had been " a regular [interstate] trader in this city for
the last twenty-six years ", was at " his old stand, corner of Esplanade and
Chartres streets, " opposite the house of [trader] John B. Smith."—*Picayune*,
Jan. 1, 1859. Notwithstanding these 26 years of trading in New Orleans,
his name does not appear in any of the several N. O. directories at hand,
for his home was in Alexandria, Va.

Thomas E. Matthews, presumably the Natchez trader of 1852-53, late in
1860 acquired Smith's slave-depot at 47 Esplanade street.

R. H. Elam was also trading at Natchez and Jackson, Miss.

ferred: if a trader specialized in negroes from any State except Louisiana, it was from Virginia; if from two, Virginia was one and South Carolina was likely to be the other.[5] The many slaves brought from Missouri and Kentucky were rarely advertised as such because less desirable.

It was much to prosper and to be generally known in one's county and State; it was vastly more to be known to sellers as far away as the Eastern Shore of Maryland and to buyers in Texas, and to deal with " famous " planters and to fancy oneself their friend. Such, at different times, were Franklin and Armfield, the Woolfolks, Bolton, Dickins & Co., the Forrests and divers others. Such, too, were the Campbells, B. M. and Walter L., whose possession and goodwill of perhaps the best old stand in Baltimore soon enabled them to develop a large business and establish a reputation for paying the highest cash prices. Then small-town buyers were glad to advertise as their agents. Originally they purchased only in Maryland and Virginia, but in 1860 they had " a large supply of all classes of negroes * * * imported from Virginia, Maryland and Georgia ", and " during the whole season were receiving " large lots of the choicest negroes " to be had in those States.[6] The senior partner made the purchases and the junior partner managed the sales. Some interstate traders, without becoming residents, went to the same city year after year,

[5] Here is an advertisement of a resident trader whose name was in the *Directory for 1856*, but it did not tell what his business was:—

"*For Sale.* VIRGINIA NEGROES.—Just arrived, a fine lot of Virginia Negroes, comprising Field Hands, Cooks, Washers and Ironers.—J. W. Boazman, 166 Gravier Street."—New Orleans *Picayune*, Sept. 23, 1860.

Owings & Charles, 76 Baronne street, also had a choice lot of negroes and would " be receiving fresh supplies during the season of the best negroes that can be bought in the Virginia and Carolina markets ".—*Picayune*, Mar. 2, 1859. Presumably the senior member of this firm was R. M. Owings, who at 9 Chalmers street, Charleston, opposite the Mart, was advertising for 100 likely negroes of from 12 to 25 years of age.—Charleston *Courier*, Nov. 18, 1859.

[6] N. O. *Commercial Bulletin*, Sept. 28, 1860.

NEGROES.

Sale of Negroes.

On the 1st of October next my house will be opened and a large supply of all classes of Negroes offered for sale, imported from Virginia, Maryland and Georgia. Afterwards, during the whole season, the supply shall be kept good by the receipt of large lots of the choicest Negroes to be had from the above States. Apply at 54 Baronne street, between Common and Gravier, and two squares west of the St. Charles Hotel. [o6 59—9m⁋] WALTER L. CAMPBELL.

Just Received.

Forty very likely young NEGROES, consisting of Field Hands, Mechanics, Seamstresses, House Servants, &c., and for sale, for cash or good city paper. Apply to C. F. HATCHER,
o19—tf 195 Gravier street, New Orleans.

Negroes for Sale.

Having removed from Esplanade to the corner of Baronne and Gravier streets, two squares west of the St. Charles Hotel, where I will keep constantly on hand a choice lot of Maryland and Virginia Negroes, consisting of Field Hands, House Servants, Mechanics, Cooks, Washers and Ironers, Seamstresses, &c.; all of which will be sold low for cash, or on time for good city acceptances.
n8 59—6m ⁋ J. M. WILSON.

Carolina and Virginia Negroes for Sale.

I have received Fifty Carolina and Virginia Negroes, consisting of Field Hands, Cooks, Washers and Ironers; also, two No. 1 Blacksmiths one No. 1 Bricklayer, five good Carpenters, and one good Cooper. Will be receiving fresh gangs every month during the season, which I will sell low for cash, or good 12 months city acceptances. Persons wishing to purchase would do well to give me a call before purchasing elsewhere. Apply to
H. F. PETERSON, 15 Perdido street,
o24—6m⁋ between St. Charles and Carondelet.

C. F. Hatcher,

No. 195 Gravier street, New Orleans, La.—Liberal Advances made on Property placed in my hands for Sale—Slaves—Texas, Mississippi and Louisiana Lands Bought and Sold:
C. M. JOHNSON, Superintendent Slave Depot.
NOTICE TO MERCHANTS, PLANTERS, TRADERS and Owners of Slaves—Having made extensive alterations and accommodations on my old stand, I am now prepared to receive and accommodate from two to three hundred slaves, for sale on commission. I can also accommodate the owners with good board and comfortable rooms, on reasonable terms. Those having business in my line would do well to call and see for themselves before looking elsewhere, as the inducements I offer are unequaled. A good stock of Negroes for sale will be constantly kept on hand, consisting of Field Hands, Mechanics, House Servants, Seamstresses, Nurses, Hair Dressers, &c. C. F. HATCHER.
New Orleans, September 26, 1859. a28 59—1y

R. H. Elam,

(Formerly of Natchez, Mississippi,)
Has located at No. 58 Baronne and 176 Gravier street, New Orleans, two squares in the rear of St. Charles Hotel, where he now has a large lot of SLAVES for sale, which will be regularly recruited by fresh importations during the season.
It is only necessary for my old customers to know where to find me. To others I would say, please give me a trial. o14—6m

Committed,

To the Jail of Greene County, Ala., on the 30th day of June, 1859, a negro man named JIM, who says he belongs to John Studman, who lives in the fork of Red and Black Rivers, and says his master's shipping point is Clark's Depot or Landing on Red River. Said boy is about 30 or 35 years old, weighs about 175 or 180 pounds, 6 feet 1½ inches high, scar on his right wrist, which produced a little stiffness in the little finger of the same hand; color black; full beard.
The owner is hereby notified to come forward, prove property, pay charges and take him away, or he will be dealt with as the law directs.
W. R. HARDAWAY, Sheriff.
Eutaw, July 1, 1859. a24—6m

For Sale.

Just arrived, with a choice lot of VIRGINIA and CAROLINA NEGROES, consisting of Plantation hands, Blacksmiths, Carpenters, Cooks, Washers, Ironers and Seamstresses, and will be receiving fresh supplies during the season, which I offer for sale, for cash or approved paper.
JOHN B. SMITH,
At the old store, cor. Esplanade and Chartres sts.,
a21—o3md & W New Orleans La.

Negroes for Sale.

Just arrived, with 100 Negroes, from Virginia, consisting of Field Hands, House Servants, and Mechanics; and will be receiving fresh lots every month. All of which are offered on accommodating terms at my old stand, corner of Esplanade and Chartres streets, near the Mint. Omnibuses running on Royal and Chartres streets all pass my house.
o3md & W⁋ JOSEPH BRUIN.

Slaves for Sale.

I have received near one hundred Negroes on consignment, of all classes—several likely families which I wish to sell, cheap for cash, or its equivalent. In addition to the above I have since received fifty more Negroes—two of which are first rate Blacksmiths. C. M. RUTHERFORD,
o9—3m No. 68 Baronne street.

Slaves for Sale.

Having permanently established myself in this city, I shall keep constantly on hand a full supply of Negroes, selected for this market, comprising Mechanics and House Servants of every description, and choice Field Hands. My stock already purchased is large, and will be added to as required during the season. Will be sold low for cash or approved city acceptances. A. WIESEMANN,
o3—3m 177 Gravier street.

WEBSTER & HOLMES,
Wholesale and Retail Druggists,

ADVERTISEMENTS BY NEW ORLEANS SLAVE-TRADERS
From the Supplement to the *Picayune*, January 4, 1860

renting the same quarters or boarding their negroes at some jail or depot until all were disposed of. Others flourished most where they were least known, and after advertising or displaying their stock for a season, departed to return no more. Not so the Campbells. Each was steadily resident and active in his special place. Whenever practicable, they avoided the risks to health from penning up negroes in depressing idleness. They had a physician regularly visit those kept in Baltimore, and he worked some of the " trusties " on his farm, pending shipment to New Orleans.[7] Most of the New Orleans traders believed in quick sales, large profits and leaving the risks to others; and negroes not sold by late spring were commonly disposed of at reduced prices, to avoid the jeopardy of close confinement and illness during the depressing heat of a New Orleans summer. The Campbells made a virtue and a profit out of a very different practice; they established a farm in a healthy and accessible region about eighty miles north of New Orleans, where the slaves that were not sold by June could cheaply and profitably be kept and trained while becoming acclimated. There, too, the little children, the " breeding women " and the ailing of all kinds could be cared for until most salable. During the long and hot season, when the Southern metropolis was avoided, persons needing slaves were invited to come to the farm. Thus Walter L. Campbell, as he advised the public in five New Orleans newspapers, had " negroes for sale all the time ". Still better, he was able to reopen his yard in October with a supply of more than 100 that were ablebodied, trained, fully acclimated and very valuable.[8]

[7] This physician lived near New Market, Md., and owned Fred Fowler, who ran away when he heard that he was to be sent South.—5 *Journal of Negro History*, (Oct., 1920), 477.

[8] It was characteristic of the standing of the Campbells that when Congress in 1862 adopted compensated emancipation in the District of Columbia and appointed a commission to carry out the law, B. M. Campbell was invited over from Baltimore to help the commissioners decide as to prices, $300 being the maximum allowed by law.—Edw. Ingle, *The Negro in the D. C.* (J. H. Univ. Studies), 16-18.

Of the traders in the photostated group, C. F. Hatcher, Thomas Foster and C. M. Rutherford belonged to a class that, theoretically at least, preferred the usual two and one-half per cent commission for buying or selling for others. They sought slaves of all kinds, and each had a jail and a yard. One of them laconically explained his business thus:

"C. M. RUTHERFORD, COMMISSION AGENT FOR THE SALE OF SLAVES, OFFICE AND YARD, No. 68 Baronne street, New Orleans." [9]

Foster was one of the best known of his class. Finally he was not able to resist the temptation to speculate, and selling on commission became a secondary consideration.

C. F. Hatcher illustrated how an enterprising trader could quickly rise, perhaps without speculation or considerable risk. In 1856 he was superintendent of a slave-depot at 195 Gravier street belonging to J. L. Carman & Co., " auctioneers ".[10] By 1860 he was advertising throughout the South to inform " merchants, planters, traders and owner of slaves " that he had made extensive alterations in his stand and was prepared to receive from 200 to 300 slaves to sell on commission; that he could furnish slaveowners with good meals and comfortable rooms at reasonable rates, and that he should constantly keep a good stock of all kinds of slaves for sale, including nurses, hairdressers, etc. As was common, he offered liberal advances on all property placed in his hands; but he must be first choice or none: he would not receive slaves that had been in other yards or depots.[11] His pride was his new and " very commodious show-room ". He also dealt in real estate, especially land in Texas, Mississippi and Louisiana,[12] and advertised his slave-trading business in

[9] Memphis *Avalanche*, Feb. 29, 1860.
[10] *Picayune*, Jan. 5, 1856.
[11] *Picayune*, Aug. 1, 1860, and about daily from 1859.
[12] Richmond *Enquirer*, Dec. 3, 1859; Charleston *Mercury*, the Savannah

leading marts for New Orleans supplies. To his establishment all might come with their slaves, get board and lodg-
ing and find buyers—exactly as drovers and ranchmen
bring their carloads of steers or sheep to the stockyards
and live at the drover-hotels. Not to be outdone by Campbell, he kept his office open summer and winter and also
had a farm or large slave-yard in the piny woods, nearer
and more accessible than Campbell's. Prospective buyers
needed only to call at 195 Gravier street, examine the descriptive list of his stock and then take a short ride on
train or boat.[13]

" Orders from commission merchants respectfully solicited ", said Thomas Foster's advertisement. That refers to a phase of slave-trading then little noticed by the
public and now almost forgotten. The agent that disposed
of a planter's crop and bought for him supplies not easily
obtained near home was called his commission merchant
or factor. The accounts were expected to be settled annually. The sugar planters were within easy reach of
New Orleans and usually went there at least once a year
for business and pleasure. It was quite different with the
cotton planters in northern and western Louisiana, eastern
Texas, Arkansas and Mississippi. If they sent their produce and orders to New Orleans, their commission merchant or factor also bought or sold slaves for them according to whether they had a surplus or a marked deficit with
him. And he dealt with a regular trader, a commission
merchant or an auctioneer.[14]

To inspect some of the depots, pens, yards, booths or
salesrooms and to attend a large public sale of slaves was
one of the first aims of visitors from afar. In 1856-1860
there were at least 25 such places within a few squares of
the St. Charles Hotel, and nearly all were on Gravier

Republican and the Nashville *Republican Banner*, all in Jan., 1860, and in
many other newspapers, including the New Orleans *Le Courrier*, 26 juin, 1860.

[13] *Picayune*, Aug. 1, 1860.

[14] This paragraph is based on notes of an interview, in 1902, with an old
New Orleans factor, who described his experiences before 1860.

(where there were not less than 11 or 12), Baronne (where there were 6 or more), Magazine or Common streets. In the French quarter there were about half as many, mostly on Esplanade street near the corner of Chartres or in the neighborhood of Exchange Place and St. Louis street.

On a Mississippi River steamboat a youth from Ohio met a clerk from New Orleans and accepted his invitation to call at 71 and 73 Baronne street. The Ohioan was surprised to find there a large building bearing the sign,

| VIRGINIA SLAVES FOR SALE HERE. | [15]

Subsequently the resident showed the visitor through several other principal marts. The first question asked strangers was, " Do you want to buy some niggers? " At one place the keeper rang a little bell such as school-teachers use. Promptly " from their stables at the rear of the building, the stock came marching [in], in two files, the one of men and boys, the other of women and girls." There were also three or four babes in arms. " The tallest in each line headed the column, then the next in height, and so on down to the toddlekins at the foot of the class. The files stood ranged along opposite walls, as if drawn up for a spelling match. They were dressed in coarse stuff, an appropriate, simple uniform being provided for each sex." Just then appeared three sugar-planters to purchase some fieldhands. " They walked up and down the rows, making many inquiries, and examining closely the human chattels they expected to buy. We learned that a good Knight of Labor was worth about $1,500. One of the planters picked out a number of slaves, male and female, who, one by one, stepped from the ranks, and stood huddled together in a group. There was much chaffering as to the price of certain children who, being regarded as incumbrances,

---

[15] The place was conducted by David Wise.—*N. O. Merchants' Diary & Guide for 1857-58*, p. 58.

mere colts or calves, were thrown in for good measure
* * * ''.[16]

When Charles Mackay entered one of the show-rooms he
was greeted with: "*Achetez-moi. Je suis bonne cuisi-
nière et couturière. Achetez-moi!*" From the other side
of the room some of the men also entreated him to buy
them. One, apparently white, and supposed to be an Irishman, of the quality of county Cork—got up from his seat
as the visitor passed, and, with an unmistakable brogue,
said: " I am a good gardener, your honour. I am also a
bit of a carpenter, and can look after the horses, and do
any sort of odd job about the house."—" But you are jok-
ing; you are an Irishman?"—" My father was an Irishman ", he answered.—" Is there not a mistake here?" the
visitor inquired of the owner of the slave-depot. " This
is a white man."—" His mother was a nigger ". That
was conclusive, no matter how light one might be. " We
have sometimes much whiter men for sale than he is. Look
at his hair and lips. There is no mistake about him." [17]

Another English traveler, when in New Orleans in 1855,
went to a trader's booth with a planter who wished to buy
three slave women. About 60 slaves were in what re-
minded him of a country school-room. " The most of them
were from Virginia and seemed anxious to get masters ".
At the head of one line was a woman with a child in her
arms and who was pregnant and had been separated from
her husband in Alabama. " Buy me, master, I am a good
fieldhand and can work at anything ", or a similar appeal
came from everyone on whom the visitor looked. He erroneously inferred that this eagerness to be sold was because " they must find the confinement irksome ".[18]

Why those files according to sex and in a descending
line? For the convenience of purchasers and to eliminate
family ties. One negro was selected here, one there, and

[16] [W. H. Venable], *Down South before the War*, 17-19.
[17] 1 Mackay, 316-18.
[18] Robert Russell, *North America*, etc., 277-78.

11

then urgent appeals to take another on account of kinship or marriage might be considered. A cheerful, pleading humility in slaves was often influential. But the urgency of their efforts to sell themselves was prompted by prospects of rewards or punishments. An ex-slave, a blacksmith's apprentice, speaking of his experience in a New Orleans yard, told the author that when a buyer came to the office, all of the kind asked for were put in line, and, he added: " Ef yo' talked up bright an' smaht an' was sol', p'r'aps de niggah-tradah'd give yo' a dollah ". Another Virginia slave, bought in an Esplanade street pen by an owner of a brickyard, made this explanation: " Pussuns had ter be on dere p's an' q's an' showin' off so as to sell well when some one come ter buy 'em, an' ef yo' didn't put on dat pleasin' look, yo' 'd pay fer it when de pussuns went out o' de ya'd. An' ef dey sol' yo' on trial an' yo' was brought back, yo' 'd be 'mos' killed." [19]

Miss Bremer saw " nothing especially repulsive in these places excepting the whole thing "! The " groups of colored men and women, of all shades between black and light yellow ", standing or sitting unemployed at the doors, indicated the nature of the business within. She believed that they were well fed and clothed. She noticed that the slightest kind or jocose word called forth a sunny smile, full of good humor. She also went to see " some of the rooms in which the slaves were lodged for the night, and which were great garrets without beds, chairs or tables." [20] As a rule, in all such places the floor was the only bed, a dirty blanket the only covering, a miscellaneous bundle the only pillow.

C. E. Girardey & Co. advertised in far-away Charleston that they " WANTED, FOR A LOUISIANA SUGAR PLANTATION, several gangs, varying from 50 to 150, of good PLANTATION

[19] From notes of interviews with ex-slaves Nathan Ross and Washington Taylor (see *ante* p. 279 n.), in Donaldsonville, La., in May, 1902. See also *Key*, 162.

[20] Bremer, 2 *Homes of the New World*, 202-204.

NEGROES, accustomed either to the culture of Cotton or
Rice. Planters having such, and wishing to secure them a
good home, will forward full descriptive lists—lowest possible cash price—when deliverable, at once or after the
crops, and most accessible route from Charleston of their
whereabouts." [21]   That was a cleverly worded means of
obtaining supplies wholesale; for, as we know, masters
preferred a planter and cash, if no considerable reduction
in price was required.   A few months later Girardey &
Co. were offering a Georgia-coast gang of 67, to be sold
in one or two lots. [22]   Of course they did not restrict
themselves to gangs or families.   Their office was at 37
Magazine street, but most of their large vendues were at
the City Hotel, on the northeast corner of Common and
Camp streets.   There at noon, February 21, 1860, one
could have found them selling at auction, " singly and in
families ", " 84 choice plantation slaves, 33 being from
one plantation near Georgetown, South Carolina ". [23]   On
many other days they likewise sold large numbers, such
as " 40 choice slaves, young and very likely ", " 54
prime slaves ", " 57 choice plantation slaves " [24] and 12
" choice family slaves ".   This last meant not that they
were to be kept in families, but only that they were
domestic servants.   The eldest was but 23 and the youngest two were Louisa, a " very smart house-servant ",
aged 11, and Jim, " very handy and intelligent ", aged
12.   Except a hairdresser and her babe of 22 months, all

---

[21] *Courier*, Aug. 31, 1859, and other days.

[22] " A Gang of Sixty-Seven Choice Plantation SLAVES, IN Families, from
one Plantation in Southeastern Georgia, accustomed to the culture of Rice and
Sea Island Cotton, all raised on the Estate of the late Gen. Clinck.—This Gang
will be sold in one or two Lots, on favorable terms, to approved Planters,
deliverable here or in Savannah. The negroes are strictly prime. Apply to
C. E. GIRARDEY & CO."—*Picayune*, Jan. 27, 1860.

[23] *Delta*, Feb. 18, 1860. The terms were "twelve months' credit, for approved factors' acceptances, bearing eight per cent interest ".

[24] Respectively *Delta*, Jan. 3, Dec. 23, 1860; *Picayune*, Oct. 17, 1860.

were sold separately.[25] On another day they sold at auction " Gracieuse, aged about 32, a creole speaking French and English, one of the best creole cooks in the city ", with her two boys, 5 and 3 years of age.[26] As if to illustrate what slave-selling might come to, they offered this speculation to the highest bidder:—

" The slave girl CATHERINE, a dark griffe, aged 13 years, very likely; is subject to fits, and supposed to be occasioned from tape worm. Not guaranteed except in title.—Terms—Cash." [27]

Perhaps the largest slave-seller in New Orleans during the 'forties and the 'fifties—for auctioneers often out-traded the regular traders—was Joseph A. Beard. In appearance he was of the butcher or saloon-keeper type— " a short, thick man, with a red face ". He became known as " Major Beard, the great slave-auctioneer of New Orleans ". Like other traders, he often changed partners. Late in the 'fifties his office was at 38 Magazine street and most of his vendues were at Bank's Arcade, hard by, which was one of the five or six most popular marts [27a]; but he willingly went wherever profit invited. By 1859 his auctions were conducted by Gardner Smith, at first a silent

[25] *Picayune*, Oct. 4, 1860. They also had for sale privately " 50 choice slaves just arrived, comprising likely young men, women, boys, girls, fieldhands and house servants."—*Commercial Bulletin*, Oct. 9, 1860.

[26] *Delta*, Oct. 25, 1860.

[27] *Picayune*, Oct. 13, 1860. Among 10 slaves whom they sold at auction singly, Jan. 11, 1859, were " SARAH, black, aged about 13 years, a very likely house girl, good child's nurse, an orphan; also her brother TOM, black, aged about 6 years ", and also George, a very likely orphan of 11 years.—All were fully guaranteed.—*Picayune*, Jan. 11, 1859.

[27a] Ebenezer Davies (*American Scenes and Christian Slavery* (London, 1849), 48 ff.) gives a good account of some sales by Beard, Calhoun & Co. in Bank's Arcade, in 1848. Out of 12 " lots " three were of married couples, two with one or more children. The auctioneer—presumably Beard, " a sleek-looking fellow, with a face that indicated frequent and familiar intercourse with the brandy-bottle "—discribed one " lot " as " a young piece of city goods—the girl Cornelia. * * * She is well known in the city, and has always belonged to some of the best families. * * * She is sold for no fault, but simply for want of money."—*Ibid.*, 50, 52, 53.

partner. In January, 1859, Gardner Smith sold for Beard & Co., at Bank's Arcade, 13 " valuable Creole slaves ", which usually meant that they were mulattoes, spoke French and had French names.[28] Early in 1860 the firm was Beard, Pitts and Gardner Smith. A few months later Gardner Smith & Co., at 81 Common street, combined the businesses of slave-auctioneer, regular trader and keeper of a slave-yard and boarding-house for masters and traders—for " gentlemen who wish to stay in the house with their slaves "![29] Beard's successful understudy was planning to rival Hatcher,—but the Civil War was only a few months off.

Julian Neville was another great auctioneer; and another great auction-mart, " The American Exchange ", was in the St. Charles Hotel. Neville had apparently outstripped all competitors by 1860. His advertisements of sales of real estate and negroes sometimes covered nearly an entire page of the *Picayune*—more space than those of all other auctioneers together.[30] Because good sugar plantations required expensive machinery as well as trained laborers, it was often advantageous to sell all together; to divide them was like dividing a factory. At the St. Charles it was least difficult to attract men with experience and capital sufficient for such enterprises. The sale of " Belle Chasse " was an example. This plantation was about a nine-mile drive from New Orleans. Judah P. Benjamin, distinguished as lawyer, planter and United States Senator, had been half-owner of it, and on it had built what was called one of the best plantation houses in Louisiana. By purchases in 1853 and 1854, amounting to

[28] They were Andrinette, about 40, "and her six children", aged from 5 months to 18 years, and Euphemie, about 42, and her five children, aged from 14 months to 18 years. All 13 were mulattoes. Nothing was said about sales by "families" nor of husbands or fathers.—*Picayune*, Jan. 6, 1859. In the 'forties Beard's office was on Camp opposite Natchez st.—*Directory for 1842*, p. 25.

[29] *Picayune*, Oct. 11, 1860.

[30] *Picayune*, Feb. 4, 5, 22, 1860.

nearly $168,000, Samuel Packwood acquired the whole. About five years later, he died. As usual, the heirs could not afford to operate such an estate. " Belle Chasse " must be sold at auction. Fortunately for the 161 negroes, —as the number was by the day of the sale,—the entire property was disposed of *en bloc*, March 10, 1860. That it brought $250,000 warrants the belief that the best mart and the best auctioneer had been chosen. For such success and distinction the title of captain or major would have been deemed inadequate. Therefore, if never before, Neville was " Colonel " [31]—a title usually reserved for men owning many slaves or supposed to have marked social, political or military standing.

McCerren, Landry & Co. were so prosperous that they fitted up Masonic Hall, at the corner of St. Charles and Perdido streets, as an " auction mart " with " a large, commodious and attractive salesroom, with spacious accommodations for slaves ". Local editorial items called attention to their Tuesday and Saturday sales of real estate, slaves and various other kinds of property. Here is a sample:

"McCerren, Landry & Co., auctioneers, sell at their auction mart, at 11 o'clock a neat two-story brick dwelling, in the First District, on Triton Walk. Also several slaves, a splendid sorrel trotter and two mares." [32]

This selling of negroes, beasts and many other kinds of property at the same time was common everywhere, almost necessary, and gave slavery a very inhuman aspect. And the slaves were scattered much more widely than the beasts. Paid advertisements in Charleston, Montgomery, Jackson (Mississippi), Nashville and Memphis newspapers announced that 136 slaves, " selected by Mr. Nich. Lewis

[31] " Colonel Neville also sold yesterday, the well-known ' Bellechasse Plantation ', situated in the parish of Plaquemines, on the right bank of the river, about five and a half leagues [by the river] below the city, for $250,000. E. J. Zunts, Esq., is the purchaser."—*Picayune*, Sunday, Mar. 11, 1860.

[32] *Picayune*, Feb. 11, 1860.

[their deceased master]; out of many thousand ", would be sold near Huntsville, Alabama, in January, 1860, to the highest bidders, along with " 47 head of mules and horses, 54 head of cattle, the oxen, stock hogs, killing hogs and 90 head of sheep ".[33] In front of Ferguson & Wilkinson's auction store, Norfolk, were sold 3 horses, 2 carts, 1 fine buggy, 20 cases of boots, 6 or 8 casks of hams, 5,000 cigars, etc. and " a likely negro girl 19 years old with a likely boy child of 18 months ".[34] Some combinations were still more grotesque. At the courthouse door in Covington, Georgia, on the first Tuesday in April, 1852, the sheriff delivered to the highest bidders two negroes, Nelson, about 32 years of age, Rachel, about 45, " also, a roan mule, about eight years old, and one sorrel mule, about seven or eight years old, and one two-horse wagon; levied on * * * to satisfy two mortgage fi fas " etc.[35] At Montezuma, Macon county, Georgia, January 9, 1860, there was a public sale of about 100 " young and likely " negroes: " amongst the number [were] four good carpenters, two plantation black-smiths, a superior pressman—having had several years experience in printing offices in Macon—and a first rate ostler. * * * Also, a fine lot of mules and horses, together with ' Morgan Comet ', a superior young stallion, from Vermont." [36]

Two English ladies, the Misses Turnbull, were much shocked in New Orleans by a handbill announcing a raffle for several things, including a mulatto seamstress and lady's-maid, 18 years of age, together with a horse, wagon

[33] Memphis, Tenn., *Weekly Avalanche*, Dec. 13, 1859.

For the public sale of 140 slaves—" a finer parcel of negroes was never before offered for sale at this place "—and a large number of valuable mules of the estate of Thomas M. Cowles, at the Artesian Basin, Montgomery, see the Montgomery *Confederation*, Jan. 2, 1860.

M. Schulken likewise sold slaves, mules, etc., and his N. C. turpentine plantation.—Wilmington *Journal*, Jan. 9, 1860.

[34] Southern *Argus*, Jan. 18, 1855.

[35] Milledgeville, Ga., *The Southern Recorder*, Mar. 16, 1852.

[36] Augusta, Daily *Constitutionalist*, Jan. 7, 1860.

and other things.[37]   It was something to attract " sports ".
Success prompts repetition and imitation.   " The enterprising and go-ahead Colonel Jennings has got a raffle
under way now, which eclipses all his previous undertakings in that line ", said the New Orleans *True Delta*.   It
was for " the celebrated trotting horse ' Star ', buggy and
harness " and a " stout mulatto girl ' Sarah ', aged about
twenty years, general house servant." [38]

The yellow slave girls gave special interest to such raffles.
Inter-race sexual immorality was one of the worst features
of slavery.   A Southern judge and ex-Confederate soldier
wrote to the author that " the moral results of slavery,
in its most favorable aspects, are unprintable ".   We are
here concerned with only the printed evidence of the trade
in slave girls and young women for sexual purposes, in
addition to work as servants.   In small numbers and of
varying complexions they were to be seen in nearly all
Southern markets.   Traders gladly exhibited them and
were proud of the high prices they commanded; visitors
were curious to see them and sure to tell about them
later.   Miss Bremer wrote of some in Richmond: " In
another ' jail ' were kept the so-called ' fancy girls ' for
fancy purchasers.   They were handsome fair mulattoes,
some of them almost white girls." [39]   Her comment on
those seen in Augusta, Georgia, was: " Many of these
children [from 12 to 20 years of age] were fair mulattoes,
and some of them very pretty.   One girl of twelve was
so white, that I should have supposed her to belong to the
white race; her features, too, were those of the whites.
The slave-keeper told us that the day before, another girl,
still fairer and handsomer, had been sold for $1,500.   These
white children of slavery become, for the most part, vic-

---

[37] The Turnbulls', 2 *Amer. Photographs*, 52.   Phillips, *Amer. Negro Slavery*,
192, cites a raffle for a girl of 13.
[38] *Key to Uncle Tom*, 182, quotes the full details.
[39] 2 Bremer, 535.

tims of crime, and sink to the deepest degradation." [40]
This item appeared in an editorial article in the Memphis *Eagle and Enquirer,* June 26, 1857:

" A slave woman is advertised to be sold in St. Louis who is so surpassingly beautiful that $5,000 has been already offered for her, at private sale, and refused."

To gamblers, traders, saloonkeepers, turfmen and debauchees, owning a " fancy girl " was a luxurious ideal.
And Longfellow's lines described what was supposed to be no rarity among traders taking a considerable number of purchases to the New Orleans market:

" The Slaver led her from the door,
He led her by the hand,
To be his slave and paramour
In a strange and distant land! "

New Orleans—where thousands of sporting men and voluptuaries lived and other thousands came for the racing season, the Carnival and dissipation—was fully tenfold the largest market for " fancy girls ". The prospect of great profit induced their conspicuous display. At the mart where the planter came to buy when the Ohio youth was

[40] 1 Bremer, 373. For some in Washington, D. C., see *ante* pp. 50-51, 57.
The numerous reports of very high prices for girls without either children or special skill were significant. See *post* pp. 357, 357 n.-358 n.
W. D. Smith of Williamsport, La., offered $100 for the recovery of his runaway mulattress, Livinia, aged about 27. " She is very intelligent and pretty good looking. She is remarkably well provided with clothes of fair quality, and had on when she left a white silk bonnet. It is probable that she will endeavor to find a hiding place in the city or some of the coast towns, as she has lived in almost all of them ".—*Picayune,* Jan. 2, 1859, Sunday supplement.
At the same time and place A. Lauraine of 96 Canal st., New Orleans, offered the same amount for the recovery for his runaway Elizabeth: " She is in color black * * * has a fine suit of hair, stands erect, speaks French and English well, and in appearance [is] handsome; weighs about 130 pounds ".
See *Key,* 183, for the cases of Julia and Fanny; Stowe's *Life of Harriet Beecher Stowe,* 201, for the case of Eliza Buck; *Narrative of Wm. W. Brown,* 34, for the beautiful and nearly white slave girl trader Walker bought in Mo. and took to New Orleans.

inspecting it, a handsome quadroon girl, gaily dressed and adorned with ribbons and jewels, sat in a show-window to attract attention. "She, too, was for sale, as a choice house-servant, at a high price on account of her beauty. As our friend the planter was about to leave the premises he glanced at this girl, and asked what the trader would take for her. Being told, he shook his head, leered at the slave, and said, with an oath, ' Too expensive '." Charles Casey, an English traveler, saw " a beautiful quadroon girl, neatly dressed and very intelligent ", sell for $2,000 in Evans's Arcade, in New Orleans, at a time when field-hands brought from $600 to $800.[41] And " Ole Charley " Logan bought a bright mulatto girl, Violetta, for $600., in Columbia, South Carolina, took her to New Orleans in one of his coffles and sold her for $1,500.[42]

In April, 1848, between 70 and 80 slaves attempted to escape to the North from Washington on a schooner called the " Pearl ".[43] It was overtaken near the mouth of the Potomac, the would-be runaways were lodged in a Washington jail and most of them met the usual fate in such cases—they were " sold South ". Among them were six intelligent and superior mulatto children of Milly and Paul Edmondson—Mary and Emily (16 and 14 years of age) and four of their brothers. The father had been freed many years previously. The slave mother and her 14 children were the inheritance of a feeble-minded maiden lady whose property was cared for by her guardian. The six Edmondson children and many other unfortunates of the " Pearl " were sold to the firm of Bruin & Hill. Since 1834 Joseph Bruin had been an interstate trader in New Orleans, getting his supplies in Maryland and Virginia, just like George Kephart; and since 1836 he had covetously

---

[41] *Two years on the Farm of Uncle Sam*, 263.

[42] Julian Selby (*ante* p. 241) knew her in Columbia and after the Civil War chanced to meet her in New Orleans.

[43] See *Personal Memoir of Daniel Drayton*, 24 ff.

watched the growing Edmondson children, for he had been promised an opportunity to buy them if they should be for sale. Now the time that they feared and he hoped for had come. He paid $4,500 for these six and put them in his jail in Alexandria, Virginia.[44] The lady for whom Mary Edmondson had been working offered Bruin $1,000 for her, which was much more than she cost. He answered that he could get twice that much for her in New Orleans. In a few weeks the six Edmondson children and about 40 other slaves were shipped from Baltimore to New Orleans, where the girls were required to stand on an open porch fronting the street so as to attract the attention of possible purchasers. One of the girls in the yard, who had been sold conditionally for the worst of purposes and was soon returned as unsatisfactory, was mercilessly flogged. Owing to the effect of yellow fever on the trade, Bruin soon concluded to send those unsold back to Baltimore. Before the end of the summer Mary and Emily were again in Bruin's Alexandria jail.

Meantime philanthropic efforts had been made to buy some of the Edmondsons out of slavery, and one of the boys was soon purchased for $900. Finally the old father, Paul Edmondson, resolved to go to New York and try to collect enough money to pay for Emily and Mary. Bruin & Hill gave him a general letter of introduction, September 5, 1848, offering to sell the two girls for $2,250. If $1,200 should be paid, or satisfactory assurances received, within 15 days, then the girls would be kept in Alexandria 25 days longer before being sent to the South Carolina market, along with others. The time elapsed and the coffle was made ready. At the last moment, Emily and Mary, who had become favorites with Bruin's family, were al-

[44] For details about Bruin, the Edmondsons and Emily Russell see Mrs. Stowe's *Key to Uncle Tom's Cabin*, 155-70.

One of the ex-slaves the author interviewed in Donaldsonville in 1902 was sold from Bruin's New Orleans pen; and an old negro met near the battle-field of Bull Run in 1903 named Bruin as the Alexandria trader he used to hear most about.

lowed to remain until later. As the others marched off—
the men handcuffed together and the women and children
following—they were compelled to sing, aided by fiddles
and banjoes, so as to prevent an expression of their actual
feelings and to deceive on-lookers. Paul Edmondson soon
returned, accompanied by a representative of the Abolitionists in New York that had been aroused by the elo-
quence of Henry Ward Beecher and had contributed the
required $2,250. Bruin signed the papers and gave
Mary and Emily each a five dollar gold piece. Instead
of being sold as " fancy girls ", they were taken to New
York to be educated.

Quite different was the fate of another Emily—Emily
Russell, also a pretty mulatto girl and one of the unfortunates of the " Pearl ". She had hoped to reach her
mother, a washwoman who had saved enough to buy her
own freedom and go to New York. Emily and several
others seem to have been taken first to a Baltimore slave-
pen and not placed in Bruin's in Alexandria until early in
January, 1850. Learning that they were presently to be
sent to New Orleans, Emily appealed to her mother, who
besought the financial aid of Abolitionists. They agreed
to contribute to the purchase of Emily and perhaps others,
if obtainable for a reasonable price. The traders answered
thus :—

"Alexandria, Jan. 31, 1850.

* * * "All I have to say about the matter is, that we paid very high
for the negroes and cannot afford to sell the girl Emily for less than $1,800.
This may seem a high price to you, but, cotton being very high, consequently slaves are high. We have two or three offers for Emily from
gentlemen from the South. She is said to be the finest-looking woman in
this country. As for Hagar and her seven children, we will take $2,500.
for them. Sally and her four children, we will take for them $2,800.
You may seem a little surprised at the difference in prices, but the difference in the negroes makes the difference in price. We expect to start
South with the negroes on the 8th February, and if you intend to do anything, you had better do it soon.—Yours, respectfully,

Bruin & Hill."

Not cotton, but being " the finest-looking woman in this country " and having " two or three offers for Emily from gentlemen from the South ", made her so valuable, as was shown by asking only $2,500 for Hagar and her seven children. It was impossible for the philanthropists to collect any one of these sums in the few days before the starting of the coffle overland afoot. Emily had to accompany the others. What stupid recklessness to begin such a march in February! About midway on it, Emily died. When her mother, knowing why the girl was so prized, heard of her death, she exclaimed: " The Lord be thanked! He has heard my prayers at last! "

It was at the French Exchange, in the rotunda of the St. Louis Hotel, that superior-looking girls, varying from mulatto to octoroon, were most often to be seen on the auction-block. French was generally spoken, the whole setting was Creole and all the more strange and fascinating to Northern visitors. This hotel stood near the center of the old city and covered almost the entire square bounded by St. Louis, Chartres, Toulouse and Royal streets. Less costly and impressive than the St. Charles, it was so superior in *cuisine*, in the size and the attractiveness of its ball-rooms, that the gayest social functions were held there. An arcade 127 by 40 feet extended from St. Louis street to a grand rotunda, 80 feet in diameter, with galleries around it and crowned by a lofty dome, letting in a blaze of light and having a very ornamental ceiling. On the sides were pillars 50 feet in height and on the walls were " works in *chiaroscuro*, representing various successful actions gained during the struggle for independence ". The floor was of variegated marble. Extending nearly half-way around the rotunda was a marble bar, which, with its decorations and equipments, was said to be the finest and largest then known. The number and the vivacity of its patrons betokened the superlative quality of the drinks served there.

Opposite the bar were half a dozen small platforms with marble desks for auctioneers. About them, on busy days, were casks of wine, bales, kegs, boxes, crates, furniture, bric-a-brac, books, groceries, drygoods and nearly everything that comes into an auction-mart. The sales of general merchandise began at ten o'clock. Soon the auctioneers were shouting, gesticulating, turning quickly from side to side, sometimes speaking merrily, sometimes almost eloquently. The Creoles called them *encanteurs,* the old French word, instead of *crieurs à l'enchère,* the modern term. Like the announcements of sales by order of any Louisiana court, these *encanteurs* twice said everything that was important—once in each language. Some of them did so with such speed and facility that there seemed to be a simultaneous flow of two distinct streams of words.

What most persons came to see was the slave-auctions. Looking down from the circular galleries on the moving scenes, it was very noticeable that a large proportion of the slaves were of a light color and seemed more intelligent than those in marts outside of New Orleans. At about eleven o'clock, different groups had been brought in from the yards on Esplanade, Moreau, Baronne, Gravier and Common streets and lined up ready for inspection. At one side of the rotunda there were rooms where slaves might be locked up for any temporary purpose and where the scrutiny of men or women might be as close as anyone wished. In no other market was inspection more important than in New Orleans, where the worst in health and character, as well as the best, were gathered.[45]

[45] An old Creole attorney, known as an authority on the law and custom of slave-trading, when asked by the author if it was common to strip the woman, answered: "If the prospective bidders had any doubts, they would strip them, especially the nice looking quadroon girls."

J. B. Walton, one of the busy auctioneers, offered the following to the highest bidder, at the St. Charles Hotel Exchange, Feb. 11, 1860: "LIZZIE, a good-looking and sprightly mulattress, aged about 20 years, a good house servant and nurse; sold without any guarantee whatever. Terms—Cash on the spot."—*Picayune,* Feb. 11, 1860. Here some expert's judgment of the slave's qualities and condition was important.

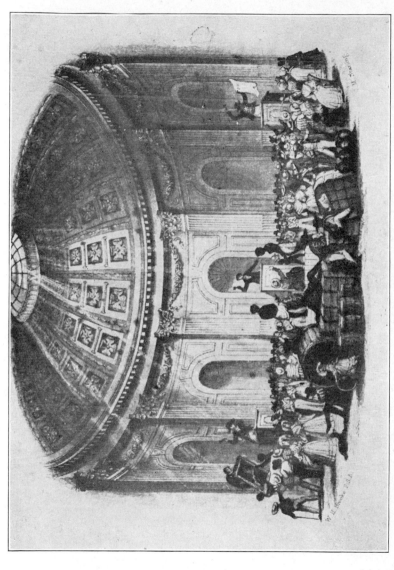

A Slave-Auction at the French Exchange, in the Rotunda of the St. Louis Hotel, New Orleans

From Buckingham's *Slave States*

Auctioneers never felt more important than when selling slaves, and for the *encanteur* there was no place like *la Bourse de l'Hotel St. Louis à midi*—the French Exchange at noon. He assumed his most impressive mien, puffed himself up and his wooden mallet made his marble desk ring out a warning that the important hour to begin the slave-sales had arrived. "*Et maintenant, messieurs, commençons l'encan de ces esclaves de valeur*". The chatter of voices lessened and many persons drew near him as he ordered a slave to mount the nearest appropriately sized box or crate. Here is an apparently realistic account of an auction of a young mother and her two year old boy. She was "very sprucely dressed in a dark bombasine gown, which set off her waist and shoulders to great advantage", and a white cap with lace knots and gay ribbons gave her a coquettish air. The *encanteur* was profuse in praise of mother and child, "and shadowed forth the perfections, both of her mind and body"; she was, moreover, "a good Christian and an accomplished cook"! * * * "*Deux cents gourdes!* Why bless me! * * * *Elle en vaut au moins mille.* And then look at that boy! *Dans quelques ans il sera fort comme un lion ce gamin là!* " * * * " Four hundred dollars! "—* * * " You show your good sense, sir: *on voit que vous vous y connoisez.* * * * Amanda Mix, step forward a little more: there, set the child down, and let the gentlemen see how firm you stand on your cornstalks! There is a beautiful picture! You need not blush, Amanda " (shouts of laughter, in which the ebony beauty heartily joined); " you deserve the compliment. Why, gentlemen, there has not been so splendid a lot in this market within my recollection." Soon the bidding reached $550. " I say, here is a woman of most excellent parts—young, well proportioned and strong; as tractable as a lamb; extremely honest and industrious; with a child that, in a very few years, will be a mine of wealth to its proprietor; and yet for these inestimable articles the paltry sum of five hundred and fifty dollars only has been offered! * * *—" Six hundred dollars!"—Doubtless by pre-arrangement, the auctioneer called on her to draw out from her bosom a neatly folded recommendation. " This is to certify that Amanda Mix is a most excellent servant, always obedient, never grumbles, is seldom sick, and is exceedingly fond of children." Phrenology, then in vogue, was the facile plaything of small wits. The auctioneer felt the heads of the mother and the child and declared that each bore strong evidence of philoprogenitiveness and divers other qualities valuable in slaves. Then a fresh gushing of praise.—" Six hundred and seventy-five dollars!"—" Gentlemen, the matter is creeping to a close: *allons, courage, encore une fois!*" Yet notwithstanding so many merits, mother and child were sold for $700.[46] That was because the year was about 1840. Had it been near the end of the 'fifties they might have brought thrice as much but the other features would have been about the same.

Forty years after the last slave was sold in this once notorious St. Louis Hotel, the building was standing— standing battered like a haunted house with ten thousand curses on it. Window panes were out, locks were broken and doors were nailed up with rough boards or fastened in some crude way. The many " For Rent " signs had so long in vain appealed to the public that they were tattered and yellow from despair. Of the rooms once occupied by flourishing shopkeepers, all save one were empty, except of dirt and rubbish, and that one contained several piles of rusty and forgotten junk. Finally a caretaker was found—a pale Creole, dressed in black and looking both sad and famished. First, one should see the grand halls for receptions and balls, where even the wealthiest guests of the St. Charles gave their most ambitious entertainments. The dome was indeed large, but when it so impressed travelers, that of the National Capitol had not

[46] Tasistro, 1 *Random Shots and Southern Breezes*, 88-92.

been constructed and that of the Library of Congress had not been thought of. After the days of slavery the floors of the second and upper stories were extended under the dome. This made the old rotunda dark. In 1902 it was damp and mouldy; the wood was in decay, and the marble pavement—once clicking to the step of innumerable idlers, visitors, speculators and planters, as well as to the heavy tramp of slaves in their new shoes—was loose, broken, and, in places, destroyed. There stood the formerly grand and gorgeous bar—almost black with humid dirt. Here was an auctioneer's stand from which, it was believed, hundreds of slaves had been sold. In that side-room with barred windows many had been locked up before and after sale. It was almost as damp and gloomy as a dungeon cell. In moving about in it one aroused swarms of strange flying insects. Yes, undoubtedly, from this room — — but then it may have been light and dry. The once gay and busy arcade was only less dismal than the rotunda.

Across Chartres street an aged Creole was complacently sitting in front of his secondhand furniture-store. It was all an old, old story and true. He himself had seen " tousan' an' tousan' o' nagr' " sold right there in the rotunda in the days when the light streamed down from dome to pavement. The law in Louisiana did not allow young children to be parted from their mothers, but he had often seen families auctioned off, no two of whose members went to the same buyer. Mulatto girls would sometimes bring from $2,000 to $2,500; the best hairdressers might sell for as much as $3,500, for they could each earn many hundreds a year for their owners by going to regular patrons. (The New Orleans ladies prided themselves on an artistic *coiffure,* daily.) He also spoke of several of the double-tongued *encanteurs,* especially Vignie.

To have forgotten Vignie would have discredited his recollections, for Vignie was better known in the French quarter than Beard, and only less well known in the American quarter. At one time, he was, perhaps the most prosperous auctioneer in New Orleans and alone did nearly three-fifths as much business as the whole firm of Beard & May.[47] His total commissions in the best years probably exceeded $10,000 or $15,000—more than thrice what those sums would mean today. Certainly a large part came from the sale of slaves. Before 1860 he was selling less often in the French than in the American quarter, where the trade was rapidly increasing. But he and other *encanteurs* continued frequently to chant the praises of *esclaves de valeur* at the French Exchange until stopped by the Civil War.

[47] In a dull quarter of 1851 his gross sales of all sorts amounted to about $264,000, whereas Beard and May's were about $430,000.—25 *Hunt's Merchants' Magazine*, 364. In the last quarter of 1859 Vignie stood eighth, with sales amounting to $146,000; J. Neville & Co., first, with $366,000; Girardey & Co., second, with $352,000; Beard, Pitts & Gardner Smith, tenth, with $112,000.—*Picayune*, Jan. 12, 1860.

The auctioneer's commission varied from 2½% to ½% according to the amount and the character of the sale.—*Revised Stats. La., 1856*, p. 21, sec. 22.

CHAPTER XVI

HIGH PRICES AND "THE NEGRO-FEVER"

Southern soldiers in the Great War " to make the world safe for democracy " must find it hard to conceive of the social and economic notions of their forebears. How much stranger to the rest of the world! Early in the eighteen thirties, Ingraham wrote of the Southwest: " Cotton and negroes are the constant theme—the ever harped upon, never worn out subject of conversation among all classes."[1] With growing intensity from year to year, especially in the cotton belt, they were discussed in the streets of every village and city, in the stages, on the steamboats and the trains, under the planter's portico and on the farmer's " gallery ", at the tavern bar, and, most of all, among the medley of men about the county courthouse. A serious-minded Scotch traveler in 1857 recorded this epigrammatic judgment: " Niggers and cotton—cotton and niggers; these are the law and the prophets to the men of the South."[2] Southerners firmly believed, as one of them wrote: " This alliance between negroes and cotton, we will venture to say, is now the *strongest power* in the world; and the peace and welfare of Christendom absolutely depends [*sic*] upon the strength and security of it."[3]

The largest percentages of profit came, as we know, not from slave labor on the regular cotton crop but from the rearing of slaves when their value was rapidly augment-

---

[1] 2 *The Southwest*, 86.

[2] Stirling, *Letters from the Slave States*, 179. Less seriously Carlton H. Rogers (*Incidents of Travel in the Southern States and Cuba*, 247) wrote: " The topic most frequently discussed is cotton and ' niggers ', which being rather a dry subject, those engaged in it were often obliged to resort to the bar, to lubricate their vocal organs, so that they may be understood by those around them."

[3] 29 *De Bow*, 139.

ing, and still more from transforming virgin soil into cotton plantations. This transformation quickly increased the value of the land fivefold, sometimes tenfold; but it could not be repeated in the same place, like a crop, and only a small fraction of the slaves were employed in this work. Yet the public, accustomed to believe common talk, to think in the superlative and to make rules out of exceptions, viewed the vast onward sweep of ax, fire, plow and hoe, closely followed by white fields of cotton, as the normal and exclusive result of slave labor. Illusions naturally grew into delusions. Slaves, much more than land, cotton, rice or sugar, came to be popularly considered the standard of value and prosperity, at once the safest investment and the most profitable speculation; and accordingly slavery was cherished as the greatest good. Consequently the price of slaves was absurdly inflated and planting rested largely on uneconomic bases.

A reminiscent judge in Georgia illustrated the great change in the relative value of livestock and slaves between the period before the invention of the cotton-gin and the middle of the nineteenth century by saying that testators were once careful to bequeath to their daughters livestock, rather than slaves, because more valuable.[4] As has been noticed, Jefferson sold some slaves instead of more land, which he called " the only sure provision for my children ". Before the end of the 'fifties slaves were so dear and the prices obtained for horses, mules (nearly twice as valuable as horses), cattle and sheep were relatively so low that they were seldom widely reported, except to point a contrast. A sound pickaninny, by the time it could run about, was worth fully as much as two or three ordinary workhorses. A prime fieldhand in the Southwest would sell for more than 10 or 15 horses, sometimes for that many mules, or for scores of cattle, sheep and hogs, which were grouped and sold like " job lots ". In the latter part of

[4] Wylie, ed., *Memoirs of Judge Richard H. Clark*, 154.

the 'fifties a prime fieldhand almost anywhere would have brought more than $929.50, which was all that the Gadsden estate received for 67 head of cattle, 19 sheep and a stallion.[5] That shows the great profit of slave-rearing.

In Maryland and Virginia, prime male fieldhands, such as were valued at less than $300 about 1790, readily sold for from $1,000 to $1,200, and sometimes much more, by 1860. There were, of course, marked fluctuations and the prices were often highly speculative; for, as Chief Justice Ruffin of North Carolina said, " There can be no positive correctness in setting a value on a slave. One man will give or take fifty or one hundred dollars more or less in the purchase of one than another man will." [6] And credit for a few years doubled the margin of uncertainty. Thus prices rose approximately fivefold in seventy years, and nearly threefold in half that time. Professor Phillips says that they " well-nigh quadrupled in the

---

[5] Gadsden's administrator's account.

"SALE DAY.—✴ ✴ ✴ Horses brought from $100 to $150; buggies, $75 to $150. One negro woman, $1400; one woman and three children, $2700; one boy, $855; one boy, $1030."—*Charleston* Tri-weekly *Mercury*, Dec. 10, 1859, quoting the Newberry *Sun* about prices in Newberry, S. C.

"Prices of Negroes &c. At a recent sale of the estate of W. W. Belcher, says the Abbeville, S. C. *Banner*, made by Capt. F. P. Robertson, Auctioneer, Ninety head [!] of negroes sold for an average of $1000. ✴ ✴ ✴ Mules sold unusually high, one bringing $250, one $220, one $216, and the whole lot of about 54 head were near averaging $175. Cattle, common stock, brought $20, $25, $30 and $35 per head."—Savannah *Republican*, Jan. 30, 1860.

At Albany, Ga., 120 slaves of the Paul E. Tarver [or Turner] estate sold for an average of $1,083.87 and the 31 mules (several of very high grade, one selling for $306 and several for $275) brought an average of $203.19, 65 cows $9.00 per head. The total for the stock and $1,208 for cotton seed was $8,303, whereas the slaves commanded more than $136,000.—Augusta *Chronicle etc.*, Jan. 8, 1860.

In the inventory of the " Belle Chasse " sugar estate (*ante* p. 325), made in March, 1859, 55 male slaves of all ages (except infants listed with their mothers) were appraised, separately, as worth a total of $54,450, or almost $1,000 each. Many prime fieldhands were rated at $1,500. Each kind of livestock was grouped: 60 mules, $6,000 [an average of $100]; 50 head of cattle, $1,160; 14 sheep, $35.

[6] 2 Catterall, 97.

three score years of the nineteenth century ''. Edmund
Ruffin was conservative in estimating, in 1859, that they
had doubled since 1844, and he expected that they would
continue to rise.[7] (In Mississippi and Louisiana they ranged
from 30 to 70 per cent higher than in Maryland and Virginia) and up the Red River and beyond they were at least
10 or 20 per cent higher still. With many variations,
there was a general rise from Delaware to Texas.

Because land in the Southwest was fertile, boundless
and cheap, much of that in the old slave States steadily
depreciated and was not easily sold; often great tracts,
with houses and barns, were abandoned. It was just the
reverse with slaves: there was never half enough of them;
their value rapidly increased, and they could be moved to
the place where they would command the most cash or
their labor be most productive. Before 1860 servants, mechanics and good male fieldhands above forty-five years
old could be sold for much more than they had cost 25 or
30 years earlier. Senator and ex-Governor James H.
Hammond of South Carolina exclaimed in a speech to his
neighbors, in October, 1858: '' Why, in this identical quarter of a century our slaves have doubled in numbers and
each slave has more than doubled in value. (The very
negro who, as a prime laborer, would have brought $400
in 1828, would now, with thirty years upon him, sell for
$800.'' [8]) Much of the value and fancied security of slave
property depended on advancing prices. The risks might
have been greatly lessened if the offers of numerous life-
insurance companies, with agencies in all cities, had generally been availed of. But why think of risks when prices

[7] 26 *De Bow*, 649, 657. Presumably referring to the period 1830-60, D. R.
Hundley, a literary zealot for slavery, wrote: `` But suddenly came the great
demand for cotton; negroes advanced in value from $500 to $1,500 a piece
* * * .—*Social Relations in Our Southern States* (1860), 253. No two esti-
mates entirely agree, for they are based on different data. See Phillips,
Amer. Negro Slavery, 370 ff., 410; Hammond, *Cotton Culture*, 51-52; Schaper,
Sectionalism and Representation in South Carolina, 391.

[8] *Speeches and Letters*, 345.

were continually mounting? " The peculiar institution ",
according to Hundley and thousands of others, had become " decidedly the most profitable and safe investment
in the whole country ". And Senator Hammond, leaving
nothing to be added, said: " The rock of Gibraltar does
not stand so firm on its base as our slave system." [9] The
only question was as to the degree of profit.

That but partly explains the so-called economic condition of " the peculiar institution "—peculiar almost beyond belief, when thought of as existing until after the
middle of the nineteenth century in the republic that considered itself to be the sole personification and the last
hope of Liberty enlightening the world. Not only real
estate, but also stocks, bonds and all other personal property were little prized in comparison with slaves. As dots
or other family presents they were more coveted than silver or gold and represented affectionate, even religious,
sentiments and supposed guaranties of choicest comforts
and largest profits.[10] Absurd as it now seems, slaves, especially girls and young women, because of prospective increase, were considered the best investment for persons
of small means and for trust funds for widows and
orphans.[11] The least that a slaveholding farmer hoped to
leave his children, especially his daughters, was a young
female slave, who was expected to be highly profitable.[12]

[9] Hundley, 254; Hammond, 345.

[10] In connection with such gifts, this verse was often mentioned with
unction: " And ye shall take them as an inheritance for your children after
you, to inherit them for a possession; they shall be your bondmen for ever
* * * ."—Leviticus, ch. 25, v. 46.

[11] " The Southern slaves, regarded as property, were the most desirable investment open to the generality of people that has ever been known."—J. C.
Reed, The Brothers' War, 433. Mr. Reed also wrote to the author, March 24,
1906, that " a probate judge or chancellor was generally prone to advise that
representatives of estates, applying for authority to invest, place the funds in
negroes, and preferably young women. That tells the potency of slave
property in its area."
See also V. V. Clayton, White and Black etc., 51.

[12] The will of a North Carolinian, who died in 1847, provided " that his

This ever-present expectation of great profit from future increase was the basis of the strongest financial objection to getting rid of slavery within a few generations by declaring free all children born of slaves after a specific date in the future. Thomas R. R. Cobb, perhaps the highest authority, wrote summarily, about 1857: " In a slaveholding State, the greatest evidence of wealth in the planter is the number of his slaves. The most desirable property for a remunerative income is slaves. The best property to leave to his children, and from which they will part with greatest reluctance, is slaves. Hence, the planter invests his surplus income in slaves. The natural result is, that lands are a secondary consideration. No surplus is left for their improvement. The homestead is valued only so long as the adjacent lands are profitable for cultivation." [13]

To own many slaves and enjoy all the advantages to be derived from them, one must have large fields producing crops of tobacco, cotton, rice or sugar cane; one must be a planter. Accordingly to be a planter—and all planters were popularly supposed to be rich—was the dream of childhood [14] and the supreme gratification of old age—the acme of every ambition, whether one " began " as a lawyer, clergyman, physician or merchant; for " it was the condition that came nearest to the shadow of the colonial aristocracy which yet remained." [15] According to popular notion, it was synonymous with luxurious ease and social

five younger daughters should * * * have a negro girl each, and, if his negroes should not increase to a sufficient number in time, that some of the other negroes should be sold for the purpose of procuring the girls."—2 Catterall, 166.

[13] *Law of Negro Slavery*, p. ccxv.

[14] When a child, R. M. T. Hunter was given the choice of a pony or a slave boy. He chose the slave, of course.—Hunter's *R. M. T. Hunter*, 30. Virginia F. Boyle says (*Devil Tales*, 141) that when a slave was born on a certain plantation, the mother was visited by the planter's wife, accompanied by her children, who bore presents " and put in their claims to the little black baby with many excited arguments ". Similar occurrences were numerous.

[15] Grayson, *Life of James L. Petigru*, 136-37.

distinction. To be slaveless was at least to appear to be
cheerless, to have a drudge for a wife and children without
opportunities. To buy or to hire a slave, even a child, was
to take a step forward and upward and to begin to be commanding; one was no longer a " poor white ".[16] To own
a score of slaves made it evident that one had advanced well
toward the " upper class " and the " aristocracy ". What
did the " upper class " and the " aristocracy " mean to
the great mass of the white people? An old Georgian,
whose experience, standing and recollections fitted him to
answer, said to the author: " If a man could sit on his
porch and see fifty niggrahs ride his mules in from work—
that was aristocracy. But if he went broke and had to sell
a niggrah, a ' buck ', his reputation was gone and he could
not borrow a dollah." Fortunes laboriously earned in
professions or business often rapidly dwindled after slaves
and lands were bought; but that did not appreciably lessen
the general desire.

Slaves were the criterion of riches, social status and all
that these represented to persons without them.[17] There
were, indeed, large slaveowners that did not always pass
for gentlemen, but who before 1860 ever heard of a slaveless " Southern gentleman "? Had it been said that a
certain lawyer was " worth $100,000 ", invested mainly in
bonds and bank or railroad stocks, and that a certain cotton, tobacco, rice or sugar grower " had 100 slaves "—
rarely unencumbered and the number commonly exag-

---

[16] Hundley called slaveowning the greatest ambition of the Southern yeoman,
the thrifty poor white, and illustrated his point by this dialogue between such
a man and his first slave: " Jeff! you, Jeff! Come here, you big black
nigger, you! " When Jeff responded with, " Bres God, Mas'r, what's de
marter? ", his novice of a master answered: " O nuthin, *I only wanted to see
how 'twould sound jist—that's all!* "—Hundley, *Social Relations etc.*, 198.
Olmsted, *Texas*, pp. xvi-xvii, explains the fashion of slaveholding.

[17] " The increase of them is the general standard of your worldly prosperity "
etc.—Quoted by Olmsted, 2 *Cotton Kingdom*, 216. " It was a wealthy neighborhood; two of the trustees * * * were worth a hundred negroes apiece "
* * * .—Rev. Dr. Thornwell of S. C. in 25 *De Bow* 421. Burke, *Reminiscences
of Georgia*, 119, and many others speak of slaves as a measure of wealth.

gerated—it would have been taken for granted that the two men were about equally rich, for $100,000 was riches then; but " 100 slaves " denoted a " large planter ", a " patrician ", with high " social standing " whereas $100,000 in stocks and bonds, even without debts, signified little except so much property. " There was always connected with the ownership of slaves a sense of pride and independence, a supposed badge of superiority, that attracted men." It was " a passport to society. The man or the woman who owned one hundred slaves was everywhere an honored person. The owners of great plantations, stocked with slaves, were the most influential men in the State. They everywhere received homage. They were untitled nobility. The merchant might be as wealthy, but he ranked below the ' great planter '." [18] McDuffie of South Carolina, although the son of a non-slaveowner, said in 1835 that the slaveholding and landholding classes formed a gentry that rendered unnecessary " an order of nobility and all other appendages of a hereditary system of government ".[19] Such an announcement as, " Mr. Gregg is a large [South Carolina] planter, and is here [Richmond] to buy more slaves for his plantation " [20] was a recognition of his superiority. And no matter how often it was proclaimed that ' slave-traders are hated " nor how well it was known that a visiting planter was to purchase exclusively from them, it did not lessen his prestige. Had a South Carolinian come to engage a builder and to obtain materials for constructing a public school, a hotel or a bank, his presence would have been of little, if any, public interest.

There were many enterprises in the South more remunerative than any phase of slaveholding except slave-

[18] Temple, *East Tennessee etc.*, 84, 254. Judge Temple of Knoxville, Tenn., was a slaveowner and an able and impartial historian, from whose conversation and correspondence the present author derived much pleasure and benefit.

[19] Ingle, *Southern Side Lights*, 19.

[20] Richmond Semi-weekly *Enquirer*, Jan. 25, 1861.

rearing and turning rich wild land into plantations, but they lacked distinction and could not be exploited socially. To rise above them one must own negroes and a " plantation ". Virtually everybody was expecting or hoping to prosper, at some time, by the purchase, the increase, the mortgaging, the hiring out, the inheritance or the sale of slave property. Work and thrift not being in favor with persons much in need of them, there was a feverish desire to buy slaves to the limit of possible credit and in the spirit of speculation. Yet, apart from rising prices, based on a limited supply and a surely increasing demand, slaves, individually, were very precarious investments: they could not be standardized and designated in market quotations like stocks and bonds, livestock and merchandise; they might any day become gravely ill or die. The only " exchanges " were the numerous unconnected auction blocks and still more numerous private jails or pens. The usual descriptions according to age, sex and habitual occupation left unnoticed qualities that might be most important—honesty, industry, good habits, and their opposites. Because of the wide margin of uncertainty, there was always much risk in purchasing, unless one had special information. Nevertheless there was an almost irresistable fascination about the thought of acquiring slaves.

De Bow summed it up in a few words: " The universal disposition is to purchase. It [slave property] is the first use for savings, and the negro purchased is the last possession to be parted with. If a woman, her children become heirlooms and make the nucleus of an estate." [21] Accordingly negroes and a plantation were a matter of course, as soon as possible, and " after that, it was more negroes to work more land to the end of the chapter ".[22] Planters were proverbially impatient to mortgage their crops to buy more slaves to make more cotton to buy more

[21] 30 *De Bow*, 74.
[22] Reuben Davis, *Recollections of a Mississippian*, 156.

slaves. A genial old South Carolinian, reminiscing at four
score about the luxurious calm of the rice-planter's existence—although few of them, as he laughingly confessed,
dared to plan a long trip or any considerable extra expense
without first consulting their factors about further credit
—mentioned with lingering pride: " My factor used to
say to me, ' Colonel, are you *nevah* goin' to stop buyin'
niggrahs ? ' "

Even when prices were highest, the markets in the
Atlantic border slave States were often overflowing, for
the profit on slave labor was correspondingly reduced, and
creditors were impatient to have accounts liquidated.
Extravagance, carelessness, misfortune and death brought
thousands of slaves into the market, for they were the
chief security, the most salable and the major part of all
agricultural property. From November to March, many
estates, large and small, were dissolving and slaves were
scattering as if, like the seasons, such things were the
order of nature; and other estates, farther south or west,
were forming or expanding with the slaves purchased,
often less for the value of the crops they might raise than
for speculation or the satisfaction of owning more and
more.

In a world of such conditions, such fancies, such illusions, the slaves of a deceased planter were at a large premium, for they gave special prestige and were likely to be
superior. The Mobile *Advertiser* of January 18, 1860, may
have exaggerated in saying that at an administrator's sale
slave property " always sells for at least one-third more
* * * than it is actually worth ". But the desire to buy was
so great, even when one could not obtain good security,
that some auctioneers, like Vignie in New Orleans, found
it necessary to advertise that prospective purchasers must
in advance of the sale make known the names of their in-
dorsers.[23]

[23] N. O. *Picayune*, Feb. 16, 1856.

It was a proud day for a quondam overseer that could be conspicuous on such occasions. To outbid rivals and get a few of the most desirable slaves from some large estate, to be able to tell neighbors and visitors that his coachman had belonged to a certain planter-statesman, or that these stalwart fieldhands were the best of a cotton gang that their former master had selected in various markets and at numerous sales, or that his cook had belonged to a once rich Creole—any of these would be good evidence of marked social progress. If some of the older men recounted the circumstances when he was " overseein' " in the neighborhood, then " when he bought his first ' nigger ' ", and, later, how additions had annually come by purchases and births, it made him still more a model for the slaveless, because he had demonstrated what was possible, if one could get started. There was hardly a courthouse village or a crossroads postoffice in all the agricultural regions of the South where men were not looked up to mainly on account of their owning slaves. And they seemed to say to the non-slaveholders: " This is the road to riches and social recognition."

Slaves being a common interest, in fact or fancy, about no other subject was it so easy to start a conversation in which all present were prone to take an active part. The question that everybody, except the hopeless " poor whites ", wished answered as often as possible was, " How are niggrahs sellin'? " Between counties, between States, distant States, there was no information so welcome orally or in the press. What important news had little Warrenton in the upland to give to Alexandria sleeping by the Potomac? The answer was:

"WARRENTON ITEMS.—Slaves sold enormously high on Court day, and New Year's. A negro man brought $1,275, and one woman $1,300, and a girl, fourteen years old, $1,150. Tolerably tall." [24]

Prices in Texas and Louisiana were of about as much con-

[24] Alexandria *Gazette and Va. Advertiser*, Jan. 10, 1859.

cern to South Carolinians and Georgians as those in Kentucky and Missouri were to Alabamians and Mississippians. Prices in Virginia were of special import, for they were supposed to represent a fair minimum.[25]

In the spring of 1852, before the excitement over prices was general, an announcement that the slaves of a deceased planter in Wilcox county, Alabama, had been sold at auction for an average cash price of $700 and that an old slave above sixty years of age brought more than $1,000, was capped by this triumphant climax: " *Niggers are niggers* now, especially the Atwood *niggers* ".[26] Two years later the Montgomery *Journal* reported what it called " the highest prices which we have ever noticed " for common fieldhands and children of the McLemore estate: 18 slaves, ten of whom were children of from 2 months to 7 years of age, sold for $14,195; a boy of 7 brought $760; one of 12, $710; a youth of 17, $1,374, and a woman of 37, with six children, from 2 to 7 years, $5,000. They were sold " by the auctioneer General Carroll ".[27]

These superlative prices of 1854 in the Southwest were in a few years surpassed in the selling States, where slaves were most plentiful and least expensive. The Montgomery *Confederation* had a much prized news item when it reported in January, 1859, that the poorest as well as the best slaves both of a living and of a deceased master in Virginia were commanding very high prices at auction— a boy of 15, $1,188; one of 18, $1,395; girls of 10 to 16,

[25] Any report like the following was considered very significant: " A few days ago, 21 slaves belonging to the estate of Wm. Pendleton, consisting of old and young men, women, and children, not regarded as above ordinary, were sold at Lynchburg, Va., at the average price of $553. One negro man without a trade sold for $1028; a woman with a child ten months old sold for $950; and a girl aged eleven years for $600. On the public road of Virginia slave men are hiring at from $120 to $150 per year."—Milledgeville *Southern Recorder*, Jan. 20, 1852.

[26] Huntsville, Ala., *Southern Advocate*, Mar. 10, 1852.

[27] 30 *Hunt's Mchts' Mag.* (April, 1854), 500.

from $792 to $1,275.[28] Before the end of the year there were reports of still higher prices in Virginia and in North Carolina:

"HIGH PRICES FOR NEGROES

At a sale of negro property last week, in Davie county, says the Charlotte *Democrat,* one fieldhand brought $1,640; another $1,600; and a girl sixteen years old $1,400. They were bought by traders. At a sale of slaves in Mecklenburg county, Va., a few days since, twelve, including three infants, one Albino, two infirm, and ages ranging from 7 to 50 brought $11,485." [29]

A point being made of sale to traders, the master's name was carefully omitted. Traders paying $1,600 and $1,640 for fieldhands in the old States must have expected to receive considerably more than $2,000 for each, if sold in Louisiana or Texas.

To have been present at an auction of a planter's slaves where such prices were obtained was as much a matter of pride as to have seen a race in which some famous horse had " broken the record ", or to have heard a joint-debate where there had been an exchange of personalities that led to a challenge. If an editor had unhappily missed such an occasion, he counted himself fortunate indeed if able to quote the auctioneer's account of it,[30] for his readers were always eager for such news.

Phenomenal prices were obtained in many instances even in South Carolina in 1859 and 1860. At the sale of the 31 slaves of the Philip Cromer estate in the Abbeville region a mother and child were sold at auction for $1,900, a

[28] At the same time a " negro woman, almost blind in both eyes, a negro girl blind in one eye, and a small child—all scrofulous and of the same family—were sold in a lot for $850."—*Confederation,* Jan. 15, 1859.

[29] Raleigh Tri-weekly *N. C. Standard,* Dec. 7, 1859.

[30] " THE NEGROES sold here on Monday last, belonging to the estate of Mr. Robert N. Ellis, brought very high prices. We were not present at the sale, but understand from John B. Williams, who was the Auctioneer, that one negro man brought $1,859, and three others over $1,800 each. Terms, 12 months credit, without interest.—Greensboro *Beacon.*"—Montgomery Daily *Confederation,* Jan. 3, 1859.

mother and three children for $3,005, and a girl for $1,705,
whereas a male fieldhand brought $150 less.[31]   Two days
later still better news was announced:

"BIGGEST SALE YET. -The Commissioner's sale of the Youngblood
negros on Monday last was 'hard to beat'.   Thirty-six slaves, ten or
twelve of the lot being children under eight years of age, and two or three
over forty, brought very nearly thirty-eight thousand dollars." [32]

During the first week of January, 1860, there came from
three different counties reports of prices that must have
set imaginations ablaze: $1,630 for a common fieldhand
" and others went at corresponding rates "; $1,795 for a
" fellow 40 years old ", and $1,605 for another of 21;
$1,105, $1,150 and $1,200 for three boys of 10 years, and
$1,045 for a girl of 10; one gang of 13 sold at an average
of $1,020, and another of 16 at an average of $1,086.50;
and " seven boys, from 14 to 38 years of age ", brought
an average of $1,540.[33]   Among 104 of a deceased planter's
slaves " 45 were children under ten years of age ", " some
of the adults were likely and first-rate—some were very
far from it ".   " A very large number of persons attended
from this and the surrounding districts (counties), and
the biddings were animated and ran high "—to a total of
$100,350 and an average of $964.90 per slave.[34]

In January, 1860, the Reverend James Petigru Boyce, a
professor in the Southern Baptist Seminary at Greenville,
South Carolina, and formerly a distinguished pastor in
Columbia, paid $3,500 for " George, a likely fellow, said
to be a good joiner and carpenter ".   The professor, who

[31] Charleston Tri-weekly *Mercury*, Dec. 8, 1859.
[32] Charleston Tri-weekly *Mercury*, Dec. 10, 1859, quoting the Edgefield
Advertiser.   The same number announced that in Winnsboro, a blacksmith,
22 years old, brought $2,500, a crippled boy, 16, $1,020, Nancy about 10, $765,
all belonging to the estate of a "colonel"; and a boy of about 12 owned by
Mrs. Durham sold for $915 cash, "notwithstanding the inclemency of the
weather, [for] a considerable crowd was in attendance".
[33] Charleston *Mercury*, Jan. 7, 1860, in an article entitled "NEGROS IN
THE COUNTRY".
[34] Charleston *Courier*, Jan. 11, 1860, quoting the Unionville *Times*.

had inherited commercial, not planting, riches, must have
been as well versed in slaves as in theology, for he was
almost immediately offered $4,000 for his carpenter.[35]

Joseph Bond was called the wealthiest and largest cotton grower in Georgia. He was, indeed, as Judge Clark
described him, " a lordly planter, with his hundreds of
slaves and his thousands of rich acres ", for in the southwestern part of the State he owned six plantations comprising nearly 20,000 acres and 566 negroes—worth a total
of more than a million dollars, apart from his real estate
and personal property elsewhere. In 1858 he produced
" 2,170 bales of cotton which would at present [January,
1859] rates bring him over $100,000. A neat little in-
come." So the Macon *Telegraph* reported, rightly with
much pride,[36] although that was gross income. His city
house, " for a long time the grandest home in Macon, even
in Georgia ", still crowns the brow of the impressive hill
of Vineville and like a Greek temple overlooks old Macon.
Between planters and their former overseers ill feelings
were not rare. An overseer that had worked for Joseph
Bond, but in March, 1859, was in charge of a neighboring
plantation, committed some offense in relation to one of
Bond's slaves, which the master violently resented. There
were two very different stories. Certain it is that Bond
rode forth in a frenzy of anger to chastise the overseer,
found him mounted, knocked him off his horse, and, while
cudgeling him, was fatally shot by him. Bond's chief
pride and pleasure, sympathetically remarked the Macon
Telegraph, were in " his plantations and the comfort and
happiness of his people ", and he was " noted for his great
care and attachment to them ". The tender relation " between a good and humane master and his faithful servants ", said the Montgomery *Confederation*, was " but
little inferior to that of parent and child "; and such an

---

[35] Charleston *Mercury*, Jan. 28, 1860.
[36] Quoted by the Savannah *Republican*, Jan. 26, 1859.

12

instance as this would better explain it " than [would] all the effusions of Mrs. Stowe and the abolition crew combined." [37] The sad incident was the occasion for much touching sentiment. Mention the phrases, " planter with hundreds of negroes ", " thousands of acres ", " attachment to his people ", and every mind would soon evolve a picture—usually a very fanciful one. All the graver was the reflection on Joseph Bond's act when, as Judge Clark said, " two successive grand juries found ' no bill ' upon the indictments, and the overseer stood acquitted of the crime ".

Within eight months after Bond's death an advertisement announced that his more than 550 slaves—about one-fourth more than the Pierce Butler sale—would be sold at auction before the courthouse door in Albany, Georgia, on January 3, 1860, " and continued to each successive day ". They were described as under good discipline, acclimated, well trained to the cultivation of corn and cotton and " as likely a gang as will ever be offered again, perhaps in any of the States South ".[38] It was literally and prophetically true. No other planter's estate is known to have marketed so many at one time. It is the supreme example of " patriarchal "—dissolution. Reports were awaited with impatience, near and far. After the auction had continued throughout two days, and 536 of the 566 slaves had been sold, it was announced that the average price was $1,025. A " girl " offered " as unsound brought $1,800 "; a sound one of 17 and a " boy " of 20 [39] were sold together for $3,600; a male fieldhand of 30, $2,005; several " boys ", over $2,000 each; a " boy " with wife and child, $4,500; and one of the executors paid $16,000.10 for parents with their eleven children, from 5

[37] For the different points see *Memoirs of Judge Richard H. Clark*, 30-31, 156-58, and the Montgomery *Daily Confederation*, March 29, 1859, which also quoted the Macon *Telegraph* of Mar. 15, 1859.

[38] Augusta, Ga., *Constitutionalist* continued the detailed advt. for many weeks.

[39] The terms " girl " and " boy " were often extremely vague.

to 18 years of age, all "average negroes ".[40] The 19,388 acres of the six plantations sold for $468,892.24, or an average of about $24 an acre.[41] Presumably the equipments of these plantations, the stock and the remnants of corn, fodder, etc. sold for not more than about $25,000. The 566 slaves must have brought a total of about $580,150, or nearly $90,000 more than all the rest of the plantation property. This shows what slave-rearing might mean to the largest planters.

In Brooks county, Georgia, an unspecified number of slaves averaged $1,566.37; $2,445 was paid for Bess and two children, $2,515 and $3,114 for two men presumably of some class above that of fieldhands. These were called the highest Georgia prices yet noticed.[42] News of the sale of a selected gang of 108 railroad builders (of whom 25 were women and 10 were children) that averaged $1,364, one of whom, a mechanic, brought $2,500, caused the Savannah *Republican* of January 14, 1860, much enthusiasm and it gratefully mentioned the person to whom it was indebted for the information. Still more remarkable was its report about the public sale of an ordinary plantation gang of 81 (all but about 20 of whom were women and children) who averaged $1,100. Over $2,000 was obtained for each of several men, $1,465 for a girl of 11 and $1,385 for another a little younger. Think of the profit of rearing children at even half those prices!

[40] Augusta, Ga., *Chronicle and Sentinel*, Jan. 8, 1860, quoting the Albany *Patriot*.

[41] Charleston Tri-weekly *Mercury*, Dec. 15, 1859, gave the average price per acre for each plantation.

[42] Augusta, Daily *Constitutionalist*, Jan. 17, 1860, quoting the Thomasville *Enterprise*.

"Twenty negroes were sold in Sparta on Tuesday last, belonging to the estate of James Derby, that averaged $919. Leaving out five of them, an old one and the children, the other fifteen averaged $1128."—Augusta, Ga. *Chronicle and Sentinel*, Jan. 12, 1860. The same newspaper, three days later, quoted an article from the Bainbridge *Argus* saying that negroes from 3 to 50 years old, belonging to an estate were sold there on the 3rd at an average of nearly $1148.

In general the prices increased as one advanced to the lower Southwest. High " offers for one's bargain " and the excess of prices obtained above appraisals emphasized the opportunities for speculation. At Marshal Court House, Texas, early in 1857, about 30 slaves sold for an average of nearly 50 per cent higher than their appraisals.[43] " A tip-top Negro blacksmith was sold in this city yesterday for the sum of $2000, and the purchaser was offered shortly after, $500 for his bargain," said the Austin, Texas, *State Gazette* of October 15, 1859. In Louisiana in July and August, 1858, seven slaves at public sale brought an average of $1,538 and without guarantee as to soundness; a man of 36 years sold for $1,835; another, 26, $2,050; one of 50, $1,225, and a woman of 20, $1,300.[44]

" Frequent notices occur in the newspapers of high prices paid for negroes ", said the Greenville *South Alabamian* of February 12, 1859, but it thought that the highest mark had been reached when fieldhands and children of the Thigpen estate sold for an average of $1,309 each; Henry, 29, brought $2,400 and Stephen, 27, $2,431.[45]

Even the certainty of secession apparently did not lower prices; and when special credit could be obtained, they mounted highest. Such was the case at an executor's sale in Columbia county, Florida, where 50 negroes, " big, little, old and young " were sold at an average of over $1,200, with a credit of two or three years,—but, of course, not

---

[43] Three men, two 22 and one 23, each appraised at $1,200, brought $1,765, $1,890 and $1,910.—22 *De Bow*, 349, gives all the figures. For the children see *post* p. 358.

[44] 25 *De Bow*, 493.

[45] Quoted by the Savannah, Ga., *Republican*, Feb. 16, 1859. Some of the prices received for a mother and children and for children are cited *ante* p. 83 and *post* p. 357, note 48.

At Mobile, in Jan., 1860, the 33 slaves of the Harmon estate averaged $1,145, which was higher than it would have been but for the unusual credit of twelve months.—Mobile *Advertiser*, Jan. 18, 1860.

without securities and notes bearing interest from the date of the sale.[46]

The prices commonly received for children were very significant. In the latter part of the 'fifties children of from 8 to 10 years of age sometimes sold for more than prime fieldhands and ordinary mechanics had cost ten or twelve years earlier.[47] Young children might be bought for any one of many reasons; but, as their labor was worth hardly more than their "board and keep" and was rarely needed, they were most desirable as speculations. Instead of being shocked by this traffic, journalists and the public manifested the liveliest curiosity about the prices obtained, no matter how far away, for they conclusively showed both that slave-rearing was extremely profitable in the early years and that children were eagerly bought at hazardous valuations.[48]

[46] Charleston *Courier*, Nov. 26, 1860, quoting *Florida Dispatch*.
17 slaves were sold at auction separately in Carrollton, Miss., at an average of a little less than $1,200, only two days before that State passed its ordinance of secession.—N. O. Daily *True Delta*, Jan. 19, 1861.

[47] "Two little negro girls, respectively seven and twelve years of age, sold in Petersburg, Va., last Tuesday, at $725 and $770."—Richmond, Semi-weekly *Examiner*, Jan. 6, 1857.
Five little children of the Jesse Gill estate, Wade county, N. C., 1860: Emeline, 7, $635; Rachel, 4, $475; Ruffin, 8, $810; Leah, 5, $700; Samantha, 4, $400.—Charleston *Mercury*, Oct. 15, 1860.
At a chancery sale at Lebanon, Tenn., in 1859: Sally, 8, $1,051; Emeline, 7, $1,051; John, 14, $1,575; Tabby, 15, $1,501; Prince, 10, $860; Bobb, 7, $800.—41 *Hunt's Merchants' Magazine*, 774.
In different counties in Ky.: Emma, 12, $865; Ellen, 12, $800; Elizabeth, 11 (one-eyed), $406; Sanford, 9, $700; Arabel, 10, $690; Bettie, 3, $260.—McDougle, 3 *Jour. Negro Hist.*, 234-35. At Franklin, Ky., in Aug., 1859, children of the estate of Thomas Layne, deceased, were sold on a credit of 12 months, as follows:—two boys of 11, $1,365 and $1,305; two boys of 9, $1,170 and $1,000; girl of 7, $1,075.—41 *Hunt's Merchants' Magazine*, 774.
Trexler cites these high prices in Mo.: boy, 11, $795; girl, 12, $942; girl, 3, $400; boys 9, 7, 5, $550 and $300; girl, 9, $450; boy, 4, $321. He also cites appraisals in 1859 that were about as high.—*Slavery in Missouri*, 40-41.

[48] Some children of the Thigpen estate sold as follows: Henderson, 14, $1,900; Isum, 11, $1,350; Esther, 13, $1,541; Terrill, 9, $1,105; Polly, 12, $1,625; Prissy, 15, $1,515; Mary, 15, $1,420. "We may also remark that the

It was large planters, persons with slaves to sell and fanatically proslavery journalists that were most enthusiastic about high prices. If buyers often seemed not less so, it was because they wished to anticipate a still further rise. Henry Laurens wrote in 1755 that South Carolinians "growled in the gizzard a good deal" at paying high prices for Africans. A century later, farmers and small planters in the Southwest, especially in Louisiana, Missis-

negroes selling highest were purchased outside the family connections."— Savannah *Republican*, Feb. 16, 1859.

Of the Harmon estate slaves, Andy, 13, brought $1,725; Lize, 10, $1,160; Manda, 12, $1,405.—Mobile *Advertiser*, Jan. 18, 1860.

The advt. of the auction of Marshal Court House (*ante* p. 356) mentioned no relationships whatever, except that children of four or less years were sold with their mothers. The following named children were sold singly at an average of more than 36% above their appraisals:

		Appraised	Sold			Appraised	Sold
Caroline,	11,	$800	$1,100.	Sarah,	9,	$600	$890.
Frank,	9,	600	805.	Dick,	7,	500	650.
Little Allick,	7,	500	810.	Sam,	3,	200	450.
Catharine,	10,	705	700.	Phoebe,	10,	500	655.
Flora,	6,	500	695.	Ben,	6,	350	405.

—22 *De Bow* (April, 1857), 439.

Here are more samples of high prices obtained for adults and children in Texas in 1859-60:—

At an administrator's sale in Rusk, Cherokee co., a man, about 38, brought $1,325; a woman with an infant, $1,308; a girl, not 14, $1,403, and a boy, 17, $1,527. "Another girl, 12 years of age, found a ready master at the cool price of $1,255, and a boy of the same age, went—going—going—*gone*—at $1,155. A bright-eyed little lad, not yet out of his swaddling clothes, brought $485; and another lad, only 8 years old, *actually* sold for $1,002."—Quoted by Austin, Tex., *State Gazette*, Feb. 19, 1859.

At a sale for division (on three months' time) in Giles co., Tex., slaves whose sexes were not mentioned brought the following prices: one, 28, $1,500; one, 26, $1,650; one, 18, $1,800; one, 9, $1,056; one, 7, $1,005; one, 13, $1,005. —Austin, Tex., *State Gazette*, Mar. 26, 1859.

At an administrator's sale (on twelve months' time) in Palestine, Tex., a man, 21, brought $2,015; a man, 43, a woman, 45, and a child, 11 months, $2,525; a girl, 15, $1,635; a boy, 10 or 12, $1,236; a girl, about 8, $850; a girl, about 6, $501.30; a boy, about 3, $500; a boy, 9 or 10, $1,230; a man, about 35, $2,206. * * * "These are the highest prices we recollect ever to have been paid for negroes. The negroes are all field and house hands."—Palestine, Tex., *Trinity Advocate*, Mar. 14, 1860.

sippi and Texas, demanded cheaper labor and complained that the border slave States and the Carolinas had almost a monopoly of the supply of slaves, which made the price nearly prohibitive and agriculture unprofitable. The political conditions were still more discouraging. In comparison with the rapid growth of population in the North, the South was in a decline. Proslavery control of the House of Representatives was gone forever, and without a large increase of cheap slaves territorial expansion and more slave States would be impossible—which meant that the Senate also would become antislavery before many years.

It was urged that both conditions could be improved by reopening the African slave-trade. Fire-eating orators and journalists advocated it. A few daring adventurers planned to risk their necks for the money expected to be made out of each cargo. Southern leaders in Washington undertook to hamper and end the special efforts made by the United States Government in conjunction with Great Britain to stop the African slave-trade on the high seas. The agitators and the adventurers easily held public attention, although the movement, except in Mississippi, Louisiana and Texas, was superficial and did not appeal to intelligent planters nor to shrewd politicians. Planters perceived that cheap Africans would mean a depreciation in the value of slave property; and politicians foresaw that advocacy of the foreign slave-trade would alienate Northern Democrats and thereby hasten the dreaded supremacy of the Republican party. Yet rumors of alleged importations from Africa and of many more soon to arrive, were frequently reported in the Southern press.

But the only fully authenticated cargo successfully brought directly from the Dark Continent to the South during the latter half of the 'fifties was on the "Wanderer", a fast yacht turned into a slaver.[49] Early in

[49] In July, *1860*, the "Clotilde" brought 103 Africans into the Bay of Mobile, where they were transshipped and taken about 50 miles up the Alabama River

December, 1858, it landed about 420 near Brunswick, Georgia, and most of them were soon shipped to and up the Savannah River and put ashore in South Carolina, almost opposite Augusta. Charles A. L. Lamar, of a good Georgia family but a brazen-faced and vociferous soldier of fortune, was the head of the enterprise.[50]

The South was much stirred by Lamar's bold venture, and many persons triumphantly claimed that the African slave-trade had been successfully reopened. Every bit of news or rumor about imported Africans was printed and read as if of great moment. Shortly before Christmas, 1858, "quite an excitement was produced in" Atlanta "on account of the arrival, by the Georgia Railroad train, of forty negroes, said to be direct from Africa. They were under the control of Mr. Thack Brodnax, a gentleman we have long known", wrote the editor of the *Intelligencer*. Although this "gentleman" said that they were natives of South Carolina, the editor evidently inclined to the popular belief that they were part of the "Wanderer's" cargo.[51] Meantime two other Africans, who had been put in charge of an express company and started for south-western Georgia, were seized in Macon and taken to Savannah. The item about them gravely ended with these words: "They are males, about 17 and 21 years of age."[52] Not boys or men, but only males, as if they were of some

to be landed. It seems much less likely that the "Clotilde" obtained its small cargo in Africa than in Cuba or from some slaver in neighboring waters, which were the sources of most if not all the small cargoes supposed to have been occasionally smuggled into States on the Gulf. The main facts about the "Clotilde" were quickly made known to the Department of Justice; but, presumably on account of the presidential campaign then raging, prosecution was delayed, and secession soon intervened.

[50] It was trumpeted as a success, although Lamar wrote: "You are aware that it is a risky business. *I lost two out of three.* * * * I have been in for 'grandeur', and been fighting for principle. Now I am in for the dollars".— 143 *N. Am. Review*, 459.

[51] Atlanta *Intelligencer*, Dec. 24, quoted by the Jackson *Mississippian* of Dec. 31, 1858. Twenty Africans that were sold for $12,000 in Marksville, La., (Savannah *Republican*, Feb. 1, 1859) were presumably of this lot.

[52] Savannah *Republican*, Dec. 30, 1858.

previously unknown but peculiarly useful species of wild beast. And at the South Carolina State Fair in 1859 two were exhibited, given a silver goblet,[53] and viewed with hardly less curiosity than if they had been two of the gorillas Paul Du Chaillu had recently discovered. Yet half of South Carolina's entire population was of not very remote African parentage; scores, if not hundreds, of natives of the Dark Continent, like General Gadsden's Tom, were still living in that State, and a decade or two earlier there must have been thousands of them.

Was there not somewhere consciousness of the folly of the passion for slaves and more slaves? Yes. Solemn warnings were both numerous and—without effect. " Dr. Franklin's motto, ' Let well enough alone ', has not been followed ", said the Milledgeville *Southern Recorder,* as early as February 24, 1852, " and in the vain attempt to make a hasty fortune by speculating in negroes, the planter has worsted his condition. Let him now settle the reckoning of his past folly as best he can, and profiting by the past, avoid the like error in the future." In 1854 the Montgomery *Journal* expressed the opinion that prices for slaves were " ranging far above their legitimate point ", and that when tilled land was selling at $20 an acre and negroes at " $1,000 per head ", the raising of cotton would not pay.[54] The Charleston *Mercury* in 1856 pointedly called attention to the anomaly that within the previous few years slaves had advanced 50 per cent. in price and had accordingly increased the capital employed in planting, without any corresponding increase in its profits.[55] At no time in the 'fifties, except 1857, was cotton as high as in 1839, when slaves cost not more than two-thirds or three-fourths as much as in 1858-60.[56] The absurdity of the

[53] Montgomery *Confederation,* Nov. 19, 1859.

[54] Quoted in 30 *Hunt's Merchants' Magazine* (April, 1854), 500.

[55] Quoted by Chambers, *Amer. Slavery and Colour,* 207.

[56] Hammond, *Cotton Industry,* 395; Phillips, *Amer. Negro Slavery,* table opposite 370.

actual condition was concisely expressed in the common phrase, " high-priced negroes and low-priced cotton ". " It is too much the custom for planters to anticipate their crops in dollars and cents, and shape their liabilities accordingly ", said the Mobile *Register,* January 19, 1859. " The demand for laborers is good, but we do not think that it justifies the exorbitant and high rates which prevail, although the South was never more solvent than now."

But the trumpeting of high prices and the joy of imagining that slavery was triumphant and that negroes would enrich their owners—these continued unrestrained. What! " Slavery not profitable "! " Times hard "! Consider these prices:—

" HARD TIMES.—As an evidence of the extreme *hardness* of the times, we may mention the negroes sold from the block in this city, on Tuesday last (twelve months' credit,) at the following figures: one negro man for $1,512; negro boy $1,111; old negro man $899; old do., $850; one woman, diseased, $750; with several other negroes, ranging above $1100. At McDonough, Henry county, on the same day, we are told that upwards of $50,000 worth of negro and other property was sold at enormously high prices." [57]

" HIGH PRICES FOR SLAVES.—Nine negroes belonging to the estate of A. D. Alexander, comprising a boy, 3 men and 5 girls, were sold at Charlotte C. H., on Monday last. They brought $10,530, an average of $1,170 cash—which considering the ' hard times ', we think a *crack* sale." [58]

The innumerable reports of high prices had made doubts seem preposterous. William J. Grayson, who had convinced thousands that he had done for slavery what Long-

[57] *American (Griffin) Union.*—Savannah *Republican,* Jan. 13, 1858.

[58] Petersburg, Va., *Express.*—Savannah, Ga., *Republican,* Jan. 13, 1858.

Reporting that at an administrator's sale " an ordinary boy ", 20, brought $2,000, and one of 23, $1,800, the *Central Texan* asked " Who complains of hard times? "—Austin *State Gazette,* Feb. 19, 1859.

The high prices obtained at Marshal Court House were prefaced thus: " In proportion with the assaults of free labor, has risen and rises the value and influence of the products of the slave, and of [the] consequence of the slave himself."—22 *De Bow* (1857), 439.

fellow and Whittier had done for freedom[59]—said with
equal truth and satisfaction: " While slavery is attacked,
the slave rises in value. The property assailed is estimated more highly every day. The confidence of the garrison steadily increases under the enemy's fire."[60] That
was brilliant and conclusive, then. " While in Montgomery on Monday we saw negroes sold and hired at tremendous high rates ", proudly reported the editor of the
Atlanta *Intelligencer*. " Judging from all the above the
' irrepressible conflict ' of Mr. Seward has not as yet arrived, or made such serious headway as to lessen the value
of the ' peculiar institution '. * * * If ' trifling politicians '
think she [the South] loves the Union more than her own
Institutions, and will sacrifice the latter to preserve the
former, why they are mistaken—that's all."[61] Nearly a
century and a quarter earlier it had been remarked: " Negroes may be said to be the bait proper for catching a
South Carolina planter, as certain as beef [is] to catch a
shark. How many under the notion of 18 months credit,
had been tempted to buy more negroes than they could
possibly expect to pay [for] in 3 years! "[62] Long before
1860 that bait was good all over the lower South.

This was not only the excitement of speculation based on
an infatuation about prices that were largely ficticious;
it was a widespread economic and social aberration.
" There is a perfect fever raging in Georgia now on the
subject of buying negroes ", said the Milledgeville *Federal Union* of January 17, 1860. " Several sales which
have come under our eye within a month past afford an
unmistakable symptom of the prevalence of a disease in
the public mind on this subject. * * * Men are borrowing

---

[59] His long poem *The Hireling and the Slave* was very popular. It and a
copy of the Bible were the only books " Belle Brittan " could find on the boat
between Savannah and Charleston in 1858.—*On a Tour* etc. 126.

[60] 28 *De Bow*, 48.

[61] Quoted by Phillips, 2 *Plantation* etc., 72.

[62] *Ibid.*, 51.

money at exorbitant rates of interest to buy negroes at exorbitant prices.'' Slaves were then twenty-five per cent higher, " with cotton at ten and one-half cents than they were two or three years ago, when it was worth fifteen or sixteen cents. Men are demented upon the subject. A reverse will surely come.'' This disorder was aptly called " the negro-fever ".[63] It was contagious and had spread like talk of secession.

[63] Augusta *Chronicle and Sentinel*, Jan. 21, 1860; Wilmington Daily *Journal*, Jan. 26, 1860; Phillips, 2 *Plantation* etc., 73.

CHAPTER XVII

THE STATUS OF SLAVE-TRADING

In the Old South, slave-trading was as lawful as any other business. To have stopped it in any State would have made slavery there moribund. If the National Government had at any time before 1861 forbidden the interstate slave-trade, secession would have been precipitated in every Southern State, except Delaware. This was because such a prohibition would have been considered destructive of what was generally regarded as a vital part of the social and economic organization of the South. Slave-trading and slavery were mutually necessary.

The Charleston *Mercury's* assertion—that " slaves * * * are as much and as frequently articles of commerce as the sugar and molasses which they produce "—and Dr. Wyeth's opinion—that " the selling and buying of negroes was as common in the cotton-belt of the South at this period as the buying or selling of horses or cattle, or any other merchantable live product "—these truly described the general prevalence of slave-trading.

Forrest's joint biographers called it " one of the strangest of paradoxes " that the Southern people, " while earnestly impressed with the belief that not only the prosperity of their section was linked with the preservation of slavery, but also the perpetuity of those traits of which they were proudest ", nevertheless " looked with disfavor upon traffic in slaves. Selling their slaves at pleasure or purchasing of the dealer, they were yet prone to disparage his avocation. This probably arose, at first, from personal causes. But there were many dealers who overcame the prejudice by their individual worth and standing " * * *.[1] As has been noticed, Forrest illustrated this, and was benefited rather than hampered by his slave-

[1] Jordan & Pryor, *Forrest*, 26.

trading: having acquired riches and popularity by it, he was elected alderman.

A Southern judge, a slaveholder and more than 40 years old when the Civil War began, in his ripe old age wrote to the present author: "In the South the calling of a slave-trader was always hateful, odious, even among slave-holders themselves. This is curious, but it is so." A trader's children recovered, to some extent, but there was ever a *thin* cloud resting on them, which they could not get rid of. We had two or three slave-traders in this section, and, although their children were taken into society, it was no uncommon thing to hear the sly remark— "his or her father was a slave driver". After naming one of these traders, who became rich, the judge continued: "He made, by his cruelty to his slaves, an unenviable reputation. His daughters—three of them—all married (in this town) gentlemen of excellent character and of excellent families. Two of them live here now, and are taken into the best society, and are worthy to be, yet they can never outlive the memory of their father's calling, however excellent they may be." Had this father been a notoriously dishonest and cruel overseer or a cheating and drunken factor, however, prosperous and rich, the remarks about him would probably have been more bitter and not less injurious to his children. Thus the criterion seems to have been not slave-trading, but chiefly the qualities and traits of the trader; yet that was not all.

Enlightened persons, except in the Southern States, and many even there, condemned slavery and were shocked by some of the public manifestations of slave-trading, and it was impossible for anyone to make a rational defense of them. Although these worst features could not be prohibited without weakening slavery, they could be and were condemned morally. Accordingly there was cultivated a firm belief that these generally condemned worst features comprised all the objectionable slave-trading there was, and that whatever was bad about it was hated by all good Southerners as well as by the rest of the civilized world. If for a moment we accept this reasoning and ignore facts to the contrary, it will be interesting to notice how this belief served as a shield. /

(All the objectionable features of slave-trading were assumed to be typified by the supposed acts and the character of what was popularly called a " nigger trader ". The conception was not, of course, an accurate composite: no one person possessed half of the alleged traits, and yet few regular traders were without some of them. This " nigger-trader " was a brutal, keen speculator, a ruthless sharper. He watched for bargains at the public and the private jails; he started the bidding at the auctions, but dropped out if there was ambitious competition, for he would purchase at only the lowest prices and sell at the highest. He often had, and always pretended to have, ample cash, but seemed meanly sparing of it.[2] He was conspicious and inquisitive in public places and on public occasions—on sale-days and during the session of the county court, at the musterings, the barbecues, the joint debates and even the Fourth of July celebrations, where " liberty ", " freedom " and " State sovereignty " were on every tongue —collecting scraps of news or gossip about the fortunes and misfortunes of farmers, planters, professional men and merchants that might be induced to buy or compelled to sell slaves.) He was intrusive and impertinent privately, eager to argue that a certain sum of money would be much more useful than the services of some boy or girl, cook or hostler, or that a " breeder ", a carpenter, a blacksmith, a drayman, a barber or a hair-

---

[2] W. Ballard Preston, a Va. delegate to the Commercial Convention in Montgomery, in 1858, said that he had recently attended a sale of an estate in Va. where 86 slaves were sold at an average of $702; but that only five of them were bought by traders, although 16 traders were present, with half a million dollars in their pockets.—24 De Bow, 595. He did not tell how he knew the amount of their cash.

dresser would surely be a good investment. He bubbled over with assurances and recent instances designed to relieve all doubts and to encourage all expectations, whether he wished to buy or to sell, although his largest profits often came from children separated from their mothers, or *vice versa,* and the palming off of unsound or vicious slaves as " prime " and " of good character ". To planters able to buy, he was obsequious; before slave-owners needing cash, or plain farmers, mechanics or tradesmen that had saved it so as to join the slaveholding class, he posed as benevolently willing to furnish what was desired. He negotiated as secretly as any hypo-critical master wished, and hastened away at night, so as to prevent sad partings and escape public notice, but treated his purchases like so many sheep or refractory cattle. Imagine a compound of an unscrupulous horse-trader, a familiar old-time tavern-keeper, a superficially complaisant and artful, hard-drinking gambler and an ignorant, garrulous, low politician, and you will get a con-ception that resembles the Southern ante-bellum notion of the " nigger-trader ".[3]

A trader, or any other person, suspected of having even part of these qualities was, of course, shunned and re-garded with disgust. A pawnbroker, a drover, a " money-shark " or a peddler with like traits would have been shunned still more. Visitors to the South were con-tinually told that " all traders were hated by respectable persons " and " could never go into society ". This seemed to imply that, except for their business, their social standing might have been good. In fact, no livery-

---

[3] When going down the Mississippi River Thomas Hamilton often had to sit at table next to a slave-trader, who had " the soul of a brute ". " He ate, he drank, he voided profusion of tobacco juice, he swallowed brandy every half hour of the day, and passed three-fourths, both of day and night, in gambling * * * [yet] no one on board talked about freedom so loudly or so long as this slave-dealer."—*Men and Manners in America,* 332-33. See also Hundley, *Social Relations* etc., 139 ff.

stable-keeper, no petty merchant, no common mechanic, whatever his virtues, his prosperity or his public-spirit, could " go into society "; and quite apart from their occupation most regular slave-traders were much less fit " to go into society ". No person of dignity would have thought of drinking with a shoemaker or a blacksmith although they were not " hated ". But the honest and clever large trader—about in proportion to his business, and therefore in proportion as he deserved to be " hated ", if all trading was hateful—provided wine and spirits for his callers and clients, who welcomed the courtesy. His advertisements were in the city directories and the best newspapers, and were often given special notices. He was a middleman, obtaining from old masters what he disposed of to new: the masters sold and bought; he bought and sold. He had friendly business relations with planters, farmers, bankers and merchants of all kinds, and was well spoken of. Many besides Austin Woolfolk and Forrest publicly and without offense appealed to and thanked their " patrons and friends "; and the most prosperous general agents, as has been shown, advertised with lists of the names of highly respectable citizens for whom they had hired out slaves. In plantation management the blame for whatever went wrong was usually put on the hired overseer. This relieved the planter of all moral responsibility. Likewise the " nigger trader " was made the scapegoat for the conspicious evils of slave-selling, while the large traders, the small speculators and occasional sellers for gain or current expenses, the " brokers ", the auctioneers, the general agents, the commission merchants and others were virtually ignored. Thus there were traders and traders besides " nigger traders ".

Apart from the opponents of slavery, numerous in every Southern State, the only persons that " hated traders " of all kinds were slaves, the " hate " being mainly fear, for a trader betokened separation from kindred and old associations, and a dreaded uncertainty. Slave mothers cautioned their children to keep out of sight of everyone suspected of being a trader or his agent; and they frightened unruly pickaninnies into obedience by saying: " De spekilatah is comin' and I'ze gwine ter let 'im hab yo', sho '! " [4]

When E. S. Abdy was at a hotel in Warrenton, Virginia, a very attentive resident told him how happy and contented the slaves were, and pointed out with abhorrence a rich trader who had long lived there but, it was alleged, was not recognized by any respectable person.[5]   It was not explained how he could have grown rich in that very respectable community unless many masters had sold slaves to him. A few hours by stage brought Abdy to Orange Court-House, of which he wrote:

" I now found that the hotel, where we had breakfasted most luxuriously, was kept by a ' trader '; who, so far from sharing the fate of his brother-merchant at Warrenton, had all the profits of the business without its odium; was in high favor with visitors from the South, and was not a little respected by his neighbors. His gains from this diabolical traffic must be enormous; as he has been known to make a thousand dollars in the course of a week, by buying and selling his fellow-creatures, as bullocks are disposed of in Smithfield-market." [6]

According to the best contemporary information in Baltimore, Austin Woolfolk—" the justly celebrated "— had made himself very rich by the trade. Professor E. A. Andrews's explanation was: " The business is conducted by him, and by the other regular traders, in such a manner, that there is never any suspicion of unfairness in regard to their mode of acquiring slaves." Andrews was credibly informed that Woolfolk, instead of being a demon, was " a most mild and indulgent master, and an upright

[4] Milly Edmondson said:—" I never see a white man come on to the place that I didn't think, ' There, now, he's coming to look at my children '; and when I saw any white man going by I've called in my children and hid 'em, for fear he'd see 'em and want to buy 'em."—*Key*, 156.

[5] Abdy, 2 *Journal* etc., 209-10. This trader was probably a member of the firm of J. M. Saunders & Co., agents of Franklin & Armfield.

[6] *Ibid.*, 215.

and scrupulously honest man ", whose word was implicitly trusted. After extensive inquiries in different cities Andrews wrote: " I am convinced * * * that the traders exhibit more proofs of humanity in their dealings, than a large portion of those from whom they purchase." [7] An unusually liberal, thrifty but uneducated small planter in northern Mississippi considered some of the slave-dealers honorable men; " *high-toned gentlemen*, as ever he saw, some of 'em was ".[8] A clergyman testified in the Bolton trial that for fifteen years he had been acquainted with the murdered McMillan—who kidnaped and sold the free negro—and that his character was supposed to be good. " I never knew McMillan to be rejected from respectable society. I have walked with him in the street without feeling disgraced by it. It is true that he was a tavern-keeper and a slave-trader—occupations not much esteemed there." [9]

The most successful large slave-traders held their heads high, confidently proclaiming their own virtues and admitting no sins. They welcomed visitors, even Abolitionists, to their pens so that their good qualities might become widely known. Many others besides the tender-hearted John Busk of Baltimore and Corbin Thompson and Bernard M. Lynch of St. Louis pretended to be almost missionaries of humanity. They were masters of cant, and supplied their patrons with ready-made excuses. Slave-dealers with comfortable jails advertised the fact and let negroes outside come at least to the gate to see their kindred and friends, clean and well-dressed, cheered by instrumental music, song and games, and luxuriating in well-fed idleness. When slaves were out after curfew and wished to escape arrest and punishment, some traders would receive them for the night, treat them well, advise

[7] *Slavery* etc., 80, 81, 152. [8] Olmsted, *Back Country*, 153.
[9] Memphis *Appeal*, Apr. 7, 1858. Mrs. McMillan testified that her husband kept his slaves in the basement of his kitchen.—*Ibid.*

their masters in the morning and make only a slight charge, if any. Whatever would spread among slaves a good opinion of such traders was likely to be employed. One of the most effective tricks was to put out decoys to tell of the advantages of being bought by this kind-hearted trader, who made a specialty of finding good homes for " servants ". Respectable masters did not like to have it known that they sold their slaves to traders; but if slaves were told that misfortune would compel their sale, that they might choose any purchaser that would pay a fair price, and if they chose a trader that " wanted them for servants for a rich planter " in Alabama or Mississippi— that precluded all reproach, for it could be said that the slaves had chosen their future master, happily a good planter. That was satisfactory to all in the beginning and might even be true, although not the whole truth. In any case, there was considered to be no semblance of " hated " slave-trading about it.

Hope H. Slatter was a good example of the thoroughly sophisticated large trader. He may have been surpassed by others, but his traits are worth noticing. In 1841, the poet Whittier and Joseph Sturge, an English fellow-Quaker, called on Slatter, then the largest slave-merchant in Baltimore.[10] He received them courteously and soon showed that he knew human nature and the virtue of soft answers and moral airs. He told them that his mother had for fifty years been a member of the Methodist church; that he had been reared accordingly and, although not a church-member, had never sworn an oath nor committed an immoral act in his life; that no one was more in favor of compensated emancipation, but he held that while the law permitted the trade, slave-selling was no worse than slaveholding; that he had freed his head-slave's wife and had promised to free him—who was so reliable that the business and jail were frequently left to

[10] *Ante* pp. 38-39.

his care for weeks—if he continued to conduct himself well a few years longer; that he (Slatter) never divided families, but, of course, could not control what happened before he bought or after he sold; that slaves often came to him and asked to be purchased, and by complying he was not infrequently the means of transferring them from bad to good masters; that when he had any suspicion that a negro offered to him was not a slave, he had the case investigated by the antislavery man that accompanied Whittier and Sturge. To employ such an investigator was shrewd business foresight; for if a reputable trader was detected in attempting to sell a free negro in lieu of a slave, a false title for a true, ruin was almost certain, as Isaac Bolton's case demonstrated. Had these gentle Quakers known that for years Slatter had been dealing in children of from seven years of age, they would have mixed several grains of salt with this self-praise. They went away much impressed, but soon received a rude shock: they were credibly informed, that Slatter had recently purchased a free negro's slave wife and child and had sent them off to New Orleans, after the free negro had offered to buy them and while he was struggling to obtain the money.[11]

In 1848 Slatter had a car-load of 50 slaves (of whom 20 or more were unsuccessful fugitives of the " Pearl ") at the old Baltimore & Ohio station in Washington, until after 1900 at the northeast corner of New Jersey Avenue and C street, northwest, only two or three squares from the Capitol. He was about to take them to Georgia to sell. An antislavery observer wrote with much feeling:

" About half of them were females, a few of whom had but a slight tinge of African blood in their veins, and were finely formed and beautiful. The men were ironed together, and the whole group looked sad and dejected. At each end of the car stood two ruffianly-looking personages, with large canes in their hands * * *. While observing this old, gray-headed villain [Slatter, who was standing in the middle of the car], * * *

[11] Sturge, 45-48.

the chaplain of the Senate entered the car,—a Methodist brother,—and took his brother Slatter by the hand, chatted with him for some time, and seemed to view the heart-rending scene before him with as little concern as we should look upon cattle. * * * Some of the colored people outside, as well as in the car, were weeping most bitterly. I learned that many families were separated. * * * A husband, in the meridian of life, begged to see the partner of his bosom. He protested that she was free—that she had free papers, and was torn from him, and shut up in the jail. He clambered up to one of the windows of the car to see his wife, and, as she was reaching forward her hand to him, the black-hearted villain, Slatter, ordered him down. He did not obey. The husband and wife, with tears streaming down their cheeks, besought him to let them converse for a moment. But no! a monster more hideous, hardened and savage, than the blackest spirit of the pit, knocked him down from the car, and ordered him away." [12]

Some of the Abolitionists were glad to believe that Joseph Bruin's treatment of the Edmondson children indicated that he had good qualities.[13] It does not appear that he made any pretensions of extra humanity. Where Abolitionists had cash to buy negroes out of slavery to prevent their being taken to the Southern market, he was willing to realize his profits at once and avoid all trouble and risk. His being one of the earliest subscribers to Dr. Bailey's *National Era* helped him to remain in negotiable relations with such philanthropists. And because a slave's unsuccessful attempt to escape to the North almost certainly resulted in his sale to a trader, Bruin was not acting contrary to his own interest when he was bondsman for a man arrested for assisting a runaway.

Hundley, who was thoroughly Southern and proslavery, showed the hypocrisy of the affectation of hatred of slave-traders, by saying that many rich and respectable men,

" who are bold as the boldest in denouncing the common, vulgar, ignorant Negro Trader, do yet privily advance the funds necessary to enable the latter to carry on his business, and usually take the lion's share of the profits. These are the respectable well-to-do Southern Yankees, who have

---

[12] Daniel Drayton, *Personal Memoir*, 59-60.
[13] *Key*, 165, 167.

a position in society to maintain, and who would as soon be considered guilty of highway robbery as of participating in the vulgar traffic of buying and selling slaves. Still they do not scruple to sell a man from his wife, provided they can do so on any plausible pretext, and have reason to believe that they will at the same time make a few pennies more by such heartlessness." [14]

The commission merchants nearly everywhere made it a part of their business to buy and sell slaves for others for a definite percentage. This, like the other branches of their business, was understood to be strictly regular; and because the planter had no fear that commission merchants would be either dishonest or make excessive charges, there was no prejudice against them. They did not go about the country buying or selling slaves, nor were they often seen with the slaves they handled, and they were not even thought of as slave-traders; but being such, in fact, it is not strange that some with ample cash invested it in the most profitable kind of slave-trading. If they had not kept their speculations secret, the planter would have feared being cheated—which was what had caused him to shun known speculators and to give orders for slaves to his commission merchant—and then he would have treated his commission merchant accordingly. It was the supposed dishonesty of the " nigger trader " quite as much as his objectionable personal traits, that caused him to be shunned and " hated ". Auctioneers and " brokers " were often patronized instead of regular slave-speculators, and were viewed quite differently. Principals and agents in such cases were alike interested in keeping the prejudice against " nigger-trading " turned away from their own

[14] *Social Relations in Our Southern States*, 145-46. "The slave-dealers cannot have been fiends in human form, for such would have gone speedily bankrupt. The social stigma laid upon them can hardly have been so stringent as tradition tells, for many a planter and perhaps most of the general merchants turned a trade on favorable occasion, and sundry citizens of solid worth and esteem can be identified as regular participants."— Phillips, *Old South*, 158.

transactions. And when the respectable large traders were dealt with, this prejudice was turned away from them also.

Honest and fairly humane trading of itself, especially if on a large scale, seems never to have lowered the standing of a man of good family, and it always improved that of men of humble origin. It was so, especially in Charleston, from early in the seventeenth century. Professor Wallace, admirable in his independence and lucidity, writes of the colonial period: " The importation of slaves, both on their own account and as agents for the ' American merchants ' of England, was * * * the practice of numbers of Charleston merchants of the highest business and social standing. Not only was there no moral condemnation of this crime against humanity, but the importer was entirely free from the social disadvantage which attaches to many occupations whose morality and necessity are universally recognized."[15] After tireless and very successful researches Miss Elizabeth Donnan says: " Of Charleston's [commission] merchants there were few, if any, whose names did not sooner or later appear affixed to notices of negro sales. Before the Revolution at least one hundred firms had offered cargoes for sale * * * . The negro merchants were men of substance and standing in the community." " Nothing can be more certain than that not the slightest social stigma rested upon these men [about half a dozen slave-merchants Pelatiah Webster met in Charleston] because of their trade."[16] The ex-

---

[15] Wallace, *Henry Laurens*, 74.

[16] 33 *American Historical Review* (July, 1928), 810, 811.

Advertisements that the present author has found in turning files of the newspapers mentioned, show that the commission merchants whose names follow engaged in the slave-trade in Africans, if not also in the "African trade":—

Ball, Jennings & Co.; [George and Josiah] Smith, [Daniel] De Saussure and [Edward] Darrell.—Phillips, *Am. Negro Slavery*, 41. This Daniel De Saussure was the father of the Chancellor of S. C.—*Memoir etc. Henry Wm. De Saussure*, p. 7 ff. (1841).

ceptional opportunities for gain, for becoming a planter
and for close contact with planters explain why this was.[17]
In the middle of the nineteenth century there were, presumably, very few if any merchants in Charleston that
had as good social standing as Louis D. DeSaussure,
Capers & Heyward and several other Broad or State

J. Vesey & Co., 27½ Bay, sold cargoes at Mrs. Dewees's yard, 43 Queen
st.—*S. C. Gazette and Genl. Advtr.*, Sept. 16-20, 1781.

A. Wilkinson & Co.—*Ibid.*, Jan. 13-15, 1784.

Gervais & Owen.—*Ibid.*, Feb. 21-24, 1784.

John Mitchell, "in Mr. Bourdeaux's yard, at No. 48 on the Bay".—
Gazette of State of S. C., June 10, 1784.

Daniel Bourdeaux.—*Ibid.*, June 17, 1784.

John Price & Co., Miller & Robertson, and Tunno & Cox were all agents for
African cargoes sold at Savannah.—*City Gazette* etc., July 4 and Aug.
26, 1796.

Laurens, about Dec., 1764, turned over most of his commission business
to Price, Hest & Head.—Wallace, *Laurens*, 69. McCrady, while ignoring that
Henry Laurens extensively dealt in African slaves—Miss Donnan says (33
Amer. Hist. Rev., 812) that he was "probably the most famous of all
Charleston slave dealers"—emphasized the fact that Gabriel Manigault
always rejected that branch of the commission-merchant's business; but he
refers to the fact that Joseph Wragg, the father of William, who had
a distinguished career in S. C., "was likewise a merchant. He dealt largely
in the slave trade, as the *Gazette* mentions in announcing his death".—
McCrady, *S. C.*, 1710-76, 102, 103, 107.

These were engaged in at least the domestic slave-trade:—

"HORT and WARLEY HAVE FOR SALE, A Number of very valuable and
handsome NEGROES (Just Imported) [perhaps from the West Indies].
Among whom are Sempstresses, Cooks, Washers and Ironers, and some Field
Slaves, which they will dispose of for Cash or Produce at Market Price."—
The Gazette of the State of South Carolina, Jan. 1, 1784.

Currie & Norris.—*Royal Gazette*, May 2-5, 1781.

John and Adam Tunno, 48 Bay.—*Ibid.*, Aug. 25-29, 1781.

Brian Cape, 84 Church street.—*Ibid.*, Dec. 19-22, 1781.

Blair & Wallace.—*Ibid.*, July 3, 1782.

Saml. Prioleau, jun., & Co.—*S. C. Gazette* etc., May 10, 1783.

Cudworth, Waller & Co. (They seemed to be doing the largest slave-trading
business.)—*S. C. Gazette* etc., May 17, 1783.

Smith, De Saussure & Darrell.—*S. C. Gazette* etc., July 15, 1783; *Gazette
of State of S. C.*, Oct. 4, 1784.

[17] In colonial days the commission on ordinary business was 5%, but on the
African trade it was 10% minus the expenditures for coasting fees, loading,
etc.—Wallace, *Laurens*, 75. Few could resist such percentages.

street slave-traders.[18]   Thomas Ryan and J. S. Riggs, although State street traders, were not only elected aldermen but were also chosen by their colleagues (including a Ravenel, three drygoods merchants, a factor and several mechanics) as members of the committee of three to edit the [real estate] *Census of Charleston for 1861.* One of the five trustees of the Unionville academy in Tennessee, where Wm. F. King taught school, was a prominent slave-trader.[19]   When traders prospered, were honest, thrifty and bought plantations, like Forrest, the Woolfolks, Isaac Franklin and many others, they enjoyed the essentials of respectability.[20]   The hiring out of slaves, whether by owners or their agents, resembled a distinction rather than a disgrace.   And Captain Joseph Bryan, Georgia's largest trader, who seems to have engaged in all branches of slave-trading—even receiving into his private jail one or more Africans unlawfully imported— was not put in the hated class, but maintained a good business and social position, for he was of an excellent family, popular and believed to be honest.   Had he notoriously acted like a typical " nigger-trader ", nothing could have preserved his high standing.

[18] The author learned from contemporaries of DeSaussure and Capers & Heyward that these men seemed never to have been thought of as traders, but merely as brokers, incidentally selling slaves "only in the settlement of estates", which was counted as good fortune.   One who as a boy had seen auctions at Ryan's Mart, and remembered DeSaussure as highly respected, had entirely forgotten it if he had ever heard that DeSaussure dealt in slaves. With Thomas N. Gadsden it was somewhat different: antislavery literature as early as 1839 made him notorious as a trader and erroneously alleged that he was the brother of Gen Jas. Gadsden.—[Theo. D. Weld] *Slavery As It Is,* 174.   Such notoriety would, of course, cause later believers in the tradition that all traders were hated to assume that Gadsden's standing must have been damaged.

[19] *Ante* p. 290; *Reminiscences,* 100.

[20] See *ante* p. 296, note, about Mason Harwell's respectability;   p. 131, about the "Business Mirror" in the Lexington, Ky., *Directory.*   "John R. White of Howard county [Mo.] was a wealthy planter of good repute who dealt in slaves", says Trexler, *Slavery in Mo.,* 47.   See also *ibid.* pp. 45, 46 for various opinions.

If honest and well-mannered traders had been hated, a judge of the highest character in Mississippi would hardly have volunteered the information that he had bought a slave of Forrest; nor would a judge in another State have written to the author: " He [a famous trader] was a personal friend of my father and first came to my attention .* * * when he purchased * * * my nurse Emaline, which intensely excited my childish indigation." Nor would those Virginia churches have paid their pastors for more than half a century by the hiring out of purchased slave girls and their numerous offspring. Nor would auctioneers, general agents, brokers and commission merchants so eagerly have engaged in slave-trading; nor would factors, bankers, investors and merchants, in their different ways, have been so ready to associate themselves with its financial operations. And how could it have been hateful to trade honestly in the most coveted and prestige-giving property, which guardians and trustees, by order of the courts, bought for widows and orphans? Moreover, if slave-trading, apart from the " nigger-trading " type, had been hateful, how could there have been such widespread curiosity about high prices and such eagerness to speculate by buying slaves on credit, confident that the rapid rise in price together with the natural increase would produce an enormous percentage of profit? It was almost exactly like the present-day purchasing of speculative stocks on margin, expecting that extra dividends and " split-ups " will soon result in great gain.

Not less conclusive was the attitude of Southern newspapers. " The printer " or " the editor " was a willing intermediary, a mediating agent, and, for small sales, was often preferred to the regular trader or the formal agent when secrecy and economy were desired. The leading journals gratefully received and conspicuously displayed advertisements of regular traders and others to sell, buy or hire out slaves. All favorable phases of slave-trading were of prime interest to readers and, therefore, were welcome subjects for the ready editorial pen.[21] The Savannah *Republican's* greeting to Joseph Bryan—" Good prices to the Captain and good homes to the negroes "[22] —and the Richmond *Enquirer's* editorial article about " Our Slave Market " demonstrated that slave-trading was recognized as both an honorable and an important business. The editor of the Atlanta *Intelligencer* seemed proud to be able to say that the trader in charge of 40 Africans brought in on the " Wanderer " was " Mr. Thack Brodnax, a gentleman whom we have long known ".[23] Leonidas W. Spratt, editor of the Charleston *Standard* and the great champion of reopening of the African slave-trade, said in the Southern Commerical Convention at Vicksburg in 1859, that the profits of that trade would compensate for the risks. " There is honor, also, and my friend Lamar already hoists the slave-trade flag and floats it from his masthead " * * *.[24] The Charleston *Mercury* of January 18, 1860, contained these six notices in immediate sequence: two referring to two gangs of slaves that had been advertised to be sold at the Mart that day; one about the presentation of bills against a certain French bark; another about a noon-day prayer-meeting; and two about the candidacies of Major Edward McCrady, Jr., the future historian, and of Colonel L. M.

---

[21] The Memphis *Eagle and Enquirer* carried an advertisement of, and reported the prices obtained by, a slave-trading auctioneer whose business was in the basement of its building.—Nov. 15, 1855.

The New Orleans *Picayune* advised its readers thus:

" N. Vignie, auctioneer, sells this day at the City Hotel, a No. 1 engineer, two calkers, and other slaves worthy of the attention of buyers."

" Planters and house keepers will do well to attend the sale at auction, this day, by Messrs. C. E. Girardey & Co., at 12 o'clock, at the City Hotel, of a choice lot of slaves, comprising field hands and house servants. See catalogues."—Respectively Jan. 12 and Oct. 17, 1860.

[22] *Ante* p. 224.

[23] *Ante* p. 360.

[24] 27 *De Bow*, 212.

Hatch for colonelcies of certain South Carolina regiments. In the Montgomery *Confederation* of January 15, 1859, the advertisement of S. N. Brown, one of the city's largest and best known regular traders appeared in the column next to and almost touching an advertisement of the " Alabama Bible House ", with the names of all its officers. And the first two items in the *Confederation's* column of city news, Sunday morning, January 8, 1860, were as follows:—

"BISHOP ELLIOTT.—This gentleman preaches today at the Protestant Episcopal Church."

"NEGROES AT PRIVATE SALE—Mr. M. J. Saffold offers some valuable negroes at private sale. See his advertisement."

Two days later the public was likewise advised that a certain person in Aberdeen, Mississippi, wished to sell 150 negroes and that Bishop Elliott had on Sunday " delivered a most eloquent sermon to a very large congregation ". This time the slave-advertisement came first.

Where such things were possible, frequent and passed without causing comment, honest traders without offen sive personal qualities could not have been hated. It all came virtually to this: whatever respectable persons thought needful in buying or selling slaves was not viewed as having any taint of " hated " slave-trading; yet it early became a fully credited tradition, implicitly accepted generation after generation, that " all traders were hated".

CHAPTER XVIII

ESTIMATES AS TO NUMBERS, TRANSACTIONS AND VALUE

To quote obviously extreme figures or guesses without discrediting them seems to approve them, when one ought to be mindful of the old witticism: " You say, ' Figures won't lie ', but you forget that liars will figure." And unless Solomon spoke with greatly mistaken haste, it is well to scrutinize figures, especially when they are called statistics and are used for propaganda.

Because there is hardly anything worthy of the name of statistics and bearing directly except on certain features of the domestic slave-trade at different times and places, it is all the more serious to give any standing to fanciful conjectures. The most nearly reliable and extensive bases for calculations about this trade are the United States decennial census reports of the population between 1790 and 1860.[1] Otherwise the general elements for mathematical precision do not exist. To obtain the prerequisites for a solvable problem one must employ some assumptions known to be inexact. The most that the circumstances permit will be to use relevant facts, probabilities and careful judgment, sometimes only careful guesses, so as to make reasonable, lucid speculations and estimates. One must use numerals because the problems are in them; but, of course, no amount of figuring can make *facts* or produce statistics; speculations necessarily remain such, however reasonable they may seem. Accordingly *statistics* and a *statistical* argument are expressly disclaimed. At best, this can be little, if any, more than a careful study in approximations.

---

[1] It is hoped that the table (opposite this page) of the slave population in the Southern States (and of their free negro population where the increase was considerable) will facilitate an understanding of the estimates. Delaware has been left out of the calculations as negligible.

SLAVE POPULATION IN THE SOUTHERN STATES.

	1790	1800	1810	1820	1830	1840	1850	1860
Ala.				41,879	117,549	253,532	342,844	435,080
Ark.				1,617	4,576	19,935	47,100	111,115
Del. [Delaware is not used because abnormal and unimportant.]								
Free Negroes	3,899	8,268	13,136	12,958	15,855	16,919	18,073	19,829
Slaves	8,887	6,153	4,177	4,509	3,292	2,605	2,290	1,798
Total	12,786	14,421	17,313	17,467	19,147	19,524	20,363	21,627
Fla.				......	15,501	25,717	39,310	61,745
Ga.	29,264	59,406	105,218	149,656	217,531	280,944	381,682	462,198
Ky.								
Free Negroes	114	739	1,713	2,759	4,917	7,317	10,011	10,684
Slaves	12,430	40,343	80,561	126,732	165,213	182,258	210,981	225,483
Total	12,544	41,082	82,274	129,491	170,130	189,575	220,992	236,167
La.			34,660	69,064	109,588	168,452	244,809	331,726
Md.								
Free Negroes	8,043	19,587	33,927	39,730	52,938	62,078	74,723	83,942
Slaves	103,036	105,635	111,502	107,397	102,994	89,737	90,368	87,189
Total	111,079	125,222	145,429	147,127	155,932	151,815	165,091	171,131
Miss.		3,489	17,088	32,814	65,659	195,211	309,878	436,631
Mo.								
Free Negroes			607	347	569	1,574	2,618	3,572
Slaves			3,011	10,222	25,091	58,240	87,422	114,931
Total			3,618	10,569	25,660	59,814	90,040	118,503
N. C.	100,572	133,296	168,824	204,917	245,601	245,817	288,548	331,059
S. C.	107,094	146,151	196,365	258,475	315,401	327,038	384,984	402,406
Tenn.	3,417	13,584	44,535	80,107	141,603	183,059	239,459	275,719
Texas.							58,161	182,566
Va.								
Free Negroes	12,866	20,124	30,570	36,883	47,348	49,842	54,333	58,042
Slaves	292,627	345,796	392,516	425,148	469,757	448,987	472,528	490,865
Total	305,483	365,920	423,086	462,031	517,105	498,829	526,861	548,907

—Census 1870, Population, pp. 7 and 6.

The general purposes here are: (1) to explain the method to be used, and to give various illustrations of it; (2) to test by it some estimates made by others, and (3) to attempt to estimate roughly the number of the slaves and of the transactions and the total value involved in the slave-trading for an average year during the 'fifties.

Maryland and Virginia were almost exclusively slave-exporting States. Texas was wholly an importing State; Florida and Arkansas were at first only a little less so. The Carolinas, Kentucky and Missouri early began exporting and increased it, while continuing importations in variously lessening degrees. Until after the Mexican War, Georgia did not export many, and Alabama, Mississippi and Louisiana imported almost exclusively—except when a few thousand were taken to Texas and interstate markets, like those of Mobile, Natchez and New Orleans, resold to neighboring States—but subsequently more and more slaves were removed from all those States to Arkansas and Texas in the hope of obtaining still cheaper land and more profitable opportunities to raise cotton.

Because of the movement of slaves out of or into each State, the precise natural increase in any State is not known; but the approximate natural increase in the whole South, especially during 1830-60, can easily be calculated. By omitting Delaware, as negligible, and by deducting from the slave population of 1850 the 58,161 in Texas, which did not belong with the natural increase of the South for 1840-50, we find that the increase from 1830 to 1840 was a trifle less than 24.2 per cent; from 1840 to 1850 it was a little more than 26.6 per cent, and from 1850 to 1860 it was a little more than 23.4 per cent. The much smaller movement of the slave population during 1840-50 than during 1830-40 and 1850-60 is supposed to have been the main cause of that decade's larger percentage of increase. Of course the percentage of natural increase was not exactly the same in any two States, but the variations were presumably slight. A large majority of the slaves taken to the Southwest were of the most reproductive ages, but the change of climate and the harder labor must have somewhat checked reproduction for a year or two. In Maryland, Virginia and Kentucky, where reproduction, instead of the crops, was the chief profit and the labor was comparatively light, the unfavorable severity of winter probably did not prevent the natural increase from equaling that of the Southwest.[2]

To estimate the number of slaves removed, between 1830 and 1840, from a wholly exporting State or taken into a wholly importing State, one should add to the slave population at the beginning of the decade the 24.2 per cent natural increase for the decade, or multiply by 1.242. If this sum (or product) is less than the actual slave population at the end of the decade, there were exportations; if more, there were importations. In case of exportations, the difference between the *natural* or prospective population of 1840 and the *actual* population of 1840 was apparently the sum of the exportations and the natural increase on them. Being unable to discover how many left annually, we must assume that the number was uniform; consequently, on an average, all exportations were out of the State five years. Accordingly their natural increase was only half of 24.2 per cent, 12.1 per cent. Knowing the sum of the exportations and their natural increase and that this increase was 12.1 per cent, we need only to divide that sum by 1.121 to learn the number of the apparent exportations. By deducting these exportations from that sum we get the number of the apparent natural increase. But in most States and decades, special influences required additions to or subtractions from such exportations and natural increase, in order to get closer approximations.

Virginia's slave population in 1830, . . . 469,757,
with a natural increase of 24.2 per cent, . . . 113,681,
should have risen, without exportations, to . . 583,438

[2] See *ante* p. 71 for Dew's opinion.

by 1840; but it was only . . . . 448,987, showing apparent exportations and their natural increase amounting to . . . . 134,451. As the difference between the natural and the actual slave population has been assumed to be the sum of the exportations and their increase, it is obvious that if there were emancipations and successful runaways, these with their increase should be deducted. Knowing that there were many such cases, but without information as to their number, we assume that there were at least 2,000. A 12.1 per cent natural increase added makes . . . . . 2,242. This subtracted from 134,451 gives . . . . 132,209, the supposed total of the exportations and their increase. By dividing 132,209 by 1.121 we get the estimated number of the exportations for the decade, ... 117,938,[3] or an annual average of nearly 11,800. The exports were probably less than that early in the 1830's—when Dew, Thomas Jefferson Randolph, Jesse Burton Harrison and others made their surprisingly good guesses [4]—much more in 1835 and 1836 and considerably less thereafter.

In violent contrast with these estimates was that alleged to have been repeated as hearsay by the Wheeling *Virginia Times:*

" We have heard intelligent men estimate the number of slaves exported from Virginia within the last twelve months [probably from the summer of 1835] at 120,000, each slave averaging at least $600, making an aggregate of $72,000,000. Of the number of slaves exported, not more than one-third had been sold, (the others having been carried by their owners who have removed) which would leave in the State the sum of $24,000,000 arising from the sale of slaves!" [5]

---

[3] The problem can be expressed by the following equation: $469,757 \times 1.242 - 448,987 - 2,242 [2,000 \times 1.121] \div 1.121 = 117,938.$

[4] Henry Berry estimated that 9,500 were exported annually (speech of Jan. 20, 1832, in the Virginia House of Delegates, p. 7) and Thomas Marshall thought the average about 10,800 (speech of Jan. 14, 1832, in Va. House of Delegates, p. 8).

[5] Quoted in 51 *Niles' Register* (Oct. 8, 1836), 83, without naming the date or the place of publication of the *Va. Times.*

13

A longer quotation, without naming the place of publication, shows that this report of alleged estimates was only incidental (and all the more unreliable) to urging the establishment of numerous banks, for which, it was argued, ample capital was to be found in " the immense amount of money that has been brought into the State by the sale of slaves ".[6] When less than 120,000 were exported during the decade, it is ludicrous to suppose that 120,000 left the State in one year.

Following the method already explained—taking the respective natural increase for each decade and deducting 2,000, with respective increase, for runaway and emancipated slaves, we find that during 1840-50 the exportations were 82,632, or about 8,200 annually; that during 1850-60 they were 80,572, or slightly more than 8,000 annually.[7] Thus according to the method employed, Virginia's exportations during the three decades 1830-60—117,938, 82,632 and 80,572—seem to have been 281,142, or an annual average of 9,371.

It is equally easy to estimate the importations into exclusively, or almost exclusively, buying States. Without

---

[6] Quoted in "Fourth Annual Report Am. Anti-Slavery Soc.", 2 *Quarterly Anti-Slavery Mag.* (July, 1837), 409.

Apparently following Theo. D. Weld's *Am. Slavery As It Is*, 184, (New York, 1839) or *Slavery and the Internal Slave Trade* (London, 1841), pp. 12-13, both documents of the Amer. Anti-Slavery Soc., many scholars, including J. R. Spears (*Amer. Slave-Trade*, 182-83), M. B. Hammond (*Cotton Industry*, 50-51), W. H. Collins (*Domestic Slave Trade*, 52) and G. S. Callender (*Selections from the Econ. Hist. U. S. 1765-1860*, 307), have accepted this estimate as a valuable historical opinion given by the Wheeling. *Va. Times.* The Librarian of the Wheeling (now W. Va.) Public Library and the State Librarian of Va. have each very obligingly advised the author that they have searched in vain for evidence that a *Virginia Times* was ever published in Wheeling. The Richmond *Va. Times* is the only one of which any trace has been found.

[7] These equations show the problems:—

1840-50: 448,987 × 1.266 — 472,528 — 2,266 [2,000 × 1.133] ÷ 1.133 = 82,632.
1850-60: 472,528 × 1.234 — 490,865 — 2,234 [2,000 × 1.117] ÷ 1.117 = 80,572.

The deductions would be larger but for allowances made for the recapture of runaways and for kidnaped free negroes sold into slavery.

other influences, natural increase at 24.2 per cent would
have raised Mississippi's slave population of

1830, ... 65,659,
to 81,548
by 1840, but it was 195,211,
showing importations and increase amounting to 113,663.
Probably at least 1,000 were exported. These with their
12.1 per cent increase, making 1,121,
would raise the 113,663 to . . . . 114,784.
Dividing this sum of the apparent importations and their
increase by 1.121, we obtain the number of the estimated
importations, ... 102,394,
or an annual average of 10,239.

In the next two decades Mississippi's exportations, especially to Texas and Arkansas, were much larger, presumably at least 3,000 during 1840-50 and not less than
8,000 during 1850-60. By the same method, using the slave
populations and the supposed exportations, each with the
appropriate percentage of increase, it is supposed that the
importations during 1840-50 were 58,375, or about 5,800
annually, and for 1850-60 were 56,560, or about 5,600
annually.[7a]

Much like the estimate of the *Virginia Times*, and about
as widely and unwisely credited, was that attributed in 1837
to the Natchez *Courier* " of recent date ", saying that the
States of Alabama, Arkansas, Louisiana and Mississippi
had imported 250,000 slaves in 1836.[8] The total slave
population in 1830 of these then almost wholly importing
States was . . . . 297,372.

[7a] The problems may be indicated as follows:—
  1840-50: 195,211 × 1.266 subtracted from 309,878 + 3,399 [3,000 × 1.133] ÷
  1.133 = 58,375.
  1850-60: 309,878 × 1.234 subtracted from 436,631 + 8,936 [8,000 × 1.117] ÷
  1.117 = 56,560.

[8] 2 *Quarterly Anti-Slavery Mag.* (1837), 411. *Slavery and the Internal
Slave Trade,* 13, made a direct but dateless quotation. The use of quotations
from newspapers without giving the dates was very common in those days;
see H. C. Carey's *The Slave Trade, Domestic and Foreign,* 112-15.

A natural increase of 24.2 per cent would have
raised it by 1840 to 369,366;
but it had actually become   637,130,
which showed importations and increase of . . 267,794.
The exportations (mainly to Texas) with their increase
probably amounted to at least . . . . . .   5,000.
By adding these two figures we obtain the total of the importations and their increase, ...   272,794.
Dividing this by 1.121 gives the estimated importations for
the decade, ...   243,348,
nearly 7,000 less than the alleged number of the importations in one year!

The exportation of slaves from Kentucky has also been
erroneously represented. Much as Jesse Burton Harrison
welcomed Dew's estimate about Virginia's exportations,
so Cassius M. Clay, an antislavery leader, welcomed that
of Robert Wickliffe, a proslavery politician, made in a
speech in the Kentucky legislature in 1840—that over
60,000 slaves had been exported in the seven years 1833 40,
or 8,571 annually. For different reasons the figures suited
both sides. Apparently thinking them too large, but inad-
vertently employing the word *sales* instead of *exportations*,
Professor Asa Earl Martin wrote: " The evidence, however, seems to indicate that such sales exceeded 5,000 per
year ".[9] Even this was excessive.

For the three decades 1790 to 1820 Kentucky's importations—counting the natural increase of each decade at 25
per cent, instead of the excessive percentages of the
United States Census, which include all importations, legal
and illegal, from abroad and Florida's 15,501, counted in
1830—were respectively, in round numbers, about 22,000,
26,000 and 23,000. Similar figuring, *without counting
any exportations*, shows that Kentucky's importations and
their increase during 1820-30 were . . . . .   6,798.
Presumably the exportations and their increase were not

[9] Martin, *Anti-Slavery Movement in Ky. prior to 1850*, 89.

less than 3,375,
which would raise the 6,798 to . . . . . . 10,173.
Dividing by 1.125 gives the apparent importations
as 9,042,
less whatever the number of the emancipated and successful runaway slaves.

But it is the exportations during 1830-40 that are to be
estimated. The greater prices and agricultural attractions
in Alabama, Mississippi, Louisiana and Missouri were lessening Kentucky's importations and augmenting its exportations. Its slave population in 1830, 165,213,
with a natural increase of 24.2 per cent, should have
become 205,194
by 1840, but it was only 182,258,
which indicates exportations and their increase,
without counting the importations, amounting to 22,936.
From 1833, importations were forbidden, except by immigrants coming with their slaves and by residents obtaining title " by will, descent, distribution, or marriage, or
gift in consideration of marriage ".[10] Residents and
traders, in anticipation of the prohibition of 1833, may have
imported 2,000 and thereafter have smuggled in not less
than 1,000. During the decade 1,000 more may have come
from inheritances etc., and actual settlers may have
brought in 1,000, making the total importations 5,000, which
the natural increase for five years would have raised
to . . . . 5,605.
This would make the apparent exportations and their
increase . . . . 28,541.
Our calculations have assumed that more than the natural increase was evidence of importations and that less
denoted exportations. In a slave State the increase of free
negroes beyond a natural percentage signified that there
had been emancipations. These lessened the slave popu-

[10] See *ante* p. 272.

lation and seemed to indicate exportations but, of course, were not. To correct this discrepancy they must be deducted from exportations. Kentucky's free negro population of 1830, ... 4,917, would normally have increased by 1840 to . . . 6,106, but it was actually . . . . 7,317, showing a surplus of 1,211, made up of emancipated and successful runaway slaves and their increase. All these had remained in Kentucky. Probably there were enough more on the other side of the Ohio to make the total 2,500. Subtracting this number from 28,541 we obtain the number of the exportations and their increase 26,041. Dividing this by 1.121 gives the number of the exportations during 1830-40, ... 23,230, or 2,323 annually—not one-third as much as Wickliffe's estimate and less than half that of Professor Martin.

Kentucky's slave population of 1840, 182,258, with an increase of 26.6 per cent, should have become . . 230,738 by 1850, but it was only . . . . 210,981, or . . . . 19,757 less. As the prohibition against residents buying and importing for use was not repealed until 1849, perhaps their lawful and all unlawful importations did not amount to more than 2,000, and the importations by settlers and from inheritances etc. may each have been about 1,000, thus making a total of about 4,000. These with their natural increase amounted to about 4,532 and raised the apparent exportations to . . . . 24,289. The free negro population of 1840, 7,317, would normally have increased to 9,263, but it was 10,011, or 748 more. Probably there were enough more, with increase, north of the Ohio to require a deduction of . . . . 1,500, which would reduce the exportations and their increase to . . . . 22,789. This divided by 1.133 gives the actual exportations as . . . . 20,113, or an annual average of about 2,000. If this seems too low an estimate, it should be remembered that there was a general decline in the movement of the slave population in that decade.

Kentucky's slave population in 1850, 210,981, with
a 23.4 per cent increase, should have become . . 260,350
in 1860, but it was only 225,483,
showing. apparent exportations and natural increase amounting to . . . . 34,867.
Although there were no longer any restrictions on importations, except for sale, it is doubtful, on account of greater attractions to Missouri and especially to Texas, if Kentucky's importations of all kinds were more than 4,000 (half of the number being involved in slave-trading), which a natural increase of 11.7 per cent would raise to   4,468.
This added to 34,867 indicates apparent exportations and increase amounting to . . . . 39,335.
The Kentucky constitution of 1850 provided that the general assembly should pass laws to prevent slaves from remaining in the State after emancipation. This was complied with in 1851 and 1852.[11] The effect is shown by the fact that the free negro population of 1850, 10,011, which ought to have increased by 1860 to 12,353, was actually only 10,684, which shows that 1,669 expected to be in Kentucky were elsewhere. Except those that were increase, most may have been negroes that had obtained their freedom in a previous decade and had been frightened away. In any case, the decrease gives no clue to the number of runaway and emancipated slaves during 1850-60. As the laws and the growing sentiment against free negroes may have increased the number of successful runaways and not lessened that of emancipations, it seems reasonable to assume that they and their increase were as numerous as in the previous decade, ... 1,500.
Subtracting 1,500 from 39,335, we get the supposed total

[11] 1 Catterall, 276.

of the exportations and their increase, . . . 37,835;
and dividing this by 1.117 gives the number of the exportations, 1850-60, ... 33,871,
or an annual average of nearly . . . . . 3,400.
As in Maryland, the growth of a moral sentiment against
slavery was probably increasing emancipations, at least
by wills, and warning needy slaveholders that it would be
best to sell for export while prices were high.

In 1850, ex-Governor James H. Hammond, wishing to
show how seriously South Carolina had suffered on account of the removal of whites and slaves, argued
that 83,000
slaves, 8,300 annually, had been taken out of the State
between 1830 and 1840, and as many during the next decade.[12] He employed the excessive United States Census
rate for 1820-30, about 30 per cent, instead of the average
rates—24.2 per cent for 1830-40, and 26.6 per cent for 1840-
50. He would have gone still farther afield if he had not
overlooked the fact that the slaves imported from other
States—presumably fully 10,000 during 1830-40, when the
Neals and others were regularly taking their coffles to
South Carolina, 6,000 during 1840-50, and 4,000 during
1850-60—were additions to the population and, with their
respective five-year natural increases, entered into the
problems. South Carolina's 315,401
slaves in 1830, with 24.2 per cent increase, should have
become 391,728
by 1840, but there were only 327,038,
that is 64,690
less. This is the apparent total of the exportations and
their increase. But if there were 10,000 importations, with
their 12.1 per cent increase, we must add . . 11,210,
which raises the actual total to . . . . . 75,900.
This divided by 1.121 gives . . . . . . 67,707,[13]

[12] 8 De Bow, 502, 516.
[13] 1830-40: 315,401 × 1.242 — 327,038 + 11,210 [10,000 × 1.121] ÷ 1.121
= 67,707.

the number of the exportations, or an annual average of
about 6,700
(without making a small deduction for emancipated and
runaway slaves), instead of Hammond's 8,300. By the
same process, using the appropriate figures for the respective decades, the total exportations for 1840-50 seem to
have been . . . . 31,636,[14]
or an annual average of 3,163; and for 1850-60, 69,052,[15]
or an annual average of 6,905, both without any deductions.

During 1850-60 South Carolina exported slightly less
than 18 per cent of its slave population of 1850, to Virginia's slightly more than 17 per cent; but Virginia, with
a much larger population, retained the lead, for it surpassed South Carolina by about 11,520 exportations during the decade.

A committee of the South Carolina House of Representatives, to whom was referred what Governor Adams had
said in his message of 1856 about reopening the African
slave-trade, estimated in its report, 1857, that 234,638
slaves were exported from Maryland, Virginia, Kentucky,
North Carolina and South Carolina during 1840-50. That
was supposed to represent all the slaves that those States
had been able to spare, 1840-50, for the increasing demands
of planting, and high prices were regarded as a demonstration of a very insufficient supply. The more numerous
and higher priced the exported slaves in the past, the more
obvious the need of cheap Africans to extend and render
more profitable the production of cotton, rice and sugar,
and to give the South more political power to protect slavery. In estimating the 234,638 the committee figured the
natural increase at 30 per cent,[16] when 26.6 per cent should
have been used; they took the total slave population of

[14] *1840-50:* 327,038 × 1.266 — 384,984 + 6,798 [6,000 × 1.133] ÷ 1.133
= 31,636.

[15] *1850-60:* 384,984 × 1.234 — 402,406 + 4,468 [4,000 × 1.117] ÷ 1.117
= 69,052.

[16] Report of the committee, pp. 27-28.

the five States in 1840 and added 30 per cent; from the sum they subtracted the slave population in 1850 and concluded that the result was the number of the exportations, instead of being the total of the *exportations and their increase.* And there were no additions for importations in any State nor any deductions for emancipations and runaways. The net result was that their estimate was more than 50,000 excessive, according to the method employed here.

Thomas Ellison, a British authority on the cotton trade and the author of a careful study of slavery in connection with the economic and political history of the United States, estimated that during the decade 1850-60 Alabama, Arkansas, Florida, Georgia, Mississippi, Louisiana and Texas imported [from the other States] more than 263,000 slaves, worth about $1,000 each—a total of $263,000,000.[17] He added the correct natural increase of 23.4 per cent to the slave population of these States in 1850 and subtracted the sum from their population in 1860; but, like the South Carolina committee and many other persons that have dealt with these questions, he concluded that the *difference* indicated the *importations,* instead of the *importations plus the natural increase on them.* This oversight caused a mistake of . . . . 27,665. He also overlooked the smugglings from Cuba and Africa, which with their increase may possibly have amounted to a few thousand, at most . . . . 5,000.[18] Accordingly his estimate of 263,000 was . . . 32,665

---

[17] *Slavery and Secession in America, Historical and Economical* (London 1861), 223. He used the words "imported" and "paid", but the context clearly shows that he had in mind the whole number and value of the slaves annually brought into these cotton-producing States. His estimate is considered in this sense. The present author uses the Census figures, from which Ellison's vary somewhat; perhaps he wrote before the Census of 1860 was published.

[18] That is more than anyone has ever accounted for in a manner that will bear scrutiny. The author is familiar with, but discredits, the speculations and conclusions of Mr. Du Bois and Mr. Collins about the alleged vast numbers of Africans smuggled into the South during this and some previous decades. Apart from the " Wanderer "—for the " Clotilde " (*ante* p. 359 n.-

excessive and should have been . . . . . . 230,335.
Moreover, he must have been thinking of prices in 1859 and
1860 when he counted $1,000 an average price for importa-
tions of all ages; $800 would be a liberal average for the
decade. Thus the 230,335 at $800 each were worth $184,-
268,000,—$78,732,000 less than Ellison's estimate. And
this reduced estimate, like Ellison's original, entirely overlooks the slave-trading between these seven States, which
was considerable, as we shall see.

After quoting the Portsmouth, Virginia, *Transcript*
about the passing of carloads of slaves from the eastern
shore of Maryland and Delaware,[19] the Montgomery, Alabama, *Confederation* of January 13, 1859, said:

"We ourselves have observed the enormous influx of negroes upon the

---

60 n.) seems to have entirely escaped their notice—their conclusions about
smugglings during the 'fifties are based almost exclusively on rumors, hearsays,
expectations, sometimes mere canards or hoaxes, and on erroneous assumptions
that the fitting-out of slavers in the U. S. and the capture of these or others
with Africans and flying the U. S. flag meant that the cargoes were for the
Southern States, instead of for Cuba or Brazil. The following passages illustrate Mr. Collins's credulousness and method in making up figures:— " About
1860 it was stated that twenty large cities and towns in the South were depots
for African slaves and sixty or seventy cargoes of slaves had been introduced
in the preceding eighteen months. [Before accepting this rumor, published by
the American Anti Slavery Society, Mr. Collins should have tried to find some
of the alleged " twenty depots for African slaves " and some of the " sixty or
seventy cargoes ",—except that of the " Wanderer ", of which unquestionable
particulars were given in the leading newspapers.] It was estimated in 1860
that eighty-five vessels which had been fitted out from New York City during
eighteen months of 1859 and 1860, would [!] introduce from thirty thousand
to sixty thousand annually.

" From what has been said it seems to us certain that at least 270,000 slaves
were introduced into the United States from 1808 to 1860 inclusive. These
we would distribute as follows: Between 1808 and 1820, sixty thousand; 1820
to 1830, fifty thousand; 1830 to 1840, forty thousand; 1840 to 1850, fifty
thousand and from 1850 to 1860 seventy thousand. We consider these very
moderate and even low estimates."—*Domestic Slave Trade*, 19-20. 70,000
smuggled Africans " a very moderate and even low estimate " for 1850-60!
But when he came to make up his figures for that decade he was content with
" deducting 50,000 illicitly imported " (*Ibid.*, 65), which the present author
considers at least 45,000 excessive.

cotton and sugar growing regions for the last two months and more. We suppose that the daily shipments by the railroads from Augusta, south and west alone, have not averaged less than some two hundred during this time, and they are sitll coming at that, if not at a greater ratio. There never has been anything like it before. We think it would be a moderate estimate to say, that the negroes imported into the cotton States this season will be able to make 200,000 bales of cotton in the next crop."

In a few days the editor of the Mobile *Register* employed, perhaps only reëchoed, about the same expressions, except that he reported the average daily shipments of 200 as having continued for *three* months (which indicated 18,000), and, he added:

* * * "the tide of emigration by way of other points is proportionately as great. * * * We are unable to say in figures the number of slaves imported into the cotton States, this season, but if the calculation be true that the crop of 1859 will be increased 200,000 bales, in consequence of this additional labor, some reasonable estimate as to numbers may be made, by supposing that each hand will be equal to four bales—we will have 50,000 as the number." [20]

Undoubtedly it was such estimates that caused *Hunt's Merchants' Magazine* to say, late in 1860: " There are no statistics to show the actual numerical amount of this withdrawal [of slaves]. We have heard it stated at 60,000 annually from all the non-cotton slaveholding States." [21] Obviously this " annually " referred only to the conditions since the winter of 1858-59; and authority for this estimate, based on mere conjecture, was carefully reported as hearsay. Hearsay as to figures was likely to be very inaccurate, especially at that time of intense curiosity about high prices. Von Halle, whose dragnet caught about everything in books, pamphlets and periodicals, referred to, but did not quote, that magazine as if it had seriously estimated that 60,000 had been imported.[22] It seems not

[19] *Ante*, p. 291.
[20] *Register*, Jan. 19, 1859. The Savannah *Republican* of Feb. 3, 1859, quoted and commented on the *Register's* opinions without questioning them.
[21] 43 *Hunt's Mchts.' Mag.*, 642.   [22] *Baumwollproduktion*, 283.

improbable that as many as 60,000 slaves were taken to the cotton States during a single year near the end of the decade, when the movement was greatest, but not in any other year of that period; the difference is great.

No one has ever suggested a method for finding what proportion of the slaves transported from one State to another were taken by original masters or their heirs for their own use. When the *Virginia Times* supported the absurd opinion that 120,000 slaves had been removed from Virginia in one year, it unwisely surmised that " not more than one-third had been sold ".[23] About 1840, the executive committee of the American Antislavery Society thought that " by far the greater proportion, perhaps four-fifths or more " of the slaves sent out of the selling States were " supplied by the internal slave trade ".[24] Dew confidently said that " the largest portion of slaves sent out of Virginia is sent through the operation of our internal slave-trade ".[25] That was near the height of the prejudice in the Southwest against the interstate traders, when planters most commonly went to Maryland and Virginia to make their purchases, which was not counted as slave-trading. Collins, leaving out this important feature of the interstate trade,[26] believed that " at least three-fifths of the removals of slaves from the border slave States to those farther South from 1820 to 1850 were due to emigration " [i. e. transported by emigrants], but he later added that " it might be fair to reduce the number estimated to have been carried South by emigrants to one-third or one-half " during the 'fifties.[27] In 1859 Edmund Ruffin wrote that when slaves in Virginia were disposed

[23] *Ante*, p. 385.

[24] *Slavery and the Internal Slave Trade in the U. S.*, p. 13.

[25] *Ante*, pp. 71-72.

[26] " We have not taken into account the slaves brought by planters themselves independently of the traders."—*Domestic Slave Trade*, 62n.

[27] *Ibid.*, 62, 66-67.

of for debt etc. " nearly all sold must be sent abroad "—
to States where their labor would be profitable. " It is
supposed that the annual draft and deportation thus made
on our stock, already exceed in number all the increase in
slaves in Virginia by procreation." [28] This was an under-
statement, if he meant the condition in 1859, when he was
giving special publicity to his belief that it was unprofitable
to buy fieldhands for use in Virginia. From the evidence
—admittedly meager and largely circumstantial—that the
present writer has been able to find, he supposes that,
in the 'fifties, when the extreme prejudice against the
interstate traders had abated and their inadequate supplies were eagerly purchased, fully 70 per cent of the slaves
removed from the Atlantic and the border slave States to
the Southwest were taken after purchase or with a view to
sale, that is, were objects of slave-trading. Accordingly 70
per cent will be counted here in the long-range interstate
trade and less percentages for less remote interstate trading.

In agriculture it was the number of slaves that was
counted. In slave-trading it was the number of the sales
and the hirings that were significant: one slave sold five
times might be as important in the trade as five slaves each
sold once. Consequently the trade may best be measured
by transactions. Settling in a State with the slaves one
had reared or inherited did not involve any slave-trading.
If a user in one State purchased directly of an original
owner in a distant State, which was *relatively* seldom in
the 'fifties, there was but one transaction. If he purchased
from a large trader, there were at least two transactions,
and as many more as the transactions back to the original
owner. The large interstate traders would have preferred
to buy from estates of planters as often as they sold to
planter-users in the Southwest, if slaves of such estates
had not usually commanded premiums, which could not be
added to the prices in the distant markets. The major

[28] 26 *De Bow* 650.

parts of their supplies seem to have been chosen from the
stocks of regional large traders (often actual or nominal
agents), including the most enterprising brokers, auctioneers and private jailors, in the cities of the Atlantic and
the border slave States. And the energetic, ubiquitous
itinerant buyers, knowing the requirements and ample cash
of the large interstate traders, offered them the best. If,
when the interstate traders were selling, at Macon, Montgomery, Memphis, Natchez or New Orleans, an agent, a
commission-merchant or a small trader participated, there
was at least one more transaction, and there were often
others before a slave was settled up the Red River or in
Texas. Accordingly it seems moderate to count an average of three transactions per slave in the long-range trade.

Reverting to Ellison's estimate for 1850-60, as reduced
to 230,335, and taking 23,033 as the average number of
slaves annually imported into the Florida-Texas group and
counting 70 per cent of these as sold three times, indicates
that there were   48,369
transactions in this interstate trading. But these were the
lesser part of all that occurred in an average year in the
'fifties. The others must be sought (1) in other interstate
trading—(a) between the States of the Florida-Texas
group; (b) between the other States of the South, except
negligible Delaware; (2) in the trade that was entirely
within each of the fourteen States and exclusive of transactions already counted, and (3) in all hirings.

The interstate trading merely in the Florida-Texas
group was far from slight. Remember three things: that,
as a rule, slaves were dearer and opportunities to use them
profitably on cheaper fertile land were greater in Florida
and Alabama than in Georgia, still greater in Mississippi
and Louisiana, and, in some respects, greatest in Arkansas
and Texas; that extravagance, speculation, carelessness,
death and other influences in all these States threw large
numbers of slaves on the market; and that virtually every-

where traders, planters, farmers, merchants and professional men were agog for " more niggers ". Prospective buyers were often ready to go long distances and it was common to advertise in remote newspapers the sale of some gangs and to send others to New Orleans to be disposed of.[29]

Georgia continued to make considerable importations down to 1860.[30] It was cheaper for Georgia planters to buy slaves in or from Maryland, Virginia and the Carolinas than to purchase those of Georgia, who were often sold in large numbers to the newer States, especially from the Memphis and the New Orleans markets during the 'fifties. Undoubtedly the exportations were much more numerous than the importations.[31] By obtaining the difference between Georgia's natural and its actual population in 1860 and assuming, as the signs seem to warrant, that as many as 8,000 had been imported into the State during the decade, and adding these with their 11.7 per cent increase, and dividing the result by 1,117, we get 15,875 as Georgia's apparent exportations. If we allow 875 for emancipations and successful runaways, both few, there remained 15,000 [32] as actual exportations, or an annual average of 1,500. Because the slaves exported from one State to another in the Florida-Texas group were more often taken by original owners than in the long-range interstate trade, 50 per cent, instead of only 30, should be counted. Of the 50 per cent,

[29] In the same column with Girardey & Co.'s New Orleans advt. of Gen. Clinch's Ga. gang (*ante* p. 323) one B. M. Bradford of Aberdeen, Miss., was offering two gangs, amounting to 150 negroes, for sale. In the *Picayune* of Jan. 8, 1859, Julian Neville announced that he would sell 63 Miss. slaves at auction on the 12th, but on the 11th he reported that they had been disposed of at private sale.

[30] See *ante* pp. 200n., Goulden's opinion, and 246 ff.

[31] Many besides the Forrests and Bolton, Dickins & Co. in Memphis and Thomas Foster, Joseph A. Beard & Co. and the Campbells in New Orleans sold Ga. slaves. Neville had a gang of 70 " from one cotton plantation in Georgia ", to be sold at auction Jan. 1, 1860.—*Picayune*, Jan. 1, 1860.

[32] *1850-60:* $381{,}682 \times 1.234 - 462{,}198 + 8{,}936 \; [8{,}000 \times 1.117] \div 1.117 - 875 = 15{,}000.$

750 annually, involved in slave-trading probably there were not more than two transactions per slave. This would make an annual average of . . . . 1,500 transactions. Florida, Alabama, Mississippi, Arkansas and Louisiana together presumably had at least 50 per cent more transactions than Georgia, say . . 2,250, which would mean a total annual average of . 3,750 transactions between the States of this group.

The interstate trading exclusively between Maryland, Virginia, Kentucky, Missouri, North Carolina, South Carolina and Tennessee remains to be estimated. Maryland's importations were negligible. Few, if any, persons with slaves were settling in Virginia, and hardly any Virginians were going to the markets of the other States to buy for their own use. Of the many hundred slaves annually taken from Maryland and North Carolina to Virginia markets, with the expectation of sale to the Southwest, probably not less than 200 were purchased and retained in Virginia, mainly as servants or skilled laborers. As there were rarely more than two transactions per slave, and often only one, an average of one and one-half transactions will be counted, in all, ... 300.

The supposed 2,000 slave-trading importations into Kentucky during 1850-60,[33] or 200 annually, were of such short range that they should not be counted as more than one and one-half transactions per slave, or . . . . 300.

Expectations of political and economic advantages to slavery unduly encouraged slaveholding immigrants to Missouri during 1830-60, but the actual conditions were often disappointing and many slaves were sold, especially in the 'fifties. This partly accounts for the numerous large traders there buying for the lower Southwest. The difference between what Missouri's slave population would naturally have become by 1860, ... 107,878, and its actual population of that year, . . . 114,931.

[33] *Ante* p. 391.

indicates importations and increase amounting to   7,053.
There were as many more as the actual exportations and
their 11.7 per cent five-year natural increase. 15,000 with
natural increase making   16,755,
would seem to be a moderate estimate for 1850-60. It
would raise the apparent total to . . . .   23,808.
The free negro population of 2,618 in 1850 would naturally
have become 3,230 by 1860; it was 3,572, or 342 more.
Emancipations and successful runaways (aided by antislavery men determined to make Kansas a free State and
to get revenge for Missouri's efforts to establish slavery
there) were, with their increase, perhaps four or five times
that many, but, say, a total of . . . . .   1,400.
Deducting these would leave   22,408
importations and their increase, of which the importations
were . . . .   20,060.
The slight evidence of strictly slave-trading importations
into Missouri compels the belief that these were exceptionally few. Accordingly perhaps not more than 30 per cent of
all importations, at 1.25 transactions per slave, should be
counted here. This would mean . . . . .   7,522 [34]
transactions, or an annual average of 752.

Tennesseeans, like Georgians, continued to import considerable numbers of slaves because cheaper than those
of Tennessee, for whom there was a large demand in the
Southwest. The State's slave population of 1850 (239,459)
would naturally have become   295,492,
by 1860, but it was only   275,719,
which showed apparent exportations and increase of 19,773.
It was as much larger as the number of the importations,
presumably not less than 8,000, and their 11.7 per cent increase, amounting to   8,936,
which made a total of . . . .   28,709.
This divided by 1.117 gives   25,683

[34] *1850-60:* 87,422 × 1.234 subtracted from 114,931 + 16,755 — 1,400 ÷
1.117 × .30 × 1.25 = 7,522.

as the number of the exportations, or 2,568 annually.[35] This was exclusive of the importations that were sold to other States. Thus Tennessee had become a largely slave-exporting State. But it is the supposed 8,000 importations, an annual average of 800, that we are concerned with. Counting 60 per cent—instead of 70 as in the long-range trade with the Florida-Texas group—as being involved in the slave-trade with two transactions per slave, would make   .   .   .   .   9,600.

At least a few Carolina planters and other users continued to purchase Maryland and Virginia slaves because often cheaper or better, especially the servants and the mechanics. The total importations, during 1850-60, into North Carolina may have amounted to 2,000 and into South Carolina 4,000, making 6,000 in both, or 600 annually. As there were hardly any persons settling there with slaves, we count 60 per cent of the importations as in the trade and two transactions per slave, making   .   .   720

Apart from all these interstate transactions was the wholly *intra-state* trade in slaves that had been born or had lived long in the State where they were sold and retained. Such cases were numerous in all States but the numbers varied widely. In Texas this intra-state trade was relatively slight because newcomers and children made up a large majority of the slave population. To the other extreme, in Virginia, the Carolinas and Kentucky, it was very large, for it included all sales not directly or indirectly associated with importations or exportations. Where slaves were commonly the best, and often the only available, security for debts or special needs, large numbers of them had to be sold. Nearly everywhere more were desired. And " the negro fever ", the prestige of having them for servants and the supposed profit of owning them, if only to hire them out—these were prevalent influences

[35] Below the border slave States, except in La., the emancipated and successful runaway slaves were so few that they may be considered negligible here.

that resulted in purchases where cash or credit could be obtained. The petty merchant, the mechanic and the small farmer always coveted some of the slaves that the happy-go-unlucky "planter" or his estate had to sell. And planters were usually desirous of obtaining some of the slaves of deceased neighbors. Much of this intra-state trading was inconspicious or even private and little known. But the whole is believed to have involved as many *slaves* as all the *interstate* trading, an annual average of at least 19,839.[36] It is supposed that there were about one and one-fourth transactions per slave, or a total of . . 24,798.

Then the hirings. They were common, considered socially important or financially profitable nearly everywhere. Counted by the year, their value was relatively small—usually representing from about one-tenth to one-fifth of what the slave would sell for. They must annually have numbered from several hundred to a few thousand in each of the largest cities, and every little city had many and nearly every village had some.[37] A large proportion of them were employed, of course, in agriculture, in building railroads, digging canals and ditches of all sorts and

[36] This figure is obtained from the annual averages, thus:

	Slaves	Percentage involved	Numbers dealt in
Fla.-Tex. group's trading with rest of the South (p. 399)	23,033	70	16,123
Ga.'s interstate trading in its group (p. 400)	1,500	50	750
That of others in this group (p. 401)	2,250	50	1,125
Va. (p. 401)			200
Ky. (p. 401)			200
Mo. (p. 402)	2,006	30	601
Tenn. (p. 403)	800	60	480
N. C. and S. C. (p. 403)	600	60	360

19,839

[37] Many of the negroes who swarm in the cities * * * belong to planters, or others, who [not needing their slaves' services] hire them to citizens, as mechanics, cooks, waiters, nurses &c". * * *.—(Ingraham) 2 *The Southwest*, 250.

making highways. The number and the activity of the agents—who attended to only part of the hirings—compel the belief that fully 5,000 slaves were annually hired out in Richmond alone, for work in or not far from that city. In Virginia the hirelings of all ages probably numbered at least 15,000 annually in the 'fifties. And the entire number in all the thirteen other States could hardly have been less than three times as many more, making a total of . . . . 60,000.

Perhaps the significance of all these estimates of different kinds of slave-trading can be made clearer by attempting to express their approximate values in dollars, as if the transactions had been about agricultural products or manufactured goods passing from original producers to wholesalers, then to middlemen and on to ultimate consumers. We have already counted the following *average annual transactions* in the decade 1850-60:

(1) the importations into the Florida-
        Texas group 48,369
(2) the interstate trading there . . . 3,750
(3) the interstate trading exclusively
        within the border States, the
        Carolinas and Tennessee . . . 3,032
        making the total interstate tran-
        sactions 55,151
(4) the *intra-state* trade 24,798
(5) the hirings . . . . 60,000.

The average price put on a transaction does not represent profit, but the capital involved, as in case of real estate. It is supposed that the following average prices are about right for the respective classes of transactions:

$800 for each of the 55,151 transactions in the interstate trade, representing a total of $44,120,800
$600 for each of the 24,798 transactions in the intra-state

trade, representing $14,878,800
and $100 for each of the 60,000 hirings represent-
ing . . . . $ 6,000,000.
This shows a grand total indicating an annual average
involved in the different kinds of slave-trading amounting
to . . . . $64,999,600.
In 1859-60, when sales and prices were at the maximum and
" the negro-fever " was raging, more than twice this average, or possibly $150,000,000, may have been reached in a
single year.

At that time, $100,000,000 was relatively a fabulous inter-
est to the South. It represented about one-twenty-fifth of
the entire value of the nearly four millions slaves. And
slave-trading was vastly more important than this suggests: it was absolutely necessary to the continuance of
this most highly prized property and to the economic,
social and political conditions dependent on it.

THE END.

INDEX

407

H